Reconfiguring Thomistic Christology

In this book, Matthew Levering unites eschatologically charged biblical Christology with metaphysical and dogmatic Thomistic Christology, by highlighting the typological Christologies shared by Scripture, the Church Fathers, and Aquinas. Like the Church Fathers, Aquinas often reflected upon Jesus in typological terms (especially in his biblical commentaries), just as the New Testament does. Showing the connections between New Testament, Patristic, and Aquinas's own typological portraits of Jesus, Levering reveals how the eschatological Jesus of biblical scholarship can be integrated with Thomistic Christology. His study produces a fully contemporary Thomistic Christology that unites *Ressourcement* and Thomistic modes of theological inquiry, thereby bridging two schools of contemporary theology that too often are imagined as rivals. Levering's book reflects and augments the current resurgence of Thomistic Christology as an ecumenical project of relevance to all Christians.

MATTHEW LEVERING holds the James N. and Mary D. Perry Jr. Chair of Theology at Mundelein Seminary. He is the author of over thirty books, including *Aquinas's Eschatological Ethics and the Virtue of Temperance* (2019) and *Paul in the "Summa Theologiae"* (2014).

CURRENT ISSUES IN THEOLOGY

General Editors:

Iain Torrance
Pro-Chancellor of the University of Aberdeen

David Fergusson
University of Edinburgh

Editorial Advisory Board:

David Ford   *University of Cambridge*
Bryan Spinks   *Yale University*
Kathryn Tanner   *Yale Divinity School*

There is a need among upper-undergraduate and graduate students of theology, as well as among Christian teachers and church professionals, for a series of short, focussed studies of particular key topics in theology written by prominent theologians. Current Issues in Theology meets this need.

The books in the series are designed to provide a 'state-of-the-art' statement on the topic in question, engaging with contemporary thinking as well as providing original insights. The aim is to publish books which stand between the static monograph genre and the more immediate statement of a journal article, by authors who are questioning existing paradigms or rethinking perspectives.

Other titles in the series:

Holy Scripture   John Webster
The Just War Revisited   Oliver O'Donovan
Bodies and Souls, or Spirited Bodies?   Nancey Murphy
Christ and Horrors   Marilyn McCord Adams
Divinity and Humanity   Oliver D. Crisp
The Eucharist and Ecumenism   George Hunsinger
Christ the Key   Kathryn Tanner
Theology without Metaphysics   Kevin W. Hector

Reconsidering John Calvin   Randall C. Zachman
God's Presence   Frances Youngman
An Incarnational Model of the Eucharist   James M. Arcadi
The Providence of God   David Fergusson
Reading the Bible Theologically   Darren Sarisky
Divine Action and the Human Mind   Sarah Ritchie Lane
Law and the Rule of God: A Christian Engagement with Shari'a   Joshua Ralston
Human Anguish and God's Power   David H. Kelsey
Rethinking Paul: Protestant Theology and Pauline Exegesis   Edwin Chr. van Driel
Humility of the Eternal Son: "Reformed" Kenoticism and Repair of Chalcedon   Bruce Lindley McCormack
Why the Cross? Divine Friendship and the Power of Justice   Ligita Ryliškytė
Reconfiguring Thomistic Christology   Matthew Levering

"In this book, Levering not only documents the contemporary reemergence of Thomistic Christology. He also contributes to it significantly by underscoring the biblical and typological framework of St. Thomas' Christology. He does so while illustrating manifold connections between Aquinas' scriptural exegesis and that of many contemporary biblical interpreters, in a contribution that is both original and sorely needed, restoring unity to regions of theology that are often separated artificially. This is a bold work of theological faith and historical reason, contemporary biblical exegesis and classical scriptural theology, yet another illustration of the judicious insight and tangible charity of Matthew Levering as a central protagonist of theology in our era."

Thomas Joseph White, OP, Rector,
Angelicum, Rome

"The very conception of this book a reading of Thomistic Christology through the lens of Thomas' use of biblical typologies is a brilliant and inspired breakthrough that promises to break down entrenched boundaries between systematic Christology, modern biblical exegesis, and Thomistic studies. The realization of this conception throughout this book brings this daring promise to a compelling and richly rewarding fulfillment. This is ressourcement theology at its finest, as deeply recuperative of the riches of the Christian tradition as it is creatively and impactfully responsive to the present moment."

Khaled Anatolios, John A. O'Brien Professor of Theology,
University of Notre Dame

MATTHEW LEVERING
Mundelein Seminary, Illinois

Reconfiguring Thomistic Christology

CAMBRIDGE
UNIVERSITY PRESS

Shaftesbury Road, Cambridge CB2 8EA, United Kingdom

One Liberty Plaza, 20th Floor, New York, NY 10006, USA

477 Williamstown Road, Port Melbourne, VIC 3207, Australia

314–321, 3rd Floor, Plot 3, Splendor Forum, Jasola District Centre, New Delhi – 110025, India

103 Penang Road, #05–06/07, Visioncrest Commercial, Singapore 238467

Cambridge University Press is part of Cambridge University Press & Assessment, a department of the University of Cambridge.

We share the University's mission to contribute to society through the pursuit of education, learning and research at the highest international levels of excellence.

www.cambridge.org
Information on this title: www.cambridge.org/9781009221498

DOI: 10.1017/9781009221504

© Cambridge University Press & Assessment 2023

This publication is in copyright. Subject to statutory exception and to the provisions of relevant collective licensing agreements, no reproduction of any part may take place without the written permission of Cambridge University Press & Assessment.

First published 2023
First paperback edition 2026

A catalogue record for this publication is available from the British Library

ISBN 978-1-009-22145-0 Hardback
ISBN 978-1-009-22149-8 Paperback

Cambridge University Press & Assessment has no responsibility for the persistence or accuracy of URLs for external or third-party internet websites referred to in this publication and does not guarantee that any content on such websites is, or will remain, accurate or appropriate.

Contents

Acknowledgments		*page* viii
	Introduction	1
1	Contemporary Thomistic Christology	26
2	Christ the New Adam: The New Creation	61
3	Christ the New Isaac: The Eschatological Temple	104
4	Christ the New Moses: The Eschatological Exodus	139
5	Christ the New Joshua: The Eschatological Promised Land	179
6	Christ the New David: The Eschatological Kingdom	227
	Conclusion	285
	Bibliography	295
	Index	327

Acknowledgments

The idea for this book came about through an invitation from Dominic Legge, O.P. and the Thomistic Institute in Washington, DC to deliver the annual Aquinas Lecture at the Dominican House of Studies in January 2021. I chose the topic of Thomas Aquinas on Christ the New Adam. I was able to deliver this lecture in person and to receive the encouragement of many Dominican friends along with laypeople who attended the event. Particular thanks go to Reginald Lynch, O.P., Nicholas Lombardo, O.P., and Br. Charles Marie Rooney, O.P., and to the many other wonderful Dominicans who raised valuable questions at the talk and during conversations afterward.

Via Zoom, I participated in Ave Maria University's February 2021 "Hope and Death" conference, and delivered a paper on the topic Christ the New Isaac; I thank Scott Hahn, Michael Dauphinais, and Roger Nutt for the invitation. For the Eighth Day Institute's June 2021 Florovsky-Newman week – focused in 2021 on baptism – I spoke on Christ the New Joshua. I thank Matthew Umbarger, Erin Doom, Joshua Papsdorf, Chad Raith, Marcus Plested, and all who participated in this in-person ecumenical event. In June 2021, I gave three in-person lectures drawn from my book manuscript to the Religious Sisters of Mercy in Alma, Michigan. I thank Mary Christa Nutt, R. S. M., Prudence Allen, R. S. M., and the other Sisters whose intellectual gifts and deep Catholic piety were so inspiring and helpful.

Many friends helped me with correcting and improving this manuscript. David Moser, now Assistant Professor of Theology at

Dordt College, read an early draft and saved me from embarrassing Christological errors. Andrew Hofer, O.P., offered crucial corrections. Thomas Joseph White, O.P., rector of the Angelicum, was a reader of the manuscript for Cambridge. He made a number of invaluable contributions to the manuscript, assisting in balancing the typological with the ontological. Michael Barber of the Augustine Institute read a late draft of the manuscript and, in addition to correcting the biblical material, showed me that Aquinas understood Christ to be the New Moses. Jörgen Vijgen, Belgium's preeminent Thomist, gave me important materials for my work on Christ the New Joshua. With Jörgen and Piotr Roszak, I coedited a special issue of *Studium* on "Biblical Thomism," and a portion of Chapter 5 has appeared as "Christ the New Joshua," *Studium* 24 (2021): 117–36. Richard Ounsworth, O.P., generously corrected my survey of his important book. Without the above friends, this book would be far poorer.

Let me also thank Beatrice Rehl and David Fergusson for their support for the publication of this book at Cambridge in David's series. It is a privilege to work with them and to have this book included in the series. I thank Marial Corona for generously doing the bibliography with her customary skill. Caitlyn Trader did the index, a time-consuming labor for which I am grateful. The editorial staff at Cambridge copy-edited the book and managed the production process with skill and professionalism.

For making possible the writing of this book, I have Mundelein Seminary to thank, and especially Jim and Molly Perry, the wonderful benefactors who endowed the chair I hold. None of my work would be possible without my wife Joy, with whom I pray the prayer of Tobias and Sarah: "Blessed are you, O God of our fathers, and blessed be your holy and glorious name for ever. Let the heavens and all your creatures bless you" (Tobit 8:5).

I dedicate this book to Dominic Legge and his colleagues at the Thomistic Institute; may they be blessed! Fr. Dominic lives in service to others, marked by serenity and humility and good humor,

ACKNOWLEDGMENTS

sharing the wisdom of Christ with all and sundry. Of Fr. Dominic and his colleagues, it can truly be said that they live by the psalmist's words: "As for man, his days are like grass; he flourishes like a flower of the field; for the wind passes over it, and it is gone, and its place knows it no more. But the mercy of the Lord is from everlasting to everlasting upon those who fear him" (Ps 103:15–17).

Introduction

This book has a simple argument: Contemporary Catholic and Protestant Thomistic Christology is an immensely promising development, and it should now be enhanced by a fuller integration of biblical typologies (the New Adam, New Isaac, New Moses, New Joshua, and New David) in order to do justice to the New Testament's eschatological portraits of Jesus.

When I first conceived this book, I intended to argue that Thomas Aquinas should have included more attention to the New Testament's Christological typologies in his *tertia pars*, because this would have allowed him to do fuller justice to the eschatological character of Jesus' identity and mission. Aquinas knew these typologies well, and he could have integrated them into his *tertia pars*. On reflection, however, I realized that my concern is not actually with Aquinas himself in his time and place but with contemporary Thomistic Christology. In order to fully convey Jesus' eschatological identity and mission, Thomistic Christology needs to incorporate the typological materials found especially in Aquinas's biblical commentaries. This is not a competition between the *tertia pars* and the biblical commentaries, since, as we will see, the eschatological insights conveyed by the typologies are present in their ontological core within the *Summa theologiae*. The reconfiguring that I propose in this book is a matter of figural enhancement and augmentation, not of laying new foundations. My proposal accords with Thomas Joseph White's call for theologians to "seek a progressive unification of classical Christological 'science' and modern historical study," in order to integrate the results of historical and dogmatic approaches "into one coherent narrative."¹

Given an understanding of history that allows for God's providence, the fact that the divine Messiah recapitulates the central figures of Israel's Scriptures will come as no surprise.² Among the Church Fathers, Irenaeus is representative in teaching that "the treasure hid in the Scriptures is Christ, since He was pointed out by means of types and parables."³ For their part, contemporary biblical scholars recognize that for Second Temple Jews and for the New Testament authors, "God is the mastermind of a vast divine economy that includes both external past-tense events and their inscripturation."⁴ The New Testament portrays Jesus as the "new" or eschatological Adam, Isaac, Moses, Joshua, and David. For Christians, just as the "New" Testament fulfills but does not negate or replace the "Old,"

---

¹ Thomas Joseph White, O.P., "The Precarity of Wisdom: Modern Dominican Theology, Perspectivalism, and the Tasks of Reconstruction," in *Ressourcement Thomism: Sacred Doctrine, the Sacraments, and the Moral Life. Essays in Honor of Romanus Cessario, O.P.*, ed. Reinhard Hütter and Matthew Levering), 92–123, at 116–17. Among the questions that White raises is one at the heart of my project: "What is the relation between his [Jesus's] eschatological message concerning the Kingdom of God and the revelation of his own identiy as the Son of God?" (116). As White emphasizes in his *The Incarnate Lord: A Thomistic Study in Christology* (Washington, DC: Catholic University of America Press, 2015), 61, appreciation for historical research into Jesus does not here substitute for the gift of faith by which Jesus is known personally.

² In the New Testament (and, even more, in the Church Fathers and Aquinas), Jesus eschatologically recapitulates the male figures, while Mary/Church recapitulates the central female figures, beginning with Eve. It could also be argued that Jesus eschatologically recapitulates various female figures in the Old Testament, but this is not the path taken by the New Testament. For discussion of Mary and typology, see Joseph Ratzinger, *Daughter Zion: Meditations on the Church's Marian Belief*, trans. John M. McDermott, S.J. (San Francisco: Ignatius Press, 1983); and Louis Bouyer, *The Seat of Wisdom: An Essay on the Place of the Virgin Mary in Christian Theology*, trans. A. V. Littledale (London: Darton, Longman & Todd, 1960).

³ Irenaeus, "Against Heresies," Book IV, chapter 26, in *The Apostolic Fathers, Justin Martyr, Irenaeus*, ed. Alexander Roberts and James Donaldson, vol. 1 of Ante-Nicene Fathers Series (Peabody, MA: Hendrickson, 1995), 315–567, at 496.

⁴ Matthew W. Bates, *The Hermeneutics of the Apostolic Proclamation: The Center of Paul's Method of Scriptural Interpretation* (Waco, TX: Baylor University Press, 2012), 121.

so also Jesus is the eschatological fulfillment of these central Old Testament figures without negating their own distinctive narrative histories and identities.[5] Thus the New Testament's "figural Christology" requires what Richard Hays terms "reading backwards."[6]

Indebted to the Church Fathers, Aquinas gave explicit attention in his writings to Jesus as the New Adam, Isaac, Moses, Joshua, and David according to the New Testament's literal sense. Yet, contemporary Thomistic Christology has paid relatively little attention to Jesus' eschatological fulfillment of these types. Given that "the 'reign of God' is the clear and unmistakable central theme of Jesus' work,"[7] the question is how to ensure that the reign of God is also a central theme of Thomistic Christology. The theme is by no means absent from Aquinas's Christology. The *tertia pars* of the *Summa theologiae* lacks a distinct *quaestio* on Jesus as King or on the inauguration of the kingdom of God. But the theme of the reign of God, and the ontological reality expressed by that phrase, appears frequently within Aquinas's Christological reflections, especially in his discussions of Jesus as the eschatological Moses, Joshua, and David.

My argument is that by incorporating and expanding upon Aquinas's reflections on the Christological typologies, contemporary Thomistic Christology can meet the challenge identified by White and laid down by the biblical scholar John Meier in the first volume of his *A Marginal Jew*: "[F]aith in Christ today must be able to reflect on itself systematically in a way that will allow an appropriation of

---

[5] The New Testament does not name Jesus as the "New Adam" – Paul employs "last Adam" or "second" Adam in 1 Corinthians 15. Nor does the New Testament speak of the "New" Isaac, Moses, Joshua, or David. In this book, however, I will employ these phrases in order to signify the eschatological recapitulation of these figures by Jesus. On the Christian meaning of "Old" and "New" when applied to the two Testaments, see R. W. L. Moberly, *The Old Testament of the Old Testament: Patriarchal Narratives and Mosaic Yahwism* (Minneapolis, MN: Augsburg Fortress, 1992), 158–59.

[6] See Richard B. Hays, *Reading Backwards: Figural Christology and the Fourfold Gospel Witness* (Waco, TX: Baylor University Press, 2014).

[7] Gerhard Lohfink, *The Forty Parables of Jesus*, trans. Linda M. Maloney (Collegeville, MN: Liturgical Press Academic, 2021), 223.

the quest for the historical Jesus into theology. The historical Jesus, while not the object or essence of *faith*, must be an integral part of modern *theology*."[8] The "historical Jesus" portrayed by Meier and others is an eschatological prophet who understood himself to be inaugurating the kingdom of God. It is this eschatological Jesus that the New Testament's (and the Church Fathers' and Aquinas's) typological Christology depicts in richly nuanced ways. It does so from within a providentially unified understanding of history that does not subscribe to the limits imposed by modern historiography. This providential understanding of history resonates with contemporary Thomistic Christology, which shares Paul's view that "nothing – that is to say, no human, no spiritual power, no geographical space, no era of time, and not even death – ultimately stands outside the reach of God's sovereign control."[9]

After an introductory chapter that appreciatively sketches the contemporary ecumenical resurgence of Thomistic Christology, each of the five main chapters takes up one typological motif (the eschatological New Adam, New Isaac, New Moses, New Joshua, and New David), exploring its role in the New Testament and in the Church Fathers and addressing how Aquinas employs it. Each chapter also identifies places in the *tertia pars* of the *Summa theologiae* where further integration of the typological motif might strengthen contemporary Thomistic Christology. Each chapter has a concluding section titled "An Ontological Note," in which I supplement the chapters' typological-eschatological emphasis by briefly examining Aquinas's insights into the ontological realities expressed respectively by the phrases "New Adam" (Christ's human perfection under grace), "New Isaac" (atonement), "New Moses" (law and grace), "New Joshua" (the state of glory), and "New David" (the mystical body and Christ's Headship of grace).[10]

---

[8] John P. Meier, *A Marginal Jew: Rethinking the Historical Jesus*, vol. 1, *The Roots of the Problem and the Person* (New York: Doubleday, 1991), 198–99.

[9] Bates, *The Hermeneutics of the Apostolic Proclamation*, 122.

[10] Here may be the place to recall the medieval practice of exegeting Scripture according to the four causes, so as to penetrate to the ontological realities under discussion

In proposing to "reconfigure" Thomistic Christology by integrating these typologies more fully, I am concurring with the judgment of Romanus Cessario and Cajetan Cuddy that Thomistic theologians should "receive the essential philosophical and theological principles from the Angelic Doctor and then apply these sound principles to the unique questions, challenges, and requirements that their own period raises."[11] As noted, I am responding especially to modern New Testament scholars' questions, challenges, and insights about Jesus' eschatological understanding of his identity and mission. For contemporary New Testament scholars, one of the clearest elements of the New Testament is "that Jesus was remembered as preaching about the kingdom of God and that this was central to his message and mission."[12] Biblical scholars also affirm that "Jesus' talk of the kingdom was blended with the much older imagery of inheriting the land of promise," that is, imagery related to the exodus.[13] Jesus' eschatological renewal of the Temple and the end of the exile are other frequent themes.[14]

---

in scriptural texts. For background, focusing on the relation of divine and human authorship, see Timothy Bellamah, O.P., "*Tunc scimus cum causas cognoscimus*: Some Medieval Endeavors to Know Scripture in Its Causes," in *Theology Needs Philosophy: Acting against Reason Is Contrary to Human Nature*, ed. Matthew L. Lamb (Washington, DC: Catholic University of America Press, 2016), 154–72.

[11] Romanus Cessario, O.P., and Cajetan Cuddy, O.P., *Thomas and the Thomists: The Achievement of Thomas Aquinas and His Interpreters* (Minneapolis, MN: Fortress, 2017), xii, xvii.

[12] James D. G. Dunn, *Jesus Remembered* (Grand Rapids, MI: Eerdmans, 2003), 387.

[13] Dunn, *Jesus Remembered*, 386. For the influence of the exodus upon New Testament writings and thought-patterns (as distinct from claims about the historical Jesus' own worldview), see for example Teresa Morgan, *Roman Faith and Christian Faith: Pistis and Fides in the Early Roman Empire and Early Churches* (Oxford: Oxford University Press, 2015), 504–05.

[14] For background to the theme of the eschatological end of exile, see Judith H. Newman, *Before the Bible: The Liturgical Body and the Formation of Scriptures in Early Judaism* (Oxford: Oxford University Press, 2018), 95. This theme has been a central element in N. T. Wright's work, as spelled out especially in Wright's

For the purpose of developing these eschatological dimensions of Jesus' identity and mission from within Thomistic Christology, I argue that the above-named five biblical typologies, well known to Aquinas, can serve as a bridge for joining Aquinas's Christology to modern biblical scholarship's emphasis on Jesus as the eschatological Davidic king who restores his people, renews the Temple, and leads the new exodus. Contemporary Thomists have perceived how profoundly Aquinas integrates Scripture and the Church Fathers into his theology, but Thomistic Christology still needs to assimilate more explicitly the eschatological aspects that shape the New Testament's portraits of Jesus.[15] Therefore, my chapters propose enrichments to Thomistic Christology flowing from explicit attention to the typologies, and I show how such enrichments can be set forth in relation to the *tertia pars*.

---

programmatic *The New Testament and the People of God* (Minneapolis, MN: Fortress, 1992). For further discussion, see Brant Pitre, "Excursus: N. T. Wright and 'the End of the Exile,'" in *Jesus, the Tribulation, and the End of the Exile: Restoration Eschatology and the Origin of the Atonement* (Grand Rapids, MI: Baker Academic, 2005), 31–40, where Pitre argues that "while Wright is absolutely right about the importance of the 'exile,' he is fundamentally wrong in his understanding of it" – since Second Temple Jews living in the land do not appear to have considered themselves to be in "exile," but instead they focused on the fact that the Assyrian exile of the northern ten tribes had never been resolved and they awaited "the restoration of all twelve tribes of Israel in a final Return from Exile, under the headship of a messianic king" (32, 38).

[15] See, for example, Roger Nutt and Michael Dauphinais, eds., *Thomas Aquinas, Biblical Theologian* (Steubenville, OH: Emmaus Academic, 2021); Piotr Roszak and Jörgen Vijgen, eds., *Reading the Church Fathers with St. Thomas Aquinas: Historical and Systematical Perspectives* (Turnhout: Brepols, 2021); Michael Dauphinais, Andrew Hofer, O.P., and Roger W. Nutt, eds., *Thomas Aquinas and the Greek Fathers* (Ave Maria, FL: Sapientia Press, 2019); Leo J. Elders, S.V.D., *Thomas Aquinas and His Predecessors: The Philosophers and the Church Fathers in His Works* (Washington, DC: Catholic University of America Press, 2018); Michael Dauphinais, Barry David, and Matthew Levering, eds. *Aquinas the Augustinian* (Washington, DC: Catholic University of America Press, 2007); and Michael Dauphinais and Matthew Levering, eds., *Reading John with St. Thomas Aquinas: Theological Exegesis and Speculative Theology* (Washington, DC: Catholic University of America Press, 2004).

INTRODUCTION

Lest there be any misunderstanding, let me firmly reject the all-too-common idea that Thomistic Christology is overly philosophical. In fact, the metaphysical richness of Aquinas's Christology and of contemporary Thomistic Christology is greatly needed for any serious reflection on who Jesus is, what he accomplished, and what he continues to accomplish today. In Chapter 1, I survey a number of contemporary Catholic and Protestant thinkers who have reflected deeply upon Aquinas's Christology and who have retrieved its metaphysical and theological relevance. I single out recent books by Adonis Vidu and Thomas Joseph White, while describing the work of many other important contributors as well, such as Jean-Pierre Torrell and Dominic Legge. It is noteworthy that scholars with deep Eastern sympathies such as Rowan Williams, and Eastern Catholics such as Khaled Anatolios, have also recently drawn upon Aquinas's Christology in fruitful ways. My first chapter makes clear that the purpose of my book is not to undermine contemporary Thomistic Christology but to augment it. Recognition of Jesus' humanity, which Paul Gondreau and others have shown is so central to Aquinas's Christology,[16] requires today a focused attention on the way his teaching comports with the eschatological dimensions of New Testament Christology.

I propose augmenting Thomistic Christology along *typological* lines because Aquinas himself employed these typologies and because they have a strikingly eschatological import. Of course, given the biblical and patristic testimony, all theologians – not only Thomists – should have a strong interest in exploring Jesus Christ as the eschatological New Adam, New Isaac, New Moses, New Joshua, and New David. As Joseph Ratzinger says of one of these types, along lines that can be extended to the other four:

---

[16] See Paul Gondreau, "The Humanity of Christ, the Incarnate Word," in *The Theology of Thomas Aquinas*, ed. Rik Van Nieuwenhove and Joseph Wawrykow (Notre Dame: University of Notre Dame Press, 2005), 252–76.

"[I]t is important to emphasize that Jesus adopts the tradition of Sinai and thus presents himself as the new Moses."[17]

Biblical Scholarship and Typology

Before proceeding, let me offer some further background to my proposal. One of the most influential New Testament scholars of the past fifty years, E. P. Sanders, reconstructs Jesus' self-understanding as follows: "Through him, Jesus held, God was acting directly and immediately, bypassing the agreed, biblically sanctioned ordinances, reaching out to the lost sheep of the house of Israel with no more mediation than the words and deeds of one man – himself."[18] For Sanders, Jesus understood himself to have "full authority to speak and act on behalf of God," and Jesus experienced his relationship to God to be uniquely intimate.[19]

Sanders's remarks are only partly correct, in my view. He is correct about Jesus' authority and intimacy with the Father. But it is not the case (as Sanders elsewhere helps to show[20]) that Jesus simply "bypassed" Torah and Temple or that Jesus reached out to his people in a way that bypassed the mediation of Israel's Scriptures. On the contrary, Jesus fulfilled, rather than bypassed, Israel's covenantal law and cult.[21] Jesus' words and deeds are unintelligible without the mediation of Israel's Scriptures. This can be seen throughout

---

[17] Ratzinger is here writing as Pope Emeritus Benedict XVI: "The Catholic Priesthood," in *From the Depths of Our Hearts: Priesthood, Celibacy, and the Crisis of the Catholic Church*, trans. Michael J. Miller, ed. Nicholas Diat (San Francisco: Ignatius Press, 2020), 23–60, at 32.

[18] E. P. Sanders, *The Historical Figure of Jesus* (London: Penguin, 1993), 236–37.

[19] Sanders, *The Historical Figure of Jesus*, 238.

[20] See E. P. Sanders, *Jesus and Judaism* (Minneapolis, MN: Fortress, 1985).

[21] For discussion of this point, addressing supersessionist and exegetical concerns, see the chapters on "Torah" and "Temple" in my *Engaging the Doctrine of Israel: A Christian Israelology in Dialogue with Ongoing Judaism* (Eugene, OR: Cascade, 2021).

the New Testament, not least in Paul's devotion to Jesus. As Robin Scroggs remarks, "Paul believes that the eschatological age has been inaugurated by a man who embodies God's intent for all men – an intent thwarted by the first Adam, fulfilled by the Last."[22] Scroggs calls this belief Paul's "Adamic Christology."

From the Church Fathers onward – most certainly including Aquinas – Christians have upheld this Adamic Christology. Moreover, Adam is not the only figure from Israel's Scriptures who helped Jesus and the apostles to illuminate the meaning of Jesus' words and deeds. King David has a central role as well, since Jesus is repeatedly described as the Messianic king in the line of David. So do Melchizedek, Abraham, Isaac, Moses, Joshua, and Solomon.[23]

But should these Old Testament figures matter to Christology today? In Sanders's view as a historian, they should not. No doubt Jesus thought of himself as uniquely God's "viceroy," helping to inaugurate the imminent kingdom of God,[24] but for Sanders there is no need to describe Jesus as a New David or New Adam. Sanders offers an illustration of what is wrong with such typological Christology. He states that according to the Bible, "God called Abraham in 1921 BC, Moses led the Israelites out of Egypt around 1500 BC, and David flourished about 1030 BC.... An approximate parallel today to the gospel's treatment of Jesus would be to describe Elizabeth II by saying that she is heir to the throne of William the Conqueror, that she fulfills the promise of King Arthur."[25] When the New Testament authors affirmed that Jesus fulfilled the work of Moses and David, they reflected a commonplace manner

---

[22] Robin Scroggs, *The Last Adam: A Study in Pauline Anthropology* (Philadelphia: Fortress Press, 1966), ix.
[23] For the connection of Abraham and Jesus, see Mary Healy, *Hebrews* (Grand Rapids, MI: Baker Academic, 2016), 241.
[24] Sanders, *The Historical Figure of Jesus*, 248.
[25] Sanders, *The Historical Figure of Jesus*, 83.

of thinking in Second Temple Judaism, but for Sanders this cannot be taken seriously today. In Matthew 16:14, for example, the people imagine that Jesus might be the return of Elijah or Jeremiah!

Sanders represents a standard historical viewpoint when he dismisses as mere invention Matthew's references to Jesus as the New Moses or Luke's references to Jesus as the New David. Yet, Sanders considers that a significant amount of truth about Jesus can still be discerned in the Gospels, notwithstanding all the typology. He states, "Echoes of Jewish scripture are everywhere in the gospels, but nevertheless no one would ever mistake the Jesus of the gospels for either Moses or David.... [T]he gospels *claim* a connection between Jesus and David, but they do not present Jesus as being in the least like David."[26] Surely Sanders is correct that Jesus did not do a lot of the things done by Moses and David, both of whom killed other people, for example. In fact, Sanders recognizes that the evangelists "thought that Jesus had gone beyond Moses and was a different sort of king from David. Thus we do not get a cardboard pop-up depiction of Jesus as a new Moses or David."[27] But Sanders still thinks that the historical Jesus must be separated from the typological overlay by which the evangelists sought "to convince readers that Jesus fulfilled God's promises to Israel" and that Jesus is the "universal saviour who fits into Jewish salvation history."[28] According to Sanders, the historian must do the "patient spadework to dig through the layers of Christian devotion and to recover the historical core."[29]

However, Sanders's approach has an evident weak spot. Namely, assuming that God exists and is the provident Creator – assumptions that are quite reasonable[30] – why could not the incarnate Lord

---

[26] Sanders, *The Historical Figure of Jesus*, 89.
[27] Sanders, *The Historical Figure of Jesus*, 90.
[28] Sanders, *The Historical Figure of Jesus*, 90.
[29] Sanders, *The Historical Figure of Jesus*, 280.
[30] Against the notion that these assumptions require revealed theology per se, see the arguments in my *Proofs of God: Classical Arguments from Tertullian to Barth* (Grand Rapids, MI: Baker Academic, 2016).

actually be in a real and fully historical way the New Adam (inaugurating a new creation), the New Isaac (fulfilling the sacrificial cult of the Temple), the New Moses (teaching God's law, mediating between God and his people, and establishing the new covenant[31]), the New Joshua (leading God's people across the Jordan of death to the fullness of the Promised Land), and the New David (inaugurating the kingdom of God)? For Sanders, this may be all very well as *theology*, but the historian cannot pay attention to it. The historian must "distinguish one kind of truth from another, and ... study only the second, mundane kind," namely, the "bit of ordinary history within the grand framework of salvation history."[32]

What if, however, the ordinary history at issue actually *is* "salvation" history? Sanders assumes that the "ordinary history" of Jesus of Nazareth is obscured by the salvation-historical typologies. But what makes this assumption true, unless one deems *a priori* that Jesus is not the incarnate Lord or that history has no providential unity? While affirming the possibility of "Jesus' own conscious

---

[31] On the new covenant, see, for example, Michael J. Gorman's observation about Matthew 26:27-28, in Gorman, *The Death of the Messiah and the Birth of the New Covenant: A (Not So) New Model of the Atonement* (Eugene, OR: Cascade, 2014), 36-37: "[I]n this dominical claim we should probably hear echoes of at least three scriptural texts and themes – the Passover/Exodus, the blood of the covenant (Exod 24:6-8), and the new covenant and its forgiveness (Jer 31:31-34) – plus, in light of Matthew's ransom text (Matt 20:28 = Mark 10:45), the suffering servant's death (Isa 53:12).... This *forgiven* and *forgiving* new-covenant community embodies, indeed fulfills, the two tables of the law." See also Morna D. Hooker, *Not Ashamed of the Gospel: New Testament Interpretations of the Death of Christ* (Grand Rapids, MI: Eerdmans, 1994), 59, 67.

[32] Sanders, *The Historical Figure of Jesus*, 91. For the procedures involved, see Ernst Troeltsch's 1898 essay, "Historical and Dogmatic Method in Theology," in *Religion in History*, trans. James Luther Adams and Walter F. Bense (Minneapolis, MN: Fortress, 1991), 11-33. Against Sanders's view of history, see especially *The New Testament and the People of God*, 81-144. See also, from a somewhat different standpoint, Robert Morgan, "Christology through Scriptural Interpretation through New Testament Theology," in *Christology and Scripture: Interdisciplinary Perspectives*, ed. Andrew T. Lincoln and Angus Paddison (London: T&T Clark, 2007), 58-83.

imitation of scriptural types," Sanders holds that such imitation did not express an underlying truth about Jesus.[33]

This is a common viewpoint among scholars today, many of whom find Scripture's typologies to be implausible, arbitrary, and historically anachronistic. I grant that some of the Old and New Testament's typological links may well be arbitrary, just as there are instances of patristic and medieval typological or allegorical exegesis that are implausible.[34] But I think the five Christological types presented here, which are not invented by the Church Fathers but are found in the New Testament's literal sense, can be demonstrated to be reasonable entailments of Jesus' status as the eschatological Messiah. In my view, Christians should affirm these typological portraits to be historically true about Jesus, rather than mere metaphors.[35]

---

[33] Sanders, *The Historical Figure of Jesus*, 85. For Sanders, "The more parallels there were between Jesus and characters or prophecies in Hebrew scripture, the more likely Matthew, Mark and Luke were to invent still more. They may have reasoned that if there were six similarities, there probably had been a seventh. I think that there is no doubt that they did invent some, though the possibility of overlaps, or of Jesus' own conscious imitation of scriptural types, means that we must often be uncertain" (85). Without engaging the question of the historicity of the typological fulfillment, Anthony Le Donne argues that Sanders should have integrated typology more fully into his portrait of Jesus, since Jesus' worldview was typologically saturated: see Le Donne, *The Historiographical Jesus: Memory, Typology, and the Son of David* (Waco, TX: Baylor University Press, 2009), 4–5.

[34] For background, see, for example, Lewis Ayres, "'There's Fire in That Rain': On Reading the Letter and Reading Allegorically," in *Heaven on Earth? Theological Interpretation in Ecumenical Dialogue*, ed. Hans Boersma and Matthew Levering (Oxford: Wiley-Blackwell, 2013), 33–52; and Henri de Lubac, S.J., *Medieval Exegesis*, vol. 1, *The Four Senses of Scripture*, trans. Mark Sebanc (Grand Rapids, MI: Eerdmans, 1998).

[35] See Gilbert Dahan, "Thomas Aquinas: Exegesis and Hermeneutics," in *Reading Sacred Scripture with Thomas Aquinas: Hermeneutical Tools, Theological Questions and New Perspectives*, ed. Piotr Roszak and Jörgen Vijgen (Turnhout: Brepols, 2015), 45–70. Dahan notes that in studying Aquinas's biblical interpretation, it is useful to "distinguish between the historical books of the Old Testament, entailing a literal reading and an allegorical (figurative) reading; the prophetic books,

Put simply, Jesus really is the eschatological (and therefore "New") Adam, Isaac, Moses, Joshua, and David. To call him the Messianic Son of David or the Last Adam is not a mere metaphor. This entails that from the beginning, in God's plan, Jesus is the one to whom the earlier figures inchoately pointed, since "it is a law of Biblical exegesis that the types in Scripture derive ... their meaning and value from the anti-types to which they refer. Adam is therefore entirely subordinated to Christ."[36]

In critical dialogue with Sanders, N. T. Wright has argued that the New Testament's worldview in this regard should be taken much more seriously by contemporary historians – and by contemporary theologians. The New Testament authors would not be surprised to find that their faith-filled understanding of Jesus as fulfilling God's covenants with Israel in the midst of history is difficult to accept for modern secular historians. But Wright argues that to understand the historical Jesus requires understanding how

---

principally entailing a literal reading (in a Christological sense); and the New Testament, entailing a literal reading and a spiritual (somewhat tropological) reading" (54). If one is reading the New Testament texts that portray Jesus as the eschatological Adam (or Isaac, Moses, Joshua, David), then this is the literal sense – and it is no mere metaphor, since Jesus eschatologically recapitulates these personages. Note that Jesus does not eschatologically recapitulate everything in the lives of these Old Testament personages but only the parts that befit his saving work, allowing for his radical newness. See also Timothy Bellamah's observation that Theodore of Mopsuestia, who held that only five Psalms literally refer to Jesus Christ, was condemned by Constantinople II in 553, "with the result that Aquinas considered the prophetic literal sense a matter of doctrine and the denial of it a matter of heresy" (Bellamah, "*Tunc scimus cum causas cognoscimus*," 168). Summarizing the import of *Summa theologiae* I, q. 1, a. 10, Bellamah adds that for Aquinas "the literal sense is the one intended by the author, and ... the author of Scripture is God.... [A]ny text of Scripture may convey several senses, because such signification lies within the capacity of its divine author, namely, God," and also because the human author can speak prophetically (and literally) about future realities (Bellamah, "*Tunc scimus cum causas cognoscimus*," 169).

[36] Thomas Merton, *The New Man* (New York: Farrar, Straus and Giroux, 1961), 132. I have excised one word (marked by "..."): "all."

in Jesus "the symbols and stories of Israel had been fulfilled in a shocking and decisive manner."³⁷ This at least was the claim made by the New Testament authors, by the first Christians, and in various ways by Jesus himself. When one reads the New Testament, one perceives that its authors continually show us the truth about Jesus typologically, in light of the central figures of Israel's Scriptures, beginning with Adam. The authors of the New Testament understood these figures to be part of "the saga of God's election, judgment, and redemption of a people through time," and they understood Jesus to have recapitulated and perfected the missions of these figures through his eschatological fulfillment of God's covenants with Israel.³⁸

Thus, Wright maintains that underlying the Gospel narratives about Jesus' life, death, and Resurrection, we see in a fulfilled and transformed way "the *narratives of Israel's vocation*: Abraham's call and covenant, Moses' Exodus and Tabernacle, David's and Solomon's victories and Temple."³⁹ For his part, the biblical theologian Thomas Schreiner takes us back to Adam: "Jesus is the true Adam, who exercises the rule that Adam was supposed to carry

---

[37] N. T. Wright, *History and Eschatology: Jesus and the Promise of Natural Theology* (Waco, TX: Baylor University Press, 2019), 197. See also Francis Watson's observation, spelling out the consequences of Gerhard von Rad's approach: "The 'Old Testament', as Christian scripture, only comes into existence in the moment of absolute newness represented by Jesus, and should be interpreted on the basis of its moment of origin; only the antitype makes the types visible as such" (Watson, *Text and Truth: Redefining Biblical Theology* [Grand Rapids, MI: Eerdmans, 1997], 207; cf. 212–19 for criticism of Brevard Childs's effort to preserve a "relatively independent status" for the Old Testament within the Christian Bible).

[38] Richard B. Hays, *The Conversion of the Imagination: Paul as Interpreter of Israel's Scripture* (Grand Rapids, MI: Eerdmans, 2005), xvi. Hays specifies what he means by inaugurated eschatology: Paul "identifies the church as standing precisely at the temporal juncture in which the old age has lost its claim upon us but the new age is present only proleptically.... The story is not over yet, and the church should imagine itself to be, analogously to Israel in the wilderness, a pilgrim people that has not yet arrived at its promised destination" (188).

[39] Wright, *History and Eschatology*, 237.

out."[40] Jesus thereby overcomes the consequences of human sin and death.[41] Brant Pitre emphasizes the theme of the new exodus in the Gospel narratives. He contends that Jesus "identified himself as the eschatological Moses, whose prophetic signs would not only signify the new exodus spoken of by the prophets, but actually set it in motion."[42] Joshua Jipp directs us toward Jesus as the eschatological David, known through "royal honorific[s] such as Christ, Son of David, Branch, the Lion of Judah, shepherd, King, and so on."[43] These typological Christologies are the means by which the New Testament authors communicate eschatological truths about Jesus. Francis Watson nicely sums up the point: "Old Testament conceptuality establishes the preconditions for the intelligibility of Jesus' person and work."[44]

In his masterwork *Echoes of Scripture in the Gospels*, Hays addresses the challenge mounted by scholars such as Sanders. Hays remarks that historical-critical scholarship "characteristically judges that the New Testament's Christological readings of Israel's Scripture are simply a big mistake."[45] Influenced by Hays, I offer three observations in response. First, these central figures of Israel's

---

[40] Thomas S. Schreiner, *The King in His Beauty: A Biblical Theology of the Old and New Testaments* (Grand Rapids, MI: Baker Academic, 2013), 438.

[41] For background, see Jeffrey S. Siker, *Sin in the New Testament* (Oxford: Oxford University Press, 2020). As Siker observes, the New Testament presents "sin as the fundamental human dilemma from which we need to be saved by God. The mechanism for such salvation within Christian tradition is always linked to the life, death, and resurrection of Jesus ... [T]he death of Jesus was the primary focus for how the early Christians came to understand God's extension of forgiveness of sins, as well as the defeat of the power of sin and sin's consequence, death" (172–73).

[42] Brant Pitre, *Jesus and the Last Supper* (Grand Rapids, MI: Eerdmans, 2015), 514.

[43] Joshua W. Jipp, *The Messianic Theology of the New Testament* (Grand Rapids, MI: Eerdmans, 2020), 16.

[44] Watson, *Text and Truth*, 218. Watson adds that this point does not mean that Jesus "can be adequately 'explained' on this basis," along lines that would reduce him to a mere extension of Old Testament figures (218).

[45] Richard B. Hays, *Echoes of Scripture in the Gospels* (Waco, TX: Baylor University Press, 2016), 3.

Scriptures shed light upon Jesus' words and deeds.⁴⁶ Did Jesus say or do anything that suggests a parallel with Adam? Yes, he inaugurated Israel's restoration and thereby stands at the center of a renewed creation. Did Jesus say or do anything that suggests a parallel with Isaac? Yes, he made clear that he was to shed his blood, in obedience, as the Father's beloved Son, thereby enacting the perfect sacrificial offering. Did Jesus say or do anything that suggests a link with Moses? Yes, he taught with unique authority, correcting Torah when needed; and he symbolically presented his ministry as a new exodus, in which his twelve disciples represent the twelve tribes of the people of God. Did Jesus say or do anything that suggests a link with Joshua? Yes, in accord with his baptism in the Jordan and through his death and Resurrection, he crossed over into the fullness of the Promised Land at the head of the people of God.⁴⁷ Did Jesus say or do anything that lays claim to Davidic royal authority? Yes, he preached the kingdom of God and did so as the one whose work is central to its inauguration.

Second, our contemporaries are unlikely to be able to make sense of Jesus as the Christ unless we retrieve the role of these typologies in illuminating his eschatological work. As Christopher Seitz says, "The challenge of our day is how to see in Jesus' death and raising actions truly in accordance with the Scriptures of Israel. For that, we shall need to return to typological and figural senses."⁴⁸ If we Christians are going to teach about the real Jesus Christ, who brings God's

---

⁴⁶ My point in this paragraph is not to claim that Jesus consciously thought of himself, so far as historical criticism can discern, as the New Adam or the New Isaac (and so on). Instead, I maintain that Jesus said and did things that make comprehensible (and justifiable) these typological connections as found in the New Testament.

⁴⁷ For relevant background, see Pitre, *Jesus and the Last Supper*, 166-67, 188.

⁴⁸ Christopher R. Seitz, *Figured Out: Typology and Providence in Christian Scripture* (Louisville, KY: Westminster John Knox, 2001), 47. See also the contention of Aidan Nichols, O.P.: "The fundamental promise-fulfillment format of the Bible is why the kind of exegesis we call 'typological' is the sort that best befits its unique genius" (Nichols, *Lovely, Like Jerusalem: The Fulfillment of the Old Testament in Christ and the Church* [San Francisco: Ignatius Press, 2007], 167).

plan to eschatological fulfillment, we must use the two-Testament Bible to underscore that Jesus taught and did things that enable us to recognize him as of universal relevance (the New Adam), as possessing definitive royal authority in establishing justice (the New David), as accomplishing the perfect offering in self-sacrificial love (the New Isaac), as teaching the authoritative law of love and enacting the new covenant (the New Moses), and as leading human beings into the true Promised Land (the New Joshua). If much of the Old Testament "is simply bewildering to modern Christians," as Leroy Huizenga remarks,[49] then this requires a Christology that unlocks the whole of Israel's Scriptures and covenantal life.

Third, Christianity stands or falls upon the existence and providence of God. Indeed, these two realities are the main point of much of Israel's Scriptures, so much so that the Letter to the Hebrews maintains in its chapter on the scriptural heroes of faith that "whoever would draw near to God must believe that he exists and that he rewards those who seek him" (Heb 11:6). The covenantal God enters into a relationship with his people in order to show them who he is (and, of course, *that* he is) and in order to show them that he cares for them and is trustworthy, despite their sufferings. The providential convergence of the two-Testament scriptural witness in the figure of Jesus Christ is what would be expected if Jesus is the incarnate Lord. No wonder Seitz remarks, "The crisis in [biblical] hermeneutics is in reality a crisis involving God's providence."[50] One way that God shows his fidelity consists in his shaping of Israel's history and Scriptures to illuminate the person and work of Jesus.[51]

---

[49] Leroy A. Huizenga, *Loosing the Lion: Proclaiming the Gospel of Mark* (Steubenville, OH: Emmaus Road, 2017), 19.
[50] Huizenga, *Loosing the Lion*, 33.
[51] See also, from a different angle than the one pursued here, Gregory R. Lanier's study of Luke's application to Jesus of various metaphors that are "significant OT/Jewish ways of *conceptualizing* the identity of God" (Lanier, *Old Testament Conceptual Metaphors and the Christology of Luke's Gospel* [London: T&T Clark, 2018], 222).

INTRODUCTION

Thomism, *Ressourcement*, and Typology

As noted above, although Aquinas does not fully exploit the Christological typologies in the *tertia pars* of the *Summa theologiae* – although even if he does observe that Christ's death on a Cross fulfills "very many figures" found in Israel's Scriptures[52] – the typologies appear more centrally in Aquinas's biblical commentaries. Moreover, Aquinas treats Christ as the New Melchizedek in the *tertia pars*'s question on Christ's priesthood. Thus, the fact that Aquinas's theology is scientific, in an Aristotelian sense (while also employing reasons of fittingness[53]), does not prevent Aquinas from decisively employing Christological typology within his *sacra doctrina*.

Aquinas states that "all the senses are founded on one – the literal – from which alone can any argument be drawn, and not from those intended in allegory."[54] It may seem that the New Testament typologies are the spiritual sense (specifically, the allegorical sense), and for Aquinas "nothing necessary to faith is contained under the spiritual sense which is not elsewhere put forward by the Scripture in its literal sense."[55] But in fact Aquinas makes clear that "the literal sense is what is first intended by the words whether properly speaking or figuratively."[56] Given this definition, the typologies that are most

[52] Thomas Aquinas, *Summa theologiae*, trans. Fathers of the English Dominican Province (Westminster, MD: Christian Classics, 1981), III, q. 46, a. 4.
[53] See Aidan Nichols, O.P., "St. Thomas Aquinas on the Passion of Christ: A Reading of *Summa Theologiae* IIIa, q. 46," *Scottish Journal of Theology* 43 (1990): 447–59.
[54] Aquinas, *Summa theologiae* I, q. 1, a. 10, ad 1.
[55] I, q. 1, a. 10, ad 1. Franklin T. Harkins states, "Following the most common medieval classification, Aquinas divides the spiritual sense into the allegorical, the moral or tropological, and the anagogical. The allegorical sense is that according to which 'the things of the Old Law signify the things of the New Law' (I.1.10 co.). For Aquinas, as for premodern exegetes generally, Christological interpretations of the Old Testament fall within the ambit of the allegorical" (Harkins, *Thomas Aquinas: The Basics* [London: Routledge, 2021], 35).
[56] Thomas Aquinas, *Commentary on the Book of Job*, trans. Brian Thomas Becket Mullady, O.P., ed. The Aquinas Institute (Lander, WY: The Aquinas Institute for the Study of Sacred Doctrine, 2016), ch. 1, lect. 2, p. 14.

notable for Christology belong to the New Testament's literal sense. According to the literal sense of various New Testament texts, Jesus is the New Adam, New Isaac, New Moses, New Joshua, and New David. Although he transcends these Old Testament personages, they are "types" of him and he eschatologically recapitulates and fulfills their missions.

In the patristic and medieval eras, as Hans Boersma says, "Christian readers were convinced of the providential guidance of God throughout history. So they would be more likely to regard similarities between various events reflected in different [scriptural] passages as the result of God's faithful character rather than as mere historical coincidence."[57] We should do the same in our reading of Scripture. Even more pointedly, Ephraim Radner advises: "If … the Word is indeed the living hand that shapes events, then we should rightly seek the meaning of such events in their figural identity."[58] We should not expect to be able to understand Jesus as the Christ outside of his figural identity. For example, if Jesus were not the New David, he could not have brought Israel's covenants to eschatological fulfillment. Indeed, as Matthew Barrett says, "Jesus' own Christological reading of the Old Testament, one imitated by his disciples," is typologically structured.[59]

In the mid-twentieth century, *Ressourcement* theologians and neoscholastic theologians argued about what place to give to biblical typologies and the spiritual senses. While otherwise being close collaborators in the retrieval of typological awareness, the Jesuits Jean Daniélou and Henri de Lubac sharply disagreed with each other about whether typology can or should be distinguished from

---

[57] Hans Boersma, *Sacramental Preaching: Sermons on the Hidden Presence of Christ* (Grand Rapids, MI: Baker Academic, 2016), 51.

[58] Ephraim Radner, *Time and the Word: Figural Reading of the Christian Scriptures* (Grand Rapids, MI: Eerdmans, 2016), 8.

[59] Matthew Barrett, *Canon, Covenant and Christology: Rethinking Jesus and the Scriptures of Israel* (Downers Grove, IL: IVP Academic, 2020), 37.

allegory (Daniélou thought so, de Lubac thought not).[60] Among the views condemned in Pope Pius XII's 1950 encyclical *Humani Generis* is the view that "the literal sense of Holy Scripture and its explanation, carefully worked out under the Church's vigilance by so many great exegetes, should yield now to a new exegesis, which they are pleased to call symbolic or spiritual."[61] Some neoscholastics feared that if biblical history were interpreted typologically in a vigorous manner, then the defense of the historicity of the biblical narratives could be imperiled. With regard to Christology, this reasonable fear should lead us to recognize the need for a defense of the historicity of the New Testament's witness to Jesus,[62] but there is no need to play down the typologies woven into the fabric of the New Testament.

In an earlier book, *Participatory Biblical Exegesis*, I argued in favor of a typologically rich understanding of "history," and thus of the literal sense, due to history's participation in divine providence.[63] I was indebted to Francis Martin, who remarks that "the persons of Israel share proleptically but metaphysically in the reality of Christ," and so "the relation between Jesus and Moses or David is *analogical* and not merely intertextual."[64] Although my arguments in *Participatory*

---

[60] See Jean Daniélou, S.J., *The Lord of History: Reflections on the Inner Meaning of History*, trans. Nigel Abercrombie (Chicago: Henry Regnery, 1958); and Henri de Lubac, S.J., "'Typologie' et allégorisme," *Recherches de science religieuse* 34 (1947): 180–226.

[61] Pope Pius XII, Encyclical *Humani Generis*, §23, at www.vatican.va/content/pius-xii/en/encyclicals/documents/hf_p-xii_enc_12081950_humani-generis.html.

[62] See, for example, Brant Pitre, *The Case for Jesus: The Biblical and Historical Evidence for Christ* (New York: Image, 2016). See also my *Did Jesus Rise from the Dead? Historical and Theological Reflections* (Oxford: Oxford University Press, 2019).

[63] See my *Participatory Biblical Exegesis: A Theology of Biblical Interpretation* (Notre Dame: University of Notre Dame Press, 2008). See also, more recently, T. Adam Van Wart, "Aquinas's Eschatological Historiography: Job, Providence, and the Multiple Senses of the Historical Event," *Pro Ecclesia* 30 (2021): 32–50.

[64] Francis Martin, *Sacred Scripture: The Disclosure of the Word* (Naples, FL: Sapientia Press, 2006), 274. See also Jeremy Holmes, "Participation and the Meaning of Scripture," in *Reading Sacred Scripture with Thomas Aquinas*, 91–113. I think that such typologies need not be grounded in a historical referent although they may well be. Even

Biblical Exegesis fit with *Ressourcement* theology, I advanced the arguments on Thomistic grounds. Despite significant philosophical differences (where the neoscholastics were largely in the right) and despite significant differences in historical erudition (where the *Ressourcement* theologians had the upper hand), these two movements of twentieth-century theology should complement each other.

My approach in the present book brings together neoscholastic or Thomistic insights with *Ressourcement* insights into figural Christology. My approach may also help to further unite Protestant and Catholic Thomistic Christologies, by highlighting biblical theology in a manner congruent with Reformed theologians' emphasis on Scripture, while doing so in a way befitting Catholic (and Orthodox) emphasis on the importance of patristic exegesis. Overall, I strive to contribute to what Piotr Roszak and Jörgen Vijgen have called "Biblical Thomism" – defined not as something *other than* "Thomism" but as an effort "to understand and employ the praxis of *sacra doctrina*, as exemplified primarily by Thomas Aquinas" in light of "the pivotal role of Scripture in such a speculative engagement with Revelation."[65] In his own recent contribution to Biblical Thomism, Serge-Thomas Bonino has highlighted Aquinas's practice of a "*conversio ad Scripturas*" by which "the theologian returns to the Bible, on one hand to verify the conformity of his theology to the permanent standard that is the Word of God, and on the other hand to deepen the understanding of the Scriptures by means of perspectives opened up by theological contemplation."[66] This is the

---

if no "historical Isaac" existed, God could have providentially governed the development of the text of Genesis to ensure a typological preparation for Jesus the New Isaac.

[65] Piotr Roszak and Jörgen Vijgen, "Introduction," in *Towards a Biblical Thomism: Thomas Aquinas and the Renewal of Biblical Theology*, ed. Piotr Roszak and Jörgen Vijgen (Pamplona: EUNSA, 2018), 11–20, at 14. The present book can be seen as a companion to my earlier work of constructive Thomistic Christology, *Christ's Fulfillment of Torah and Temple: Salvation according to Thomas Aquinas* (Notre Dame: University of Notre Dame Press, 2002).

[66] Serge-Thomas Bonino, O.P., *Saint Thomas d'Aquin, lecteur du* Cantique des Cantiques (Paris: Cerf, 2019), 137. I employ here the translation of Bonino's book

standpoint from which my "reconfiguring" of Thomistic Christology in an eschatological key will proceed.

Conclusion

Hays has encouraged contemporary theologians and biblical scholars to appreciate "the revisionary figural ways that the four Gospel writers actually read Israel's Scripture."[67] Similarly, Jeffrey Pulse calls upon the Christian Bible's readers "to identify the various biblical motifs that weave their way through the entirety of the biblical narrative…. These motifs show the unity of the narrative as they connect all Scripture – Genesis to Revelation – into one story."[68] The Gospels' figural reading practices have dogmatic significance, insofar as they shed light on Jesus' Incarnation, teaching, Cross, and Resurrection. Just as typologies are important for Scripture's presentation of the mysteries of Christ, so also can they contribute much to Thomistic Christology.

On this basis, my book sketches a typological path for Thomistic integration of contemporary eschatological portraits of Jesus' person and work. Thomists can agree with Dale Allison's claim that "Jesus was an apocalyptic prophet."[69] Jesus understood himself to be proclaiming and inaugurating the eschatological kingdom, healing the fallen creation and restoring his people. Allison notes that "the major theme of Jesus' preaching was the kingdom of God" and

---

done by Andrew Levering, forthcoming as *Reading the Song of Songs with St. Thomas Aquinas* (Washington, DC: Catholic University of America Press). See also Stéphane Loiseau, *De l'écoute à la parole. La lecture biblique dans la doctrine sacrée selon Thomas d'Aquin* (Paris: Cerf, 2017).

[67] Hays, *Echoes of Scripture in the Gospels*, 4.
[68] Jeffrey Pulse, *Figuring Resurrection: Joseph as a Death and Resurrection Figure in the Old Testament and Second Temple Judaism* (Bellingham, WA: Lexham, 2021), 278.
[69] Dale C. Allison, Jr., *Constructing Jesus: Memory, Imagination, and History* (Grand Rapids, MI: Baker Academic, 2010), 31.

that "Jesus himself is, in the canonical Gospels, the eschatological king, or destined to be such."[70]

As noted above, Aquinas affirms that Jesus is the Messianic king who has inaugurated the eschatological kingdom of God, even if Aquinas does not give this point an explicit place in the *tertia pars*. As we will see, explicit reflection on Jesus as the New David would be helpful for contemporary Thomistic Christology (Chapter 6).

Pitre has shown that Jesus placed the new exodus at the very center of his worldview. Commenting upon the symbolism of the Last Supper, Pitre reconstructs its likely rationale: "Just as the first exodus was set in motion by the Passover sacrifice, so too the new exodus, which will usher in the kingdom, is set in motion by a new Passover – an eschatological Passover – that is accomplished by means of his own suffering, death, and restoration to life 'in the kingdom.'"[71] The new exodus theme receives a prominent place in the New Testament, and it sheds light upon many of the central aspects of Jesus' words and deeds. Attention to Jesus as the New Moses (Chapter 4) and New Joshua (Chapter 5) can enrich contemporary Thomistic Christology's reflections on various aspects of the new exodus, such as Christ's teaching and covenantal enactment (New Moses) and Christ's baptism and Ascension (New Joshua).

Jesus in the Gospels strongly associates himself with the Temple. Anthony Le Donne has argued that the title "Son of David," in the Gospels, "was both Davidic and Solomonic," and he finds that "the charting of memory refraction will show how early memories of Jesus were initially shaped by typological interpretation."[72]

---

[70] Allison, *Constructing Jesus*, 244–45. For Allison, it is likely that Jesus thought of the full arrival of the kingdom as far more imminent than has actually turned out to be the case, and Allison does not give particular credence, as a historian, to Jesus being God incarnate.

[71] Pitre, *Jesus and the Last Supper*, 511.

[72] Le Donne, *The Historiographical Jesus*, 94.

Le Donne suggests that Mark 11 and Matthew 21 – Jesus' triumphal entry into Jerusalem and his cleansing of the Temple – should be read in light of Solomon the Son of David and Temple builder.[73] Michael Patrick Barber has provided further arguments along similar lines.[74] For contemporary Thomistic Christology, Christ as the New Isaac (Chapter 3) – the perfect cultic sacrifice – offers a path for engaging Christ's relation to the Temple.

Among the more pressing theological issues today are whether Christ really is the universal Savior and whether faith (implicit or explicit) in Christ is necessary for salvation. In my view, attention to Christ as the New Adam (Chapter 2) provides a way for contemporary Thomistic Christology to deepen its appreciation of Christ's Headship and to explain what it means to affirm that Christ is the universal Savior.

Aquinas's use of the New Melchizedek typology sets the pattern for my chapters. When he addresses Christ's priesthood in the *tertia pars*, he recalls the Letter to the Hebrews's statement that Jesus was "designated by God a high priest according to the order of Melchizedek" (Heb 5:10). In an insistent and evocative manner, Hebrews discusses Jesus in light of Melchizedek. After showing why Christ did not descend from the Levitical or Aaronic priesthood, Aquinas concludes his *quaestio* on Christ's priesthood (III, q. 22) by

---

[73] Jiří Dvořáček emphasizes Solomon's role in Jewish tradition as a healer and exorcist. With significant textual evidence, he argues that "when Matthew's Jesus in Matt 12,42 says 'Something greater than Solomon is here,' he alludes not only to his own person and teaching but also to his miraculous deeds, namely to his healings and exorcisms, which are deeds of wisdom (cf. Matt 11,2; 11,19) and which surpass even the healings and exorcisms of Solomon (9,33; 12,42)" (Dvořáček, *The Son of David in Matthew's Gospel in the Light of the Solomon as Exorcist Tradition* [Tübingen: Mohr Siebeck, 2016], 205).

[74] Michael Patrick Barber, "Jesus as the Davidic Temple Builder and Peter's Priestly Role in Matthew 16:16–19," *Journal of Biblical Literature* 132 (2013): 935–53. For the argument that Jesus understood David and Solomon along priestly lines – and understood himself as the "Son of David" in this sense – see Nicholas Perrin, *Jesus the Priest* (Grand Rapids, MI: Baker Academic, 2018), 152–65.

discussing what it means for Christ to be a New Melchizedek.[75] His discussion here exemplifies the value of the "reconfiguring" that I hope to encourage in Thomistic Christology today.

In sum, after an opening chapter demonstrating that the present ecumenical renewal of Thomistic Christology offers an exciting prospect, my five constructive chapters will outline a biblical, patristic, and Thomistic typological approach whose consistent purpose is to integrate contemporary Thomistic Christology more fully with the New Testament's inaugurated eschatology.

---

[75] Fred L. Horton, Jr., provides some background from the Church Fathers: "In searching the fathers, Jerome found that, except for Origen, those who dealt with Melchizedek all considered him to be a man, a Canaanite, and the king of Jerusalem. In general the function of Melchizedek for the church fathers was that of a priest of the uncircumcision, a priesthood carried on through Christ .... The great majority of writings about Melchizedek in the early church stem from writers opposing heretics who make of Melchizedek a heavenly being" (Horton, *The Melchizedek Tradition: A Critical Examination of the Sources to the Fifth Century A.D. and in the Epistle to the Hebrews* [Cambridge: Cambridge University Press, 1976], 88–89). Horton argues that Hebrews does not consider Melchizedek to be a heavenly being. Susan R. Garrett deems it likely that the authors of Genesis 14:18–19 and Psalm 110:4 thought Melchizedek to be an angel: see Garrett, *No Ordinary Angel: Celestial Spirits and Christian Claims about Jesus* (New Haven, CT: Yale University Press, 2008), 67. Garrett adds, "Jesus is never called an angel in the New Testament, and indeed he is distinguished from them in quite important ways" (Garrett, *No Ordinary Angel*, 238).

1 | Contemporary Thomistic Christology

1.1 Introduction

In this chapter, I will survey some of the most notable works of Thomistic Christology that have appeared in recent decades. These include historical works on Thomas Aquinas's Christology; dogmatic works of Reformed, Anglican, and Eastern Catholic Thomistic Christology; and dogmatic works of (Roman) Catholic Thomistic Christology. My purpose in this first chapter is to present the arguments of these books and to make clear that I associate my "reconfiguring" closely with their theological and metaphysical perspectives. Modern Christology benefits greatly from attention to the richly biblical, patristic, and metaphysical Christology offered by Aquinas.

Since I also hold that some important biblical elements should be added to Thomistic Christology as presently practiced, this makes it even more incumbent upon me to provide a detailed portrait of contemporary Thomistic Christology. If I am calling for contemporary Thomistic Christology to be reconfigured in a certain way, this proposal requires an assessment of the contributions of recent scholars in the domain of Thomistic Christology.

Before proceeding, let me add that I recognize that Aquinas's Christology was never merely ignored even by those theologians who sharply disagreed with the neoscholastic thinkers who predominated in Catholic theology between the late nineteenth century and the 1950s. To name one influential example, Karl Barth makes relatively frequent references to Aquinas in the first volume of his

1.1 INTRODUCTION

Church Dogmatics. Rather acerbically, Barth states of Aquinas that the "story that when he was engaged in the christological part of the work [the *tertia pars*] Christ appeared to him with the words: *Bene scripsisti de me, Thoma!* seems to be less in accord with the facts!"[1] Barth thinks that Aquinas, in treating of Christ, not only did so in an improper order – in the third part of the *Summa* rather than in its opening part – but also imported far too much Aristotle.[2] Barth warns that Protestant theologians must not become "so weary of Descartes that we throw ourselves into the arms of, e.g., Aristotle or Thomas."[3]

Barth goes on to say that he does not agree with Aquinas's conception of a divine "person" or with Aquinas's approach to identifying Jesus Christ in his eternal Sonship as the "Word."[4] He thinks that Aquinas's doctrine of the "Word" arises more from his anthropology than from Scripture. Barth criticizes Aquinas's account of Mary's *fiat* at the Annunciation.[5] In arguing that Jesus represented us as Priest, Barth finds Aquinas's position too weak, because Aquinas does not perceive that the category "priest" applies solely to Christ. Moreover, Aquinas does not present Christ as the Judge judged in our place: "Jesus Christ is

---

[1] Karl Barth, *Church Dogmatics*, vol. 1, *The Doctrine of the Word of God, Part 1*, 2nd ed., trans. G. W. Bromiley, ed. G. W. Bromiley and T. F. Torrance (Edinburgh: T&T Clark, 1975), 21.

[2] Indeed, as Corey Barnes and Jean-Pierre Torrell have shown, there is no doubt that Aquinas employs Aristotle in highly significant ways in the *tertia pars*'s treatise on Christ's Person and work. See Corey L. Barnes, "Aristotle in the *Summa Theologiae*'s Christology," in *Aristotle in Aquinas's Theology*, ed. Gilles Emery, O.P., and Matthew Levering (Oxford: Oxford University Press, 2015), 186–204; Jean-Pierre Torrell, O.P., *Jésus le Christ chez saint Thomas d'Aquin. Texte de la Tertia Pars (ST IIIa) traduit et commenté, accompagné de Données historiques et doctrinales et de cinquante Textes choisis* (Paris: Cerf, 2008).

[3] Barth, *Church Dogmatics*, 1.1, 195.

[4] See Barth, *Church Dogmatics*, 1.1, 437.

[5] Karl Barth, *Church Dogmatics*, vol. 1, *The Doctrine of the Word of God, Part 2*, trans. G. T. Thomson and Harold Knight, ed. G. W. Bromiley and T. F. Torrance (Edinburgh: T&T Clark, 1956), 144.

the One who was accused, condemned and judged in the place of us sinners."⁶

In the Christology and soteriology of his *Theo-Drama*, Barth's fellow Swiss dogmatician Hans Urs von Balthasar likewise cites Aquinas at important junctures, even if to criticize him. More than Barth, Balthasar finds himself in agreement with Aquinas. In his account of Christ's Person, for example, Balthasar refers to Aquinas's argument that the Person of the Son, in the economy of salvation, is a "mission." For Balthasar "the economic Trinity cannot be regarded as simply identical with the immanent," but nevertheless the incarnate Son is indeed "the Subject in whom person and mission are identical."⁷ Aquinas would surely agree, even if Aquinas's understanding of "person" and of "mission" is somewhat different than Balthasar's.

Balthasar describes Aquinas's account of Christ's knowledge in some detail, while differing from it.⁸ He disagrees with Aquinas's view that the Word's activity in the Incarnation precedes (non-temporally) that of the Spirit.⁹ In his view, too, Aquinas's position that Christ has only one *esse* is mistaken.¹⁰ Remarking that "Thomas' view of Christ's 'representation' builds on the soteriology of Anselm," Balthasar contends that the New Testament requires us to go beyond this perspective.¹¹ In his historical overview of Christian soteriology, Balthasar devotes four pages to Aquinas, arguing that

---

[6] Karl Barth, *Church Dogmatics*, vol. 4, *The Doctrine of Reconciliation, Part 1*, trans. G. W. Bromiley, ed. G. W. Bromiley and T. F. Torrance (Edinburgh: T&T Clark, 1956), 277; on Aquinas see 275.

[7] Hans Urs von Balthasar, *Theo-Drama: Theological Dramatic Theory*, vol. 3, *The Dramatis Personae: The Person in Christ*, trans. Graham Harrison (San Francisco: Ignatius Press, 1992), 157.

[8] See Balthasar, *Theo-Drama*, vol. 3, 174–75, 192.

[9] See Balthasar, *Theo-Drama*, vol. 3, 186.

[10] See Balthasar, *Theo-Drama*, vol. 3, 228n68. *Esse* in this debate is not the *esse* of predication but rather is *esse in realis*.

[11] Balthasar, *Theo-Drama*, vol. 3, 241–42.

while Aquinas does better than Anselm, he fails to grasp the radical nature of Christ's bearing of our sin.[12]

Elsewhere I have challenged some of these criticisms of Aquinas. For present purposes, however, the point is simply that Aquinas's Christology never disappeared entirely from the scene, even among its critics. No doubt, in the first few decades after the Second Vatican Council, Aquinas's Christology garnered far less interest among Catholic dogmatic theologians than it had prior to the Council. In Jon Sobrino's *Jesus the Liberator*, for example, Aquinas's contribution to Christology is summed up by including Aquinas in a list of patristic and medieval theologians who failed to take seriously enough Christ's abandonment by the Father and also by asserting, without further comment, that Aquinas's denial that Christ had faith is the result of his reliance on "a scholastic and non-biblical concept [of faith], and a type of argumentation starting from the hypostatic union."[13] Sobrino, a Spanish Jesuit who received his theological formation in the years immediately after the Council and then became a noted liberation theologian in El Salvador, does not apologize for paying only dismissive attention to Aquinas's Christology. Whereas Balthasar takes some time to criticize Aquinas and draws upon him positively in certain ways, Sobrino does not.

Sobrino's companion volume to *Jesus the Liberator* – titled *Christ the Liberator: A View from the Victims* – mentions Aquinas only once, stating that although Aquinas should be commended for devoting twenty-five questions in the *tertia pars* to the mysteries of Christ's life, contemporary theology must entirely revise Aquinas's approach, through the lens of historical-critical exegesis. For Sobrino, Aquinas has to be superseded because, like his patristic

---

[12] See Hans Urs von Balthasar, *Theo-Drama: Theological Dramatic Theory*, vol. 4, *The Action*, trans. Graham Harrison (San Francisco: Ignatius Press, 1994), 262–66.
[13] Jon Sobrino, S.J., *Jesus the Liberator: A Historical-Theological Reading of Jesus of Nazareth*, trans. Paul Burns and Francis McDonagh (Maryknoll, NY: Orbis, 1993), 155, cf. 237–38.

predecessors, he grounded himself in "doxological and not historical statements," whereas contemporary theology must focus upon "the *reality* of Jesus of Nazareth, recalling it and understanding it as *history*."[14]

In the wider Church, Sobrino's burial of Thomistic Christology in the 1990s was generally assumed to be justified. On this view, Thomistic Christology would continue to be studied by historical theologians, but no more would it be taken seriously by dogmatic theologians. How mistaken this perspective was!

1.2 The Revival of Thomistic Christology

Thomistic Christology began to revive in the 1980s when historically minded studies reintroduced the value of Aquinas's perspective. Romanus Cessario's 1982 *Christian Satisfaction in Aquinas: Towards a Personalist Understanding* and Thomas Weinandy's 1985 *Does God Change?* planted the seeds for the reintroduction of Thomistic Christology in the English-speaking world. By expositing and defending Aquinas's theology of the Incarnation and the Cross, these published dissertations made the case that Aquinas's Christology remains highly relevant. Cessario studied at the University of Fribourg under the Thomists Colman O'Neill, Servais Pinckaers, and Jean-Hervé Nicolas, and Weinandy studied at the University of London under the Anglican Thomistic theologian Eric Mascall.[15] Cessario's book has appeared in two subsequent editions (1990 and 2020), demonstrating its value. Weinandy has continued on the

---

[14] Jon Sobrino, S.J., *Christ the Liberator: A View from the Victims*, trans. Paul Burns (Maryknoll, NY: Orbis, 2001), 227–28.

[15] See Romanus Cessario, O.P., *Christian Satisfaction in Aquinas: Towards a Personalist Understanding* (Washington, DC: University Press of America, 1982); Thomas G. Weinandy, O.F.M. Cap., *Does God Change? The Word's Becoming in the Incarnation* (Still River, MA: St. Bede's Publications, 1985).

1.2 THE REVIVAL OF THOMISTIC CHRISTOLOGY

path of constructive Thomistic Christology in later books such as *Does God Suffer?* (2000) and *Jesus: Essays in Christology* (2014).[16]

In the 1990s, Jean-Pierre Torrell was at work on studies of Thomistic Christology that have exercised a notable influence throughout the Catholic world. He first published *L'Initiation à Saint Thomas d'Aquin: Sa personne et son oeuvre* in 1993, and he published its companion volume, *Saint Thomas d'Aquin, maître spirituel*, in 1996. The first book is a historical introduction to Aquinas's life and writings, and Torrell shows that "in Thomas's thought not only does the Incarnation not introduce any disruption into the schema *exitus-reditus* [that governs the *Summa theologiae*] but, on the contrary, it is only through the Incarnation that this movement achieves its fruition."[17] The second book gives full rein to Torrell's valuation of Aquinas's Christology, though by no means does Torrell neglect Aquinas's other themes. The Son is "the Father's Art and perfect Image" and is the one "through whom we come forth from the Father and return to Him."[18] The Son becomes incarnate as Jesus Christ as our Savior, model, and path to union with the Trinity. Torrell emphasizes the centrality of the imitation of Christ for Aquinas's spirituality and understanding of the moral life.

In 1999, Torrell published a landmark two-volume study, *Le Christ en ses mystères: La view et l'oeuvre de Jésus selon saint Thomas d'Aquin*.[19] This book tracks Aquinas's treatise on the mysteries of Christ's life, questions 27–59 of the *tertia pars*. Torrell covers all the topics that Aquinas investigates in this profound section of the

---

[16] See Thomas G. Weinandy, O.F.M. Cap., *Does God Suffer?* (Notre Dame: University of Notre Dame Press, 2000); Weinandy, *Jesus: Essays in Christology* (Ave Maria, FL: Sapientia Press, 2014).

[17] Jean-Pierre Torrell, O.P., *Saint Thomas Aquinas*, vol. 1, *The Person and His Work*, trans. Robert Royal (Washington, DC: Catholic University of America Press, 1996), 155.

[18] Jean-Pierre Torrell, O.P., *Saint Thomas Aquinas*, vol. 2, *Spiritual Master*, trans. Robert Royal (Washington, DC: Catholic University of America Press, 1996), 101.

[19] Jean-Pierre Torrell, O.P., *Le Christ en ses mystères: La view et l'oeuvre de Jésus selon saint Thomas d'Aquin*, 2 vols. (Paris: Desclée, 1999).

Summa theologiae. In his study, Torrell expresses a debt to the Italian scholar Inos Biffi's historical research on Aquinas's Christology, synthesized as *I Misteri di Cristo in Tommaso d'Aquino*.[20] As Torrell shows, Aquinas finds in all of Christ's words and deeds matter for inexhaustible theological reflection and spiritual meditation.[21] I should also mention Torrell's 2008 translation and commentary on the *tertia pars*, published as *Jésus le Christ chez saint Thomas d'Aquin*, as well as various essays (mainly from the 1990s and early 2000s) that were translated and published in English as *Christ and Spirituality in St. Thomas Aquinas*.[22] Torrell's historical retrieval of Aquinas's Christology helped to make it a respectable object of study again.

1.2.1 Historical, Reformed, Anglican, and Eastern Catholic Retrievals of Aquinas's Christology

Beginning in the late 1990s, a steady stream of historically erudite studies of Aquinas's Christology began to appear. Let me mention a few of them here. Michael Gorman defended a dissertation at Boston College under Matthew Lamb in 1997 that was eventually published, in a much revised form, as *Aquinas on the Metaphysics of the Hypostatic Union*.[23] Gorman clears Aquinas of the charge of rationalism in his metaphysics of the Incarnation – showing that Aquinas never pushes too far but instead tacitly grants that "our reflection must always reach a point where we must settle for something that is, in itself, not fully satisfying" – while also demonstrating that Aquinas does not reach this point too soon but instead

---

[20] See Inos Biffi, *I Misteri di Cristo in Tommaso d'Aquino* (Milan: Jaca Book, 1994).
[21] See Torrell, *Le Christ en ses mystères*, 21.
[22] See Torrell, *Jésus le Christ chez saint Thomas d'Aquin*; Torrell, *Christ and Spirituality in St. Thomas Aquinas*, trans. Bernhard Blankenhorn, O.P. (Washington, DC: Catholic University of America Press, 2011).
[23] Michael Gorman, *Aquinas on the Metaphysics of the Hypostatic Union* (Cambridge: Cambridge University Press, 2017).

fruitfully allows metaphysical inquiry to address the problems that challenge the doctrine of the Incarnation.[24] Gorman also responds to the view that Aquinas's account of the Incarnation tends toward monophysitism.[25] Around the same time, Paul Gondreau completed his doctoral dissertation under Torrell at the University of Fribourg. First published in 2002 and twice republished since (most recently in 2018), Gondreau's *The Passions of Christ's Soul in the Theology of St. Thomas Aquinas* is a tour de force of historical scholarship, exhibiting a mastery of the various sources and systematic conclusions of Aquinas's on Christ's passions. In exploring Aquinas's account of Christ's full humanity, sinlessness, and suffering, Gondreau makes clear that Aquinas "ranks as the one medieval author who paid the greatest heed to the demands of the Incarnation and who did more than anyone to shed light on the human face of God."[26]

In 2012, Corey Barnes published his dissertation, completed under Joseph Wawrykow at the University of Notre Dame, titled *Christ's Two Wills in Scholastic Thought: The Christology of Aquinas and Its Historical Contexts*. Barnes helps us to appreciate the relation of the Incarnation of the Word and the human redemptive acts of Christ. Clearly, the unity of Christ as an acting Person matters greatly for orthodox Christian understanding of how this particular man can accomplish salvation for the whole world.[27] Most recently, Dominic Legge in 2017 published *The Trinitarian Christology of St Thomas Aquinas*, a revised version of his dissertation written

---

[24] Gorman, *Aquinas on the Metaphysics of the Hypostatic Union*, 163.

[25] For this view, see Richard Cross, *The Metaphysics of the Incarnation: Thomas Aquinas to Duns Scotus* (Oxford: Oxford University Press, 2002). Cross's book gave a boost to the study of Aquinas's Christology.

[26] Paul Gondreau, *The Passions of Christ's Soul in the Theology of St. Thomas Aquinas* (Providence, RI: Cluny, 2018), iii. The first edition appeared under the same title from Aschendorff.

[27] As Barnes says, "Aquinas's repeated references to Christ's humanity as *instrumentum divinitatis* avoid Nestorian overtones precisely because he specifies *instrumentum divinitatis* as a hypostatically united rational instrument. This both eliminates a

at the University of Fribourg under Gilles Emery. In his foreword to this book, Emery notes that Legge reads "Christology in light of Aquinas's theology of the divine missions," with the result that Aquinas's Christology is unveiled as "a genuine Spirit Christology" in which the words and deeds of Christ are interiorly unified and through which we come to appreciate that, as the Gospels attest, "Christ and the Holy Spirit lead us to the Father by giving us a participation in the very relations that they have with the Father."[28] With Legge's insights in hand, Christians can discover that "'the Trinitarian shape of our salvation is derived from the Trinitarian shape of the mystery of the incarnation.'"[29]

At the same time, serious Reformed interest in Aquinas's Christology has emerged. Let me confine myself to a few notable representatives. First, Michael Allen has mined various elements of Aquinas's theology in his work. This includes devoting considerable effort in his published doctoral dissertation, *The Christ's Faith: A Dogmatic Account*, to understanding and criticizing Aquinas's view of Christ's knowledge. In his chapter on the metaphysics of the Incarnation, Allen approves Aquinas's understanding of divine transcendence (and immanence) and analogous discourse. He then shows along Thomistic lines that "the claim that divine transcendence and analogy has been overcome in the *hypostatic union* fails to honor the otherness brought within the very life of

---

Nestorian interpretation of instrumentality and elevates the soteriological role of Christ's human will" (Corey L. Barnes, *Christ's Two Wills in Scholastic Thought: The Christology of Aquinas and Its Historical Contexts* [Toronto: Pontifical Institute of Mediaeval Studies, 2012], 284). Barnes draws upon a European historical study from the period of the relative desuetude of Thomistic research: Francis Ruello, *La christologie de Thomas d'Aquin* (Paris: Beauchesne, 1987).

[28] Gilles Emery, O.P., "Foreword," in Dominic Legge, O.P., *The Trinitarian Christology of St Thomas Aquinas* (Oxford: Oxford University Press, 2017), v-viii, at v-vii.

[29] Emery, "Foreword," viii, citing Legge, 235. See also Gilles Emery, O.P., "*Theologia* and *Dispensatio*: The Centrality of the Divine Missions in St. Thomas's Trinitarian Theology," *The Thomist* 74 (2010): 515-61.

the eternal Son."³⁰ He rejects Aquinas's view that Christ did not have faith, arguing that Aquinas's understanding of "the moral and intellectual dimensions of Christ's personality" is a weak spot that can be corrected by a fuller attention to "the emphasis on history and dynamism throughout the rest of Thomas's Christology and soteriology."³¹

In his 2019 *God in Himself: Scripture, Metaphysics, and the Task of Christian Theology*, Steven Duby devotes a chapter to the Incarnation. Duby is one of the clearest and most incisive theologians writing today, and he shapes his chapter as a Thomistic dialogue with Karl Barth, T. F. Torrance, Eberhard Jüngel, Robert Jenson, and Bruce McCormack. He argues that a proper understanding of God's speaking through Scripture justifies "contemplat[ing] God from above in what Thomas calls a 'way of descent,' understanding God himself (in an ectypal manner) and then with God's own guidance framing his outward works in the light of his eternal triune life."³² In short, everything that Christ does in the flesh must be understood in light of his relation to the Father and to the Spirit, but not in such a way as to derive that relation simply from (e.g.) the Cross. The Old Testament frames Christ's identity, and the New Testament helps us to see, as Aquinas holds, that "the humanity of the Son is uniquely endowed with wisdom by the one who is the Spirit of the Son as well as the Father."³³

In his 2021 *The Same God Who Works All Things: Inseparable Operations in Trinitarian Theology*, Adonis Vidu devotes chapters to the Incarnation, Christ's "theandric" action and suffering, Christ's work of atonement, and the Spirit of Christ. The central

---

³⁰ R. Michael Allen, *The Christ's Faith: A Dogmatic Account* (London: Continuum, 2009), 117.
³¹ Allen, *The Christ's Faith*, 148–49.
³² Steven J. Duby, *God in Himself: Scripture, Metaphysics, and the Task of Christian Theology* (Downers Grove, IL: IVP Academic, 2019), 141.
³³ Duby, *God in Himself*, 151.

question that Vidu investigates is whether the three divine Persons can truly be said to be undivided in their operation *ad extra*. Are the Father and the Son distinguished from each other not only by the Father–Son relation (eternal generation) but also by distinct divine knowing and divine willing in the economy of salvation?[34] What is at stake here is the metaphysical simplicity and infinite plenitude of the Godhead. If the Son and the Father are not perfectly identical in attributes pertaining to the divine nature (such as intellect and will), then neither the Son nor the Father is the full plenitude of the Godhead. The result would be that the Father, Son, and Spirit are not infinite in being but rather each of them is limited: Where the Father's will begins, the Son's ends. On this view, they would be three finite gods.

Vidu inquires into how, if the divine Persons are not distinguished by acts *ad extra*, it makes sense to say that the Son, and the Son alone, became incarnate. In response, he draws upon Aquinas to articulate the Trinity's agency in assuming a human nature to union with the divine nature in the Person of the Son. He also asks whether there is "a specific personal causality of the Son upon this human nature, consequent upon the assumption."[35] Vidu's answer makes appeal to John Duns Scotus and to the Thomistic Christology of the Reformed theologian John Owen. He addresses the criticisms of Aquinas's position lodged by Karl Rahner and concludes along Thomistic lines: "The eternal Word remains extrinsic to the human nature in the sense that he is ontologically distinct from it, as uncreated. That said, the human nature upon its union with the Logos begins to manifest the unique mode of existence of the Logos

---

[34] See also the background and constructive insights, in light of contemporary debates about the "subordination" of the Son, provided by Scott R. Swain, "The Radiance of the Father's Glory: Eternal Generation, the Divine Names, and Biblical Interpretation," in *Retrieving Eternal Generation*, ed. Fred Sanders and Scott R. Swain (Grand Rapids, MI: Zondervan Academic, 2017), 29–43.
[35] Adonis Vidu, *The Same God Who Works All Things: Inseparable Operations in Trinitarian Theology* (Grand Rapids, MI: Eerdmans, 2021), 163.

on its own created level of existence."³⁶ Indeed, Vidu argues that Aquinas's account of the incarnate Son's *esse* – an account that in the decades after the Council fell profoundly out of favor – is in fact crucial for understanding the historical Jesus Christ. He states, "The human nature mediates the revelation of the Son because it supernaturally acquires the personal *esse* (existence) of the Son as its ultimate metaphysical foundation."³⁷

Further chapters on Christ draw heavily upon Aquinas, often in dialogue with Scotus. Vidu notes the agreement between Balthasar and Aquinas on the understanding of a person as "a particular realization of a given nature," thereby ensuring that Person and nature remain united in the Trinity.³⁸ He probes into how the Son's divine and human actions should be distinguished, arguing that "persons act from their natures" and therefore "two natures originate two sets of first acts, which come together in the one person of Jesus Christ, the eternal Logos."³⁹ Clarifying this claim further (in a Scotistic rather than Thomistic direction), he observes: "Actions do not originate at the personal level; they are perfected by the person. Thus, the incarnate Logos perfects in himself a human operation that springs from his human nature."⁴⁰ In a lengthy discussion of Aquinas's Christology, Vidu argues that Aquinas succeeds in describing a truly theandric agency in Christ. Aquinas offers a fully Trinitarian Christology, with Christ in his

---

³⁶ Vidu, *The Same God Who Works All Things*, 176.
³⁷ Vidu, *The Same God Who Works All Things*, 177. The Son reveals himself in his humanity.
³⁸ Vidu, *The Same God Who Works All Things*, 190. Vidu refers here to Balthasar's reflections on the Monothelite controversy, in Balthasar's *Cosmic Liturgy: The Universe according to Maximus the Confessor*, trans. Brian E. Daley, S.J. (San Francisco: Ignatius Press, 2003).
³⁹ Vidu, *The Same God Who Works All Things*, 193.
⁴⁰ Vidu, *The Same God Who Works All Things*, 193. For Aquinas (by contrast to Scotus), Vidu explains, "personality is a positive entity that disposes a singular nature for existence; it comes to the individual substance before and as a condition of its existence" (195).

human nature taking on the Son's filial mode of being and thus receiving everything from the Father and manifesting the Father through his human actions.[41]

I note that in unpacking the consequences of a properly Trinitarian doctrine of the atonement, Vidu turns to the Latin theology of Bernard Lonergan, specifically Lonergan's *The Triune God: Systematics*.[42] I mention this fact in order to signal the value of the current recovery of Lonergan's Thomistic Christology. Jeremy Wilkins remarks in his *Before Truth: Lonergan, Aquinas, and the Problem of Wisdom*, "Lonergan was convinced as a matter of faith seeking understanding, that Christ, throughout his human life, contemplated divine wisdom and love in the light of the glory proper to the heavenly Jerusalem."[43]

The Anglican theologian A. N. Williams's 1999 *The Ground of Union: Deification in Aquinas and Palamas* began as her dissertation at Yale under George Lindbeck. Though her section on Aquinas's Christology is short, it is notable. She begins with a helpful comparison of Aquinas's Christology with his doctrine of creation, explaining that Aquinas understands "the Incarnation as the fruit of divine desire for self-communication and union with humanity."[44] She reflects upon the ways in which the Incarnation brings human nature to its perfection, both in Christ himself and by enabling our minds – accustomed to gaining knowledge from the realm of the senses – to know God and thereby to love God. She points out that the "Incarnation," as such, is a created reality,

---

[41] In addition to Aquinas's texts and Legge's book, Vidu draws upon Gilles Emery, O.P.'s "The Personal Mode of Trinitarian Action in Saint Thomas Aquinas," *The Thomist* 69 (2005): 31–77.

[42] See Bernard Lonergan, S.J., *The Triune God: Systematics* (Toronto: University of Toronto Press, 2007).

[43] Jeremy D. Wilkins, *Before Truth: Lonergan, Aquinas, and the Problem of Wisdom* (Washington, DC: Catholic University of America Press, 2018).

[44] A. N. Williams, *The Ground of Union: Deification in Aquinas and Palamas* (Oxford: Oxford University Press, 1999), 90.

even though the term of the Incarnation is the Son and the cause of the Incarnation is the Trinity. In a sense, the Incarnation can be described as a "grace," since the union of the divine and human natures in the Person of the Son is not anything that human nature could have merited. Too strongly in my view, she maintains that for Aquinas "our destiny is a sharing of divine life as intimate as that represented by the hypostatic union. To be divine by participation through grace constitutes no second-order, derivative union with God but a union after the manner of Christ's very own."[45] Williams's emphasis on Christ's deifying centrality – and thus on the centrality of his charity (and of the Eucharist) – is welcome.

The Anglican theologian Rowan Williams's 2018 *Christ the Heart of Creation* deserves mention here for its extensive engagement with Aquinas's Christology. The introductory first chapter, which sets the stage for all that follows, is devoted to Aquinas's perspective. Williams's speculative investigation focuses on the question of how "Christology itself generate[s] a new and fuller grasp of the 'grammar' of createdness."[46] While he cautions against treating every aspect of Aquinas's Christology as "timelessly true and adequate," he nevertheless credits Aquinas's synthesis with being "the point at which the broadest range of theoretical questions was brought into view and a robust and consistent vocabulary developed for integrating these questions."[47] He argues that modern Christology could be spared many dead-ends and puzzles simply by retrieving what Aquinas has already worked out. The topics that he has in view include not only the Incarnation itself but also Christ's knowledge and grace. Regarding the Incarnation, Williams shows that what at first may seem to be overly abstract or arcane questions in the *tertia pars* turn out to be, in fact, an

---

[45] Williams, *The Ground of Union*, 92.
[46] Rowan Williams, *Christ the Heart of Creation* (London: Bloomsbury, 2018), 6.
[47] Williams, *Christ the Heart of Creation*, 7.

extraordinarily valuable "grammatical clearing of the ground so that there is no room for any notion of incarnation as a heavenly individual 'turning into' an earthly one."[48]

Khaled Anatolios, a Greek Catholic Melkite scholar, offered in 2020 an account of Christ's saving work that draws constructively upon Aquinas. In his *Deification through the Cross*, Anatolios seeks "to present the fundamental framework of a constructive theology of Christ's doxological contrition that is grounded in the Byzantine Christian tradition."[49] He observes how strongly Aquinas highlights Christ's sorrow over sin. Indeed, for Aquinas the sorrow that Christ endures on the Cross is the greatest sorrow ever experienced. As Anatolios notes, this claim may appear exaggerated, given that there seem to be ways of dying that inflict even more suffering than does the torture of crucifixion. Yet, for Aquinas, Christ's immense interior sorrow or contrition regarding each and every human sin is constitutive of the superabundant "satisfaction" that Christ offers for sin. Placing his finger on a theme that has been somewhat neglected by Thomists in their accounts of Aquinas's theology of the Cross,[50] Anatolios observes that Aquinas "speaks explicitly of the representative suffering of Christ as a contrition that transcends all other human experiences of repentance."[51] As

---

[48] Williams, *Christ the Heart of Creation*, 12. See, however, Katherine Sonderegger's concerns regarding Williams's account of the two natures, in Sonderegger, "Christ as Infinite and Finite: Rowan Williams' *Christ the Heart of Creation*," *Pro Ecclesia* 30 (2021): 98–113.

[49] Khaled Anatolios, *Deification through the Cross: An Eastern Christian Theology of Salvation* (Grand Rapids, MI: Eerdmans, 2020), 35.

[50] I am among those who have somewhat neglected it! As Anatolios points out on 334–35, a Thomist who deserves credit for perceiving this element is Bruce D. Marshall, "The Dereliction of Christ and the Impassibility of God," in *Divine Impassibility and the Mystery of Human Suffering*, ed. James F. Keating and Thomas Joseph White, O.P. (Grand Rapids, MI: Eerdmans, 2009), 246–98, at 272–73. Anatolios, like Marshall, draws especially upon Thomas Aquinas, *Summa Theologiae*, trans. Fathers of the English Dominican Province (Westminster, MD: Christian Classics, 1981), III, q. 46, a. 6.

[51] Anatolios, *Deification through the Cross*, 333.

1.2 THE REVIVAL OF THOMISTIC CHRISTOLOGY

our representative, Christ on the Cross makes satisfaction for us by experiencing the profound contrition that we should have had for each and every sin.

Anatolios combines Aquinas's insight with some elements of Matthias Joseph Scheeben's doxological or latreutic understanding of Christ's Paschal sacrifice. The combination of these two thinkers serves Anatolios's presentation of the Cross as "doxological contrition," an insight that arose for Anatolios primarily through celebrating the Byzantine liturgy. Even without drawing upon Scheeben, one can find a link between Christ's sorrow and doxology in Aquinas himself. This link is Aquinas's insistence that while sorrowing most intensely in his lower soul, Christ in his higher soul enjoyed beatific communion, praising God perfectly. Here Anatolios moves from *Summa theologiae* III, q. 46, a. 6 to q. 46, a. 8. According to Aquinas, Christ did not allow the joy he experiences in his higher soul to overflow upon his lower soul; thus his immense sorrow was not alleviated by joy but rather both were present at the same time in different ways. For Anatolios, the important thing is not parsing the psychology of this claim but rather the fact that Aquinas places front and center both immense sorrow and immense doxological praise. Anatolios describes these two elements in terms of coinherence, rather than in terms of a higher and a lower part of the soul. In Anatolios's view, Aquinas approaches this solution when he holds that if Christ did not know and praise God perfectly, then Christ could not have realized how intensely we should sorrow over sin. This is what Anatolios means by "coinherence," namely, that "during his earthly life Christ's perfect enjoyment of the vision of God was entirely intrinsic to and even constitutive of his contrition for human sin."[52]

Anatolios here shows an extraordinary penetration into and appreciation for Aquinas's theology of the Cross. As Anatolios says, "the representative contrition of Christ was itself a certain

---

[52] Anatolios, *Deification through the Cross*, 337.

mode of the 'overflow' of his glory.... Conversely, his vision of God persisted not by virtue of being oblivious of the suffering of some hermetically sealed 'lower part' of the soul but precisely in and through this suffering of Christ's contrition."[53] Anatolios argues that every moment of Christ's life combines these two elements, but the sorrow for sin is intensified on the Cross, where Christ sorrows vicariously for us. The Resurrection takes up and glorifies Christ's wounds and his contrition. Thus, the Paschal mystery "shines forth as divine forgiveness and the reconciliation of God and humanity."[54] This is a constructive argument that retrieves Thomistic Christology in a fruitful way, in accord with Anatolios's ecumenical intentions.

1.2.2 Thomistic Christology and Contemporary Catholic Philosophical Theology

Let me now mention a few examples of the contemporary interest in Aquinas's Christology within (Roman) Catholic dogmatics. Eleonore Stump's massive 2018 book *Atonement* followed upon an equally lengthy, but more strictly philosophical, set of essays published by Stump under the title *Aquinas*. Two of the essays in the latter work treat aspects of Aquinas's Christology, specifically the metaphysics of the Incarnation and the atonement.[55] But whereas in *Aquinas* Stump's primary concern is to understand Aquinas rightly – although she brings her immense creativity to the task, inevitably seeking the truth of the matter whatever Aquinas might have thought – in *Atonement* we find a fully constructive work of philosophical theology. She states, "I have tried to learn from varying interpretations of the doctrine of the *at onement* which are found in different periods in the history of the Christian theological

---

[53] Anatolios, *Deification through the Cross*, 338.
[54] Anatolios, *Deification through the Cross*, 338.
[55] See Eleonore Stump, *Aquinas* (London: Routledge, 2003), chapters 14 and 15.

tradition, but I have not adopted wholesale any one of them, not even that of Aquinas.... I am not either presupposing or defending Aquinas's interpretation of the doctrine."[56] Yet Aquinas appears in one way or another on nearly every page.

Stump divides theories of the atonement into two categories: theories that argue that God must be placated for human sin (she calls these theories "Anselmian") and theories that argue that humans must be changed in themselves (she calls these theories "Thomistic"). The "Anselmian" theories refer above all to the divine justice or the divine honor, which requires the payment of a penalty or a debt in order to be "satisfied" – a payment that the merciful God himself pays. The "Thomistic" theories refer above all to the fallenness of the human will, which is turned away from God and is in need of God's healing grace. By his love and grace exhibited on the Cross, Christ offers "a bridge that spans the gap between the condition in which sinful human beings find themselves ... and the desired union with God."[57] Or as Stump puts the matter at the end of her book, describing her own "Thomistic" theory of atonement that she calls "the Marian interpretation": "[T]he atonement of Christ is the unquenchable love of God offered to all the suffering, the self-alienated, and the evil, so that in their own beauty they might be at peace with themselves and with others and at home in the love of God."[58]

To my mind, Stump has correctly identified an element of Aquinas's understanding of Christ's Cross, but she has overlooked or rejected other elements that Aquinas includes. Her polarity between "Thomistic" and "Anselmian" is unhelpful, partly because Peter Abelard's position is much more like Stump's than is Aquinas's. Still, this does not take away from the fact that Aquinas's Christology – linked

---

[56] Eleonore Stump, *Atonement* (Oxford: Oxford University Press, 2018), 14.
[57] Stump, *Atonement*, 37.
[58] Stump, *Atonement*, 411.

with his doctrine of God, anthropology, and theology of grace – plays a highly significant role in Stump's stimulating book.

Stump's student Timothy Pawl has published two works on Christology that contain significant engagement with Aquinas: *In Defense of Conciliar Christology* (2016) and *In Defense of Extended Conciliar Christology* (2019).[59] Aquinas is a significant presence in the first volume and even more so in the second. Both volumes mount arguments employing analytic philosophy in order to show that the basic claims of classical Christological orthodoxy are intelligible. Pawl has recourse to the documents of the early Councils and to patristic theologians, but his favored interlocutor is Aquinas. In *In Defense of Extended Conciliar Christology*, he addresses various problems treated by Aquinas, including whether there could have been multiple Incarnations, Christ's interim state, Christ's freedom, Christ's temptation, and Christ's knowledge. In *In Defense of Conciliar Christology*, he asks whether it is intelligible to argue that an immutable God could become man, whether a divine Person could intelligibly subsist in two natures (divine and human), and whether Christ really is a unity. Pawl argues, "Aquinas's incarnational theology is robustly metaphysical…. Showing that a Thomistic view of the Incarnation can survive philosophical objections suggests that other, less robust views can survive, too."[60] Pawl's books are not Thomistic Christology per se, but their ample use of Aquinas within an analytic-theology defense of the claims of conciliar Christology shows the significance of Thomistic Christology within the field of analytic theology.

In three lengthy books, Olivier-Thomas Venard has constructively reflected upon Aquinas's theology of the Word. The titles

---

[59] See Timothy Pawl, *In Defense of Conciliar Christology: A Philosophical Essay* (Oxford: Oxford University Press, 2016) and *In Defense of Extended Conciliar Christology* (Oxford: Oxford University Press, 2019).

[60] Pawl, *In Defense of Extended Conciliar Christology*, 10.

1.2 THE REVIVAL OF THOMISTIC CHRISTOLOGY

of his books show his literary and hermeneutical emphasis, which he grounds in a metaphysics of the Word: *Littérature et théologie, La langue de l'ineffable*, and *Pagina sacra*.[61] For English-speaking readers, selections from these books have recently appeared as *A Poetic Christ: Thomist Reflections on Scripture, Language and Reality*. Consider for example the selection that appears as "Towards a Poetic Christology." Venard asks, "Is the admirable literary complexity of the New Testament merely the result of clever rhetorical propaganda which then calls for deconstruction, or did Jesus himself lay the foundations of this literary complexity in the course of his ministry?"[62] In answering this question, Venard turns especially to the Gospel of John but also to Aquinas. Aquinas helps him to demonstrate "the extensive fittingness between the mystery of the incarnation and the being and functionality of the sign."[63] In Venard's work, the Christology of Aquinas's *Commentary on John* plays a particularly important role. He brings Aquinas's Christology into dialogue with postmodern theorists of the sign, and he reflects upon the relationship between the Incarnation of the Word and the various human modes of participating in the incarnate Word and in the Word as such. Here Aquinas's Christology becomes important for the project of rethinking hermeneutics in general and biblical exegesis in particular.

Simon Francis Gaine's *Did the Saviour See the Father? Christ, Salvation and the Vision of God* stands out for its broad defense of Aquinas's position on Christ's knowledge. Gaine critiques the ways in which some fellow Thomists, such as Jacques Maritain

---

[61] See Olivier-Thomas Venard, O.P., *Littérature et théologie. Une saison en enfer* (Geneva: Ad Solem, 2002), *La langue de l'ineffable. Essai sur le fondement théologique de la métaphysique* (Geneva: Ad Solem, 2004), and *Pagina sacra. Le passage de l'Écriture sainte à l'écriture théologique* (Paris: Cerf, 2009).

[62] Olivier-Thomas Venard, O.P., *A Poetic Christ: Thomist Reflections on Scripture, Language and Reality*, trans. Kenneth Oakes and Francesca Aran Murphy (London: T&T Clark, 2019), 64.

[63] Venard, *A Poetic Christ*, 65.

and Jean-Hervé Nicolas, have modified Aquinas's account. What especially makes Gaine's book interesting is his insistence that Aquinas's view of Christ's beatific vision does not pose problems for Christ's growth in acquired knowledge and does not require to be "translated" into concepts via infused knowledge.[64] In dialogue with a wide range of contemporary theologians and biblical scholars, Gaine shows that Aquinas's teaching in this domain is much worthier of consideration than is generally supposed today.

The work of Emmanuel Durand also deserves attention here. Christ's Person and work receive a central place in Durand's understanding of providence in his *Évangile et Providence*, where he devotes a chapter to Aquinas's approach to providence. Aquinas offers a richly metaphysical account of divine providence in the *prima pars*; but Durand points out that for Aquinas, it is also the case that "faith in divine providence acquires a considerable importance because it implicitly contains faith in Christ the Redeemer."[65] Influenced by Thomistic Christology as well as by the perspectives of other thinkers and by his own constructive biblical theology, Durand concludes by articulating the doctrine of divine providence in a fully Trinitarian key. Further works by Durand make a similarly constructive use of Thomistic Christology, as for instance his *L'Offre universelle du salut en Christ*.[66]

In *Ecce Homo: On the Divine Unity of Christ*, Aaron Riches offers an extensive survey of the patristic developments arising from the challenge of Nestorianism. He then takes up Aquinas's Christology to address problems such as the *esse* or being of Christ and the theandric action of Christ. As he says, "Thomas Aquinas's discovery

---

[64] See Simon Francis Gaine, O.P., *Did the Saviour See the Father? Christ, Salvation and the Vision of God* (London: Bloomsbury, 2015).

[65] Emmanuel Durand, O.P., *Évangile et Providence: Une théologie de l'action de Dieu* (Paris: Cerf, 2014), 179.

[66] See Emmanuel Durand, O.P., *L'Offre universelle du salut en Christ* (Paris: Cerf, 2012).

1.2 THE REVIVAL OF THOMISTIC CHRISTOLOGY

of the conciliar texts of Ephesus, Chalcedon, and Constantinople II confirmed his own highly unitive doctrine of the hypostatic union."[67] He shows how deeply Aquinas's thought converged with the anti-Nestorian perspective of the Greek Fathers. Aquinas was fighting a Nestorian drift in the medieval West, and he employed Cyril and John of Damascus to hone his Christology. The influence of the Second Council of Constantinople increasingly appears in Aquinas's writings, in particular through the doctrine that the union takes place according to subsistence, so that Christ only has one person and one subsistence. Riches explores how Constantinople III shapes Aquinas's account of Christ's two wills and two operations. He praises Aquinas's understanding of the instrumentality of the human nature of Christ, which allows Aquinas to affirm that "Jesus works divine things humanly" and "theandrically."[68] Riches also addresses Aquinas's theology of Christ's suffering in light of Christ's beatific vision, and he advocates a reading of Aquinas's position that fits with what Anatolios terms "coinherence": "[T]he *maximos dolores* suffered by Jesus are internal to the *fruitio beata* he nevertheless enjoys."[69] Riches's work is an immensely stimulating dogmatic Christology that is as Eastern as it is Thomistic.

In addition, Aquinas's Christology has recently been praised by Catholic scholars as diverse as Aidan Nichols, Denys Turner, and Bernard McGinn.[70] But arguably the most significant contemporary retrieval of Aquinas's Christology is Thomas Joseph White's *The Incarnate Lord*. Guy Mansini has noted that in the neoscholastic

---

[67] Aaron Riches, *Ecce Homo: On the Divine Unity of Christ* (Grand Rapids, MI: Eerdmans, 2016), 155.
[68] Riches, *Ecce Homo*, 185.
[69] Riches, *Ecce Homo*, 202.
[70] See Aidan Nichols, O.P., *Discovering Aquinas: An Introduction to His Life, Work and Influence* (London: Darton, Longman & Todd, 2002); Denys Turner, *Thomas Aquinas: A Portrait* (New Haven, CT: Yale University Press, 2013); Bernard McGinn, *Thomas Aquinas's "Summa Theologiae": A Biography* (Princeton, NJ: Princeton University Press, 2014).

period, Catholic Christology was essentially an in-house theological affair in which a large role was played by Aquinas. The great figures of the *Ressourcement* movement brought an end to this in-house Christology, but the Christologies of the *Ressourcement* theologians also have deficiencies. As Mansini sees it, what was needed was to retrieve Aquinas's Christology and thus also, to some degree, neoscholastic Christology – but now in dialogue with biblical scholarship, with the great *Ressourcement* thinkers, and with Protestant and Orthodox Christologies. It is this task that White's *The Incarnate Lord* undertakes.[71]

In his book, White proposes that a metaphysically rich, explicitly creedal outlook of the kind modeled by Aquinas is necessary for a Catholic Christology. Without metaphysical realism and analogous speech about God,[72] it will be impossible to speak suitably about either the human nature or divine nature of Christ, let alone about their unity-in-distinction in Christ's divine Person. White shows that Scripture itself presumes an ontology,[73] both with regard to Christ's preexistence as Creator and Lord and with regard to his human nature. Likewise, the "hypostatic union" is not a Greek imposition upon the New Testament but rather is an affirmation arising out of the New Testament's testimony to Christ as the

---

[71] See Guy Mansini, O.S.B., "Christology in Context: Review Essay of Thomas Joseph White, O.P., *The Incarnate Lord*," *Nova et Vetera* 14 (2016): 1271–91.

[72] For further background and a constructive proposal (engaging in a detailed way with leading twentieth-century Catholic perspectives in light of Martin Heidegger's critique of ontotheology), see Thomas Joseph White, O.P., *Wisdom in the Face of Modernity: A Study in Thomistic Natural Theology*, 2nd ed. (Ave Maria, FL: Sapientia Press, 2016). For White's assessment of the positions of Barth, Przywara, and others, see White, "Introduction: The *Analogia Entis* Controversy and Its Contemporary Significance," in *The Analogy of Being: Invention of the Antichrist or the Wisdom of God?*, ed. Thomas Joseph White, O.P. (Grand Rapids, MI: Eerdmans, 2011), 1–31.

[73] See also – on how to read Exodus 3:14 (and thus the "I am" passages in the Gospel of John, although these passages also draw upon the Septuagint version of Isaiah) – Thomas Joseph White, O.P., *Exodus* (Grand Rapids, MI: Brazos, 2016), 35–44, 292–304.

1.2 THE REVIVAL OF THOMISTIC CHRISTOLOGY

incarnate Lord. Metaphysical realism about human nature is not imposed by philosophically minded Christians upon Scripture but rather flows from the New Testament's "presupposition ... that Christ shared in some way in what is common to Adam and all other human beings, the natural form or essence that is possessed by each."[74] This is not simply a Thomistic claim but one made by the Council of Chalcedon, and New Testament Christology makes no sense without it.[75]

What about the notion that the one divine Person, the Son of God, acts through his two natures? White points to Philippians 2:5–11, among other passages, as evidence that this creedal claim derives from the New Testament. The very questions that Aquinas addresses at his most "metaphysical" in the *tertia pars* arise from Scripture and require to be addressed if the New Testament portrait of Jesus is to be intelligible.

In his chapters, White takes up themes that track the order of topics in the *tertia pars*: the hypostatic union, the grace of Christ, the knowledge of Christ, the obedience of Christ, the Cross, Christ's death and descent in hell, and the Resurrection. While all of his chapters are important, I will here pay attention in particular to his "Prolegomenon: Is a Modern Thomistic Christology Possible?" and his "Conclusion: The Promise of Thomism: Why Christology Is Not Primarily a Historical Science." These bookends of *The Incarnate Lord* go to the very heart of the contemporary debates.

White's "Prolegomenon" argues that if Thomistic Christology is *not* possible, this must be because Schleiermacher and Barth, in

---

[74] Thomas Joseph White, O.P., *The Incarnate Lord: A Thomistic Study in Christology* (Washington, DC: Catholic University of America Press, 2015), 17.

[75] White, *The Incarnate Lord*, 19. Or as White later comments: "*If* we are capable of thinking theologically by grace about the reality of the incarnation, then a necessary presupposition of this fact is that we are naturally capable of thinking philosophically about the creator by way of analogical terms drawn from the creation. In other words, orthodox Christology is in no way reducible to natural theology, but it is also not possible without it" (26).

their distinct ways, are correct that Chalcedonian doctrine must now be reinterpreted in a postmetaphysical way. Accepting the early historical-critical view that Jesus cannot rightly be thought of in Chalcedonian terms, Schleiermacher argues that Jesus still has theological significance insofar as he exemplifies the intensification of human religious consciousness and brings this consciousness to its highest point. On this view, elements such as Christ's virgin birth, Resurrection, and Ascension can be reinterpreted for what they say about Jesus' exemplary religious consciousness and its impact upon ours. Jesus' divinity can be reinterpreted in terms of his followers' experience of his profound God-consciousness. White sums up the methodological presupposition: "Historical study of Jesus in what is presupposed to be a post-metaphysical age permits us to recover anew the truth of Christianity that lies behind the artifices of ontological doctrine."[76]

Against Schleiermacher, Barth argues that historical-critical studies cannot get at the truth of Jesus, which is given by the Scriptures and by the community's obedience in faith to the living Lord Jesus. Barth rejects speculation about Jesus' consciousness. Yet, White argues that Barth cannot avoid the problem identified by Schleiermacher. If classical metaphysics is false, then Chalcedonian claims – whose intelligibility is inseparable from metaphysical realism – cannot stand. Absent metaphysical realism, it necessarily follows that "the *transcendence* of God incarnate as it is understood *to be revealed in Christ* is in fact something the mind simply does not have the capacity to entertain intellectually," since we can "only conceive of the presence of the divine *in this world* univocally."[77]

White's argument is that the rejection of the power of the human mind to think metaphysically, and thereby to think intelligibly about transcendent divinity and about the distinction between the human nature and the divine nature of Christ, cripples Christology.

---

[76] White, *The Incarnate Lord*, 37.
[77] White, *The Incarnate Lord*, 47.

1.2 THE REVIVAL OF THOMISTIC CHRISTOLOGY

The solution must be to retrieve some form of Thomistic Christology – whether or not it is labeled "Thomistic." White draws from Balthasar's book *The Theology of Karl Barth*, in which Balthasar shows that (in White's words) "a natural ontology and metaphysical theology are possible and even necessary within the framework of a Christological doctrine of the God-world analogy and a Catholic consideration of the relations of nature and grace."[78] White's argument is somewhat different: He defends the possibility of natural theology (i.e., classical metaphysics) on the Christological grounds that such metaphysical range turns out to be necessary for the intelligibility of Christ as the incarnate Lord. White emphasizes that Christ does not differ from us fundamentally in terms of his human powers, for example, his human consciousness; rather he differs from us fundamentally in his "primary actuality" or "substantial being," his personhood rather than his operations.[79] For Christology, then, it is necessary to insist that "the union of God and man in Christ is substantial and not accidental. It takes place within the subsistent person of the Word, and not in the accidental operations of the man Jesus."[80] Only in this way can we truly say that the eternal Word has become incarnate. This path requires the ability to distinguish ontologically the divine and human natures and operations of Christ.

Historical study and knowledge of God by faith both have a place in Christology, but the latter (faith's knowledge) will be foundational, because it is the latter that attains "to the deepest ontological core of his person," important though "the empirical, historical-cultural conditions" of the life of Christ are.[81] As an

---

[78] White, *The Incarnate Lord*, 62n58.

[79] White, *The Incarnate Lord*, 62–63.

[80] White, *The Incarnate Lord*, 64. White notes further, "Neither Barth nor Schleiermacher, however, grasps adequately this analogical distinction, and so both think *univocally* about the being-in-act of operations (Jesus's consciousness of religious dependence, Christ's human obedience) as in some way equivalent with or susceptible to signifying formally the being in act of substantial being (the subsistent person of Christ in his unity of being with the Father)" (65).

[81] White, *The Incarnate Lord*, 58.

example, White offers historical-critical reconstructions of the sacrificial meaning of Jesus' death, including reconstructions of Jesus' own view of his death. These reconstructions are plausible and valuable, but they cannot *prove* what Jesus thought he was doing. They assist faith's knowledge of the incarnate Lord, but they do not provide its foundation. White also observes that Christology must speak about the "ontological ground of unity between Christ and the Father," given that Christ's consciousness reflects his status as the incarnate Lord who "has come to us in human nature to reveal to us the inner life of God the Trinity, and to call us to himself in the eventual vision of the divine essence."[82]

Let me now describe White's "Conclusion: The Promise of Thomism: Why Christology Is Not Primarily a Historical Science." The last subtitle says it all. As a historical enterprise, Christology begins with a study of the New Testament, then turns to the Fathers, the medievals, and so on, eventually arriving at the current debates within systematic theology. This approach presumes progress in reflection and also presumes that history itself can be the standard for what is enduringly true doctrine about Christ. Yet, history is always told by a particular narrator who values some elements more than others. The question therefore becomes pressing: What is the standard for truth about Christ? One may answer: dogma. But as soon as this is done, then it becomes clear that history is not the fundamental science involved; rather, the guiding science turns out to be *sacra doctrina*, "informed by supernatural faith in the teachings of scripture and the Catholic church."[83] Christology has to do with a historical reality and makes use of historical studies, but Christology interprets that history – explains its meaning – "in light of what unifies and transcends historical existence," namely, God.[84]

---

[82] White, *The Incarnate Lord*, 68. White concludes, "Thomistic theology invites us to overcome a problematic modern opposition between Christological ontology and the anthropological dimension of theology" (68–69).

[83] White, *The Incarnate Lord*, 468.

[84] White, *The Incarnate Lord*, 469.

1.2 THE REVIVAL OF THOMISTIC CHRISTOLOGY

White therefore seeks to reclaim a "scholastic" approach – a dogmatic, metaphysically rich Christology, "not disinterested in the most subtle indications of historical learning but above all marked (in and through such considerations) by the study of the intrinsic essence and content of the mystery of Christ."[85] I agree with this project, though in the present book I place emphasis on "in and through such [historical] considerations." It seems to me that a new scholastic Christology will need to be sure to avoid mere prooftexting of scriptural and other sources; it will need to be sure to give ample room to the voice and narratives of Scripture and to the arguments (rather than simply the conclusions) of the Fathers and Doctors of the Church. In addition, a new scholastic Christology will need to be ecumenically oriented, as White's is. Earlier scholasticisms (like modern antischolasticisms) have sometimes been too quick to dismiss opponents.

White contrasts his viewpoint with that of Edward Schillebeeckx, who holds that the truth claims made by Christians are absolute only within a particular historical context and may have to be reformulated substantively in later historical contexts. The result for Schillebeeckx is that Christology is fundamentally a historical discipline and nothing more, since "there is no access to trans-historical truths of Christology that are simply available to every age."[86] The key question in Christology becomes, then, what Christ means or should mean for us today, with "today" receiving a decisive role. It follows that every epoch reflects, in its Christology, its own faith experience of God.

As White points out, Schillebeeckx does not hesitate to interpret Jesus from within the faith experience of the time when

---

[85] White, *The Incarnate Lord*, 469.
[86] White, *The Incarnate Lord*, 477. For further background and a constructive path forward, see Thomas Joseph White, O.P., "The Precarity of Wisdom: Modern Dominican Theology, Perspectivalism, and the Tasks of Reconstruction," in *Ressourcement Thomism: Sacred Doctrine, the Sacraments, and the Moral Life. Essays in Honor of Romanus Cessario, O.P.*, ed. Reinhard Hütter and Matthew Levering (Washington, DC: Catholic University of America Press, 2010), 92–123.

Schillebeeckx was writing. On this view, a relevant Christology is one that is in solidarity with the political movements of liberation within and outside the Church. Christology becomes, fundamentally, an ethical praxis that changes and develops in accord with the supposed march of history.[87]

White shows that Schillebeeckx's project neglects a fundamental challenge to postmetaphysical modernity. Namely, how do we know that texts themselves "have some intrinsic signification that can be measured by external realities," rather than having signification imposed upon them by "interpreters"?[88] Furthermore, how do we know even that there *are* "interpreters" or stable selves, or indeed any stable realities or values whatsoever? To Friedrich Nietzsche and others, many modern thinkers are guilty of importing a metaphysics according to which there exist real and identifiable referents of texts. The alternative is that texts are fundamentally collections of linguistic signs that refer simply to desires, especially the desire for power. From a Nietzschean perspective, the question is as follows: If doctrine simply expresses a particular era's religious sensibilities, then how do we know that doctrine is not simply the expression of the will to power, rather than expressing "truth" at all? Likewise, if consciousness is reducible to culture (or prevalent semiotic signs) rather than to a "self," then how do we know that a particular set of cultural values are more than arbitrary? White points out, "If our hermeneutics are those of Nietzsche, then the

---

[87] As White says, "The hermeneuticist recovers the truth of the past by 'going forward' into new horizons of political praxis, in the name of the Gospel. The truth in question is a radically historicized one. Now unusable doctrinal concepts of a past historical age are studied in view of the elaboration of new theological concepts of the future. God is himself in some sense the subject at the heart of the church's historical life who safeguards the inner workings of this process. The church mediates the ongoing sacramental expression of a perpetual divine-human encounter by taking up into herself the ongoing dialectic of human conversation regarding truth" (White, *The Incarnate Lord*, 480).

[88] White, *The Incarnate Lord*, 481.

1.2 THE REVIVAL OF THOMISTIC CHRISTOLOGY

theological guilds that seek to challenge received doctrinal tradition through a series of 'progressive' and 'empowering' discourses are themselves adopting a morally arbitrary stance. They too give voice to a will to power."[89] White shows that the alternative is to retrieve metaphysics – real existential referents, real natures, and (in the Christian domain) real dogmatic truth.

Schillebeeckx's disciple Claude Geffré, recognizing the Nietzschean problematic, argued that the solution consists in granting that one's own perspective is relative and thereby insisting that no one interpretation of Christianity can have hegemony.[90] But, as White observes, Geffré has not perceived the true problem. For example, Geffré continued to refer to the "Spirit," but to whom or what is Geffré referring? The Personal status of the Spirit in the tri-Personal God was affirmed by the Council of Constantinople and belongs to Catholic dogma, but not if this is merely a contextual claim that cannot have hegemony over other opposite claims made before, during, and since the Council of Constantinople. Furthermore, in insisting that no one interpretation of Christianity may have hegemony, has not Geffré asserted hegemony over interpretations of Christianity that affirm the hegemonic truth of a particular interpretation? In repudiating the legitimacy of hegemonic claims, Geffré is making one himself. In such a situation, continuing with the project of dogmatic or systematic theology is useless; one might as well admit that in doing so, one is simply staking out a power-claim, not a truth claim about anything extrinsic to the "self."

As White comments, therefore, perspectivalism in theology does no more than conceal its metaphysics, namely, its teleological "ontology that emphasizes either the normativity of the inclusive political good or the celebration of the will to power."[91] It turns out to be

---

[89] White, *The Incarnate Lord*, 483.
[90] See Claude Geffré, *The Risk of Interpretation: On Being Faithful to the Christian Tradition in a Non-Christian Age*, trans. David Smith (New York: Paulist Press, 1987).
[91] White, *The Incarnate Lord*, 485.

impossible to narrate the history of theology, no matter how much one rejects enduring dogma and metaphysical realism, without some tacit account of enduring realities, such as "human nature, political justice, grammar, language, human volition, and so forth."[92] It follows that a "scholastic" theology – understood as a theology that makes enduring truth claims about reality, rather than simply canvassing historical opinions or modes of political praxis – is inevitable.

This should not surprise us. The human mind is made for knowing being, and there would be no possibility of speaking about intelligible historical change unless there were in fact "realities that exist and that have essences and properties."[93] History as such, then, cannot have primacy. Even the study of ideas is not merely a study of flux, since to identify their intelligible content "we must be able to identify what is *essential* or *determinate* in the ideas under consideration."[94] And since the narrator of any history produces his or her narrative with an end in view, the narrator thereby not only confirms the existence of teleology but also reminds us that human nature seeks various ends and that these ends or goods are inevitably evaluated in terms of a hierarchy of goods. Indeed, even Nietzsche's scorched-earth critique of

---

[92] White, *The Incarnate Lord*, 485.
[93] White, *The Incarnate Lord*, 486. White goes on to say, along Aristotelian lines that seem incontrovertible to both him and me: "The mind cannot fail to note that some existents are distinct from others ... and that the natures and characteristics of diverse realities cannot be attributed to them in simultaneously contrary senses under the same aspects at the same time.... Our implicit use of the principle of non-contradiction denotes that we perceive a world of formally determined realities that have various properties" (488). Further, White explains that "there is a distinction in all the realities we experience between ontological potency and being-in-act" (491), and he shows that in understanding realities in time (realities that are changing) "we must first grasp that these realities exist and have a given nature," a nature that in this sense "transcends" time (492). Otherwise, we could not measure change in the reality under examination. White concludes that "the objects of reason are not determined uniquely by the processes of temporal change. The intellect attains to 'that which exists,' and that which exists possesses an essential form" (492).
[94] White, *The Incarnate Lord*, 493.

teleology as an illusion continually inquired into why things are as they are (final causality) and urged people to pursue certain goals. Metaphysical realism, no matter how sternly rejected, turns up ever anew.

Returning to Christology, White observes that Jesus Christ is universally relevant for all human beings because he is the God-man, he is the Redeemer, and he has risen from the dead. These points fit with the principles of metaphysical realism: Jesus exists, he can be known in his essential identity, and he acts with an ultimate end. It follows that the Incarnation, the Cross, and the Resurrection will be at the heart of a Christology that has universal relevance. When Christians believe in these realities, they are able to understand in a deeper way the conclusions of the natural sciences about the cosmos – since Christ reveals its purpose – and they are able to integrate the reconstructions about Jesus offered by historians. Through faith in Christ, they are also able to describe the fallenness of humanity in light of its healing by Christ and its ultimate consummation in Christ. White concludes that Thomistic Christology is both speculative and practical, oriented "toward knowledge and enjoyment of the Trinity."[95] Ultimately, Thomistic Christology is wisdom, since in Christ "we come to find rest in a wisdom that surpasses ourselves, and which redeems our human history and our personal lives in time, but which also orients us toward the world to come."[96]

1.3 Conclusion

In the above, I have sought to sketch the emergence in recent decades of a new historically informed, ecumenically valuable, and

---

[95] White, *The Incarnate Lord*, 507.
[96] White, *The Incarnate Lord*, 509.

dogmatically constructive Thomistic Christology.[97] This movement emerged, in fact, just as the death knell of Thomistic Christology was sounding. There is good reason even to think that this renewed Thomistic Christology may sound the death knell of the modern Christology that had attempted to bury it. Ecumenically, the contributions of Reformed and Anglican theologians to this informal "movement" stand out, ensuring that contemporary Thomistic Christology is not solely the province of Catholic dogmaticians.[98] Although Eastern Orthodox theologians have yet to tap into Aquinas's Christology, A. N. Williams's observation certainly includes Christology: "The ground that Aquinas and Palamas share is vast compared to the points at which they diverge."[99]

More could be said about this movement of contemporary Thomistic Christology. For example, the contributions surveyed above could be organized more systematically. They represent different guiding principles for soteriology. Some of the authors focus on the hypostatic union; some on the two natures of Christ; some on Spirit Christology, inclusive of Christ's "capital" grace and his perfection of knowledge; and some on Christ's meritorious life and death as the principle of redemption. It would be

---

[97] A further instance of the impressive renewal in Thomistic Christology has just recently appeared, in a volume containing many richly informative and constructive essays: see Michael Dauphinais, Andrew Hofer, O.P., and Roger W. Nutt, eds., *Thomas Aquinas and the Crisis of Christology* (Ave Maria, FL: Sapientia Press, 2021).

[98] For historical parallels, see Manfred Svensson and David VanDrunen, eds., *Aquinas among the Protestants* (Oxford: Wiley-Blackwell, 2017); and Matthew Levering and Marcus Plested, eds., *The Oxford Handbook of the Reception of Aquinas* (Oxford: Oxford University Press, 2021). For Orthodox contributions to this history, see, in addition to the relevant chapters of *The Oxford Handbook of the Reception of Aquinas*, Marcus Plested's *Orthodox Readings of Aquinas* (Oxford: Oxford University Press, 2012). See also two works that could have profitably been added to this chapter, although their focus is not Christology per se: Charles Raith II, *Aquinas and Calvin on Romans: God's Justification and Our Participation* (Oxford: Oxford University Press, 2014); and Edgardo Colón-Emeric, *Wesley, Aquinas, and Christian Perfection: An Ecumenical Dialogue* (Waco, TX: Baylor University Press, 2009).

[99] Williams, *The Ground of Union*, 175.

1.3 CONCLUSION

worthwhile to compare these perspectives with the guiding principles of other contemporary Christologies, so as to show still more clearly why this movement is of constructive importance. Exploring in more detail the various Thomistic Christological emphases would also strengthen my case that the typological Christologies truly refer to the ontological reality of Christ and his saving work, rather than being mere metaphors or implausible stories.

In addition, expanding the above discussion of contemporary Thomistic Christology could assist in demonstrating how the New Testament typologies themselves enrich our understanding of Christ and salvation. The "kingdom of God," the "new exodus," and the renewed Temple can be expressed in ontological terms. But it adds something crucial to express them in narrative-typological terms. The typologies help to connect us with the historical figure of Jesus and to enable us to appreciate the various dimensions of our discipleship to, and sacramental inclusion in, Christ's Pasch as members of the "Israel of God" (Gal 6:16). The typologies help to ensure that ontological reflection on Jesus Christ and salvation does not float free of the late Second Temple context in which Jesus lived and in which the New Testament took shape. The typologies also make clear that Jesus is not merely "the perfect *homo religiosus*" but rather is the incarnate Lord bringing salvation history to its goal.[100] As Bruce Marshall emphasizes, his are "the actions and sufferings of the Word of power who upholds all things."[101]

In his *Heavenly Participation*, Hans Boersma remarks, "Time and time again, the church fathers and medieval theologians explained the events reported in the Old Testament as 'future mysteries' (*futura mysteria*) or 'future sacraments' (*futura sacramenta*),

---

[100] Bruce D. Marshall, "God Almighty in the Flesh: Christology and the Crisis of Faith," in *Thomas Aquinas and the Crisis of Christology*, 345–67, at 348.
[101] Marshall, "God Almighty in the Flesh," 349.

referring to Jesus Christ and to the church."[102] It was not only the Fathers and medievals who did this; the New Testament did so too in its literal sense regarding Jesus. This shared pattern explains why Aquinas's own writings are seamlessly filled with so many references to Scripture and the Fathers, including the typological portraits of Jesus the New Adam, New Isaac, New Moses, New Joshua, and New David. Thus, my "reconfiguring" of Thomistic Christology depends upon the fact that Aquinas's own metaphysical and dogmatic Christology is already figurally rich. If Thomistic Christology is to be reconfigured, therefore, it cannot be reconfigured in such a way as to imperil the metaphysical and dogmatic insights that I have noted in this chapter. A test for whether my proposal succeeds will be its reception among the theologians whose works I have examined above.

In the following five chapters, I explain my typological path for adding a more explicitly eschatological inflection to contemporary Thomistic Christology, building upon and augmenting Aquinas's reflections on Adam, Isaac, Moses, Joshua, and David as figures of Jesus Christ. Piotr Roszak and Jörgen Vijgen point out, "The typically modern separation of speculative theology and biblical exegesis is foreign to the mind of Thomas Aquinas."[103] Aquinas learned this unity from the Church Fathers, who made frequent recourse to the New Testament's typological–eschatological portraits of Jesus. In this regard, the path that I propose involves encouraging contemporary Thomistic Christology to follow even more fully the example set by Aquinas himself.

---

[102] Hans Boersma, *Heavenly Participation: The Weaving of a Sacramental Tapestry* (Grand Rapids, MI: Eerdmans, 2011), 39.

[103] Piotr Roszak and Jörgen Vijgen, "Introduction," in *Towards a Biblical Thomism: Thomas Aquinas and the Renewal of Biblical Theology*, ed. Piotr Roszak and Jörgen Vijgen (Pamplona: EUNSA, 2018), 11–20, at 11.

2 | Christ the New Adam

The New Creation

2.1 Introduction

The doctrine of the Incarnation can seem highly abstract, even if for a good purpose. In questions 2–6 of the *tertia pars* of the *Summa theologiae*, Thomas Aquinas devotes thirty-six dense articles to the Incarnation. He first inquires into the union itself. Did the union of God and man take place in the natures, resulting in a *tertium quid*? Or did the union take place in the divine Person, and if so, is this the same as saying that it took place in the divine *suppositum* or *hypostasis*? If it took place in the Person/*hypostasis*, does this mean that after the Incarnation the divine Person has changed? If it has not changed, can we really say that the divine Person actually subsists in two natures (divine and human)? Does the Word take the place of the soul in Jesus Christ, or is Jesus' humanity characterized by a soul–body unity like everyone else's? If the latter, would not Jesus be a human "person," in which case the divine Person would not be the fundamental principle of unity, and Jesus would have not only two natures but also two "persons"? Is the union of the human nature and the divine nature in the Person of the Son an "accidental" union, meaning that the human nature is not really united to the Word any more than clothes are united to a man?

Many more such questions follow in Aquinas's treatment. I have surveyed the contents of only seven of the thirty-six articles contained in questions 2–6. One can see how metaphysically dense these questions are. Although Aristotle and various Church Fathers and Councils are quoted many times by Aquinas in the above seven articles, he does not quote Scripture even once.

Aquinas is not to blame for the abstractness or metaphysical difficulty of these questions. As is well known, the same questions are found in the Church Fathers, and they constitute the very heart of the Christological controversies resolved by the early Ecumenical Councils. Questions such as these are necessary, as the Fathers realized, in order to clarify and specify what is meant when we affirm with the Gospel of John: "In the beginning was the Word, and the Word was with God, and the Word was God…. And the Word became flesh and dwelt among us, full of grace and truth" (Jn 1:1, 14). Aidan Nichols has rightly remarked that Aquinas's presentation of these matters "sums up the true mind of the Fathers and Councils."[1] We should be grateful that, as Nichols says, Aquinas uses "his profound philosophy of being – his metaphysics – to underpin the teaching of the Fathers – and especially the teaching of St. Cyril of Alexandria (influential on the Third, Fourth, and Fifth Councils) who so strongly emphasized the unity of the person of Christ as God made man."[2]

Unsurprisingly, Réginald Garrigou-Lagrange's commentary on the *tertia pars* reflects a similar philosophical density, though infused even more than Aquinas's own text by references to historical controversies, including controversies from the centuries after Aquinas's death. Garrigou-Lagrange begins by listing and explaining the various Christological errors advocated by heretical Christians in early and more recent centuries. In treating the metaphysical questions about the hypostatic union, Garrigou-Lagrange regularly pauses to offer scriptural foundations. For example, regarding the mode of union (*Summa theologiae* III, q. 2, a. 1), Garrigou-Lagrange adduces the following four biblical passages that he thinks show

---

[1] Aidan Nichols, O.P., *Deep Mysteries: God, Christ, and Ourselves* (Lanham, MD: Lexington Books, 2019), 23.
[2] Nichols, *Deep Mysteries*, 23.

Christ to be truly God and truly man: Isaiah 9:6, John 14:6, Philippians 2:6, and 1 John 1:1. As he explains with regard to Philippians 2:6: "Here we have the twofold form or nature, namely, of God and the servant, each distinct, without confusion (of natures)."[3]

Similarly, Bernard Lonergan's *De Verbo incarnato* contains over two hundred pages reflecting upon the metaphysics of the Incarnation before turning to equally difficult problems such as Christ's grace and knowledge. Lonergan devotes his opening reflections on Jesus as true God and true man not only to stating the thesis and its opponents but also briefly to adducing the biblical evidence. When he turns to the biblical evidence, Lonergan is attuned to modern issues. For instance, he states that "the New Testament itself does not make use of just one manner of conceiving but of many, and these unfold little by little"; and he further contends that "if the teaching of the New Testament is not understood according to its own conceptualities, there will be no understanding of the Fathers or the problems resolved at the councils."[4]

Reflecting upon biblical foundations, Lonergan argues that the title "Son of man" is a "prospective pattern," whereas the affirmations of Christ's divinity or of his identity as the New Adam (and similar affirmations) involve a "retrospective pattern" or an "inverse retrospective pattern," moving retrospectively behind Jesus' earthly life to his preexistence, or moving from the retrospective

---

[3] Réginald Garrigou-Lagrange, O.P., *Christ the Savior: A Commentary on the Third Part of St. Thomas' Theological Summa*, trans. Dom Bede Rose, O.S.B. (St. Louis, MO: Herder, 1957), 116.

[4] Bernard Lonergan, S.J., *The Incarnate Word*, trans. Charles C. Hefling, Jr., ed. Robert M. Doran and Jeremy D. Wilkins (Toronto: University of Toronto Press, 2016), 35. See also Khaled Anatolios, *Retrieving Nicaea: The Development and Meaning of Trinitarian Doctrine* (Grand Rapids, MI: Baker Academic, 2011), 283: "[T]he retrieval of Nicene ways of reading Scripture cannot be restricted simply to cataloguing ways in which the contents of Scripture can be marshaled toward a logical argument for speaking of God as 'three persons in one nature.' It must be a retrieval precisely of the *reading* and proclamation of Scripture in just these ways rather than using doctrinal formulation to leave behind such reading and proclamation."

affirmation of his preexistence to further affirmations about Jesus as a man either in his earthly life or in his glorified state.[5] Lonergan points to numerous biblical passages that suggest the kinds of patterns he has in view.

As an example of his practice, we may take Lonergan's thesis "The divine Word united to himself flesh animated by a rational soul." He defines his terms by appeal to John 1:1, John 1:15, and the Council of Nicea. He notes that his thesis comes from the following sources: Cyril of Alexandria's Second Letter to Nestorius, as affirmed by the Council of Ephesus; Constantinople I and III; the Council of Chalcedon; and the Council of Rome in 382. He then lists the patristic-era Christians who denied that Jesus had a soul, including the Apollinarians. When he turns to his argument, he begins by defending Jesus' claim to be true man by means of a brief appeal to two verses in Acts, three each in Matthew and Luke, four in Mark, two in Hebrews, and one each in Philippians and Romans. He then cites a wide array of Church Fathers.

This path of quick lists of citations serves a helpful purpose. One can see why both Garrigou-Lagrange and Lonergan have added this element to the presentation offered by Aquinas in the early questions of the *tertia pars*. Their purpose is to exhibit the biblical and patristic grounding of Aquinas's philosophically sophisticated distinctions.[6] As Thomas Joseph White has shown in *The Incarnate Lord*, "a Christological reflection that is more overtly metaphysical in kind can also take full and realistic account of the historical characteristics of cosmic, historical, and human reality."[7]

It is no wonder that philosophical care needs to be taken in expressing theologically the biblically revealed mystery of the Incarnation.

---

[5] See Lonergan, *The Incarnate Word*, 45, 47.

[6] I have chosen to direct attention to Garrigou-Lagrange and Lonergan, but also worthy of note, among twentieth-century scholastic Christologies, is that of Jean-Hervé Nicolas, O.P., in his *Synthèse dogmatique. De la Trinité à la Trinité* (Paris: Beauchesne, 1985).

[7] Thomas Joseph White, O.P., *The Incarnate Lord: A Thomistic Study in Christology* (Washington, DC: Catholic University of America Press, 2015), 508.

2.1 INTRODUCTION

An adequate Christology must "maintain a precarious balance of the unity of Trinitarian actions *ad extra* with the Word alone as incarnate and as causing salvation through instrumental efficiency."[8] This precision cannot be accomplished without metaphysical tools. Metaphysical analysis serves the task of understanding and communicating the scriptural witness to the radical uniqueness of Jesus Christ. What it means for there to be an "incarnation" of the divine Son, without the Son changing or becoming something different from the divine Son, has been well described by Dominic Legge: "[B]ecause of this filial mode of existing that characterizes his person [as the divine Son generated eternally by the divine Father], Christ's humanity bears the Son's personal property.... [E]verything in that humanity takes on the filial mode of the Son."[9]

What does it mean for Christ's human nature to exist in a "filial mode"? For one thing, as the incarnate Son, Christ is the New Adam, the fullness of what Adam should have been – since Adam too is identified as "the son of God" (Lk 3:38). As Mauro Gagliardi observes, Christ "was able to carry out His life as a total gift to the Father for us. In His human nature, Christ lived as Adam should have lived but did not."[10] Christ's perfect filial mode of life appears in his obedience – even to the point of giving up his life out of love,

---

[8] Corey L. Barnes, *Christ's Two Wills in Scholastic Thought: The Christology of Aquinas and Its Historical Contexts* (Toronto: Pontifical Institute of Mediaeval Studies, 2012), 332.

[9] Dominic Legge, O.P., *The Trinitarian Christology of St Thomas Aquinas* (Oxford: Oxford University Press, 2017), 112. Legge defines this "filial mode" in the Trinity as follows: "[T]he Son *has* and *is* the divine *esse* and the divine nature subsisting *as proceeding from the Father*" (112.). See also the valuable investigation of this theme in Joshua R. Brown, *Balthasar in Light of Early Confucianism* (Notre Dame: University of Notre Dame Press, 2020), especially chapter 5, "Archetypal Obedience: Balthasar's Conception of Christ's Filial Obedience as Archetypal Experience," and chapter 6, "Mission, History, and Obedience: Christ's Filial Obedience in Theo-Drama."

[10] Mauro Gagliardi, *Truth Is a Synthesis: Catholic Dogmatic Theology* (Steubenville, OH: Emmaus Academic, 2020), 269–70. Gagliardi rightly adds that as the New Adam, "Christ is much more than Adam, and not only because He is God" (270).

in faithful union with the will of his Father – by contrast to Adam's disobedience due to his desire to have immortal life on his own terms and from his own resources.

In New Adam Christology, Christ's Incarnation and his saving work, which make us God's children (or sons and daughters in the incarnate Son), are firmly joined together. It becomes clear that Jesus is truly the Savior of all humanity.[11] Intrinsic to New Adam Christology is the view that Jesus is the one who accomplishes the fulfillment of all human history. Jesus reveals the meaning of the whole human story from "Adam" onward.

My proposal for a typologically rich, eschatological Thomistic Christology therefore begins with the New Adam. Aquinas comments that "man," the Adamic race, "is called a *microcosmos*."[12] As the New Adam, Jesus' significance is even more truly cosmic. In his *Commentary on the Gospel of John*, Aquinas appreciatively reports a passage in which Augustine mystically interprets the name "Adam" to show that "Christ derived his flesh from Adam in order to gather his elect from the four parts of the world."[13] The New Adam, unlike the first "Adam," is the Lord who reveals and enacts the truth about Adam and who accomplishes the restoration of Israel and of the

---

[11] Andrew J. Byers maintains that the "filial language of ecclesiology (children of God/τέκνα θεοῦ) precipitates the filial language of christology (the only Son/μονογενής) and theology (Father/πατήρ)" (Byers, *Ecclesiology and Theosis in the Gospel of John* [Cambridge: Cambridge University Press, 2017], 62, 65). I would argue for the opposite order.

[12] Thomas Aquinas, *On Kingship: To the King of Cyprus*, trans. Gerald B. Phelan (Toronto: Pontifical Institute of Mediaeval Studies, 1949), Book Two, chapter 1, p. 53.

[13] Thomas Aquinas, *Commentary on the Gospel of John: Chapters 1–5*, trans. Fabian Larcher, O.P., and James A. Weisheipl, O.P., ed. Daniel Keating and Matthew Levering (Washington, DC: Catholic University of America Press, 2010), 157, drawing from Augustine, *In Evangelium Ioannis tractatus centum viginti quatuor*, X.12, PL 35 1473–74, www.augustinus.it/latino/commento_vsg/index2.htm; cf. Thomas Aquinas, *Catena Aurea: Commentary on the Four Gospels Collected out of the Works of the Fathers*, trans. John Henry Newman (Albany, NY: Preserving Christian Publications, 1995), 2:18–22. I owe this reference and the above one to Irenaeus Dunlevy, O.P.

whole human race, opening the way for a new creation caught up in the Trinitarian life.

Christ the New Adam lives the perfection of a human life oriented toward the Father in praise, thanksgiving, and obedience. He accomplishes what all people were created to do, by acting as the "son of God" that human beings were created to be. Rather than trying to seize divinized life for himself (as Adam did), he was "in the form of God" but humbled himself even unto death (Phil 2:6). Furthermore, since the Son is the perfect expression and image of the Father, in the words and deeds of the incarnate Son we see the Father (John 14:8–10). He is the divine Son through whom and for whom all things were created, and in whom "all the fullness of God was pleased to dwell" (Col 1:19).[14] Just as Eve was the bride of Adam drawn from the side of Adam, Christ the New Adam has established his bride the Church. Before the Fall, says Matthias Joseph Scheeben, Adam "was the direct image of Christ," but by his disobedience Adam became "the reverse image."[15] Now Christ the New Adam, the obedient and true Image of the Father, reveals what it means to be God's image and calls all humankind to live by his Spirit in configuration to him.

In the biblical prelude to his metaphysics of the Incarnation – specifically in *Summa theologiae* III, q. 1, a. 5 – Aquinas quotes a key New Adam text: 1 Corinthians 15:47. Asking why God did not simply found the whole human race at the very outset upon the incarnate Son, Aquinas answers that it befits the proper order of

---

[14] For further analysis, making connections to the Wisdom literature (Proverbs 8, Wisdom 7, Sirach 24), see Marianne Meye Thompson, *Colossians and Philemon* (Grand Rapids, MI: Eerdmans, 2005), 27–32.

[15] Matthias Joseph Scheeben, *Handbook of Catholic Dogmatics*, Book 5, *Soteriology*, Part 1, *The Person of Christ the Redeemer*, trans. Michael J. Miller (Steubenville, OH: Emmaus Academic, 2020), 49. As Abner Chou observes, "Christ's status as a second Adam is the grounds for salvation and justification ... as well as glorification" (Chou, *The Hermeneutics of the Biblical Writers: Learning to Interpret Scripture from the Prophets and Apostles* [Grand Rapids, MI: Kregel Academic, 2018], 170).

body–soul creatures to move from Adam (source of the bodily life of all humans) to the New Adam (source of the graced spiritual-bodily life of all humans). Human beings move from the physical to the spiritual, from earthly life to the life of grace and glory.

Does being the divine Son make Christ less a man – less "Adam"? On the contrary, Joseph Ratzinger asserts "that man is most fully man, indeed *the* true man, who is most unlimited, who not only has contact with the infinite – the Infinite Being! – but is one with him."[16] Hans Urs von Balthasar puts the matter in terms of love, pertaining analogically to the perfection of both human and divine life. He remarks, "The first Adam is not perfectible in himself; he must die to himself if he is to be lifted to the level of the Second and incorporated in him. That this is possible is something he owes to the Second Adam, his goal and his source."[17] The New Adam bestows the grace that elevates the human being to supernatural love, an elevation that perfects human nature. It is the God-man who is *fully* human and who perfects our humanity.

---

[16] Joseph Ratzinger, *Introduction to Christianity*, trans. J. R. Foster (San Francisco: Ignatius Press, 2004), 235. I differentiate this statement – which is amplified nicely in Aaron Riches's *Ecce Homo: On the Divine Unity of Christ* (Grand Rapids, MI: Eerdmans, 2016) – from Ratzinger's further remark, influenced by Pierre Teilhard de Chardin and Karl Rahner, that "[i]n him [Christ] 'hominization' has truly reached its goal" because "[m]an's full 'hominization' presupposes God's becoming man; only by this event is the Rubicon dividing the 'animal' from the 'logical' finally crossed for ever and the highest possible development accorded to the process that began when a creature of dust and earth looked out beyond itself and its environment and was able to address God as 'You'" (*Introduction to Christianity*, 235). For background and discussion, see Anna Elisabeth Meiers, *Eschatos Adam: Zentrale Aspekte der Christologie bei Joseph Ratzinger/Benedikt XVI* (Regensburg: Friedrich Pustet, 2019).

[17] Hans Urs von Balthasar, *Theo-Drama: Theological Dramatic Theory*, vol. 4, *The Action*, trans. Graham Harrison (San Francisco: Ignatius Press, 1994), 476. See also Joshua M. McNall, *The Mosaic of Atonement: An Integrated Approach to Christ's Work* (Grand Rapids, MI: Zondervan Academic, 2019), 30. For further background see N. T. Wright, *Jesus and the Victory of God* (Minneapolis, MN: Fortress, 1996), 615; Wright, "Adam, Israel and the Messiah," in *The Climax of the Covenant: Christ and the Law in Pauline Theology* (Minneapolis, MN: Fortress, 1992), 18–40.

Both Aquinas and contemporary Christology, therefore, give a significant place to New Adam Christology.[18] I propose that contemporary Thomistic Christology should expand the place that Aquinas gives to Christ as the eschatological New Adam. In what follows, I develop this proposal in five steps. First, with the help of contemporary biblical scholars, I examine the Gospel of Luke's testimony to the New Adam, with reference also to Irenaeus and Cyril of Alexandria and briefly to the Gospel of John. Second, I investigate some historical-critical and patristic interpretations of the New Adam according to Paul in Romans 5 and 1 Corinthians 15. Third, I explore Aquinas's commentary on these Pauline passages.[19] Fourth, I suggest specific ways in which additional attention to Christ as the New Adam could find a place within the *tertia pars* and, more to the point, within contemporary Thomistic Christology. Fifth, I identify some ways that Aquinas's *sacra doctrina* already engages the reality of Christ the New Adam.

2.2 The New Adam and the Gospel of Luke

The Gospel of Luke offers a genealogy for Jesus that runs from Joseph all the way to Adam, whom Luke calls "the son of God"

---

[18] See also Hilarion Alfeyev's discussion of Christ the New Adam in *Orthodox Christianity*, vol. 2, *Doctrine and Teaching of the Orthodox Church*, trans. Andrew Smith (Yonkers, NY: St Vladimir's Seminary Press, 2012). See also the *Catechism of the Catholic Church*, 2nd ed. (Vatican City: Libreria Editrice Vaticana, 1997), §504.

[19] The same texts by Aquinas that I treat have been exposited by Luis M. Cruz, "*Christus, novissimus Adam*. La relación Cristo-Adán en los Comentarios de Santo Tomás de Aquino a las epístolas paulinas," *Revista Española de Teología* 76 (2016): 25–107; Marie-Joseph Nicolas, O.P., "La théologie du Christ nouvel dans saint Thomas d'Aquin," *Bulletin de la Société française d'études mariales* 13 (1955): 1–13; and (in the case of Romans 5:12–21) by J. A. Di Noia, O.P., "Christ Brings Freedom from Sin and Death: The Commentary of St. Thomas Aquinas on Romans 5:12–21," *The Thomist* 73 (2009): 381–98. See also Catalina Vial de Amesti, "La muerte según los Comentarios de santo Tomás a las cartas de san Pablo," *Forum: Supplement to Acta Philosophica* 5 (2019): 339–51.

(Lk 3:38). Reading the genealogy in light of Luke 4's temptation narrative, Richard Hays has commented that in Luke 3:38 "[i]t is possible that Luke is obliquely suggesting a christological identification of Jesus as the new Adam."[20] In Hays's view, however, although Luke 3:38 may be presenting Jesus as the new Adam, "this is not a theme he [Luke] develops elsewhere."[21]

Prior to this genealogy, Luke has described the angels' promise to Mary that her son "will be called the Son of the Most High" and "will be called holy, the Son of God" (Lk 1:32, 35). Immediately after the genealogy, Luke presents Satan tempting Jesus three times, and two of these temptations begin with Satan's words to Jesus: "If you are the Son of God" (Lk 4:3, 9). With Luke 1:43 in mind ("Why is this granted to me, that the mother of my Lord should come to me?"), Kavin Rowe notes that it is "as κύριος that Luke first brings Jesus into the human realm."[22] Rowe shows that this title indicates Jesus' divine status in Luke. He states, "Luke uses κύριος to make an essential claim about the relation between Jesus and the God of Israel: Jesus of Nazareth is the movement of God in one human life so much so that it is possible to speak of God and Jesus together as κύριος."[23]

By contrast to Jesus, Adam is certainly not divine, not even as the "son of God" (Lk 3:38). Joseph Fitzmyer therefore argues that Luke does not intend a typological connection between the "son of God" Adam and the "son of God" Jesus.[24] Michael Wolter, too, denies that Luke envisions Jesus as a "new Adam," even though Wolter

---

[20] Richard B. Hays, *Echoes of Scripture in the Gospels* (Waco, TX: Baylor University Press, 2016), 419n110.
[21] Hays, *Echoes of Scripture in the Gospels*, 419n110.
[22] C. Kavin Rowe, *Early Narrative Christology: The Lord in the Gospel of Luke* (Berlin: De Gruyter, 2006), 43.
[23] Rowe, *Early Narrative Christology*, 218. Similarly, Simon J. Gathercole holds that the title "Son of God" when combined with the title "Holy One" expresses Jesus' belonging "in the divine sphere of reality" (*The Pre-existent Son: Recovering the Christologies of Matthew, Mark, and Luke* [Grand Rapids, MI: Eerdmans, 2006], 282).
[24] Joseph A. Fitzmyer, S.J., *The Gospel according to Luke (I-IX)* (Garden City, NY: Doubleday, 1981), 498.

nevertheless connects the genealogy to much of what pertains theologically to the phrase "new Adam."[25] According to Wolter, Luke aims to show that God relates to all humanity through Adam and even more through Jesus. Wolter considers that in this way "Luke uses Adam's divine sonship as a model in order to mark out the framework of meaning for understanding Jesus's divine sonship."[26] On this view, Luke makes a genealogical reference to Adam in order to indicate both that God relates to the whole of humanity through Jesus and that Jesus has a relation to God so intimate as to be comparable only with Adam's.[27]

Further insight may be obtained from Brandon Crowe's recent *The Last Adam: A Theology of the Obedient Life of Jesus in the Gospels*. In Crowe's view, the connection between Adam and Jesus in Luke 3:38 warrants asking whether there is an "Adam Christology" in the Gospel of Luke, and he thinks the answer is yes.[28] Jesus accomplishes the tasks that Adam was meant to accomplish, and so Jesus is "the complete and perfect reflection of God's image, the absolutely righteous last Adam who obtained the eschatological blessings and glory."[29]

---

[25] Michael Wolter, *The Gospel according to Luke: Volume I (Luke 1–9:50)*, trans. Wayne Coppins and Christoph Heilig (Waco, TX: Baylor University Press, 2016), 183. Wolter holds that Luke intends to present Jesus "as the divinely appointed eternal ruler over Israel" and as the promised Messianic son of David.

[26] Wolter, *The Gospel according to Luke*, 184. In *The Pre-existent Son*, Gathercole holds that the Gospel of Luke does not go as far as the Gospel of John's affirmation that Jesus Christ is the incarnate preexistent divine Creator. Gathercole does think, however, that Luke presents the Messiah implicitly as preexistent – especially in Luke 1:78, with its reference to the "dawn."

[27] Biblical scholars point out that "son of God" is a phrase found in other Second Temple texts, including a messianic text from Qumran. The "son of God" was to be God's royal representative, not actually divine. Israel itself was the "son of God," and her messianic king would preeminently be "son of God." See Wright, *Jesus and the Victory of God*, 485–86.

[28] Brandon D. Crowe, *The Last Adam: A Theology of the Obedient Life of Jesus in the Gospels* (Grand Rapids, MI: Baker Academic, 2017), 27.

[29] Crowe, *The Last Adam*, 28, with reference to G. K. Beale, *A New Testament Biblical Theology: The Unfolding of the Old Testament in the New* (Grand Rapids, MI: Baker Academic, 2011), 386.

Citing a bevy of scholars – including Darrell Bock, Joel Green, Jerome Neyrey, Craig Evans, and James Sanders – Crowe argues that Luke, in his genealogy, means to show that Jesus is the "last Adam" whose "universal relevance" compares with Adam's but exceeds it.[30] Jesus' temptations by Satan in Luke 4, following close upon the genealogy, indicate that he is the new Adam who obeys God's law rather than disobeying it as the original Adam did. Jesus adopts the obedient filial stance that should have been adopted by Adam (and by Israel).[31] In Luke 4:13, we read that "when the devil had ended every temptation, he departed from him until an opportune time." The implication is that the devil will be back, and in fact, as Crowe observes, at Gethsemane "Jesus is again tempted to forego his task of obedient suffering on the cross."[32] On the Cross, the obedient new Adam is able to tell the good thief: "[T]oday you will be with me in Paradise" (Lk 23:43). He reverses Adam's exile by reversing Adam's disobedience.

Crowe is aware that he is not the first to draw this connection. He mentions a number of Church Fathers, above all Irenaeus.[33] In *Against Heresies*, Book III, chapter 23, Irenaeus reflects upon Luke 3's genealogy and concludes that Christ recapitulates all generations of humans.[34] Humans fell in Adam, whose nature was "animal,"

---

[30] Crowe, *The Last Adam*, 28.

[31] Crowe notes that Joel Marcus and others have made the case that "son of man" also is an Adamic identification, at least in Mark. See Joel Marcus, "Son of Man as Son of Adam," *Revue biblique* 110 (2003): 38–61; Marcus, "Son of Man as Son of Adam. Part II: Exegesis," *Revue biblique* 110 (2003): 370–86.

[32] Crowe, *The Last Adam*, 31.

[33] For a less fruitful strand of patristic reflection on Adam and Christ, see the reflections on Origen and Methodius in Emanuela Prinzivalli, "Adam and the Soul of Christ in Origen's *Commentary on Genesis*. A Possible Reconstruction," *Adamantius* 23 (2017): 119–29. Prinzivalli states, "in Origen, Adam – when understood anthropologically – is seen as the (fallen) soul, or – when understood Christologically – is seen as the soul of Christ. Methodius, who opposed head-on the idea of the pre-existence of souls, has to reiterate that Adam is man as such, and it is Adam as mankind – and thus not Adam as symbol of the soul – which is assumed by the Logos" (127).

[34] See Irenaeus, "Against Heresies," Book III, chapter 23, in *The Apostolic Fathers, Justin Martyr, Irenaeus*, ed. Alexander Roberts and James Donaldson, vol. 1 of Ante-Nicene

2.2 THE NEW ADAM AND THE GOSPEL OF LUKE

whereas in Christ, whose nature as the divine Son is "spiritual," salvation arrives. Christ, not Adam, is first in the order of predestination. The very fact that there is a New Adam in whom all are saved implies that this New Adam is not merely another human – though he is fully human – but rather he is a "spiritual" man capable of saving all sinners, and thus he is the divine Word or preexistent Son who has the power to forgive sins. Irenaeus remarks, "Luke, commencing the genealogy with the Lord, carried it back to Adam, indicating that it was He who regenerated them into the Gospel of life, and not they Him."[35]

The connection between Jesus as the New Adam, Jesus' obedience as reversing Adam's disobedience, and the Incarnation of the divine Son is prominent in Cyril of Alexandria's *Commentary on John*.[36] For Cyril, the key difference between the first Adam and the New Adam is that the former "was earthly and from the earth,"

Fathers Series (Peabody, MA: Hendrickson, 1995), 315–567, at 455. See also the background (cited by Crowe) in Jan Tjeerd Nielsen, *Adam and Christ in the Theology of Irenaeus of Lyons: An Examination of the Function of the Adam-Christ Typology in the "Adversus Haereses" of Irenaeus, against the Background of the Gnosticism of His Time* (Assen: Van Gorcum, 1968), 68–82; and Ben C. Blackwell, *Christosis: Pauline Soteriology in Light of Deification in Irenaeus and Cyril of Alexandria* (Tübingen: Mohr Siebeck, 2011), 41–43. More recently, see Stephen O. Presley, "The Use of Paul in Irenaeus's Christology," in *Irenaeus and Paul*, ed. Todd D. Still and David E. Wilhite (London: T&T Clark, 2020), 65–80.

[35] Irenaeus, "Against Heresies," Book III, chapter 23, 455. For discussion of Irenaeus's theology of Adam and Christ, see John Behr, *Asceticism and Anthropology in Irenaeus and Clement* (Oxford: Oxford University Press, 2000), 57–68. Behr treats Irenaeus on Luke's genealogy at 58. Since Irenaeus was writing before Nicea, it may be asked whether he believed that Christ is fully divine. For an affirmative answer, see Anthony Briggman, *God and Christ in Irenaeus* (Oxford: Oxford University Press, 2019), 113; Michel René Barnes, "Irenaeus's Trinitarian Theology," *Nova et Vetera* 7 (2009): 67–106. See also Khaled Anatolios, *Deification through the Cross: An Eastern Christian Theology of Salvation* (Grand Rapids, MI: Eerdmans, 2020), 269.

[36] See Robert Louis Wilken, "St. Cyril of Alexandria: The Mystery of Christ in the Bible," *Pro Ecclesia* 4 (1995): 454–78; Daniel A. Keating, "The Baptism of Jesus in Cyril of Alexandria: The Re-creation of the Human Race," *Pro Ecclesia* 8 (1999): 210–22 – both cited in Crowe, *The Last Adam*, 9.

whereas the second was "life by nature."[37] The first Adam had no excuse for his flagrant disobedience, but God never intended to allow it to stand. From the outset, "God the Father planned to send us the second Adam from heaven. He sent his own Son, who is by nature without variation or change, into our likeness."[38] Since sinners could not redeem themselves, the sinless incarnate Son came to accomplish this redemption. As the incarnate Lord, he was able "to conquer death for us and to raise our entire nature with him."[39]

Cyril of Alexandria is one of the greatest masters of Christology, whose teaching on the unity of Christ has crucial implications for the Christian faith. Not only the determinations of the Council of Ephesus but also many judgments of later Councils and theologians, including Aquinas, depend upon Cyril's Christology.[40] It is significant therefore that Cyril's biblical exegesis is "controlled by" the image of Jesus Christ as the New Adam, which Cyril draws from Paul's portrait in Romans 5 and 1 Corinthians 15.[41] As Robert Wilken remarks, "The Adam-Christ typology provided Cyril with an image that was at once particular and universal. It was particular in that it spoke of Adam and Christ as unique human persons. It highlighted what Adam and Christ *did*.... But it was universal in that it presented Adam and Christ as representative figures ... whose actions have consequences for all humanity."[42] Wilken observes that New Adam Christology assists Cyril in depicting Christ as fully human

---

[37] Cyril of Alexandria, *Commentary on John*, vol. 1, Ancient Christian Texts, trans. David R. Maxwell, ed. Joel C. Elowsky (Downers Grove, IL: IVP Academic, 2013), 82, commenting on John 1:32–33.

[38] Cyril of Alexandria, *Commentary on John*, vol. 1, 82.

[39] Cyril of Alexandria, *Commentary on John*, vol. 1, 82.

[40] Indeed, Aaron Riches remarks that Garrigou-Lagrange, like Aquinas, was "impeccably Cyrillian ... in matters of Christological doctrine" (Riches, *Ecce Homo*, 14n33). Riches charges Karl Rahner with a failure to understand the Cyrillian doctrine. See Rahner, "Christology Today?," in his *Theological Investigations*, vol. 17, trans. Margaret Kohl (London: Darton, Longman & Todd, 1981), 24–38.

[41] Wilken, "St. Cyril of Alexandria," 470.

[42] Wilken, "St. Cyril of Alexandria," 471.

2.2 THE NEW ADAM AND THE GOSPEL OF LUKE

and fully divine and as sending the Spirit to reestablish humankind in pre-Fall Adamic immortality.

Abner Chou has argued that the Gospel of John "ties Christ with Adam by portraying him as a gardener after the resurrection (John 20:15)."[43] Dwelling in "a garden in Eden," Adam was commanded by God to "till the earth and keep it" (Gen 2:8, 15). The New Adam restores this garden by inaugurating a new creation. When the New Adam breathes the Spirit upon his disciples, this action parallels God's breathing the breath of life into Adam at creation (see Gen 2:7; Jn 20:22). Jerome sums up in his *Homily 87*: "When Mary Magdalene had seen the Lord and thought that he was the gardener ... she was mistaken, indeed, in her vision, but the very error had its prototype. Truly, indeed, Jesus was the gardener of his paradise, of his trees of paradise."[44] This "paradise" with its "trees" is the new Eden.

Somewhat similarly, David Litwa has persuasively argued that Pilate's statement, "Behold the man!" (Jn 19:5) echoes Genesis 3:22 and some late Second Temple texts in order to depict Jesus as the New Adam – a claim with which the Fathers would agree.[45]

In sum, there are a variety of biblical and patristic testimonies that Jesus Christ is the New Adam, the one who accomplishes – while

---

[43] Chou, *The Hermeneutics of the Biblical Writers*, 163. Although this typological connection seems persuasive to me, I note that most scholars do not mention it. Craig A. Keener, for example, writes: "That Mary thought Jesus a 'gardener' (20:15) fits the story: the tomb was, after all, in a 'garden' (19:41). Gardeners tended to belong to the poorest class.... But John may suggest an ironic allusion to the joint work of Father and Son; just as the Father was a γεωργός, a vinedresser (15:1; cf. 1 Cor 3:9), Jesus was a κηπουρός, watching his garden. But without a clearer verbal connection, the allusion seems tenuous" (Keener, *The Gospel of John: A Commentary*, vol. 2 [Grand Rapids, MI: Baker Academic, 2003], 1190).

[44] Jerome, *Homily 87: On John 13–14*, in FC 57:220, cited in Joel C. Elowsky and Thomas C. Oden, eds., *John 11–21*, Ancient Christian Commentary on Scripture Series (Downers Grove, IL: IVP Academic, 2007), 346.

[45] See M. David Litwa, "Behold Adam: A Reading of John 19:5," *Horizons in Biblical Theology* 32, no. 2 (2010): 129–43.

greatly exceeding – what Adam should have done. Let me now turn to the Bible's most explicit discussion of Christ the New Adam, in Romans 5 and 1 Corinthians 15.

2.3 The New Adam in Romans 5 and 1 Corinthians 15

Romans 5:17 presents the central element of Paul's teaching on the New Adam: "If, because of one man's trespass, death reigned through that one man, much more will those who receive the abundance of grace and the free gift of righteousness reign in life through the one man Jesus Christ." According to Paul, Adam is the origin of all human life but also the origin of all human death due to his sin. Entering into this predicament, the New Adam reverses the consequences of Adam's sin and opens up for us the life that God intended to give to Adam and to the entire human race, namely, "sharing the glory of God" (Rom 5:2).

N. T. Wright suggests that "Romans 5.6–11 has as good a claim as most passages to express the heart of Paul's theology."[46] If so, then Romans 5:12–21, in which Paul portrays Christ as the New Adam, is a passage very close to Paul's heart. In Wright's view, the image of the New Adam accords with Israel's sense of its own history and mission. God's plan involves resolving Adam's failure by electing a people in the New Adam.[47] Whether or not Wright's panoramic view is correct with respect to Second Temple Jewish understandings of Israel's election, it is clear that Paul holds that Christ the New Adam has fulfilled God's purposes in such a way that "where

---

[46] N. T. Wright, *Paul and the Faithfulness of God*, vol. 2, Parts III and IV (Minneapolis, MN: Fortress, 2013), 885.

[47] For some links between Adam, Noah, and Abraham, see also Michael Fishbane, *Biblical Interpretation in Ancient Israel* (Oxford: Oxford University Press, 1985), 372; and Jon D. Levenson, *The Death and Resurrection of the Beloved Son: The Transformation of Child Sacrifice in Judaism and Christianity* (New Haven, CT: Yale University Press, 1993), 84, 88, and elsewhere.

2.3 THE NEW ADAM IN ROMANS 5 AND 1 CORINTHIANS 15

sin increased, grace abounded all the more, so that, as sin reigned in death, grace also might reign through righteousness to eternal life through Jesus Christ our Lord" (Rom 5:20–21).

Yet, does the Adam typology of Romans 5 allow for the difference between the solely human Adam and a divine-human Jesus Christ? Certainly, there is a major functional difference between Adam and Christ: "Christ has not merely restored that which Adam lost, but has gone far beyond."[48] Christ has embodied "the love of the creator God" through his faithful obedience.[49] In Romans 5, however, Wright does not consider the Adam–Christ typology to be indicative of the Incarnation. This may seem to place the New Adam (Christ) solely on the level of Adam, at least with respect to the typology of Romans 5.[50]

What about 1 Corinthians 15, where Paul seems to go beyond function toward ontology at least in passages such as 1 Corinthians 15:47, "The first man was from the earth, a man of dust; the second man is from heaven?" What makes Jesus a "man of heaven"? Fitzmyer directs attention here to the work of Philo, born a generation before Paul. Fitzmyer asks, "Is Paul's comparison of Adam and Christ worked out in terms of Philo's interpretation of the creation of two types of human beings, one 'earthly' (*gēinos*), the other 'heavenly' (*ouranios* or *noētos, asōmatos, aphthartos*), according to the two accounts of creation in Genesis chaps. 1 and 2?"[51] In his *Allegorical Interpretation*, Philo discusses Genesis 2:7, where God creates man (Adam) from the dust and breathes life into him, in light of Genesis 1:27, where God creates man in his own image and

---

[48] N. T. Wright, "The Letter to the Romans," in *The New Interpreter's Bible*, vol. 10, ed. Leander E. Keck (Nashville, TN: Abingdon Press, 2002), 395–770, at 528.
[49] Wright, "The Letter to the Romans," 530.
[50] More promisingly, Brendan Byrne, S.J., holds that for Paul in Romans 5, Christ's obedience not only expresses his love for all human beings but also flows from "his union with the Father" (Byrne, *Romans* [Collegeville, MN: Liturgical Press, 1996], 181).
[51] Joseph A. Fitzmyer, S.J., *First Corinthians: A New Translation with Introduction and Commentary* (New Haven, CT: Yale University Press, 2008), 592.

without any description of building man from dust. Comparing the two creation accounts, Philo states: "The races of men are twofold; for one is the heavenly man, and the other the earthly man. Now the heavenly man, as being born in the image of God, has no participation in any corruptible or earth-like essence. But the earthly man is made of loose material, which he calls a lump of clay."[52] The "heavenly man" is "begotten" as God's image, whereas the "earthly man" is "made" from the dirt of the ground.[53]

Philo's meaning here has to do in part with his view of the preexistence of souls. The key point for my purposes, however, is that Philo is simply emphasizing that God lifts up earthly minds. When God breathes upon the earthly man (or earthly mind), that mind is then able to perceive and contemplate God. As Fitzmyer says, this transformation from an earthly to a heavenly mind is clearly not what Paul has in view in his comparison of Adam and Christ in 1 Corinthians 15:47.

In Fitzmyer's interpretation, Adam, the first man, stands in 1 Corinthians 15:45 simply as "the first human being created" and therefore in this sense as "the head of the human race."[54] Paul quotes Genesis 2:7 to identify Adam as a "living soul" (*psychē zōsa*) and thereby to be able to draw a contrast between Adam (existing at the level of *psychē*) and the New Adam (existing, after his Resurrection, at the level of *pneuma*). Fitzmyer concludes that Paul is describing Christ as "the Adam of the eschaton," now that Christ has his risen body that is not subject to mortality or decay.[55]

---

[52] Philo, *Allegorical Interpretation*, I, chapter XII, in *The Works of Philo: Complete and Unabridged*, rev. ed., trans. C. D. Yonge (Peabody, MA: Hendrickson, 1993), 25–37, at 28.

[53] Philo, *Allegorical Interpretation*, I, chapter XII, 28. See also Philo's *On the Creation* (*De opificio mundi*), chapter XLVI, in *The Works of Philo*, 3–24, at 19, where Philo explains that man was at first a pure soul and then God saw fit to give man a body.

[54] Fitzmyer, *First Corinthians*, 597. Fitzmyer argues that there is a contrast here with the Wisdom of Solomon 16:11.

[55] Fitzmyer, *First Corinthians*, 597.

2.3 THE NEW ADAM IN ROMANS 5 AND 1 CORINTHIANS 15

Is the difference between Adam and Christ, then, simply that Christ has a "spiritual body" (1 Cor 15:44) whereas Adam does not? If so, then the New Adam would be joined by many other New Adams (on his same level) at the general resurrection. Discussing 1 Corinthians 15:45, Fitzmyer suggests that there is something more. Christ is "the last Adam, because there will be no other head of the human race in any sense after him."[56] He is the true head of the human race because he is "the source of risen life in glory" to all others.[57] Although others will share in risen life, Christ alone is the "last Adam" or New Adam because he is the source or cause of such life in all other humans.

Of course, in 1 Corinthians 15:47, Christ is not simply the source of the Spirit but also is "from heaven," whereas Adam is only "from the earth." Fitzmyer interprets this verse not in terms of preexistence but in terms of Christ's glorified risen life and his future coming in glory: Paul has in view the "coming parousia" rather than Christ's "incarnation, as in John 3:31."[58] In John 3:31, the evangelist (or John the Baptist?) states with reference to Christ: "He who comes from above is above all; he who is of the earth belongs to the earth, and of the earth he speaks." In the context of John 1, this is a clear reference to the Incarnation and the Word's preexistence. But Fitzmyer rules out such an interpretation for 1 Corinthians 15:47.

Hays offers a similar reading. The "second man" (or "last Adam") who is "from heaven" is Jesus Christ in his risen, glorified body. He explains, "For Paul, the heavenly man is Christ, manifested in his resurrected body, who will come from heaven (cf. Dan. 7:13–14; 1 Thess. 4:16–17) *at the end* to raise his people and transform them into his likeness."[59] The comparison here between

---

[56] Fitzmyer, *First Corinthians*, 597.
[57] Fitzmyer, *First Corinthians*, 598.
[58] Fitzmyer, *First Corinthians*, 599.
[59] Richard B. Hays, *First Corinthians* (Louisville, KY: John Knox Press, 1997), 273. See also the argument of Brant Pitre, Michael P. Barber, and John A. Kincaid, *Paul, a New Covenant Jew: Rethinking Pauline Theology* (Grand Rapids, MI: Eerdmans,

the first Adam and the last Adam involves Christ's Resurrection and glorification as well as his Second Coming. Again, the comparison does not involve preexistence or Incarnation – although Paul does not rule these out.[60]

However, a number of the Church Fathers, including Augustine and Cyril of Jerusalem, interpret 1 Corinthians 15:45–49 explicitly in light of Christ's preexistence. Gerald Bray sums up their perspective: "The Lord who was heavenly became earthly that he might make heavenly those who were earthly."[61] In Book XIII of *City of God*, Augustine states that according to 1 Corinthians 15:45, Adam was a "living soul" but – unlike the Second Adam – not a "life-giving spirit." Augustine then explains how Adam, by sinning, corrupted his nature and placed it on a spiral toward death. Christ freely took to himself this mortal human nature. In his Resurrection from the dead, Christ received his heavenly body, no longer subject to death. Augustine explains 1 Corinthians 15:48's reference to the "man of heaven": "It is Christ whom the Apostle means to be understood by 'the heavenly

---

2019), 215: "While the apostle certainly affirms that the resurrection will involve the individual bodies of believers (cf. Rom 8:11), the language of the eschatological vision in 1 Corinthians 15 is *ecclesial* – he does not speak of the resurrection of 'bodies' but of 'the body.' Christ does not simply raise up individuals but the church as a whole."

[60] Regarding 1 Corinthians 15:44–49's use of the Adam/Christ typology, see also Gordon D. Fee, *Pauline Christology: An Exegetical-Theological Study* (Peabody, MA: Hendrickson, 2007), 116: "Paul's present usage seems to have been determined by two matters: (1) the Septuagint's use of the word ψυχή to describe what Adam became in creation, and (2) his conviction that what is essential to our final life is Spirit (πνεῦμα). What is different in this second use of the analogy is that Paul is no longer emphasizing Christ's humanity as in common with Adam: rather, in sharp *contrast* to Adam, whose body was subject to decay and death, Christ's *risen body* is quite the opposite. It is now 'of heaven' (even though it began on earth) and is therefore without the possibility of decay. So even though the contrast [from 1 Corinthians 15:21–22] is maintained by the language of the 'first man Adam' and the 'last Adam/second man,' the emphasis on Christ is no longer on his humanity but on his present heavenly existence in *a raised/transformed body*."

[61] Gerald Bray, "Overview of 15:45–50," in *1–2 Corinthians*, ed. Gerald Bray and Thomas C. Oden, Ancient Christian Commentary on Scripture Series (Downers Grove, IL: InterVarsity Press, 1999), 174.

2.3 THE NEW ADAM IN ROMANS 5 AND 1 CORINTHIANS 15

man', because he came from heaven to be clothed in a body of earthly mortality, so that he might clothe it in heavenly immortality."[62]

Thus, Augustine agrees with Fitzmyer and Hays that Paul here has in view Christ's risen, glorified body. But for Augustine, it is not enough to interpret Paul's reference to the "man of heaven" or the man who "is from heaven" simply as the risen Jesus Christ who will come in glory. To understand what it means for Jesus to be the "last Adam" and the "man of heaven," we must apprehend not only his risen body but also the fact that he freely took on a mortal body. Adam did not freely take on a body, because Adam was fully "from the earth, a man of dust" (1 Cor 15:48). By contrast, when the New Adam (Jesus) took on a mortal body, this did not mean that he was ever "from the earth, a man of dust." Rather, he was always "from heaven." He took on an Adamic nature freely. He took it on because, as its divine Creator, he intended to heal and elevate it. He is not, then, simply a "man of dust" who became a "man of heaven" thanks to his Resurrection. If this were so, he would not have the freedom vis-à-vis Adamic nature that is needed to heal and elevate it. In his Resurrection, he did indeed become a "man of heaven" in his flesh; however, he did so not merely as an exalted Adamic figure but as the One who had always been "from heaven," as the preexistent Son. Since he was from heaven, his death in his Adamic flesh had the power to give eternal life.

Note that both Fitzmyer and Hays affirm elsewhere that Paul considers Christ to be the preexistent Son. Commenting on 1 Corinthians 8:6 – "for us there is one God, the Father, from whom are all things and for whom we exist, and one Lord, Jesus Christ, through whom are all things and through whom we exist" – Fitzmyer brushes aside any doubt that Christ is here not preexistent or divine.[63] Hays, too, recognizes the preexistence and divinity of

---

[62] Augustine, *City of God*, trans. Henry Bettenson (London: Penguin, 1984), Book XIII, ch. 23, p. 536.
[63] See Fitzmyer, *First Corinthians*, 343.

the Son. He observes that 1 Corinthians 8:6, whether composed by Paul or (in his view, more likely) by the early Christian community, "takes the extraordinarily bold step of identifying 'the Lord Jesus' with 'the Lord' acclaimed in the *Shema*, while still insisting that 'for us there is one God.' Paul and other early Christians have reshaped Israel's faith in such a way that Jesus is now acclaimed as Lord within the framework of monotheism."[64]

Arguably, then, Augustine's reasoning that 1 Corinthians 15:47 refers not solely to the *risen* Christ but also to the *preexistent* Son is not something with which Paul would have disagreed. Paul's statements about the "man of heaven" (1 Cor 15:48–49) do not need to be read solely as referring to Christ's risen body. These statements may be read in a broader context that helps to explain the power of Christ. The fact that the New Adam is "from heaven" in the sense of Incarnation illuminates the saving power of the crucifixion and Resurrection, as well as our configuration to "the image of the man of heaven."

2.4 Aquinas on the New Adam: Romans 5 and 1 Corinthians 15

In the above, I have examined some influential understandings of Christ as New Adam found among historical-critical biblical scholars and the Church Fathers. Let me now return to Aquinas and Thomistic Christology. Réginald Garrigou-Lagrange states Aquinas's perspective on the New Adam as the incarnate Lord when he observes, in commenting upon question 1, article 2 of the *tertia pars*: "Mere man cannot offer complete satisfaction to God for his own sin or for another's."[65]

---

[64] Hays, *First Corinthians*, 140.
[65] Garrigou-Lagrange, *Christ the Savior*, 66. Even a sinless mere human – the Virgin Mary being the evident example – could not have restored the order of justice between humans and God, because "sin committed against God has a certain infinity considered as an offense," and so "condign satisfaction must have infinite efficacy," which can only be the case if the satisfaction is offered by the God-man (ibid., 67).

Similarly, Garrigou-Lagrange rejoices in the value and power of the Incarnation: "[T]he Son of God through His incarnation ... stoops down to us with sublime mercy, so that the saints are moved to tears at the thought of it."[66] This fits with the power of the New Adam, whose merciful grace far exceeds Adam's Fall.

I have already mentioned the role that Christ the New Adam has in Aquinas's discussion of the fittingness of God becoming incarnate, specifically with regard to the timing of the Incarnation. For Aquinas in *Summa theologiae* III, q. 1, a. 5, the New Adam has priority in God's plan in an absolute sense, although Adam comes first in time. Aquinas states, "it is not the spiritual which is first but the physical, and then the spiritual. The first man was from the earth, a man of dust; the second man is from heaven" (1 Cor 15:46–47).[67] Moreover, as Aquinas says in *Summa theologiae* III, q. 24, a. 4, "Christ's predestination is the cause of ours"; Christ comes first. Can Aquinas's commentaries on Romans and 1 Corinthians offer us any additional insight into the value of New Adam Christology?

Let me begin with his commentary on Romans 5:12–21. Sin and death came about through Adam, but, in God's plan, Adam was *already* a type or figure of Christ, as Romans 5:14 says.[68] Christ, therefore, has priority. In what way, then, does Adam find his model in Christ? Aquinas explains that the typological relationship is centered

---

[66] Garrigou-Lagrange, *Christ the Savior*, 95.
[67] Jean-Pierre Torrell, O.P., employs an example from Chartres Cathedral to illustrate the New Adam's priority: "At the north portal of the Cathedral of Chartres, we see God creating the first man, His eyes fixed on the New Adam. And it is in accord with the latter image that he fashions man" (Torrell, *Saint Thomas Aquinas*, vol. 2, *Spiritual Master*, trans. Robert Royal [Washington, DC: Catholic University of America Press, 2003], 125).
[68] See also Peter of John Olivi's brief commentary on Romans 5:14: "Christ is Adam's image or likeness if understood by way of opposition. For just as in Adam all die, so in Christ all are brought to life. Or it could be understood as a direct correlation, because just as Adam is the beginning of all by nature, so Christ is the beginning of all by grace" (Peter of John Olivi, "Romans 5," in *The Letter to the Romans*, trans. and ed. Ian Christopher Levy, Philip D. W. Krey, and Thomas Ryan, The Bible in Medieval Tradition Series [Grand Rapids, MI: Eerdmans, 2013], 134–43, at 139).

upon the fact that Adam and Christ are both the source of something for all other humans. Adam, however, is primarily a negative source: the source of sin and death. Aquinas names two other similarities between Adam and Christ. Both are conceived without sexual intercourse, and both are the source of their bride. God places Adam in a deep sleep and removes Adam's rib, from which God forms Eve (Gen 2:21–22). Similarly, when Christ is in the sleep of death, a Roman soldier pierces his side and from his side flow blood and water: the Church-constituting sacraments of baptism and the Eucharist.

From the beginning, then, God wills for the Adamic history of sin and death to be resolved and superseded by the "history of grace [progressu gratiae]" in and through the New Adam.[69] Grace is "Christ's gift" that heals the wounds caused by sin and draws God's people into eternal life.[70] Christ's grace flows from "the immensity of the divine goodness."[71] In its divine power to heal and elevate human beings, Christ's grace is far stronger than Adam's sin. The New Adam gives the free gift of "the remission of sin" and of the divinizing good "superadded beyond the remission of sins."[72] Christ therefore is more truly the head of humanity.[73]

---

[69] The quotation comes from Thomas Aquinas, *Commentary on the Letter of Saint Paul to the Romans*, trans. Fabian Larcher, O.P., ed. J. Mortensen and E. Alarcón (Lander, WY: The Aquinas Institute for the Study of Sacred Doctrine, 2012), §430, p. 147. See, for further discussion, Roger W. Nutt, "From Eternal Sonship to Adoptive Filiation: St. Thomas on the Predestination of Christ," in *Thomism and Predestination: Principles and Disputations*, ed. Steven A. Long, Roger W. Nutt, and Thomas Joseph White, O.P. (Ave Maria, FL: Sapientia Press, 2016), 77–93; and Michał Paluch, O.P., *La Profondeur de l'amour divin. Évolution de la doctrine de la predestination dans l'oeuvre de saint Thomas d'Aquin* (Paris: J. Vrin, 2004), 238–44, expositing *Summa theologiae* III, q. 24. See also Legge, *The Trinitarian Christology of St Thomas Aquinas*, 82.

[70] See Aquinas, *Commentary on the Letter of Saint Paul to the Romans*, §431, p. 148.

[71] Aquinas, *Commentary on the Letter of Saint Paul to the Romans*, §431, p. 148. See Di Noia, "Christ Brings Freedom from Sin and Death," 391.

[72] Aquinas, *Commentary on the Letter of Saint Paul to the Romans*, §432, p. 148.

[73] For discussion of Adam's headship and Christ's, see François Daguet, *Théologie du dessein divin chez Thomas d'Aquin. Finis Omnium Ecclesia* (Paris: J. Vrin, 2003), 271–79, on "Le Christ-tête et Adam-principe: les deux capitalités."

In this context, Aquinas quotes John 1:16, "from his fullness have we all received, grace upon grace." Justification is far greater in its effects than is the condemnation that comes through Adam's sin. Through grace, believers enter into "the kingdom of life."[74] This life is not mere earthly life. Rather, the "kingdom of life" is a sharing in Christ's life. It is "eternal life" as understood in the Gospel of John: namely, a sharing in the Son's life with the Father, through the incarnate Son's crucifixion and Resurrection. Quoting John 10:10, where Jesus describes himself as the good shepherd and says, "I came that they may have life, and have it abundantly,"[75] Aquinas calls life in Christ "the eternity of life."[76] Thus the New Adam shares life in a manner typologically comparable to, but far better than, how Adam shared life with all humans.

However, is not Adam's sin much more effective with respect to the scope of its impact? The corrupted life that Adam passes on to us is present in all humans; we are all subject to sin and death. Grace, by contrast, seems to be making a much lesser impact. Aquinas offers a twofold answer to this difficulty. First, the power of Christ's grace is superabundantly sufficient for all humans. By his Cross and Resurrection, Christ opens the door to communion with God for everyone. People can refuse the gift, but that does not mean that the gift, in itself, is not universally efficacious. Second,

---

[74] Aquinas, *Commentary on the Letter of Saint Paul to the Romans*, §439, p. 150.
[75] Cited in Aquinas, *Commentary on the Letter of Saint Paul to the Romans*, §441, p. 150.
[76] Aquinas, *Commentary on the Letter of Saint Paul to the Romans*, §441, p. 150. Daguet remarks that "the Word, from before the incarnation, [is] the invisible head of humankind in the order of grace. The Word, prior to the incarnation, exercises an invisible government upon humankind, through the life of grace. By the incarnation, the Word does not cease to be head in the order of grace but, through the assumption of human nature, he confers a visible mode to his headship and his government. The Word is no longer head only according to his divine nature, but he becomes head also according to his human nature" (Daguet, *Théologie du dessein divin chez Thomas d'Aquin*, 273–74).

Paul may be making a simpler comparison: Just as all who share in Adam share in sin and death, so also *all* who share in Christ – no matter how many or how few people choose to do so – share in Christ's life. Justified in Christ, they become sharers in the kingdom of life, the kingdom of God. Aquinas adds that people who lived prior to Christ could be and were united to him, through faith in the one who was to come.

Commenting on Romans 5:19, where Paul compares Adam's disobedience with Christ's obedience, Aquinas briefly reflects upon the New Adam's reversal of Adam's disobedience. He notes that it may seem that Adam's sin was pride, not disobedience. In reply, he observes that pride prompts disobedience to God. In Genesis 3:17, Aquinas observes, God identifies Adam's disobedience as being the result of pride, and Philippians 2:8 describes Christ's *obedience*. Whereas Adam's disobedience came from pride, Christ's obedience came from love.

As Aquinas's citation of Philippians 2:8 suggests, Christ's divine preexistence has significance here. Adam grasps at immortality and divinity; Christ, who is divine, lays aside the prerogative of his divine status and humbles himself even to the point of accepting an utterly humiliating death.[77] In his treatise on temperance in the *Summa theologiae*, Aquinas examines humility as a virtue allied with temperance. Having treated the virtue of humility, he treats its opposed vice, pride. Citing Romans 5:12, he takes Adam's sin as the paradigmatic example of pride. Adam became proud when he coveted "inordinately some spiritual good above his measure"; in other

---

[77] For discussion see Gilles Emery, O.P., "Kenosis, Christ, and the Trinity in Thomas Aquinas," *Nova et Vetera* 17 (2019): 839–69; and Jeffrey M. Walkey, "'Putting on' the Lord Jesus Christ: Thomistic Reflections on Kenosis and the Christ Hymn as a Model for Mystagogical Formation," in *Initiation and Mystagogy in Thomas Aquinas: Scriptural, Systematic, Sacramental and Moral, and Pastoral Perspectives*, ed. Henk Schoot, Jacco Verburgt, and Jörgen Vijgen (Leuven: Peeters, 2019), 61–82. See also my *Paul in the "Summa Theologiae"* (Washington, DC: Catholic University of America Press, 2014), chapter 9.

2.4 AQUINAS ON THE NEW ADAM

words, he desired to be like God by his own power.[78] He sought to grasp deification. This is important because it indicates the place of the Incarnation, with its divine humility, in the reversal of Adam's disobedience.

Aquinas concludes his treatment of Paul's Adam/Christ typology in Romans 5 by commenting on Romans 5:21's teaching that God has ensured that "as sin reigned in death, grace also might reign through righteousness to eternal life through Jesus Christ our Lord." Here Aquinas looks back to Romans 3:24 and forward to Romans 6:23, and he also cites John 10:28, "I give them eternal life, and they shall never perish." The context for John 10:28 is the Incarnation and the unique status of the Son in relation to the Father, since in John 10:29–30 Jesus adds: "My Father, who has given them to me, is greater than all, and no one is able to snatch them out of the Father's hand. I and the Father are one."

Thus, the Son of God comes in the flesh, to give both the forgiveness of sins and "eternal life," namely, intimate communion with the Trinity. Aquinas hammers home this point by quoting once more from John's Gospel: "For the law was given through Moses; grace and truth came through Jesus Christ" (Jn 1:17). The New Adam is able to ensure that grace reigns "to eternal life" (Rom 5:21) because, as the incarnate Lord, he can bestow eternal communion with God. For Aquinas, the New Adam of Romans 5 is the same one who "became flesh and dwelt among us, full of grace and truth" (Jn 1:14).

Let me now turn to Aquinas's discussion of the New Adam Christology of 1 Corinthians 15. Aquinas begins his commentary on 1 Corinthians 15:21–22 by highlighting the dignity that God gives to humanity. God could have redeemed humanity without any

---

[78] Thomas Aquinas, *Summa theologiae*, trans. Fathers of the English Dominican Province (Westminster, MD: Christian Classics, 1981), II-II, q. 163, a. 1. See the discussion of this point in my *Aquinas's Eschatological Ethics and the Virtue of Temperance* (Notre Dame: University of Notre Dame Press, 2019), chapter 6.

human help; God could simply have wiped away sin by fiat. But this would have left Adam as the head of the human race and would have meant that Adam's disobedience was never reversed from within the human race. For Aquinas, it is therefore fitting that God send the Redeemer as the New Adam, fully human.[79]

In commenting on 1 Corinthians 15:22 Aquinas cites two passages from the Gospel of John, namely, 5:26 and 5:28. These passages show that Christ's causality of eternal life has a twofold dimension. On the one hand, Christ is able to cause our eternal life because he is truly risen in his glorified humanity. But on the other hand, his divinity – his unique relation as Son to his Father – also bears upon his ability to cause eternal life, including the glorification of his human nature. In John 5:26 and 5:28, Jesus states with regard to the coming resurrection of the dead: "For as the Father has life in himself, so he has granted the Son also to have life in himself.... Do not marvel at this; for the hour is coming when all who are in the tombs will hear his voice." It follows that all are to "be made alive" (1 Cor 15:22) in Christ not only because Christ is risen but also because the Son (begotten of the Father and possessed of the divine nature) has "life in himself" (Jn 5:26). Thus, as with Romans 5, Aquinas unpacks the Adam typology of 1 Corinthians 15:21–22 in light of the Gospel of John's doctrine of Incarnation.[80]

Commenting on 1 Corinthians 15:45–49, Aquinas begins by briefly reflecting upon 1 Corinthians 15:45's reference to Genesis 2:7, "The first man Adam became a living soul." According to Genesis 2:7, as Aquinas observes, this happened when God breathed the breath of life into Adam's flesh. Aquinas takes this to be an image of the animation of the body by the soul. He specifies that God's

---

[79] See Thomas Aquinas, *Commentary on the First Letter of Saint Paul to the Corinthians*, trans. Fabian Larcher, O.P., Beth Mortensen, and Daniel Keating, ed. J. Mortensen and E. Alarcón (Lander, WY: The Aquinas Institute for the Study of Sacred Doctrine, 2012), §931, p. 352 (1–396).

[80] See Aquinas, *Commentary on the First Letter of Saint Paul to the Corinthians*, §932, p. 353.

breath here is not the Holy Spirit. Rather, for Adam to be a "living soul" simply means that Adam is animated. Thus, the condition of the first Adam is one of normal earthly life, whereas "the last Adam became a life-giving spirit" (1 Cor 15:45). Aquinas thinks Paul chose the term "last" because Jesus establishes the final destiny of Adam: There can be no further advance. In the first Adam, humans are bound to sin and death; in the last Adam, humans receive "glory and life."[81] Glorified life is the greatest possible good, since it is a share in the Trinity's own life.

To underline this point, Aquinas quotes three biblical texts. The first is Isaiah 53:3, which in the RSV reads, "He was despised and rejected by men," but which in the Vulgate (as Isaiah 53:2) describes the Suffering Servant as "despised and the last of men." This connection between "last" in the sense of "despised," on the one hand, and "last" in the sense of exalted and unsurpassable, on the other, nicely conveys the glory-in-humiliation of Christ's Cross, a Johannine theme (see John 13:31–32).[82] Aquinas also quotes two verses from the Book of Revelation, both of which describe Christ as the "last" in a manner that makes clear that he is divine. The point is that Jesus is able to be the "last Adam" because he is the divine Son incarnate. He stands not only at the beginning of history as the Creator of Adam but also at the end of history as the one who heals Adam's sin (and the sin of all children of Adam) and as the one who causes the eternal life of all the redeemed.

In the same context, Aquinas identifies another comparison between Adam and Christ. In his original creation as depicted in Genesis 2, Adam was perfected by the infusion of the soul. This made Adam into what Paul in 1 Corinthians 15:46 calls a "physical"

---

[81] Aquinas, *Commentary on the First Letter of Saint Paul to the Corinthians*, §992, p. 374.
[82] As Richard Bauckham comments, "glory is a theme that John uses, very distinctively among the New Testament writers, to highlight, by paradox, the extraordinary nature of the love of God for the world in going to the lengths of Jesus's abject dying in the pain and shame of crucifixion" (Bauckham, *Gospel of Glory: Major Themes in Johannine Theology* [Grand Rapids, MI: Baker Academic, 2015], 43).

being, or "a living soul." By contrast, Jesus' humanity is perfected by the work of the Holy Spirit so as to be "a life-giving spirit" (1 Cor 15:45). Jesus is not only "living," but also "life-giving."[83] Because as the divine Son he uniquely received the Spirit, he has the power to pour out the Spirit upon all others: He has "life-giving power."[84] Aquinas here again appeals to texts from the Gospel of John: John 1:16 and John 10:10. Recall that in his commentary on Romans 5, Aquinas similarly employs John 10:10, "I came that they may have life, and have it abundantly." Aquinas also appeals to the Creed, with its confession of faith "in the life-giving Holy Spirit."[85]

Yet, does it really make sense for the one who is a "life-giving spirit" to come *last*? Just as he does in the *tertia pars*, Aquinas inquires here into why Jesus would come late in the course of human history. In reply, Aquinas reiterates that "it is not the spiritual which is first but the physical, and then the spiritual" (1 Cor 15:46). In the natural world, Aquinas explains, "in one and the same thing, the imperfect is prior to the perfect."[86] God's plan of grace does not overturn nature but heals and elevates it.

When Aquinas turns to 1 Corinthians 15:47 – the crucial text for New Adam Christology – his interpretation accords with that of the Fathers.[87] Recall that 1 Corinthians 15:47 states, "The first

---

[83] Aquinas, *Commentary on the First Letter of Saint Paul to the Corinthians*, §993, p. 374.
[84] Aquinas, *Commentary on the First Letter of Saint Paul to the Corinthians*, §993, p. 374.
[85] Aquinas, *Commentary on the First Letter of Saint Paul to the Corinthians*, §993, p. 374.
[86] Aquinas, *Commentary on the First Letter of Saint Paul to the Corinthians*, §994, p. 375. Daria Spezzano comments on III, q. 1, a. 5: "When Thomas says in a5 that the timing of the Incarnation was fitting 'on account of the order' of our furtherance in good, using the text from 1 Corinthians 15:46–47 as his authority, he seems to be implying that it was necessary for human nature to proceed from its state of imperfection in Adam to its perfection in Christ, in that Christ is both himself perfectly spiritual and the principle of spiritual perfection for others" (Spezzano, *The Glory of God's Grace: Deification according to St. Thomas Aquinas* [Ave Maria, FL: Sapientia, 2015], 164–65).
[87] This of course is no surprise. As Robert Louis Wilken remarks with respect to Aquinas's *Commentary on Romans*, "Thomas had at his disposal earlier commentaries on Romans as well as other writings of the fathers in which Romans is cited frequently. In some cases it is evident that his way of handling a particular text was

man was from the earth, a man of dust; the second man is from heaven." Modern commentators, as we have seen, generally interpret "from heaven" as referring to the risen Christ who will come from heaven. For Aquinas, by contrast, Jesus is "a life-giving spirit" because he comes "from heaven" as the preexistent Son: This is why he uniquely bears and bestows the Spirit who transforms and exalts the children of Adam. Aquinas thinks that when Paul says that the "second man" (the New Adam) is "from heaven," Paul has in view the Incarnation, even if Paul does not use the word.[88] Given that Jesus is the incarnate Son of God possessed of the divine nature, he uniquely possesses the Spirit and is properly called "heavenly." Aquinas comments that given who Jesus is, "he ought to have such perfection that it is fitting it come from heaven, namely, spiritual perfection."[89] Here again Aquinas draws a link from Paul to John. In support of Jesus' "spiritual perfection," he cites John 3:31: "He who comes from above is above all."[90]

Larry Hurtado has observed that in numerous "citations of Old Testament passages which originally have to do with God, Paul applies the passages to Jesus, making him the *Kyrios*."[91] Although he notes that a few scholars (preeminently James Dunn) deny that Paul teaches Christ's preexistence, Hurtado remarks that "the overwhelming majority of scholars in the field agree that there are at

---

suggested by other writers, often St. Augustine" (Wilken, "Origen, Augustine, and Thomas: Interpreters of the Letter to the Romans," in *Reading Romans with St. Thomas Aquinas*, ed. Matthew Levering and Michael Dauphinais [Washington, DC: Catholic University of America Press, 2012], 288–301, at 293). A similar point is made by Di Noia in "Christ Brings Freedom from Sin and Death," 385, specifying that Ambrose and Augustine are the key Fathers behind Aquinas's treatment of Romans 5.

[88] See Aquinas, *Commentary on the Letter of Saint Paul to the Romans*, §995, p. 375.
[89] Aquinas, *Commentary on the Letter of Saint Paul to the Romans*, §995, p. 375.
[90] See the discussion of Ben Witherington III on John 3:31 in Witherington, *John's Wisdom: A Commentary on the Fourth Gospel* (Louisville, KY: Westminster John Knox Press, 1995), 110.
[91] Larry W. Hurtado, *Lord Jesus Christ: Devotion to Jesus in Earliest Christianity* (Grand Rapids, MI: Eerdmans, 2003), 112.

least a few passages in Paul's undisputed letters that reflect and presuppose the idea of Jesus' preexistence."[92] Thus, there is no reason to bracket divine preexistence – of the kind attested most explicitly by the Gospel of John – from the New Adam Christology found in 1 Corinthians 15:47. Certainly, Paul's claim that "the second man is from heaven" resonates with the fact that the New Adam is indeed risen and glorified in heaven and will come from heaven. But the phrase "from heaven" has a polyvalent meaning here. It includes Christ's divine preexistence. As Aquinas says, the New Adam (or "last Adam") can be a "life-giving spirit" to all humanity precisely because he is "from heaven" both in his divine preexistence and in his glorified humanity at the right hand of the Father.

Aquinas specifies that Paul, in describing Jesus (or the "second man," the New Adam) as "from heaven," does not mean to say that Jesus brought his body from heaven, as though Jesus preexisted eternally as a man. This is denied by Scripture, which teaches that Jesus is conceived by and born of Mary. In Galatians 4:4, Paul states that Jesus is "born of woman" and that this same Jesus is God's "Son" whom God "sent forth."[93] As Aquinas puts the matter, Jesus in 1 Corinthians 15:48 "is called the man from heaven, not that he will have borne his body from heaven, since he will have assumed it from the earth, namely, from the body of the Blessed Virgin, but because the divinity (which was united to the human nature) comes from heaven, which was prior to the body of Christ."[94]

For Aquinas, the mortality of Adam – though caused by the loss of original justice due to sin – is in an important sense

---

[92] Hurtado, *Lord Jesus Christ*, 119. For Dunn's viewpoint, see James D. G. Dunn, *The Theology of Paul the Apostle* (Grand Rapids, MI: Eerdmans, 1998), 266–93. Hurtado goes on to criticize Dunn's viewpoint, but Hurtado insists that it is Jesus himself whom Paul considers to be preexistent, rather than a preexistent (and now incarnate) Wisdom.

[93] This quotation of Galatians is mine, not Aquinas's.

[94] Aquinas, *Commentary on the First Letter of Saint Paul to the Corinthians*, §995, p. 375.

natural.⁹⁵ It is natural for earthly bodies to age and decay, because of the matter of which bodies are made. Aquinas thinks this is what Paul means by saying that we bear "the image of the man of dust" (1 Cor 15:49). We are naturally mortal; our bodies do indeed decay and return to the earth.⁹⁶ Thus it is Christ who, as the Lord, brings true immortal life to humans, because Christ is not held by death but rises to glorified life.⁹⁷ Aquinas cites Romans 6:5, "For if we have been united with him in a death like his, we shall certainly be united with him in a resurrection like his."⁹⁸ In short, Aquinas is well aware of the link that Paul draws in 1 Corinthians 15:48–49 to the *risen* Christ.

Aquinas further explores 1 Corinthians 15:49 by reflecting upon the life of grace. The fact that "we have borne the image of the man of dust" means that we are mortal human sinners, and, in this way, "the likeness of Adam is in us."⁹⁹ But in Christ, we now and in eternal life "also bear the image of the man of heaven." We do this now through grace. In this regard, Aquinas cites Romans 8:29's teaching

---

⁹⁵ For Aquinas on death, see Randall S. Rosenberg, "Being-toward-a-Death-Transformed: Aquinas on the Naturalness and Unnaturalness of Human Death," *Angelicum* 83 (2006): 747–66; and the treatment of Aquinas in David Albert Jones, *Approaching the End: A Theological Exploration of Death and Dying* (Oxford: Oxford University Press, 2007). On debates surrounding the relationship of "original justice" to sanctifying grace, see chapter 2 of Daniel W. Houck, *Aquinas, Original Sin, and the Challenge of Evolution* (Cambridge: Cambridge University Press, 2020).

⁹⁶ See Aquinas, *Commentary on the First Letter of Saint Paul to the Corinthians*, §997, p. 375.

⁹⁷ For Aquinas on the immortality of the soul – and its relation to the resurrection of the body – see Denys Turner, "The Human Person," in *The Cambridge Companion to the "Summa Theologiae,"* ed. Philip McCosker and Denys Turner (Cambridge: Cambridge University Press, 2016), 168–80. See also John F. X. Knasas, "Suffering and the 'Thomistic Philosopher': A Line of Thought Instigated by the Job Commentary," in *Reading Job with St. Thomas Aquinas*, ed. Matthew Levering, Piotr Roszak, and Jörgen Vijgen (Washington, DC: Catholic University of America Press, 2020), 185–219, especially 189–96; and Bryan Kromholtz, O.P., "The Spirit of the Letter: St. Thomas's Interpretation of Scripture in His Reading of Job's Eschatology," in *Reading Job with St. Thomas Aquinas*, 364–83, at 372–77.

⁹⁸ Aquinas, *Commentary on the First Letter of Saint Paul to the Corinthians*, §997, p. 376.

⁹⁹ Aquinas, *Commentary on the First Letter of Saint Paul to the Corinthians*, §998, p. 376.

about our configuration by grace to the image of Christ. Aquinas's conclusion is exhortatory: "And so we ought to be conformed to the man of heaven in the life of grace, because otherwise we will not attain to the life of glory."[100] This means being conformed to Christ's lowliness or humility. In his study of Aquinas on the New Adam, Luis Cruz remarks that Christ "wanted to be the *novissimus virorum*, the last and most despised of men, in order thus to be the *novissimus Adam*, the last and most perfect manifestation of God's love who leads Adam, and with him all men and all creation, to the height of perfection."[101]

Elsewhere in his corpus, Aquinas reflects more briefly upon Christ as New Adam. For example, in his commentary on Philippians 2:8 and in *Summa theologiae* III, q. 47, a. 2, Aquinas notes that Christ redeems humanity by his obedience, in contrast to Adam's disobedience.[102] His obedience was his perfect fulfillment of the Torah; he acted out of supreme love of God and neighbor. Freely bearing the Adamic penalty of death, he reversed it from within, so that it became the path of eternal life. As Aquinas says in commenting on Philippians 2:8 (citing Romans 5:19 in support), "It is fitting that he bring obedience into his passion, because the first sin was accomplished by disobedience."[103] In his *Compendium theologiae*, similarly, Aquinas states that "as life first became mortal through Adam's sin, immortal life made its first appearance in Christ through the atonement for sin He offered" and

---

[100] Aquinas, *Commentary on the First Letter of Saint Paul to the Corinthians*, §998, p. 376.

[101] Cruz, "Christus, novissimus Adam," 106.

[102] See Thomas Aquinas, "Commentary on the Letter of Saint Paul to the Philippians," §§65–66, in Aquinas, *Commentary on the Letters of Saint Paul to the Philippians, Colossians, Thessalonians, Timothy, Titus, and Philemon*, trans. Fabian Larcher, O.P., ed. J. Mortensen and E. Alarcón (Lander, WY: The Aquinas Institute for the Study of Sacred Doctrine, 2012), 28 (1–68). I have highlighted III, q. 47, a. 2 (especially ad 1) as central to Aquinas's understanding of Christ's work: see my *Christ's Fulfillment of Torah and Temple: Salvation according to Thomas Aquinas* (Notre Dame: University of Notre Dame Press, 2002).

[103] Aquinas, "Commentary on the Letter of Saint Paul to the Philippians," §66.

2.4 AQUINAS ON THE NEW ADAM

through his Resurrection.[104] He adds with regard to eternal life that "Christ recovered for the human race not merely what Adam had lost through sin, but all that Adam could have attained through merit."[105]

It may also be worth mentioning Aquinas's commentary on Ephesians 4:22–24, "Put off the old man that belongs to your former manner of life and is corrupt through deceitful lusts, and be renewed in the spirit of your minds, and put on the new man, created after the likeness of God in true righteousness and holiness." Here Aquinas clarifies that the "old man" is not human nature itself but rather one's vices. He then observes that there are three "spirits" that can be discerned in human minds: the Holy Spirit, the spiritual soul (i.e., the mind itself), and imagination. The call to be renewed in the spirit of our mind indicates that our mind – our soul – has been corrupted. Aquinas observes, "If Adam had not become tainted neither he nor ourselves would need a renovation."[106] In fact, Adam did fall through disobedience and our souls greatly need healing. Aquinas thus calls Adam "the primary source of oldness" for all humans.[107] By contrast, he says, "the primary source of newness and renovation is Christ."[108] Here Aquinas cites 1 Corinthians 15:22.

As noted above, in the *secunda pars* of the *Summa theologiae* Aquinas addresses Adam and Eve's sin as the paradigmatic sin of pride. Turning in this context to the New Adam, he quotes one of his favorite biblical texts, Psalm 68:5, which reads in the

---

[104] Thomas Aquinas, *Light of Faith: The Compendium of Theology*, trans. Cyril Vollert, S.J. (Manchester, NH: Sophia Institute Press, 1993), §236, p. 304.
[105] Aquinas, *Light of Faith*, §237, p. 306.
[106] Thomas Aquinas, "Commentary on the Letter of Saint Paul to the Ephesians," trans. Matthew L. Lamb, §244, in Aquinas, *Commentary on the Letters of Saint Paul to the Galatians and Ephesians*, trans. Fabian Larcher, O.P., and Mathew L. Lamb, ed. J. Mortensen and E. Alarcón (Lander, WY: The Aquinas Institute for the Study of Sacred Doctrine, 2012), 177–346, at 290.
[107] Aquinas, "Commentary on the Letter of Saint Paul to the Ephesians," §245, p. 291.
[108] Aquinas, "Commentary on the Letter of Saint Paul to the Ephesians," §245, p. 291.

Vulgate translation, "Then did I pay that which I took not away."[109] Indebted to Peter Lombard, Aquinas attributes to Augustine a comment on this verse, to the effect that "Adam and Eve wished to rob the Godhead and they lost happiness."[110] In his *Expositions of the Psalms*, Augustine argues that in Psalm 68:5 Christ proclaims: "I was paying the price, though I committed no robbery."[111] The robber is Adam, and the New Adam is the one who pays for or restores what Adam stole. For both Augustine and Aquinas, Adam attempted to steal the Godhead, by (in Aquinas's words) "[coveting] God's likeness inordinately."[112] Christ is indeed God, but Christ "did not count equality with God a thing to be grasped." Thus, the Cross of Christ is the New Adam's supremely gracious self-offering or payment of the wages (of sin) that he does not owe, whereas Adam is a "robber" but, in God's eyes, beloved and worthy of saving.[113]

To sum up: For Aquinas as for the Fathers, New Adam Christology serves as a way of tying together Incarnation, creation, fall, redemption, and eschatology. Christ is the New Adam because, as the life-giving incarnate Son, he is the creator and exemplar of Adamic humanity and the eschatological redeemer and goal of Adamic humanity. What we have seen in Aquinas's Pauline commentaries receives an explicit place in his dogmatic treatment of Christ in *Summa theologiae* III, q. 1, a. 5 (on the fittingness of the timing of the Incarnation) and q. 47, a. 2 (on Christ's obedience reversing Adam's disobedience). As Dominic Legge remarks, "The more we appreciate St Thomas's close attention to the sacred text … and the fundamental role it plays in his thought, the easier it is to dismiss the suspicion that his theology is hostage to foreign

---

[109] In the RSV, this reads: "What I did not steal must I now restore?" (Ps 69:4).
[110] II-II, q. 163, a. 2, *sed contra*.
[111] See Augustine, *Expositions of the Psalms*, vol. 3, 51–72, trans. Maria Boulding, O.S.B., ed. John E. Rotelle, O.S.A. (Hyde Park, NY: New City Press, 2001), 375.
[112] II-II, q. 163, a. 2.
[113] See III, q. 47, a. 2, ad 1.

philosophical presuppositions, or to scholastic abstractions and hypotheticals."[114]

At the same time, I note that contemporary Thomistic Christology could be filled out even further by appeal to the eschatological New Adam. For example, in III, q. 1, a. 1 Aquinas asks whether it was fitting that God should have become incarnate. He responds that the Incarnation is the highest possible expression of God's goodness in communicating himself to creatures. Here Thomistic Christology can have recourse to the theme of the New Adam, as does Vatican II's *Gaudium et Spes* when it states, "It is only in the mystery of the Word made flesh that the mystery of man truly becomes clear. For Adam, the first man, was a type of him who was to come, Christ the Lord. Christ the new Adam, in the very revelation of the mystery of the Father and of his love, fully reveals man to himself and brings to light his most high calling."[115]

Similarly, the set of dogmatic questions arising from the early Councils to which I briefly directed attention at the beginning of this chapter – questions about the union of the divine nature and the human nature in the Person of Christ (III, qq. 2–4), the fullness of the human nature assumed by the Son of God (III, qq. 5–6), and the grace of Christ (III, qq. 7–8) – could be illuminated by Christ's status as the New Adam. As we have seen, Aquinas emphasizes that the New Adam (or the last Adam) is a particularly appropriate title for Christ because he gives grace and eternal life. Christ can do this

---

[114] Legge, *The Trinitarian Christology of St Thomas Aquinas*, 238.

[115] *Gaudium et Spes*, §22, in Austin Flannery, O.P., ed., *Vatican Council II*, vol. 1, *The Conciliar and Post Conciliar Documents*, rev. ed.(Northport, NY: Costello, 1996), 922 (903–1001). The *Catechism of the Catholic Church* quotes this passage and connects it with St. Peter Chrysologus's interpretation of 1 Corinthians 15: "The second Adam stamped his image on the first Adam when he created him. That is why he took on himself the role and the name of the first Adam, in order that he might not lose what he had made in his own image. The first Adam, the last Adam: the first had a beginning, the last knows no end. The last Adam is indeed the first; as he himself says: 'I am the first and the last'" (§359, citing Peter Chrysologus, *Sermo* 117; PL 52, 520–21).

in his humanity because he is the divine Son who sends the Spirit.[116] The hypostatic union is what makes Christ the eschatological *New Adam* rather than merely another (however perfect) Adam. Likewise, Christ's fullness of grace and his grace of headship are at the very center of his status as the New Adam. Some reference to Christ as New Adam in relation to these questions of the *Summa* would enrich theological understanding of Christ's uniqueness, given that from eternity God created Adam (and Eve) in light of the New Adam: "those whom [God] foreknew he also predestined to be conformed to the image of his Son, in order that he might be the first-born among many brethren" (Rom 8:29).[117] In addition, the value of New Adam Christology for reflection upon the saving power of Christ's Passion, death, and Resurrection (III, qq. 45–56) will be evident from Romans 5 and 1 Corinthians 15.

2.5 An Ontological Note

Ontologically, the concept of the "New Adam" has to do with Christ's holy humanity as the universal source of the life of grace and glory. Aquinas explores Christ's holy humanity in terms of

---

[116] For discussion, see Legge, *The Trinitarian Christology of St Thomas Aquinas*, especially 160–68, 215–22. As Legge says, "On the one hand, Aquinas frequently identifies Christ's own perfect possession of the Holy Spirit as the source of Christ's giving the Spirit. It is because he receives the Spirit without measure that Christ gives the Spirit to the world.... On the other hand, Aquinas sometimes points to the hypostatic union: insofar as his humanity is joined to his divinity as its instrument, Christ *as man* acts in the power of the divinity" (Legge, *The Trinitarian Christology of St Thomas Aquinas*, 219). See also, on the grace of the hypostatic union and its purpose, Jean-Miguel Garrigues's "The 'Natural Grace' of Christ in St. Thomas," in *Surnaturel: A Controversy at the Heart of Twentieth-Century Thomistic Thought*, ed. Serge-Thomas Bonino, O.P., trans. Robert Williams, trans. rev. Matthew Levering (Ave Maria, FL: Sapientia Press, 2009), 103–15.

[117] See Matthew Levering, "Aquinas on Romans 8: Predestination in Context," in *Reading Romans with St. Thomas Aquinas*, 196–215.

protology and eschatology in his reflections on Christ's human nature, personal grace, grace of headship, and defects. As a sinless man, Christ in his holy humanity is like Adam (prior to the Fall), although unlike pre-Fall Adam he is subject to death. Aquinas explains how it is that Christ can truly share Adamic human nature without being subject to sin.[118] He also explains why Christ's flesh does not share in the original justice that characterized Adam and that gave him freedom from things that weaken people's resistance to sin, such as "death, hunger, thirst, and the like."[119] Christ endured things that Adam only endured after his sin; thus the condition of Christ's humanity differs from what Christians, guided by Scripture, associate with the Edenic state. But Christ is filled with the grace of the Holy Spirit and possesses "all the virtues."[120]

As the eschatological New Adam, Christ is the source of salvation for all people. Christ is not a viator seeking to know God; rather, Christ is the source of the knowledge of God for all people. In his earthly life, Christ enjoys beatific communion with his Father, without this impeding his ability to acquire knowledge and to engage in normal, culturally appropriate discourse. Aquinas denies that Christ possesses faith or hope, since "He is perfect in Himself" and "leads others to a share of His perfection."[121] Not only does he possess "grace in its highest degree" but also "the soul of Christ so received grace, that, in a manner, it is poured out from it upon others."[122]

Aquinas similarly reflects upon Christ as the head of the Church, citing Ephesians 1:22: "[God] has put all things under his [Christ's] feet and has made him the head over all things for the Church."[123]

---

[118] See III, q. 15, a. 1 and related discussions of original sin.
[119] III, q. 14, a. 1.
[120] III, q. 7, a. 2.
[121] III, q. 7, a. 4, ad 3.
[122] III, q. 7, a. 9.
[123] III, q. 8, a. 1, *sed contra*.

As the "head," Christ is the principle or cause of salvation (the kingdom of God, the new creation), which comes to us through grace. Quoting Romans 8:29, Aquinas notes that Christ's grace "is the highest and first, though not in time, since all have received grace on account of His grace."[124] Christ has the fullness or perfection of grace, as John 1:14 says. Thus he "has the power of bestowing grace on all the members of the Church, according to John 1:16."[125]

Aquinas's reflections in questions 7 and 8 of the *tertia pars* probe into what pertains to Christ as "a life-giving spirit" and "the man of heaven" (1 Cor 15:45, 48), namely, into what makes Christ "the last Adam" (1 Cor 15:45). The key point is that Christ is our head as the source of grace and glory.[126] He is the head even of people on earth who lack grace, insofar as these people are in potency to be united to him by grace. Because he is the incarnate Word, filled with the Holy Spirit, he stands as the New Adam in the order of grace. Aquinas emphasizes that "the interior influx of grace is from no one save Christ, whose manhood, through its union with the Godhead, has the power of justifying."[127]

2.6 Conclusion

Existentially, the history of Adam and Adamic human nature is a story of sin and death. When one looks at human history, with its monstrous violence and its countless victims, one has to agree with the sacred author who wrote, "God saw the earth, and behold, it was corrupt; for all flesh had corrupted their way upon the earth" (Gen 6:12). In Christ, however, everything about Adamic human nature is transformed. The divine Son has established a "ladder"

---

[124] III, q. 8, a. 1.
[125] III, q. 8, a. 1; translation slightly altered.
[126] III, q. 8, a. 3.
[127] III, q. 8, a. 6.

(Gen 28:12) between God and fallen humanity by taking on Adamic nature, bearing the penalty of death, and reversing Adam's disobedience by his own self-giving obedient love. The divine Son became the New Adam to open up for humanity the path of deification, which was the goal of God's creation from the very outset. Romans 5 and 1 Corinthians 15 draw together the history of sin and death, the history of Israel, and the grace of the crucified and risen Christ. In the New Adam, God "has made known to us in all wisdom and insight the mystery of his will, according to his purpose which he set forth in Christ as a plan for the fulness of time, to unite all things in him, things in heaven and things on earth" (Eph 1:9–10).

I have argued that New Adam Christology can assist theologians in understanding this plan of God "to unite all things" eschatologically in Christ. Christ is the eternal Son of God who is also, in his obedient love, the perfect Adamic "son of God." He redeems the human race as the one who is radically oriented toward the Father. By his saving death and Resurrection and by pouring out the grace of the Holy Spirit, he orients us toward the Father as our head. He shows the members of his mystical body what a "filial mode" of life means, drawing us into his eternal Filial life with the Father in the Spirit. As the firstborn in the order of grace, he enters into the wound of Adam in order to heal the wound and to bear our nature eternally. He is both wondrously like us and, in his uniqueness and greatness, wondrously unlike us. Integrating New Adam Christology more fully will enrich Thomistic Christology's portrait of the relation of Christ to the Trinity, creation, fall, providence and predestination, anthropology, ecclesiology, justification and sanctification, and eschatology.

Let me end this chapter with an instructive example from medieval mystical theology. Julian of Norwich received a vision of a lord and a servant. The servant, obedient at first, rushes off and sustains a terrible and disfiguring fall. In the vision, the servant also endures out of great love the consequences of this fall. Julian perceives that this servant is both Adam and the New Adam. She realizes with great joy that God's own "great goodness and his own honour require that his beloved servant, whom he loved so much, should be highly and blessedly rewarded forever, above what he would have been if he had not fallen, yes, and so much that his falling and all the woe that he received from it will be turned into high, surpassing honour and endless bliss."[128]

This is the God of surprising and shocking love, the God who loved Adam so much that he suffered Adam's penalty on behalf of all who share Adam's nature, and who united himself to Adam's nature so as to heal and exalt the human race. Compared to our "love" – we who barely can forgive anyone at all, and whose best actions contain much self-centeredness – God's self-surrendering love revealed in Christ can only astound.[129]

God showed the meaning of the vision to Julian. The "lord" is God, and the "servant" is Adam and the whole human race, because "in the sight of God all men are one man, and one man is all men."[130] The servant (Adam and the fallen human race) does not recognize how much the Lord God loves Adam. God's love for us is eternally such "that it could melt our hearts for love and break them in two for joy."[131] When God sees Adam, he simultaneously sees the whole

---

[128] Julian of Norwich, *Showings*, trans. Edmund Colledge, O.S.A. and James Walsh, S.J. (Mahwah, NJ: Paulist Press, 1978), 269. For further background, see Denys Turner, *Julian of Norwich, Theologian* (New Haven, CT: Yale University Press, 2011); and Frederick Christian Bauerschmidt, *Julian of Norwich and the Mystical Body Politic of Christ* (Notre Dame: University of Notre Dame Press, 1999).

[129] See Hans Urs von Balthasar, *Love Alone Is Credible*, trans. D. C. Schindler (San Francisco: Ignatius Press, 2004).

[130] Julian of Norwich, *Showings*, 270.

[131] Julian of Norwich, *Showings*, 271. Julian comments later: "For I saw that God never began to love mankind; for just as mankind will be in endless bliss, fulfilling God's joy with regard to his works, just so has that same mankind been known and loved in God's prescience from without beginning in his righteous intent. And by the endless intent and assent and the full accord of all the Trinity, the mediator wanted to be the foundation and head of this fair nature, out of whom we have all come, in whom we are all enclosed, into whom we shall all go, finding in him our full heaven in everlasting joy by the prescient purpose of all the blessed Trinity from without beginning. For before he made us he loved us" (Julian of Norwich, *Showings*, 283).

Adamic race, with regard to which he has profound compassion, and sees the New Adam, with regard to whom he has profound joy. God's joy consists in seeing how the New Adam willingly endures out of love the painful consequences of Adam's fall. God's compassion and mercy prevent the Adamic race from falling into "endless death."[132] God has created humans not to dominate them but to dwell in them as in his own city or his own home. When this city or home fell into disrepair, God became the New Adam in order to repair it. When the servant stands before God, Julian sees how unworthy in outer garments the servant is, but she also sees that interiorly the servant is worthy in love. This worthy servant is the New Adam, and his love is from the Holy Spirit.

The end of this vision is a marriage. From eternity, the Son of God willed to become incarnate in order to pour out the love of the Father and the Son – the love that is the Holy Spirit – upon fallen humanity so as to repair and exalt us as his Bride forever.[133] Having died on the Cross, risen from the dead, and ascended to the Father, the New Adam in Julian's vision no longer looks like a mere servant but rather is "richly clothed in joyful amplitude."[134] The New Adam is already "at peace with his beloved wife, who is the fair maiden of endless joy."[135] May the entire race of Adam and Eve rejoice!

---

[132] Julian of Norwich, *Showings*, 274.
[133] See Brant Pitre, *Jesus the Bridegroom: The Greatest Love Story Ever Told* (New York: Random House, 2014).
[134] Julian of Norwich, *Showings*, 278.
[135] Julian of Norwich, *Showings*, 278.

3 | Christ the New Isaac

The Eschatological Temple

3.1 Introduction

Criticizing the notion that the Orthodox East prioritizes the Resurrection while the Catholic West prioritizes the crucifixion, the Orthodox theologian John Behr insists that Christ's crucifixion and Resurrection must not be separated in the minds of believers. Behr shows that the crucifixion and Resurrection impenetrate each other: "God's vindication of the crucified Jesus, not letting his holy one see corruption in the grave (Acts 2.25–32; Ps 16.10), does not remove from sight or sideline Jesus' death on the cross, but enables us to see this death as the voluntary self-offering of the innocent servant of the Lord.... Christ has trampled down death *by death*."[1] Thomas Aquinas recognizes this same unity of the Cross and Resurrection. He makes this unity clear, for instance, when discussing why Christ rose with his scars: The scars are part of Christ's glorification, because they are trophies of his victory on the Cross.[2] When Aquinas inquires into the specific cause of our salvation, he answers: "Christ's Passion wrought our salvation, properly

---

[1] John Behr, *The Mystery of Christ: Life in Death* (Crestwood, NY: St Vladimir's Seminary Press, 2006), 32. Behr adds, "Christ's taking upon himself the role of a servant, voluntarily going to the Passion, does not diminish our perception of what we might otherwise have considered to be his divinity, but actually manifests his true divinity" (35).

[2] Thomas Aquinas, *Summa theologiae*, trans. Fathers of the English Dominican Province (Westminster, MD: Christian Classics, 1981), III, q. 54, a. 4. Aquinas makes this point by quoting the Venerable Bede.

3.1 INTRODUCTION

speaking, by removing evils; but the Resurrection did so as the beginning and exemplar of all good things."³

Appreciation for the unity of the Cross and Resurrection, however, must address a troubling issue: namely, God the Father's sending his Son into this world to suffer and die. At times, the Father's role has raised the charge of divine child abuse or bloodthirstiness.⁴ The biblical scholar Leroy Huizenga says of Christ: "[I]n obedience he submits his will to that of his Father" and "his Father wills his sacrificial death."⁵ Of course, Christ is not merely passive in this regard. Christ "goes his way to sacrificial death, even orchestrating events to bring it about, as if he were erecting the cross himself."⁶ Commenting on the Gospel of Matthew, Huizenga points out that "Jesus' control of events and willingness to endure sacrificial death are seen with particular clarity in two passages in the Passion Narrative with strong echoes of the Akedah."⁷

This insight of Huizenga's informs the present chapter. As many scholars have shown, Genesis 22 (the Akedah or near-sacrifice of Isaac) has much to teach about the meaning of sacrifice and testing in God's plan of salvation.⁸ Jon Levenson argues with regard

---

³ III, q. 54, a. 1, ad 3.
⁴ See for example Richard Dawkins, *The God Delusion* (Boston: Houghton Mifflin, 2006). This charge, of course, is nearly as old as Christianity, and it was given classic expression in the Middle Ages by Peter Abelard. It has recently been articulated in an important way by Nicholas E. Lombardo, O.P., *The Father's Will: Christ's Crucifixion and the Goodness of God* (Oxford: Oxford University Press, 2013).
⁵ Leroy A. Huizenga, *The New Isaac: Tradition and Intertextuality in the Gospel of Matthew* (Leiden: Brill, 2009), 240.
⁶ Huizenga, *The New Isaac*, 240.
⁷ Huizenga, *The New Isaac*, 240.
⁸ See for example R. W. L. Moberly, *The Bible, Theology, and Faith: A Study of Abraham and Jesus* (Cambridge: Cambridge University Press, 2000), chapters 3–5; Moberly, "Living Dangerously: Genesis 22 and the Quest for Good Biblical Interpretation," in *The Art of Reading Scripture*, ed. Ellen F. Davis and Richard B. Hays (Grand Rapids, MI: Eerdmans, 2003), 181–97. See also the reflections of Veronica Chiari A. Dy-Liacco, "The Jewish Tradition of the Divine Presence, Sacrifice, and Substitutive Suffering: The Background to a Catholic Understanding," *Communio* 47 (2020): 155–89.

to Jewish, Christian, and Muslim renderings of Genesis 22 that the point of the story is "Abraham's absolute commitment to God – his obedience to God, his faith in God, his love of God," which are "priceless spiritual habits whose relevance, like that of the Aqedah, has not faded."[9] No doubt, as Levenson says, believers must affirm that God can speak to us and that when God speaks we must obey, as did Abraham. Nevertheless, it seems clear to me that the immediate response to reading the opening verses of Genesis 22 should be horror at the thought that the true God could desire such a thing – and in fact God does not desire child sacrifice (see Leviticus 18:21 and 20:2–5), let alone the death of Isaac. Indeed, Bill Arnold is correct that the text is "shocking" because of "the philosophical and theological antinomy" it creates, at least until God stops Abraham's hand and tells him that it has only been a test.[10] It is no wonder that Immanuel Kant, reading Genesis 22 outside of the context of the tradition of Jewish and Christian interpretation, deems that Abraham's obedience to the command suggests not faith but rather the insanity of a religious fanatic.[11]

---

[9] Jon D. Levenson, *Inheriting Abraham: The Legacy of the Patriarch in Judaism, Christianity, and Islam* (Princeton, NJ: Princeton University Press, 2014), 112. Levenson devotes the entirety of chapter 3 of this book to the Akedah as interpreted by Jews, Christians, and Muslims. He shows that "[t]he three religious traditions through which the Aqedah is handed down have almost always bundled it with the prohibitions upon child sacrifice (and murder, of course) that make it quite illicit to duplicate Abraham's deed today" (Levenson, *Inheriting Abraham*, 111). See also Mishael Maswari Caspi and Sascha Benjamin Cohen, *The Binding (Aqedah) and Its Transformation in Judaism and Islam: The Lambs of God* (Lewiston, NY: Mellen Biblical Press, 1995); Yvonne Sherwood, "Binding-Unbinding: Divided Responses of Judaism, Christianity, and Islam to the 'Sacrifice' of Abraham's Beloved Son," *Journal of the American Academy of Religion* 72 (2004): 821–61. Notable, too, is Devorah Schoenfeld, *Isaac on Jewish and Christian Altars: Polemic and Exegesis in Rashi and the* Glossa Ordinaria (New York: Fordham University Press, 2013).

[10] Bill T. Arnold, *Genesis* (Cambridge: Cambridge University Press, 2008), 201.

[11] For this view, see Immanuel Kant, *The Conflict of the Faculties*, in Kant, *Religion and Rational Theology*, trans. Mary J. Gregor and Robert Anchor, ed. Allen W. Wood (Cambridge: Cambridge University Press, 1996), 233–328, especially 283.

3.1 INTRODUCTION

Echoing Augustine, Aquinas argues that because the just penalty of original sin is death, and because God can justly take away any human life, it follows that "by the command of God, death can be inflicted on any man, guilty or innocent, without any injustice whatever" – and therefore God's command to Abraham to kill his son was perfectly just.[12] However, the image of Abraham tying his son to the wood on the altar and standing over his son with a raised knife is hideous, and in fact God never intended that Isaac be slain. There is something intrinsically unjust about the scene until God puts a stop to it.

For some interpreters today, it may therefore seem that Isaac being tied to the wood by his own father is bad enough – no *New* Isaac is needed or desirable. Yet, the New Testament and the Christian theological tradition conceive of Christ as the New Isaac.[13] In this chapter, I contend that New Isaac Christology merits a significant place in contemporary Thomistic Christology. To make this case, my chapter proceeds in four steps. First, I explore the biblical background of the Akedah, arguing that the passivity of Isaac prepares the way for the *active* New Isaac who is Jesus Christ. Eugene Rogers aptly remarks, "Sacrifice does not mean self-immolation: it means the persistence of intention in the

---

Levenson responds to Kant at length. See also, along Kant's lines, Carol Delaney, *Abraham on Trial: The Social Legacy of Biblical Myth* (Princeton, NJ: Princeton University Press, 1998).

[12] Aquinas, *Summa theologiae*, I-II, q. 94, a. 5, ad 2, trans. Fathers of the English Dominican Province (Westminster, MD: Christian Classics, 1981). For the context of Aquinas's position, see my "God and Natural Law: Reflections on Genesis 22," *Modern Theology* 24 (2008): 151–77.

[13] For some New Testament parallels between Jesus and Isaac, see Raymond E. Brown, S.S., *The Death of the Messiah*, vol. 2 (Garden City, NY: Doubleday, 1994), 1440–43, although Brown is perhaps overly tentative. Representative of Christian theological tradition, Albert the Great deems that Isaac represents Christ's divinity (since his divinity, which remained hypostatically united to his human nature, did not die), while the ram in the thicket represents Christ's humanity: "[T]he humanity of the leader of our flock [Christ] is immolated." See Albert the Great, *On the Body of the Lord*, trans. Sr. Albert Marie Surmanski, O.P. (Washington, DC: Catholic University of America Press, 2017), 284 (Distinction 5, chapter 2).

face of resistance. It is ... not the lack of agency, but a plenary, superlative, supererogatory agency. This plenipotentiary sacrifice emerges not from an original emptiness, but from an original abundance, the fullness of the Triune God."[14] Second, I survey the biblical scholarship of Leroy Huizenga on Christ the New Isaac. Linking the near-sacrifice of Isaac to the cultic unleashing of the divine presence, Huizenga depicts the New Isaac as the eschatological fulfillment of Israel's Temple cult. Third, I turn to the Church Fathers and to Aquinas for further insights into the New Isaac as a way of entering into the intelligibility of Jesus' Cross and Resurrection, along lines that resonate with Huizenga's portrait. In this light, I discuss some ways in which Aquinas's Christology and Thomistic Christology might benefit from further integrating Christ as the New Isaac. Fourth, I point out some ways in which Aquinas's *sacra doctrina* already engages the saving realities under discussion in this chapter.

3.2 The Figure of Isaac in Scripture

In the Letter to the Hebrews, in its litany praising the faith of the great figures of biblical Israel, we find the following rendition of Genesis 22: "By faith Abraham, when he was tested, offered up Isaac, and he who had received the promises was ready to offer up his only-begotten son.... He considered that God was able to raise

---

[14] Eugene F. Rogers, Jr., *Blood Theology: Seeing Red in Body- and God-Talk* (Cambridge: Cambridge University Press, 2021), 33. As we will see, the Rabbis understood Isaac to be active rather than passive in the Akedah. For Rogers's reflections on the Akedah, see chapter 2 of his book. He emphasizes that "here, where blood is missing from the text, Christian and rabbinic traditions both can't help themselves from reading it in" (41). Rogers considers Genesis 22 to be a trickster story in which Abraham should have resisted God, who was speaking with irony in "commanding" him to sacrifice Isaac. Rogers recognizes that his reading of Genesis 22 is "unconventional" (43), and indeed I think it mistaken.

men even from the dead; hence he did receive him back and this was a symbol" (Heb 11:17–19).[15] Abraham's faith in God's promises and power receive appropriate commendation in Hebrews 11, but what about Isaac's role? Isaac's role seems entirely passive. After praising Abraham at length, Hebrews says only this about Isaac: "By faith Isaac invoked future blessings on Jacob and Esau" (Heb 11:20). Isaac appears to have significance only in relation to the much greater significance of his father Abraham and of his son Jacob. James conveys Isaac's lack of agency when he writes, "Was not Abraham our father justified by works, when he offered his son Isaac upon the altar? You see that faith was active along with his works, and faith was completed by the works" (Js 2:21).[16]

Indeed, when one looks to the book of Genesis, the passivity and relative insignificance of Isaac are striking. Beginning in Genesis 12, Abraham takes on the leading role along with his wife Sarah. Their adventures dominate the plot until Abraham's death in Genesis 25. Genesis 26 is devoted solely to Isaac's deeds, but very little happens. In Genesis 27, the focus turns to Jacob and remains there – bound up with the adventures of Jacob's children – until Genesis 35, at the end of which we suddenly find one final mention of Isaac: "And Jacob came to his father Isaac at Mamre, or Kiriatharba (that is, Hebron), where Abraham and Isaac had sojourned. Now the days of Isaac were a hundred and

---

[15] See James Swetnam, S.J., *Jesus and Isaac: A Study of the Epistle to the Hebrews in Light of Aqedah* (Rome: Pontifical Biblical Institute, 1981); Swetnam, "Isaac as Promise: A Study of the Symbolism in Hebrews 11, 19," *Melita Theologica* 55 (2004): 65–74. Swetnam concludes "Isaac as Promise" by stating that "for the author of Hebrews the risen Christ is the reality symbolized by Isaac" ("Isaac as Promise," 74). I concur but I think that the crucified Christ can also be (and is) symbolized by Isaac, insofar as Isaac was offered up (although Isaac was not killed). See also Luke Timothy Johnson, *Hebrews: A Commentary* (Louisville, KY: Westminster John Knox, 2006), 295; and Mary Healy, *Hebrews* (Grand Rapids, MI: Baker Academic, 2016), 241.

[16] See William F. Brosend II, *James and Jude* (Cambridge: Cambridge University Press, 2004), 76.

eighty years. And Isaac breathed his last; and he died and was gathered to his people, old and full of days; and his sons Esau and Jacob buried him" (Gen 35:27–29). He may have been "old and full of days," but, compared to the days and the powerful divine encounters enjoyed by Abraham and Jacob, Isaac's days are hardly worth talking about!

At Isaac's birth, there was great joy because Abraham and Sarah were past childbearing years. Genesis makes clear that his conception required a miracle. In the form of three "men" or angels, the Lord appears to Abraham at the Oaks of Mamre and makes a concrete promise: "I will surely return to you in the spring, and Sarah your wife shall have a son" (Gen 18:10). Sarah does not believe this promise, because, as Genesis 18:11 says, "it had ceased to be with Sarah after the manner of women." All this is to underscore that when Isaac was born, there was special rejoicing (see Gen 21:1–7).

Yet, despite the celebration of his entrance into the world, Isaac himself – as a distinct agent – seems to have made little impact. In the Akedah narrative, Isaac asks the question "Behold, the fire and the wood; but where is the lamb for a burnt offering?" (Gen 22:7). To this question, his father answers only that "God will provide himself the lamb for a burnt offering, my son" (Gen 22:8). There are no words from Isaac when Abraham binds him to the wood, lays him upon the makeshift sacrificial altar, and raises his knife to slaughter Isaac. Nor are there words from Isaac when he is spared. Isaac receives a reward for his passive part in the Akedah only in the sense that when he grows up he inherits the covenantal promise.

Even when Isaac has become an adult, his life seems rather passive. Isaac marries Rebekah, a close relative, because Abraham arranges it. Isaac's first sight of his future wife is almost humorously passive. We read, "Isaac went out to meditate in the field in the evening; and he lifted up his eyes and looked, and behold, there were camels coming. And Rebekah lifted up her eyes, and when

3.2 THE FIGURE OF ISAAC IN SCRIPTURE

she saw Isaac, she alighted from the camel" (Gen 24:63–64).[17] Bill Arnold notes that the book of Genesis contains an "Abraham narrative" and a "Jacob narrative," but he identifies no "Isaac narrative."[18] Even Genesis 25 and 26, which are about Isaac, belong to what Arnold calls the "Jacob narrative."

Isaac does encounter the Lord twice. In the first encounter, God commands him not to go to Egypt but to stay in the land of the Philistines, and in both encounters, God reaffirms the covenantal promises. Like Abraham, Isaac for a time hides the fact that Rebekah is his wife, due to her beauty and his vulnerability in the land of Gerar. Like Abraham, too, Isaac gets rich.[19] Isaac intervenes in a quarrel between his herdsmen and the herdsmen of Gerar and brokers a covenant of peace. He founds the city of Beersheba, almost by mistake, when his servants dig a well there. The story of the competition between Isaac's sons Jacob and Esau suggests that Rebekah is firmly the one in charge. She ensures that her favored child, Jacob, receives the blessing of the firstborn.

The best that can be said about the life of Isaac is seemingly that he was "the precious son of a great father and the beguiled father of a scheming son."[20] Thus R. R. Reno, in commenting on Genesis 26, notes that "readers seem encouraged by Genesis to draw the conclusion that Isaac matters only as a placeholder,"

---

[17] For discussion see Jack M. Sasson, "The Servant's Tale: How Rebekah Found a Spouse," *Journal of Near Eastern Studies* 65 (2006): 241–65.

[18] See Arnold, *Genesis*, 228–29.

[19] Arnold observes that Genesis 26 "is devoted to making Isaac look as much like Abraham as possible. Echoes and direct allusions to the Abraham narrative permeate the whole" (Arnold, *Genesis*, 235). In Arnold's view, Genesis 26:1–6 show Isaac's obedience to God's command, for which Isaac is rewarded.

[20] Walter Brueggemann, *Genesis* (Atlanta, GA: John Knox Press, 1982), 221. Brueggemann insists that, nevertheless, "the figure of Isaac is made the bearer of an important and distinctive theological perspective" – namely a perspective in which there is no tension or doubt regarding the divine blessing, since the adult Isaac enjoys both "the *theological claim of blessing from Yahweh* and *prosperity judged by worldly standards*" (Brueggemann, *Genesis*, 221–22).

because he "seems an almost accidental rather than intentional patriarch."[21]

Although Isaac is passive, he still has a starring role in Genesis 22. It is he, not Abraham, who is the beloved and yearned-for son promised by God. Without him, Abraham would not have a descendant through whom the covenantal promises will continue. God's promise to make Abraham's descendants into a great nation depends upon the lineage of Abraham and Sarah. God himself intervenes to ensure that Sarah can conceive a child, and that child is Isaac.

The great trial of faith undergone by Abraham involves Isaac centrally, in two ways. First, even though Abraham "believed the Lord; and he reckoned it to him as righteousness" (Gen 15:6), it was nevertheless a great trial for Abraham to wait for a son in fulfillment of God's covenantal promises. Second, Abraham undergoes a great trial by obeying the Lord's command to "take your son, your only begotten son Isaac, whom you love, and go to the land of Moriah, and offer him there as a burnt offering upon one of the mountains of which I shall tell you" (Gen 22:2). In both cases, it is the "only begotten," "beloved" son who stands at the center of the story. The coming of the son vindicates Abraham's faith in God's promises, and Abraham's free offering of the son ends up confirming the promised blessing (Gen 22:16–18).

Of course, because Isaac is merely a passive actor, he does not have the lead role. It is Abraham who resolutely confronts the dreadful and apparently irresolvable paradox described by Walter Brueggemann, who is in turn indebted to the interpretations offered by John Calvin and Martin Luther: "The *promise* of God is that through Isaac your descendants will be named (21:12; cf. Rom. 9:7).

---

[21] R. R. Reno, *Genesis* (Grand Rapids, MI: Brazos, 2010), 224, 226. Yet, Reno maintains that "Isaac cannot be dismissed as an unimportant, transitional figure" (Reno, *Genesis*, 224). For Reno, Isaac has value in showing that, in a real sense, simply passing on the covenantal inheritance is enough; we do not have to be great in the eyes of the world.

The *command* of God is that Isaac must be killed. It follows that there will be no descendants, no future."[22] God resolves this paradox by providing the ram for sacrifice.

The first Christians connected the sacrifice of the beloved son with the Cross of Jesus Christ. Paul suggests this link when he says of God: "He who did not spare his own Son but gave him up for us all, will he not also give us all things with him?" (Rom 8:32). The Gospel of John speaks of "the Lamb of God, who takes away the sins of the world" (Jn 1:29). This Passover "Lamb" is the beloved Son of God: "For God so loved the world that he gave his only-begotten Son, that whoever believes in him should not perish but have eternal life" (Jn 3:16). While Jesus is still in the womb, Mary and Elizabeth rejoice. His birth is the cause of great joy, as Isaac's was. Paul rejoices in "the redemption which is in Christ Jesus, whom God put forward as an expiation by his blood" (Rom 3:24–25).[23] The New Isaac also receives Resurrection; indeed, his Cross becomes intelligible in light of his Resurrection, just as God's command in Genesis 22 became intelligible in light of Isaac's "resurrection."

3.3 Huizenga on the New Isaac

In order to gain further insight into the biblical testimony to Christ as a New Isaac, let me turn to Leroy Huizenga's *The New*

---

[22] Brueggemann, *Genesis*, 188.

[23] For the early Rabbis' understanding of the blood of the Passover lamb and the people's sharing in the Passover, see Mira Balberg, *Blood for Thought: The Reinvention of Sacrifice in Early Rabbinic Literature* (Oakland, CA: University of California Press, 2017), 163–77. In many early Rabbinic texts, the (hypothetical) question arose as to whether a Jewish person could participate in the Passover solely through the tossing of the sacrificial lamb's blood upon the altar or whether participation in the Passover requires eating of the sacrificial lamb. Balberg notes an "undeniable resonance between the rabbinic emphasis on the blood of the Passover and the Christian interpretation of Jesus as the Passover lamb" – a resonance that arises, in her view, from "a shared interpretive tradition that associates the blood of the Passover with the covenant" (174, 176)

Isaac.[24] Scripture is the word of God and yet it is always a word that God speaks through human beings and in the context of the cultural milieu of God's covenantal people, Israel and (in the New Testament) the messianically fulfilled and reconfigured Israel, the Church.[25] Central to this revelation is the obedient death through which comes about the fullness of divine presence. Huizenga observes that "the Matthean Jesus and the Isaac of Jewish Scripture and tradition resemble each other to a remarkable degree: both are promised children conceived under extraordinary circumstances, beloved sons who go obediently and willingly to their redemptive deaths at the hands of their respective fathers at the season of Passover."[26] The conception of Isaac and the conception of Jesus are miraculous. Isaac may go willingly to his death, but in the end Abraham does not kill him. By contrast, Jesus really does get killed. The idea that it is his Father who kills him is profoundly disturbing, as I have noted above.

Arguably, part of the solution involves examining the reception of Genesis 22, especially in texts roughly contemporaneous with the New Testament. Huizenga guides us through the receptions of Genesis 22 during this period. For example, Josephus confirms the statement of 2 Chronicles 3:1 that the Akedah took place where the Temple was later built. Josephus's *Antiquities* (AD 95–96) emphasizes Isaac's active role in his own near-sacrifice. When Abraham tells him that he (Isaac) is to be the sacrificial victim, Isaac rushes

---

[24] I examine some other relevant studies (including most notably Jon D. Levenson's *The Death and Resurrection of the Beloved Son: The Transformation of Child Sacrifice in Judaism and Christianity* [New Haven, CT: Yale University Press, 1993]) in my *Sacrifice and Community: Jewish Offering and Christian Eucharist* (Oxford: Blackwell, 2005), chapter 1. See also the reflections of Alan L. Mittleman, *Does Judaism Condone Violence? Holiness and Ethics in the Jewish Tradition* (Princeton, NJ: Princeton University Press, 2018).

[25] See Joseph Ratzinger/Pope Benedict XVI, *Jesus of Nazareth: From the Baptism in the Jordan to the Transfiguration*, trans. Adrian J. Walker (New York: Doubleday, 2007), xx–xxi.

[26] Huizenga, *The New Isaac*, 2.

3.3 HUIZENGA ON THE NEW ISAAC

joyfully to the altar. The Book of Jubilees (160–150 BC) presents the Akedah as taking place at the time of Passover. Abraham's obedience "procures deliverance and blessing."[27]

Pseudo-Jubilees (also known as 4Q225, a fragment from Qumran [c. 150 BC–AD 20]) presents Isaac as anything but passive. During Abraham's preparation for the sacrifice, Isaac in Pseudo-Jubilees requests that Abraham bind him tightly so that he (Isaac) cannot mar the sacrificial offering. Isaac here shows fortitude and fidelity; he willingly goes to his sacrificial death. In response to Isaac's active faithfulness, God blesses him. Pseudo-Jubilees also links the Akedah with the Passover and thus with the exodus from Egypt. Similarly, the Akedah as a test of Isaac – and thus Isaac's active rather than merely passive role – is suggested by Judith 8:26. Judith tells her brethren in the besieged town, "In spite of everything let us give thanks to the Lord our God, who is putting us to the test as he did our forefathers. Remember what he did with Abraham, and how he tested Isaac." Indebted to James Kugel, Huizenga remarks that it seems likely that in referring to Isaac's testing, Judith has in view the Akedah.[28]

Philo in the early first century depicts Isaac as possessing all the gifts of a virtuous nature. Isaac receives God's choicest graces, and he has no vices. As such, Isaac is indeed a "son of God," begotten miraculously by God himself. Huizenga comments, "Whereas the figures of Abraham and Jacob overshadow Isaac in Genesis, in an intriguing act of interpretive inversion Isaac has effectively supplanted them in significant ways in Philo's works."[29] Philo details Isaac's virtuous precocity and emphasizes that Isaac is the "beloved" and "only" son of Abraham. Philo describes Isaac not simply as a sacrificial victim but as a burnt offering – a sacrificial mode suited to pure and undefiled sacrifices.

---

[27] Huizenga, *The New Isaac*, 88.
[28] See James L. Kugel, *The Bible as It Was* (Cambridge: Harvard University Press, 1997), 174-75; cited in Huizenga, *The New Isaac*, 94.
[29] Huizenga, *The New Isaac*, 101-02.

The late first-century text *Liber Antiquitatum Biblicarum* by Pseudo-Philo likewise makes Isaac less passive than he is in the text of Genesis 22. Isaac not only does not object but he "explicitly consents" to his sacrifice.[30] His sacrifice is depicted as a burnt offering whose purpose is atonement. Another first-century text, *4 Maccabees*, presents Isaac "as a model of courage and endurance who willingly accepts his role in the sacrifice" and who thereby makes atonement for sin through his obedience.[31]

It is not surprising, then, that Genesis 22 belongs to the interpretive background through which the first (Jewish) Christians came to understand and depict Jesus' death and Resurrection. If Isaac actively accepted his sacrificial role, then the charge of patricide is weakened. This active Isaac sets the stage for Christian understanding of Jesus Christ: God the Father did not kill him, because Jesus freely chose to go to his death for the salvation of his people. Even if the Father willed his death, so also did the incarnate Son, and both willed this not because of bloodlust but because of their perfect love for sinful Israel.

In this regard, Huizenga directs attention to the *Christus Victor* model of atonement. This might seem anachronistic, but Huizenga explains that he is thinking in terms of "the Gospel [of Matthew]'s thoroughgoing apocalypticism and in light of the association of the Akedah with deliverance from enemies heavenly and earthly (one thinks here especially of *Jubilees* and 4 Maccabees)."[32] Huizenga presses to understand such passages as Matthew 1:21, "she will bear a son, and you shall call his name Jesus, for he will save his people from their sins," and Matthew 26:28, "for this is my blood of the covenant, which is poured out for many for the forgiveness of sins." On the

---

[30] Huizenga, *The New Isaac*, 106. Huizenga directs attention to Bruce N. Fisk, "Offering Isaac Again and Again: Pseudo-Philo's Use of the Aqedah as Intertext," *Catholic Biblical Quarterly* 62 (2000): 481–507.

[31] Huizenga, *The New Isaac*, 118.

[32] Huizenga, *The New Isaac*, 272.

Cross, is Jesus (the beloved Son, the New Isaac) placating an "angry" and bloodthirsty God by bearing the punishment of sin in our place?

In answer, Huizenga suggests that one might do better to look at Jesus' warnings against his opponents, who, in Jesus' view, are ultimately driven by Satan. When Jesus' enemies (Jewish and Roman) do their worst, Satan in a sense triumphs; however, the resurrection of Jesus – reversing his enemies' crime and, beyond mere reversal, exalting and glorifying Jesus – "is the ultimate, decisive defeat of Satan and his unwitting human minions."[33] The work of the New Isaac is an entrapment in which God the Father and Jesus, working toward their shared goal (rooted in supreme love for Israel), succeed in defeating Satan and his minions once and for all, destroying the power of death from within death by rising from the dead.

Huizenga also defends Jesus' sacrificial death on another ground. Indebted to Baruch Levine and Jonathan Klawans, he inquires into the first-century Jewish understanding of sacrifice.[34] Why did first-century Jewish priests think that something good was happening when they obeyed God's commandments to ritually slaughter animals? Summarizing Levine's and Klawans's work, Huizenga notes that the Jewish priests believed that sacrifice functioned as a prescribed mode of cultically "imitating God" and "attracting and maintaining the divine presence."[35] Grave moral defilement on the part of the people could cause God's presence to abandon the Temple, undoing the good work of sacrifice. In this light, Huizenga points out that "[t]he Matthean Jesus assumes that God dwells in the temple [cf. Mt 23:21]," and Jesus himself "is the locus of the divine presence [cf. Mt 1:23; Mt 18:15–22; Mt 28:20]."[36] Matthew,

---

[33] Huizenga, *The New Isaac*, 273.
[34] See Baruch Levine, *In the Presence of the Lord: A Study of Cult and Some Cultic Terms in Ancient Israel* (Leiden: Brill, 1974); Jonathan Klawans, *Purity, Sacrifice, and the Temple: Symbolism and Supersessionism in the Study of Ancient Judaism* (Oxford: Oxford University Press, 2006), 49–73.
[35] Huizenga, *The New Isaac*, 274.
[36] Huizenga, *The New Isaac*, 277.

then, depicts Jesus (the New Isaac) accomplishing the purposes of priest, victim, and Temple and thereby ensuring that the divine presence will be with his followers. Jesus' obedient and willing sacrifice enables him to take on the function of the Temple and mediate the divine presence. Huizenga remarks, "It is not that Jesus is another locus of God's presence or a special locus of God's presence in addition to the temple."[37] Instead, in the Gospel of Matthew, Jesus condemns the Temple (as defiled) and replaces it.[38]

If the purpose of cultic sacrifice is to attract and mediate the divine presence – and if the ground of all Israel's cultic sacrifices is the Akedah, in which the beloved son of the covenant willingly accepts death at the hands of his father, only to be restored to life by God – then can Jesus replace the defiled Temple and embody the divine presence in and through his obedient sacrifice? It all sounds like a rather complicated scheme. Today we are not likely to share ancient Jewish views about cultic sacrifice and the divine presence. Has Jesus, then, been fit by Huizenga's historical research into an ancient framework that actually diminishes his relevance for us?

The answer requires appreciating the fullness of the framework and its imagery, focused as it is upon the healing of sinful separation and the establishment of communion with the all-holy God. As Huizenga says, "Jesus' resurrected body is the ultimate temple (cf. Matt 12:40 and 27:63–64)."[39] Resurrected life – the defeat of the

---

[37] Huizenga, *The New Isaac*, 280.

[38] Huizenga, *The New Isaac*, 281; see Matthew 23–26. Huizenga is drawing here upon multiple sources, especially Birgir Gerhardsson, "Sacrificial Service and Atonement in the Gospel of Matthew," in *Reconciliation and Hope: New Testament Essays on Atonement and Eschatology Presented to L. L. Morris on His 60th Birthday*, ed. Robert Banks (Grand Rapids, MI: Eerdmans, 1974), 25–35.

[39] Huizenga, *The New Isaac*, 283. I think it evident that Huizenga is correct when he adds, "In light of ... Jesus' Passover Eucharist, the Matthean Jesus' action in the temple seems to be a prophetic action portending the end of the temple-based sacrificial system to be replaced by himself as a sacrifice. Forgiveness will no longer be mediated by the temple system but by Jesus through his Church" (Huizenga, *The New Isaac*, 290).

3.3 HUIZENGA ON THE NEW ISAAC

powers of death and the merciful triumph of divine presence in the midst of sinners – is the purpose of the New Isaac's obedient sacrifice. Everything hinges upon the claim that Jesus is "something greater than the temple."[40] If Jesus truly is greater, then he can be the New Isaac who fulfills and replaces the Temple,[41] through his utterly unique sacrifice. Huizenga writes, "The temple's legitimacy is predicated on the Akedah; the Matthean Jesus' legitimacy is predicated on the claim that he is the beloved Son like Isaac, a divinely ordained sacrifice for the redemption of his people."[42] If Jesus is simply a beloved son along the lines of Isaac, ordained by God the Father to die for the people, then he is merely a repeat of the first Isaac. He stands parallel to the Temple rather than transcending it. But in fact, according to Matthew (and Huizenga), "Jesus … is God incarnate (Matt 1:18–25)."[43]

Huizenga points out that in the opening verse of the Gospel, the evangelist announces: "The book of the genealogy of Jesus Christ, the son of David, the son of Abraham" (Mt 1:1). Both identities – "son of David" and "son of Abraham" – are significant. As Stanley Hauerwas comments, in a passage quoted by Huizenga: "Matthew knows he is telling the story of one that was born a king, yet a king to be sacrificed.

---

[40] Huizenga, *The New Isaac*, 285.
[41] In my *Engaging the Doctrine of Israel: A Christian Israelology in Dialogue with Ongoing Judaism* (Eugene, OR: Cascade, 2021), I address supersessionist concerns regarding such language. Let me add here that the New Temple image in the Gospel of Matthew is inextricably linked to the theme of judgment upon the Temple due to sin (a judgment that is freely borne by Jesus on the Cross). There is a divine solicitude expressed in Jesus' becoming the New Temple. For diverse perspectives on the Temple in the New Testament, see for example Timothy C. Gray, *The Temple in the Gospel of Mark* (Tübingen: Mohr Siebeck, 2008); Peter H. Rice, *Behold, Your House Is Left to You: The Theological and Narrative Place of the Jerusalem Temple in Luke's Gospel* (Eugene, OR: Pickwick, 2016); Paul M. Hoskins, *Jesus as the Fulfillment of the Temple in the Gospel of John* (Eugene, OR: Wipf and Stock, 2007); and Egal Regev, *The Temple in Early Christianity: Experiencing the Sacred* (New Haven, CT: Yale University Press, 2019).
[42] Huizenga, *The New Isaac*, 291.
[43] Huizenga, *The New Isaac*, 278.

God had tested Abraham by commanding him to sacrifice Isaac. By beginning with 'Son of David' Matthew prepares us to recognize that this is a king who will end up on the cross."[44] This king (son of David) is the son of Abraham: the New Isaac. Huizenga shows through an analysis of Matthew 1:20–21 that the evangelist allusively compares Mary as Virgin with Sarah as barren, indicating that in both cases there was a miraculous conception. Equally important is the allusion to Genesis 22 found in Matthew 3:17, where after Jesus' baptism God the Father proclaims: "This is my beloved Son, with whom I am well pleased."[45] What does it mean to be the beloved Son not of Abraham but of God? It means that Jesus is "God with us" (Mt 1:23), and he is "worshiped" by the Magi who rejoice at seeing him (Mt 2:10–11). Immediately before the baptism scene, John the Baptist gives Jesus a divine role in eschatological judgment (Mt 3:12). From the outset, Jesus is the locus of the divine presence and the divine power, working toward the reconciliation of the sinful people with their God.[46] This is what enables him, in his crucifixion and resurrection, to be uniquely the *New* Isaac, not merely another son of Abraham. As "God with us," the New Isaac conquers Satan and unleashes the divine presence, overcoming all cultic defilement as the perfect Temple sacrifice.

---

[44] Stanley Hauerwas, *Matthew* (Grand Rapids, MI: Brazos, 2006), 17; cited in Huizenga, *The New Isaac*, 142. Huizenga also cites (on 144) Roy A. Rosenberg's intriguing insight: "Jesus is alleged by Matthew to have lived and died during the first jubilee of the fourth cycle of fourteen generations following Abraham: i.e., at the beginning of the forty-second generation following Abraham. Following this system of chronology, the sacrifice of Jesus becomes exactly parallel to the offering of Isaac, for the book of Jubilees (13:16, 17:15, 19:1) indicates that the offering of Isaac had taken place just prior to the beginning of the forty-second jubilee after the creation of the world" (Rosenberg, "Jesus, Isaac, and the 'Suffering Servant,'" *Journal of Biblical Literature* 84 [1965]: 381–88, at 387).

[45] Huizenga grants that "[m]ost modern interpreters ... discount the possibility that the Matthean baptism evokes echoes of Isaac, finding instead allusions to Ps 2:7 and Isa 42:1 in Matt 3:17" (Huizenga, *The New Isaac*, 156).

[46] See also Ulrich Luz, *Matthew 1–7*, trans. James E. Crouch, ed. Helmut Koester (Minneapolis, MN: Fortress, 2007), 96, even though Luz doubts that Matthew strictly identifies Jesus as divine.

3.3 HUIZENGA ON THE NEW ISAAC

Other passages in the Gospel of Matthew that resonate with New Isaac Christology include the following verses from Matthew's Passion narrative: Matthew 26:36, 47, and 52. These passages involve direct linguistic parallels with the Septuagint version of Genesis 22. In Matthew 26:36, Jesus tells his disciples "Sit here" (*kathisate autou*), just as in the Septuagint version of Genesis 22:5, Abraham tells the young men who have journeyed with him and Isaac, "Sit here" (*kathisate autou*). The point in the Gospel of Matthew is that no one other than Jesus (the New Isaac) will undergo the sacrifice. In Matthew 26:47, the crowd that comes with Judas bears "swords" (*machairōn*) and clubs (*xulōn*), while in the Septuagint version of Genesis 22:6 the word for the wood of the burnt offering is *xula* and the word for the knife is *machairon*. The crowd is not permitted to implement the slaughter, just as Abraham is not either; God has another plan. Lastly, in Matthew 26:52, one of Jesus' disciples stretches forth his hand (*ekteinas tēn cheira*) and draws his sword (*tēn machairon*), and in Genesis 22:10 Abraham stretches forth his hand (*ezeteinen Abraam tēn cheira*) and takes his knife (*labein tēn machairan*). In a manner similar to how God firmly stops Abraham's action, Jesus firmly stops the disciple's action. Indeed, to rely upon the "sword" or "knife" (*machairon*) is, Jesus warns, to perish by it because of its insufficiency.

Huizenga also sees a possible reference to Genesis 22 in Jesus' statement in Matthew 26:53: "Do you think that I cannot appeal to my Father, and he will at once send me more than twelve legions of angels?" Recall that in verses 11 and 15 of Genesis 22, an angel of the Lord intervenes to ensure that Abraham does not slay Isaac and to proclaim blessing upon Abraham and his descendants. In Matthew 26:53, Jesus makes clear that no angel will interfere to prevent the slaying of the New Isaac, because in his death the redemptive cultic sacrifice that blesses all nations will take place.[47]

---

[47] For the above four connections between Matthew 26 and Genesis 22, see Huizenga, *The New Isaac*, 250–60.

CHRIST THE NEW ISAAC: THE ESCHATOLOGICAL TEMPLE

Throughout Matthew 26, as Huizenga emphasizes, Jesus is presented as fully "obedient to the divine will" and as the one who is accomplishing God's ultimate purposes for the salvation of the world.[48] No doubt, "the willing obedience of Jesus in Gethsemane to endure sacrificial death reflects Isaac's willing obedience at the Akedah."[49] In his prayer at Gethsemane, Jesus three times professes his submission to the divine will in accepting his upcoming death. Other scholars such as W. D. Davies and Dale Allison have also noted some of the connections between Matthew 26 and Genesis 22, though without the detailed exposition that Huizenga provides.[50] Since these earlier scholars suggest that the referent may be either Abraham or Isaac, Huizenga offers a set of reasons for identifying the referent as Isaac. Among other things, Huizenga points out that had the disciple who drew his sword been paying attention, he would have remembered that Jesus has been identified as the "beloved son" (Mt 17:5) whose destiny is to suffer sacrificial death, in accordance with the Akedah. Jesus deliberately acts to fulfill the divine will and to ensure that "the Scriptures of the prophets might be fulfilled" (Mt 26:56; cf. Mt 26:54).

3.4 The Church Fathers on the New Isaac

Huizenga connects Jesus as the New Isaac especially with the eschatological fulfillment of the Temple. As he sums up, "Given the association of the Akedah with the temple in Jewish tradition and the significance of the temple for the Gospel of Matthew, the

---

[48] Huizenga, *The New Isaac*, 253.
[49] Huizenga, *The New Isaac*, 254.
[50] See W. D. Davies and Dale C. Allison, Jr., *A Critical and Exegetical Commentary on the Gospel according to Saint Matthew*, vol. 3, *Introduction and Commentary on Matthew XIX–XXVIII* (New York: T&T Clark, 2004), 498.

3.4 THE CHURCH FATHERS ON THE NEW ISAAC

Isaac typology may function in service of presenting Jesus as a new temple and as the decisive, ultimate sacrifice."[51] Does the exegesis of the Church Fathers resonate with this portrait? I have chosen four figures to examine briefly: Melito of Sardis, Origen, Augustine, and Cyril of Alexandria.[52] I will begin with Augustine's *City of God* and *On the Trinity*, because Augustine generally has the most influence on Aquinas. As background, however, let me mention Ambrose's praise of Isaac as one who "abounds in glory" and who is a type of Christ's birth from a virgin and of Christ's perfect sacrificial offering, in which death and restoration are combined.[53] Interestingly, Ambrose's treatise takes the Song of Songs as its model, "casting Rebecca as the Bride and Isaac, the type of Christ, as the Bridegroom."[54]

3.4.1 Augustine

In reviewing the biblical history of the people of Israel in his *City of God*, Augustine offers a short reflection on the birth of Isaac and his near-sacrifice by Abraham. Augustine reads Genesis 22

---

[51] Huizenga, *The New Isaac*, 261.
[52] See also Edward Kessler, *Bound by the Bible: Jews, Christians and the Sacrifice of Isaac* (Cambridge: Cambridge University Press, 2004). Kessler identifies at least seventeen areas of shared ground between Rabbinic and patristic interpretations of the Akedah. Among these are the fact that both Jews and Christians sought to defend God against the charge of desiring human sacrifice and the fact that both Jews and Christians interpreted the Akedah in relation to atonement.
[53] Ambrose, "Isaac, or the Soul," in *Seven Exegetical Works*, trans. Michael P. McHugh (Washington, DC: Catholic University of America Press, 1972), 10–65, at 10. Ambrose also has a treatise on Abraham in which he engages Isaac in a similar manner: see Ambrose, *On Abraham*, trans. Theodosia Tomkinson (Etna, CA: Center for Traditional Orthodox Studies, 2000). Marcia Colish notes that Ambrose had to deviate from his pattern regarding the patriarchs when it came to treating Isaac, since "[a]ctivities and events that exemplify virtue on Isaac's part are few in number in the text of Genesis" (Colish, *Ambrose's Patriarchs: Ethics for the Common Man* [Notre Dame: University of Notre Dame Press, 2005], 69).
[54] Colish, *Ambrose's Patriarchs*, 70.

through the lens of Romans and Hebrews. He highlights the following themes:

- The joy of Abraham and Sarah when they became aware of the coming of the promised son.
- The connection between Isaac's sacrificial (near-)death and the hope of resurrection. Augustine emphasizes that "Abraham is to be praised in that he believed, without hesitation, that his son would rise again when he had been sacrificed."[55] Abraham's obedience to God's command, therefore, cannot be properly understood outside resurrection faith.
- Assurance that whatever else may stand behind God's command, God does not desire human sacrificial victims.
- Isaac is the son of the covenantal promise. The true descendants of Abraham are likewise sons of the promise.
- Isaac is a "type" or "symbol" (Heb 11:19) of Jesus. Like Christ carrying his cross, Isaac carried the wood. The ram who was sacrificed in the place of Isaac was also a type of Christ. The burnt offering was a symbol of Christ's complete self-offering.

The key to the whole story is that God has promised a son whose obedient sacrifice will bring about the covenantal blessing of all peoples. In *On the Trinity*, Augustine echoes Genesis 22 when he asks rhetorically: "[W]hat greater example of obedience could be given to us, us who had been ruined by disobedience, than God the Son obeying God the Father *even to death on the cross* (Phil 2:8)? Where could the reward of obedience be shown to better advantage than in the flesh of such a mediator when it rose to eternal life?"[56] Here we see the New Isaac's eschatological Akedah.

---

[55] Augustine, *City of God*, trans. Henry Bettenson (London: Penguin, 1984), Book XVI, ch. 32, p. 694.
[56] Augustine, *The Trinity*, trans. Edmund Hill, O.P., ed. John E. Rotelle, O.S.A. (Brooklyn, NY: New City Press, 1991), Book XIII, ch. 5, p. 361.

3.4 THE CHURCH FATHERS ON THE NEW ISAAC

3.4.2 Melito of Sardis

Melito's *On Pascha* is a second-century poem that places Christ in the context of the whole of salvation history, beginning with Adam and Eve and the entrance of sin and death. The description of sin, with its destructive violence and lust, rings true. After surveying briefly some of the sins that mar human relationships, Melito notes: "Sin rejoiced in all of this, working together with death, making forays into human souls and preparing the bodies of the dead as his food.... All flesh fell under sin, and every body under death."[57] The human condition because doubly marked: on the one hand by the desire for communion and eternity, on the other hand by sin and death. It seemed as though the latter pair would have the last word, as though the desire for communion and eternity were a mere mirage, tricking foolish mortals. Melito bemoans the fallen human condition: "Humanity was doled out by death for a strange disaster and captivity surrounded him; he was dragged off a captive under the shadow of death and the Father's image was left desolate."[58]

God, of course, has other plans in Christ. Melito envisions human history and then Israel's history as a series of types or symbols preparing for Christ and enabling us to understand Christ. Among these types is Abel, the just man slain by his brother; also among these types is Isaac, bound firmly to the wood on the altar.[59]

Melito expands upon Isaac's typological role in three connected fragments. In Fragment 9, he notes that like Christ who carried the cross, Isaac carried the wood and remained silent in his hour of trial, but unlike Christ, Isaac did not actually suffer

---

[57] Melito of Sardis, *On Pascha: With the Fragments of Melito and Other Material Related to the Quartodecimans*, trans. Alistair Stewart-Sykes, 2nd ed. (Yonkers, NY: St Vladimir's Seminary Press, 2016), 66. For the dark side of Melito's work, see Alistair Stewart-Sykes, "Melito's Anti-Judaism," *Journal of Early Christian Studies* 5 (1997): 271–83.
[58] Melito of Sardis, *On Pascha*, 67.
[59] See Melito of Sardis, *On Pascha*, 68, 71.

death. Melito is well aware of the shocking character of Genesis 22. As he says, "even the type caused fear and astonishment to come upon people. For it was a strange mystery to behold: the son led up a mountain by his father, for slaughter."[60] In Fragment 9, however, Isaac is presented as not grieving about his coming suffering, because he bore everything obediently and willingly. In Fragment 10, Melito announces the sighting of the ram that, by its death, "ransomed Isaac: in the same way the Lord was slaughtered and saved us."[61] Lastly, Fragment 11 further compares Christ to the ram. The New Isaac goes beyond Isaac by actually dying a perfectly obedient sacrificial death, as the Lamb of God and the fulfillment of Israel's cult.

3.4.3 Origen

Origen's third-century *Homilies on Genesis and Exodus* contains two homilies on Isaac, one on his birth and the other on the Akedah. In discussing Isaac's birth, Origen inquires into the spiritual sense of the story. He thinks the story is spiritually describing the joy that spiritual fathers have in their sons who are begotten in the Gospel. He reads this story through the lens of Galatians 4, where Paul allegorically inquires into what it means to be a child of Sarah as distinct from a child of Hagar.

Turning to discuss the Akedah, Origen likewise seeks spiritual meanings. God gave to Abram the name "Abraham" and God promised, "I [God] have made you [Abraham] the father of a multitude of nations" (Gen 17:5). But in Genesis 22, God seems to be attacking Abraham's very identity by calling upon him to kill the son of the promise. Abraham, trusting God, cannot deny the truth of the promise, and thus he must suppose that God will resurrect Isaac. Origen thinks that Hebrews 11 accurately represents Abraham's

---

[60] Melito of Sardis, "Fragment 9," in Melito of Sardis, *On Pascha*, 92–93, at 93.
[61] Melito of Sardis, "Fragment 10," in Melito of Sardis, *On Pascha*, 93.

3.4 THE CHURCH FATHERS ON THE NEW ISAAC

thoughts. Indeed, in Origen's view, Abraham at the outset of Genesis 22 already knows about the future coming of Christ (cf. John 8).

Origen argues that the wording of the command shows that it was simply a test. Consider how God phrases the command: "Take your son, your only-begotten son Isaac, whom you love ..." (Gen 22:2). As Origen says, this phrase evokes paternal anguish, as well as anguish regarding the status of the covenantal promises. When God commands that Abraham kill Isaac on a mountain some distance away, Origen thinks that this is to add to Abraham's testing by requiring him to be tormented by sorrowful thoughts on the journey. The mountain symbolizes the difficult ascent or struggle between "love of God and love of the flesh, the charm of things present and the expectation of things future."[62] When, on the journey, Isaac asks where the sacrificial lamb is (Gen 22:7), Origen thinks that Abraham's reply – "God will provide himself the lamb" (Gen 22:8) – is made with Christ in view. But Origen also confronts us with Abraham's agony, by asking us to reflect upon how painful it is to lose a son to early death and by asking us to imagine what it would be like if we had to bind and kill our own sons. Origen suggests that fathers should take an example from Abraham's willingness to offer up his own son to death without losing faith in God.

After God stays Abraham's hand and reveals that it has all been only a test of faith, Origen compares Abraham to God by quoting Romans 8:32, "He who did not spare his own Son but gave him up for us all." God gave up his immortal Son unto death; whereas Abraham gave up a mortal son (who did not die). The offering of the New Isaac, therefore, is far greater than the offering of Isaac, and the divine Father is far greater than Abraham. Origen adds that while Isaac represents Christ, "the ram which is slain" also represents Christ.[63]

---

[62] Origen, *Homilies on Genesis and Exodus*, trans. Ronald E. Heine (Washington, DC: Catholic University of America Press, 1982), Homily VIII, p. 139.
[63] Origen, *Homilies on Genesis and Exodus*, Homily VIII, p. 145.

For Origen, Isaac represents the immortal Word, which is not killed, whereas the ram represents Christ's humanity, which is killed. As the Word, Christ in a priestly way offers his sacrificial flesh to the Father, and, in his flesh, Christ is the victim that he himself offers. Spiritually, the meaning of the story is that when we are beset by trials, we should "beget joy [i.e., Isaac]" through our struggles and we should offer this joy as a sacrifice of praise to God. When we do so, God will return our joy to us in a superabundant way. We can do this because we know the New Isaac, Jesus Christ, who was crucified and who is risen. Indeed, Origen suggests that this faith is how Abraham, too, manages to get through his own ordeal.

3.4.4 Cyril of Alexandria

Lastly, let me describe Cyril of Alexandria's early fifth-century *Glaphyra on the Pentateuch*, which includes a discussion of Genesis 22. Cyril succinctly presents the literal sense of the narrative of Genesis 22. He then examines the figurative or spiritual meaning. Even in this discussion, however, he adverts to the literal sense, commenting upon Abraham's distress and upon Abraham's reasonable expectation that some good would come from obeying God's command. He compares Genesis 22 to Christ's Cross. Clearly some powerful good came from the latter, making it worth the Father's will that Christ suffer and die.

Cyril devotes some space to contrasting Jews and Christians allegorically.[64] The fact that the two servants travel with Abraham but are not permitted to go all the way to the mountain is interpreted by Cyril as indicative of the Jewish people's refusal, after following God's Torah, to enter into the third and final age through faith

---

[64] See Robert L. Wilken, *Judaism and the Early Christian Mind: A Study of Cyril of Alexandria's Exegesis and Theology* (New Haven, CT: Yale University Press, 1971).

in Jesus Christ. The fact that the servants must stay with the donkey (Gen 22:5) suggests the irrationality of the decision to reject Christ. When Abraham does not explicitly tell his servants what he is going to do, Cyril compares this to Christ's speaking in parables to the Jewish people while explaining the parables to his disciples.

Isaac's carrying the wood parallels Christ's carrying his cross, and Isaac's being spared while the ram is slaughtered expresses the two natures of Christ, one of which dies while the other cannot die (as in Origen's reading). Cyril puts the latter point in his own terms, conveying his sense of the unity of Christ: "Although as God he was impassible and immortal, he took himself away to suffering and death, and through his own body he offered up a pleasing aroma to God the Father."[65] Christ the New Isaac thereby constitutes the perfect sacrificial offering.

3.5 Aquinas on Isaac and the New Isaac

Let me now examine some remarks of Aquinas on the Akedah. Aquinas observes that "the sacrifice of Abraham" is mentioned in "the canon of the Mass."[66] He attributes this fact to Abraham's extraordinary devotion in offering up Isaac. In his Sequence or doctrinal hymn *Lauda Sion* – part of the Divine Office of Corpus Christi that he composed – Aquinas includes the Akedah among the figural precedents of the Eucharist, along with the Passover lamb and the manna. Interestingly, he describes Isaac as actually having been sacrificed: "Cum Isaac immolator [When Isaac was sacrificed]."[67] In

---

[65] Cyril of Alexandria, *Glaphyra on the Pentateuch*, vol. 1, *Genesis*, trans. Nicholas P. Lunn (Washington, DC: Catholic University of America Press, 2018), 156.

[66] Thomas Aquinas, *Commentary on the Sentences: Book IV, Distinctions 1–13*, trans. Beth Mortensen (Green Bay, WI: Aquinas Institute, 2017), d. 8, q. 1, a. 2, qla. 2, obj. 6 (p. 333).

[67] I quote *Lauda Sion* from the Latin and English text found in Jan-Heiner Tück, *A Gift of Presence: The Theology and Poetry of the Eucharist in Thomas Aquinas*, trans. Scott G. Hefelfinger (Washington, DC: Catholic University of America Press, 2018), 218.

his *Commentary on the Sentences*, he interprets the Akedah as signifying or prefiguring Christ's death, as well as manifesting Abraham's faith and love for God.[68] When he arrives at his treatment of sacrifice in his final major work, the *Summa theologiae*, he declares: "Isaac was a type of Christ, being himself offered in sacrifice."[69]

Aquinas's position may be similar to that of the Rabbis, who frequently referred to the sacrifice of Isaac, to his being "offered upon the altar."[70] Edward Kessler explains the Jewish position, which he contrasts to patristic Christian denials that Isaac was sacrificed: "For Jews, Isaac's blood was shed and he suffered for the benefit of Israel. During the first few centuries he was associated with the resurrection of the dead and from the eighth century at the latest, the rabbis suggested that he died and was resurrected."[71]

Could the Jewish viewpoint have been known to Aquinas? Certainly Maimonides refers to "the sacrifice of Isaac."[72] In Maimonides's view, the main thing that the Akedah shows is Abraham's profound faith and love, through Abraham's "careful examination of what is due to the Divine command and what is in accordance with the love and fear of God."[73] According to Maimonides, Abraham "hasten[ed] to kill Isaac ... solely because it is man's duty to love and to fear God."[74] Maimonides goes on to explain that Abraham knew the command was truly from God because Abraham was

---

[68] This is pointed out by Tück, *A Gift of Presence*, 223. See also Aquinas's *Catena Aurea: Commentary on the Four Gospels Collected Out of the Works of the Fathers*, vol. 3, *St. Luke, Part 2*, trans. John Henry Newman (Albany, NY: Preserving Christian Publications, 1995), ch. 24, 778, where Aquinas quotes Chrysostom (commenting on Luke 24:27) as stating that "the sacrifice of Abraham, when releasing Isaac he sacrificed the ram, prefigured Christ's sacrifice."

[69] II-II, q. 85, a. 1, ad 2.

[70] See Kessler, *Bound by the Bible*, 108, citing a variety of Rabbinic sources.

[71] Kessler, *Bound by the Bible*, 134.

[72] Moses Maimonides, *The Guide for the Perplexed*, trans. M. Friedländer, rev. ed. (London: Routledge & Kegan Paul, 1904), Part III, ch. xxiv, p. 304.

[73] Maimonides, *The Guide for the Perplexed*, Part III, ch. xxiv, p. 306.

[74] Maimonides, *The Guide for the Perplexed*, Part III, ch. xxiv, p. 306.

3.5 AQUINAS ON ISAAC AND THE NEW ISAAC

a prophet, and whatever a prophet "perceives in a prophetic vision, he considers as true and correct and not open to any doubt," for reasons Maimonides explains.[75]

Commenting on John 1:29, where John the Baptist proclaims about Jesus, "Behold, the Lamb of God, who takes away the sin of the world," Aquinas thinks first of the sacrificial animals that God in the Torah commands be offered in Israelite worship. He notes that cows, goats, sheep, turtle-doves, and doves were offered sacrificially, and he deems that "[a]ll of these prefigured the true sacrifice, which is Christ, who 'gave himself for us as an offering to God,' as is said in Ephesians (5:2)."[76] Why, however, does John the Baptist identify Jesus specifically as the "Lamb"? Aquinas answers that the principal sacrifice commanded by the Torah was that of the lamb, since on a daily basis, morning and evening, a lamb was offered in the Temple. He considers that the other offerings, while no doubt important, "were in the form of additions" to the core morning and evening sacrifice of a lamb.[77] He contends that Christ is called not merely the "Lamb" but rather the "Lamb of God" because he not only has a created human nature but also possesses the divine nature. Precisely as the divine Son, he offers his human life on the Cross in a sacrificial death for the sake of sinners. Christ therefore is preeminently the "principal sacrifice."[78] Christ is utterly holy.

---

[75] Maimonides, *The Guide for the Perplexed*, Part III, ch. xxiv, p. 306. Aquinas's Jewish contemporary Nachmanides (1195–c.1270) holds that Mount Moriah is the Temple Mount and that God "commanded him [Abraham] to offer up his son in that place for that is *the mountain which G-d hath desired for His abode*, and He wanted the merit of the *Akeidah* (the Binding of Isaac) to be in the sacrifices forever" (Ramban [Nachmanides], *Commentary on the Torah: Genesis*, trans. Charles B. Chavel [New York: Shilo, 1999], 277).

[76] Thomas Aquinas, *Commentary on the Gospel of John*, vol. 1, Chapters 1–5, trans. Fabian Larcher, O.P., and James A. Weisheipl, O.P., ed. Daniel Keating and Matthew Levering (Washington, DC: Catholic University of America Press, 2010), ch. 1, lect. 14, §257, p. 104.

[77] Aquinas, *Commentary on the Gospel of John*, ch. 1, lect. 14, §257, p. 104.

[78] Aquinas, *Commentary on the Gospel of John*, ch. 1, lect. 14, §257, p. 104.

CHRIST THE NEW ISAAC: THE ESCHATOLOGICAL TEMPLE

He freely goes to his death, and in so doing "he takes upon himself 'the sins of the' whole 'world' [Jn 1:29], as is said, 'He bore our sins in his own body' (1 Pt 2:24); 'It was our infirmities that he bore, our sufferings that he endured,' as we read in Isaiah (53:4)."[79]

In commenting on John 1:29, Aquinas points out that "the Father provided man with an oblation to offer that satisfied for sins, which man could not have through himself."[80] The whole Trinity wills this path of salvation, namely, that the incarnate Son lovingly pay the penalty of sin (i.e., death) on behalf of the human race. In his holy humanity, Christ "gave himself up by a will inspired of the Father."[81] Christ both obeys the Father in going to the Cross and obeys his own divine will. It pertains to the Father (and to the one divine will of the Trinity) to permit the acts of Christ's Roman and Jewish persecutors to occur, so that Christ is abandoned to his enemies and undergoes the Cross.[82] At the same time, freely giving up his life on the Cross is precisely what Christ himself wills to do in his supreme love.[83] The Father, Son, and Spirit will only good, and nothing could be more good than the incarnate Son's freely rescuing sinners, not by bearing divine wrath but by enduring out of supreme love the penalty of sin.

Aquinas does not fill in all these details in his discussion of John 1:29 but instead attends to the conversation between Abraham and Isaac in Genesis 22. He states: "So when Isaac asked Abraham, 'Where is the victim for the holocaust?' he answered, 'God himself will provide a victim for the holocaust' (Gen 22:7)."[84] God's

---

[79] Aquinas, *Commentary on the Gospel of John*, ch. 1, lect. 14, §259, p. 105.
[80] Aquinas, *Commentary on the Gospel of John*, ch. 1, lect. 14, §257, p. 104.
[81] III, q. 47, a. 3, ad 2.
[82] See III, q. 47, a. 3.
[83] For further discussion, see Thomas Joseph White, O.P., *The Incarnate Lord: A Thomistic Study in Christology* (Washington, DC: Catholic University of America Press, 2015), chapters 6–8; and Dominic Legge, O.P., *The Trinitarian Christology of St Thomas Aquinas* (Oxford: Oxford University Press, 2017), especially chapter 7.
[84] Aquinas, *Commentary on the Gospel of John*, ch. 1, lect. 14, §257, p. 104.

3.5 AQUINAS ON ISAAC AND THE NEW ISAAC

provision is an act of divine love, providing human beings with what we desperately need but could not provide for ourselves. Aquinas attaches to his citation of the Akedah the words of Paul: "God did not spare his own Son, but delivered him up for all of us" (Rom 8:32).[85] Romans 8 is a paean to God's love, emphasizing how "there is therefore now no condemnation for those who are in Christ Jesus" and that "in everything God works for good with those who love him" (Rom 8:1 and 28). The Akedah points to this divine love. Aquinas rejoices that God has indeed provided the Lamb of God. As he says in his commentary on Ephesians 5:2 ("And walk in love, as Christ loved us and gave himself up for us, a fragrant offering and sacrifice to God"), Christ has fulfilled the animal sacrifices and Temple cult of the Old Testament.[86]

Commenting upon Hebrews 11:17–19, Aquinas provides an analysis of the Akedah in relation to Christ's Resurrection. He first defends the justice of God's command, along the lines that I mentioned above: God, the giver of life and the one against whom sin is primarily committed, can justly take life away at will. Second, Aquinas briefly defends the justice of God's putting Abraham's faith to the test. Then he turns to the reason why Abraham "was ready to offer up his only-begotten son, of whom it was said, 'Through Isaac shall your descendants be named'" (Heb 11:17–18). Clearly, if Isaac was dead, the divine promise could not come true. In addition, Sarah's age made it humanly impossible that she would bear a child to replace Isaac. God's command, if carried out, would seem to make it impossible for God to keep his covenantal promises. Yet, Abraham obeyed.

Aquinas, like Hebrews 11:19, credits this obedience to Abraham's belief that "God was able to raise men even from the dead." Aquinas considers this to be a reasonable belief, since God can work

---

[85] Cited in Aquinas, *Commentary on the Gospel of John*, ch. 1, lect. 14, §257, p. 104.
[86] See Thomas Aquinas, *Commentary on Saint Paul's Epistle to the Ephesians*, trans. Matthew L. Lamb (Albany, NY: Magi Books, 1966), ch. 5, lect. 1, p. 196.

miracles. Given that God can be counted upon to keep his promises, such a miracle is most likely: God will "revive Isaac, by whom his [Abraham's seed] would be called."[87] Although this belief is not unreasonable, it requires strong faith to remain confident in the face of death. Aquinas concludes that Abraham's trust that "God was able to raise men even from the dead" is "the greatest proof of his faith."[88]

Hebrews 11:19 states that Abraham "did receive him [Isaac] back and this was a symbol." For Hebrews 11:19, the rescue of Isaac happened due to Abraham's faith. Having tested Abraham's faith and found it strong, God returned Isaac's life to Abraham at the very last moment and instead provided a ram to be sacrificed. Like the Greek Fathers, Aquinas thinks that the ram signifies Christ in his humanity. He interprets the ram "caught in a thicket by his horns" (Gen 22:13), to be a figure of the man Christ nailed to the Cross, with the thorny thicket symbolizing Christ's crown of thorns.

Aquinas affirms that Isaac is "a figure of Christ to be crucified."[89] Christ is the New Isaac. Yet in Aquinas's commentary on Hebrews 11, it is the Resurrection that takes center stage, in accord with Abraham's faith. The Akedah thus underscores that the crucifixion of Christ (or near-sacrifice of Isaac) cannot be rightly perceived outside the Resurrection of Christ (or restoration of Isaac). As Aquinas puts it in the *Summa theologiae*'s analysis of Christ's Resurrection, just as Christ "endure[d] evil things in dying that he might deliver us from evil, so was he glorified in rising again in order to advance us towards good things."[90]

---

[87] Thomas Aquinas, *Commentary on the Letter of Saint Paul to the Hebrews*, trans. Fabian Larcher, O.P., ed. J. Mortensen and E. Alarcón (Lander, WY: The Aquinas Institute for the Study of Sacred Doctrine, 2012), ch. 11, lect. 4, §605, p. 261.

[88] Aquinas, *Commentary on the Letter of Saint Paul to the Hebrews*, ch. 11, lect. 4, §605, p. 261.

[89] Aquinas, *Commentary on the Letter of Saint Paul to the Hebrews*, ch. 11, lect. 4, §605, p. 261.

[90] III, q. 53, a. 1; translation slightly altered.

3.5 AQUINAS ON ISAAC AND THE NEW ISAAC

Could Christ as the New Isaac be of even more service to Thomistic Christology? I think so. The above discussion has relied for its references to the Akedah (and thus to the New Isaac) mainly on Aquinas's biblical commentaries. Contemporary Thomistic Christology may envision various places in the *tertia pars* that could profitably integrate Christ the New Isaac. For example, in III, q. 22, a. 2, Aquinas asks whether Christ was both priest and victim. He discusses how "the slaying of Christ may be considered in reference to the will of the Sufferer, who freely offered himself to suffering."[91] In this article, Aquinas draws upon Hebrews 5 and 10, as well as Romans 4, but he does not take advantage of the New Isaac motif that could shed light on how Christ is both victim and offerer, eschatologically fulfilling Israel's Temple cult.

Similarly, the New Isaac motif could receive a more explicit place in the discussion of Christ's Passion in questions 46–49. For instance, in question 46, articles 2 and 3, Aquinas explores why God chose the Passion of Christ as the means of salvation. He cites a number of biblical passages but none that considers Christ's Passion in light of the significance of the Akedah. In question 47, articles 1 and 2, Aquinas directly addresses the difficult issue of whether the crucifier of Christ was actually Christ himself (the incarnate Son) or else God the Father. Since this is precisely the problem raised by the Akedah, a reference to the New Isaac could fill out Aquinas's responses. The same is true for Aquinas's reflection in question 48, article 3 on whether Christ's Passion was a sacrifice.

Aquinas in his biblical commentaries shows that the Akedah (and Christ the New Isaac) has just as much to do with resurrection as with sacrificial death. In discussing whether "it behooved Christ to rise again" in question 53, article 1 of the *tertia pars*, Aquinas cites a wide variety of passages from the Old and New Testaments, but nothing related to the Akedah. Here Thomistic Christology could include the New Isaac motif. This is especially

---

[91] III, q. 22, a. 2, ad 2.

so because, as I have shown elsewhere, Aquinas's theology of Christ's Resurrection is marked by interest in bringing together Old and New Testaments, Israel, and the Church.[92] As the fulfillment of the Temple cult, the New Isaac atones for sin and opens up the fullness of life.

3.6 An Ontological Note

Ontologically, the concept of the "New Isaac" has to do with the nature of atonement. At various points in his exposition of *sacra doctrina*, Aquinas seeks to understand the ontological reality of the reconciliation of God and humanity. He argues that at its core is self-offering in love. God is the one "who did not spare his own Son but gave him up for us all" (Rom 8:32). This Pauline allusion to the Akedah appears twice in Aquinas's discussion of whether the Father delivered up the incarnate Son to his crucifixion: question 47, article 3 of the *tertia pars*. According to Aquinas, God gave Christ the fullness of grace and the most perfect charity, and this charity moved Christ to embrace the Cross as the most loving act that Christ could undertake on behalf of the whole human race. Aquinas states, "The Father delivered up Christ, and Christ surrendered Himself, from charity."[93]

When he contemplates the restoration of the fallen human race by Christ, Aquinas holds together "furtherance in good" and "withdrawal from evil."[94] Christ enables us not only to be reconciled to God but also to be elevated into the divine life. Indeed, the latter is

---

[92] See chapter 2 of my *Jesus and the Demise of Death: Resurrection, Afterlife, and the Fate of the Christian* (Waco, TX: Baylor University Press, 2012); and chapter 3 of my *Did Jesus Rise from the Dead? Historical and Theological Reflections* (Oxford: Oxford University Press, 2019).

[93] III, q. 47, a. 3, ad 3.

[94] III, q. 1, a. 2.

intrinsic to the reconciliation that God accomplishes in Christ. In the relational order of justice inscribed in creation, what humans owe to God, the giver of life, is our whole selves. The intrinsic penalty of turning away from the life-giver is death. Christ entered into this penalty by undergoing death as a perfect self-offering in love. As Aquinas says, Christ on the Cross offered "the sacrifice of one suffering out of charity" and Christ enacted perfect "charity in offering up His own flesh."[95]

This action restored the order of justice or reconciles humanity to God, through Christ's "exceeding charity" and "the dignity of His life which He laid down in atonement."[96] His offering was so great in its ontological reality – both its supreme love (and, correspondingly, its sorrow for sins) and the fact that it was the incarnate Lord who offered his bodily life out of love – that the relational order of justice was superabundantly restored. Christ thereby transformed human death from a penalty into a pathway to eternal life, where the blessed will share in God's life and love. Thus, in Christ's offering, as in the Akedah, death and restoration are united. Aquinas remarks, "Christ's Passion wrought our salvation, properly speaking, by removing evils; but the Resurrection did so as the beginning and exemplar of all good things."[97] Forever bearing his wounds, Christ even now stands before the Father – joined by the members of his body the Church – in the posture of the supremely loving self-offering that we sinners could not have achieved for ourselves.

Much more could be said about the ontological character of Christ's self-offering according to Aquinas, but it should be clear that his speculative probing of atonement in the *tertia pars* gets at the ontological heart of New Isaac Christology.

---

[95] III, q. 48, a. 3, ad 1 and ad 3.
[96] III, q. 48, a. 2.
[97] III, q. 53, a. 1, ad 3.

3.7 Conclusion

I have emphasized that at the center of Jesus' crucifixion and Resurrection is the meaning of sacrifice and God's promise of blessing, despite the depths of sin and death. The Akedah teaches us about the sacrificial worship we are to offer and about the mode of our salvation. In Isaac, we see an obedient sacrificial "death" and "resurrection" that hint at something more, namely, a greater offering by the God of covenantal love and blessing.

Sacrifice, at its core, pertains not only to offering something to God but also to the overcoming of violence and death and the establishment of everlasting communion and joy with God in love, in accord with God's own nature as love. The *New* Isaac undergoes a miraculous birth and vicarious death, along with a joyful rescue from death, and he exhibits active and free obedience, love, and covenant faithfulness. To be able to mediate the fullness of divine blessings, the New Isaac must be the "only begotten" and "beloved" son not merely of a man but *of God*. He is the sacrificial "ram/Lamb" and risen Lord who simultaneously embodies divine and human covenantal fidelity and who accomplishes the blessing of the whole world. The New Isaac freely enters into death on behalf of all, and in this self-offering he is perfectly consecrated to the Father. In this way, the New Isaac accomplishes the transcendent fulfillment of the Temple.

Jesus Christ, in going up to Jerusalem on that fateful Passover, fulfilled the logic of the Akedah as the beloved Son, unleashing the divine presence in and through a confrontation with human and demonic wickedness. He does this for us through his profound charity and absolute obedience to God the Father by the power of the Holy Spirit. Thomistic Christology will benefit from seeking him in his "Father's house" (Jn 14:2), as the eschatological New Isaac.

4 | Christ the New Moses

The Eschatological Exodus

4.1 Introduction

In *Echoes of Scripture in the Gospels*, Richard Hays subtitles his chapter on the Gospel of Matthew "Torah Transfigured."[1] Hays describes Israel's Scriptures as read by Matthew as "an elaborate figurative tapestry."[2] Matthew understands the central figures of Israel to be types of Jesus, and indeed Jesus himself is Israel; he stands in for the whole people. Jesus thereby functions as the suffering servant of Isaiah 53, so that he is "the one in whom the fate of Israel is embodied and enacted."[3]

In this chapter, I examine Jesus as the New Moses, focusing especially on the Gospel of Matthew. As Hays says, "Matthew's narrative ... produces wide-ranging echoes of Israel's traditions about Moses."[4] Both Moses and Jesus barely avoid death as infants under tyrannical rulers; both Moses and Jesus come forth from Egypt; both Moses and Jesus fast for forty days and forty nights; both Moses and Jesus proclaim authoritative teaching; both Moses and Jesus receive a theophany at the top of a mountain. In Matthew 28, the risen "Jesus' commissioning of his disciples on the mountain in Galilee is reminiscent of the commissioning of Joshua in

---

[1] Richard B. Hays, *Echoes of Scripture in the Gospels* (Waco, TX: Baylor University Press, 2016), 105.
[2] Hays, *Echoes of Scripture in the Gospels*, 108.
[3] Hays, *Echoes of Scripture in the Gospels*, 113.
[4] Hays, *Echoes of Scripture in the Gospels*, 143.

Deuteronomy 31:23 and Joshua 1:1–9."[5] As the *New* Moses, Jesus at the same time goes decisively beyond Moses in many respects.

Like Hays, Brant Pitre has shown the significance of "Jesus' implicit modeling of his actions on the figure of Moses."[6] Jesus' words and deeds as recorded in the Gospels are interpreted by Pitre "in light of the early Jewish hope for a new Moses and a new exodus."[7] He finds numerous parallels between Moses in the Torah, the Servant in Isaiah, and Jesus in the Gospels.[8] With Ben Meyer, Pitre holds that "it is highly probable that ... Jesus took the promise of a prophet like Moses (Deut 18:15, 18) to await its fulfillment in the end-time – and concretely to find this fulfillment in his own act of bringing to completion the last measure, the fullness, of revealed truth."[9] Pitre focuses especially upon the significance of Jesus' self-understanding as the New Moses for Jesus' actions at the Last Supper. Jesus held that Israel's covenantal story was building toward an eschatological fulfillment, and the figure of the New Moses was part of that eschatological vision, rooted in various texts of Israel's highly typological Scriptures. Not only the evangelists

---

[5] Hays, *Echoes of Scripture in the Gospels*, 145.
[6] Brant Pitre, *Jesus and the Last Supper* (Grand Rapids, MI: Eerdmans, 2015), 85.
[7] Pitre, *Jesus and the Last Supper*, 66. As Pitre notes somewhat earlier, "although the imagery of a new Moses or the prophet like Moses is certainly not the most abundantly attested idea in Jewish Scripture, it does occur in two of the most popular and widely read biblical books in ancient Judaism: the book of Deuteronomy and the book of Isaiah. This seems to have led the notion to become rather influential in the development of Jewish hopes for the future" (Pitre, *Jesus and the Last Supper*, 62).
[8] See Gordon Paul Hugenberger, "The Servant of the Lord in the 'Servant Songs' of Isaiah: A Second Moses Figure," in *The Lord's Anointed: Interpretation of Old Testament Messianic Texts*, ed. P. E. Satterthwaite, R. S. Hess, and G. J. Wenham (Grand Rapids, MI: Baker, 1995), 105–40.
[9] Ben F. Meyer, "Appointed Deed, Appointed Doer: Jesus and the Scriptures," in *Authenticating the Activities of Jesus*, ed. Bruce Chilton and Craig A. Evans (Leiden: Brill, 1999), 155–76, at 171; cited in Pitre, *Jesus and the Last Supper*, 56. On the same page, Pitre similarly quotes Ben Witherington III's statement that "Jesus may well have seen himself as the Mosaic prophet of the eschatological age" (Witherington, *The Christology of Jesus* [Minneapolis, MN: Fortress, 1990], 101).

but also, Pitre argues, Jesus himself saw the connections between Moses' and Jesus' words and deeds.

The present chapter proceeds in four steps in advocating that contemporary Thomistic Christology should integrate the theme of the New Moses. First, I examine patristic testimony to Jesus as the New Moses. Such testimony is rare, but there is a notable exception: Eusebius of Caesarea's creative and biblically rich *The Proof of the Gospel*. Second, at some length, I explore the New Moses Christology found in the Gospels of Matthew and John. Since these Gospels do not explicitly state that Jesus is the New Moses, discerning their New Moses Christology requires literary and historical sensitivity to the allusions present in the Gospels. I rely here especially upon Dale Allison's *The New Moses*, which prepared the ground for more recent studies and whose insights remain current.[10] Third, I suggest how appreciation of Christ as the New Moses is found in Aquinas's writings and may enhance Thomistic Christology's understanding of Christ, the sacraments, and the Old and New Law. Fourth and finally, I reflect upon the ways in which Aquinas engages the ontological realities under discussion in this chapter.

4.2 Christ the New Moses: The Patristic Witness

In *On Pascha*, Melito of Sardis observes that Christ's Paschal mystery is prefigured by Moses (exposed to die as an infant), and also by Abel, Isaac, Joseph, David, and the prophets.[11] Melito's view of typology is rather harsh toward the holy ones of Israel. He states,

---

[10] Dale C. Allison, Jr., *The New Moses: A Matthean Typology* (Minneapolis, MN: Fortress, 1993). See most recently, indebted especially to Allison but also to Pitre and others, Patrick Schreiner's *Matthew, Disciple and Scribe: The First Gospel and Its Portrait of Jesus* (Grand Rapids, MI: Baker Academic, 2019), 131–67.

[11] Melito of Sardis, *On Pascha: With the Fragments of Melito and Other Material Related to the Quartodecimans*, trans. Alistair Stewart-Sykes. 2nd ed. (Yonkers, NY: St. Vladimir's Seminary Press, 2016), 68.

"When the thing comes about of which the sketch was a type, that which was to be, of which the type bore the likeness, then the type is destroyed, it has become useless, it yields up the image to what is truly real. What was once valuable becomes worthless when what is of true value appears."[12] For his part, Origen of Alexandria argues that the Passover prefigures Christ. In light of John 3:14, Origen comments, "For if he [Christ] had said: 'Just as Moses performed the Passover in Egypt, so too must Christ suffer,' it would be incontestable that the passion took place as antitype of the passover," but in fact the serpent hung on the wood is the antitype of the Passion.[13] The Passover lamb is a type of Christ. Thus, Origen does not connect Moses typologically with Christ. Instead, Christ is the "Lamb of God" (Jn 1:36) rather than a new Moses.

Origen's portrait of Moses is appreciative, but for Origen the true exodus is for those who are spiritual, not carnal like the Egyptians.[14] Commenting on Romans 7:23, where Paul describes the "law of sin" dwelling in his members, Origen emphasizes that the Mosaic Law does not "generate the vices of sins."[15] He treats with respect the laws of Leviticus, given by God to Moses, as well as God's commandment regarding circumcision. Yet, he also holds that "the fleshly Jew keeps the law, but the spiritual man and the Jew in secret perfects it" by keeping it according to the Spirit rather than according to the letter.[16]

---

[12] Melito of Sardis, *On Pascha*, 60.

[13] Origen, "Treatise on the Passover," in Origen, *Treatise on the Passover and Dialogue of Origen with Heraclides and His Fellow Bishops on the Father, the Son, and the Soul*, trans. Robert J. Daly, S.J. (New York: Paulist Press, 1992), 27–56, at 35.

[14] See Origen, *Treatise on the Passover*, 53.

[15] Origen, *Commentary on the Epistle to the Romans: Books 6–10*, trans. Thomas P. Scheck (Washington, DC: Catholic University of America Press, 2002), VI.7.16, p. 27.

[16] Origen, *Commentary on the Epistle to the Romans: Books 1–5*, trans. Thomas P. Scheck (Washington, DC: Catholic University of America Press, 2001), II.13.7, p. 146. Admittedly, this condition – the Spirit rather than the letter – is a significant one that leads Origen into some lamentable anti-Jewish polemic. See for instance Origen, "Homilies on Genesis," Homily XIII, in Origen, *Homilies on Genesis and Exodus*, trans. Ronald E. Heine (Washington, DC: Catholic University of America Press, 1981), 47–224, at 190–91.

4.2 CHRIST THE NEW MOSES: THE PATRISTIC WITNESS

In commenting on Exodus's account of the birth of Moses, Origen does not hesitate to draw numerous connections to Christ and the Church. Even so, he again does not depict Christ as a New Moses. On the contrary, he understands "Moses" to symbolize the Torah or the Old Testament. Christ's role, then, is to help the Church to understand the Torah properly. The Church finds "Moses" (the Torah) "in the marsh lying cast off by his own people and exposed," and the Church purifies the Torah through the enlightenment brought by baptism.[17] The Torah is finally understood when read in the light of the New Testament. Origen says offensively, "It [the Torah] was dirty and enclosed in cheap and offensive meanings of the Jews until the Church should come from the Gentiles and take it up from the muddy and marshy places and appropriate it to itself within courts of wisdom and royal houses."[18] Christ is the one who raises up "Moses" by revealing the spiritual meaning of the Torah, thereby enabling Moses to become "totally magnificent, totally distinguished, totally elegant."[19]

Origen makes clear, however, that in his view the historical Moses knew the elevated meanings, the spiritual understanding of the Torah.[20] Origen's Moses believed in Christ, even while speaking and acting in figures. When Moses withdrew from the "Egypt of vices" and when he lifted up his arms in battle through "the power of the cross of Christ," then Moses conquered, "and truly that of

---

[17] Origen, "Homilies on Exodus," Homily II, in Origen, *Homilies on Genesis and Exodus*, 227–387, at 246.

[18] Origen, "Homilies on Exodus," Homily II, 246.

[19] Origen, "Homilies on Exodus," Homily II, 247. Understood rightly, Origen contends, the Torah is not susceptible to the calumnies of the Gnostics.

[20] See Origen, "Homilies on Exodus," Homily III, 252–53. Origen goes on to remark, "Do not suppose, therefore, that Moses led the people out of Egypt only at that time. Even now Moses, whom we have with us – 'for we have Moses and the prophets' – that is, the Law of God, wishes to lead you out of Egypt. If you would hear it, it wishes to make you 'far' from Pharao. If only you would hear the Law of God and understand it spiritually, it desires to deliver you from the work of mud and chaff" (Origen, "Homilies on Exodus," Homily III, 254).

which Moses gave a figure is fulfilled in us."[21] Even though Moses is not a type of Christ, he is a type of Christians and of the Church. And since "Moses" represents "Torah" and indeed is the Torah, Moses contains Christ. Comparing the rod used so powerfully by Moses to the Cross of Christ, Origen remarks: "[T]his cross which Moses, that is the Law, contains, as the Lord said: 'For he wrote about me,' this cross, I say, of which Moses wrote, after it was cast forth in the earth, that is once it came to be believed in by men, was changed into wisdom and such a great wisdom that it devoured all the wisdom of the Egyptians, that is of the world."[22]

Augustine, too, does not explicitly envision Christ as a New Moses. When Christ goes up the mountain to deliver the Sermon on the Mount, Augustine, in commenting on the description given in Matthew 5:1, does not draw a connection to Moses other than a negative contrast: "If it is asked what the 'mountain' means, it may well be understood as meaning the greater precepts of righteousness; for there were lesser ones which were given to the Jews."[23] Augustine values Moses as preeminent among God's "holy prophets and servants" who "gave the lesser precepts to a people who as yet required to be bound by fear."[24] These lesser precepts – above all the Decalogue – might have paved the way for Augustine to reflect on Jesus as the New Moses (transcending Moses' lawgiving as the Messianic lawgiver, recapitulating Mount Sinai), but Augustine does not follow this path. Instead, he simply emphasizes Christ's preeminence and the preeminence of Christ's teachings. Regarding

---

[21] Origen, "Homilies on Exodus," Homily III, 259.
[22] Origen, "Homilies on Exodus," Homily IV, 267–68. See also the background in Nicholas de Lange, *Origen and the Jews: Studies in Jewish-Christian Relations in Third-Century Palestine* (Cambridge: Cambridge University Press, 1976).
[23] Augustine, "Our Lord's Sermon on the Mount," I.1, trans. William Findlay, rev. by D. S. Schaff, in *Augustine: Sermon on the Mount, Harmony of the Gospels, Homilies on the Gospels*, vol. 6 of Nicene and Post-Nicene Fathers, First Series, ed. Philip Schaff (Peabody, MA: Hendrickson, 1995), 3–63, at 4.
[24] Augustine, "Our Lord's Sermon on the Mount," I.1, p. 4.

4.2 CHRIST THE NEW MOSES: THE PATRISTIC WITNESS

Christ's preeminence, he states that now (in Matthew 5:2) "He is said to have opened His own mouth, whereas under the old law He was accustomed to open the mouths of the prophets."[25] The fact that Christ teaches from a mountain "mean[s] that the one Master alone fit to teach matters of so great importance teaches on a mountain," but Augustine does not mention Moses.[26]

Regarding the preeminence of Christ's teachings, Augustine argues that the Jews were not yet ready for God's greatest teachings, and therefore God had to lead them through teachings about an earthly kingdom. In a manner that is negative toward the Jewish people and overly positive about most Christians, Augustine says that God "gave the lesser precepts to a people who as yet required to be bound by fear; and ... through His Son, gave the greater ones to a people whom it had now become suitable to set free by love."[27] When Jesus goes on in the Sermon on the Mount to teach with authority – saying of the Torah "You have heard that it was said," and then augmenting or even correcting the Torah, "But I say to you" (Mt 5:21–22) – Augustine does not observe that Jesus is acting here as a "New Moses." Instead, in Pauline fashion, he connects Moses with the precepts of fear that have to do with an earthly kingdom.

In *Answer to Faustus, a Manichean*, where he defends the goodness of the Old Testament, Augustine directs attention to 1 Corinthians 10:1–4: "[O]ur fathers were all under the cloud, and all passed through the sea, and all were baptized into Moses in the cloud and the sea, and all ate the same supernatural food and all drank the same supernatural drink. For they drank from the supernatural Rock which followed them, and the Rock was Christ." Being "baptized into Moses" suggests a Moses–Jesus typology, with Jesus as a new and much greater Moses, but Augustine does not mention this

---

[25] Augustine, "Our Lord's Sermon on the Mount," I.1, p. 4.
[26] Augustine, "Our Lord's Sermon on the Mount," I.1, p. 4.
[27] Augustine, "Our Lord's Sermon on the Mount," I.1, p. 4.

aspect. The "supernatural Rock" that "was Christ" clearly differs from Moses himself. Moses leads the people rather than following them, whereas the Rock is said to follow them. Augustine emphasizes that the "spiritual food," the manna, is a type of Christ.[28]

Augustine is closer to seeing a New Moses typology when, in *Answer to Faustus, a Manichean*, he comments on Jesus' saying to Nicodemus, "And as Moses lifted up the serpent in the wilderness, so must the Son of man be lifted up, that whoever believes in him may have eternal life" (Jn 3:14–15). Augustine argues that Moses, by lifting up the bronze serpent on a rod, is extending his hands "in the sign of the cross."[29] In this way, Moses makes a sign that is a type of Christ's Cross. But the connection that Augustine makes is between the bronze serpent and Christ, not between Moses and Christ. Similarly, referring to God's miraculously transforming Moses' staff into a serpent in Exodus 4:2–4, Augustine says that Christ "is made known to me in the staff of Moses, which became a serpent on the earth and prefigured his death, which came from a serpent. But the fact that, when it was grasped by its tail, it became a staff again signifies that afterwards, when he has carried out everything at the end of his work, he returns to what he had been by rising."[30]

Augustine certainly is appreciative of Moses. He strongly criticizes the Manicheans, who refuse to "listen to Moses and the prophets [cf. Lk 16:31]."[31] His faith is inseparable from the testimony of Moses. He believes that the historical Moses knew of the salvation wrought by Christ's Cross, and he thinks this is why Moses symbolized the Cross by raising the bronze serpent on a rod. But, again, Augustine does not present Christ as the New Moses.

---

[28] See Augustine, *Answer to Faustus, a Manichean*, trans. Roland J. Teske, S.J., ed. Boniface Ramsey (Hyde Park, NY: New City Press, 2007), XII.30, p. 144.

[29] Augustine, *Answer to Faustus, a Manichean*, XII.30, pp. 144–45.

[30] Augustine, *Answer to Faustus, a Manichean*, XII.28, p. 143.

[31] Augustine, *Answer to Faustus, a Manichean*, XII.4, p. 128. In his translator's "Introduction" to *Augustine's Commentary on Galatians: Introduction, Text, Translation, and Notes*, trans. Eric Plumer (Oxford: Oxford University Press, 2003),

4.2 CHRIST THE NEW MOSES: THE PATRISTIC WITNESS

As noted above, a Church Father who does portray Christ as the New Moses is Eusebius of Caesarea. In his lengthy and biblically erudite *The Proof of the Gospel* – a masterpiece that is neglected today, perhaps because of Eusebius's effusive praise of Emperor Constantine – Eusebius pays careful attention to Moses and the Mosaic Law. He thinks of the Mosaic Law as medicine ordained by God to heal the Israelites from the superstitions and idolatries of Egypt.[32] It is a law solely for the Israelites, and therefore when God redeems the whole world, he changes the Torah through Christ. Eusebius affirms that Jesus Christ lived in accordance with the Mosaic Law and thereby brought it to fulfillment and instituted the "Gospel Law," "a legislation new and salutary for all men."[33]

Eusebius highlights Deuteronomy 18:15's prophecy, from the lips of Moses, that God will raise up a prophet like Moses who must be obeyed. This prophet, in order truly to be like Moses, must be a lawgiver. Otherwise, he would be lesser than and different from Moses. Prophets such as Isaiah and Jeremiah were not lawgivers, and Joshua

---

1–121, Eric Plumer observes: "The Manichees were ... deeply offended at Moses for the curse he pronounced on Jesus when he said, *Cursed is everyone who hangs on a tree* (Deut. 21:23). Augustine responds by saying that Moses was speaking prophetically, knowing full well that for our sakes Christ would bear the curse pronounced on humanity following the sin of Adam. In other words, Moses foresaw that Christ would take upon himself our curse in order to do away with it" (64).

[32] See Eusebius, *The Proof of the Gospel*, trans. W. J. Ferrar (Eugene, OR: Wipf and Stock, 2001), Book I, ch. 6, p. 34. Eusebius believes that "Moses himself foresaw by the Holy Spirit, that, when the new covenant was revived by Christ and preached to all nations, his own legislation would become superfluous" (34).

[33] Eusebius, *The Proof of the Gospel*, Book I, ch. 7, p. 43. Eusebius comments, "For if He had been a transgressor of the Law of Moses, He would reasonably have been considered to have rescinded it and given a contrary law: and if He had been wicked and a law-breaker He could not have been believed to be the Christ. And if He had rescinded Moses' Law, He could never have been considered to be One foretold by Moses and the prophets. Nor would His new Law have had any authority. For He would have had to embark on a new Law, in order to escape the penalty of breaking the old. But as a matter of fact He has rescinded nothing whatever in the Law, but fulfilled it" (Eusebius, *The Proof of the Gospel*, Book I, ch. 7, pp. 43–44).

was neither a prophet nor a lawgiver. Jesus Christ was a lawgiver, "giving a Law to all nations" and perfecting and fulfilling the Mosaic Law with authority.[34] In Eusebius's view, emphasizing the preeminent value of antiquity, Jesus' law is the same as that known to Melchizedek and the other holy men and women who lived before the Mosaic Law. Yet Jesus has written his law of holiness upon the hearts of his followers, thus fulfilling Jeremiah 31's prophecy.[35]

In Book III of *The Proof of the Gospel*, Eusebius returns to Deuteronomy 18:15 and 18:18, arguing again that Jesus is the expected prophet like Moses. Eusebius offers an extended comparison of Moses and Jesus, showing that Jesus is indeed the New Moses. Moses was the greatest leader of the people of Israel, the first and only lawgiver, and the teacher of the true worship of the one God. Jesus did what Moses did, but now for the whole world. He was the first to teach the true worship to the whole world and the first lawgiver for the whole world. Moses authenticated his authority by means of miracles; so, in a greater way, did Jesus. Moses delivered the Israelites from Egyptian slavery; Jesus delivered the whole human race from slavery to idols. Moses promised a holy land and a holy people; Jesus makes a greater promise in both regards, by promising "the heavenly country which suits souls that love God," that is, "the kingdom of heaven."[36]

Continuing in the same vein, Eusebius notes that Moses fasted forty days and forty nights, and so did Jesus the New Moses. Moses fed the people miraculously in the wilderness, and so, repeatedly, did Jesus the New Moses. Moses walked dry-shod across the Red Sea; Jesus outdid him, walking on top of the sea. Moses controlled the sea miraculously, and so did Jesus by calming the sea. Moses descended Mount Sinai

---

[34] Eusebius, *The Proof of the Gospel*, Book I, ch. 7, p. 45.
[35] Eusebius states: "The one wrote on lifeless tables, the Other wrote the perfect commandments of the new covenant on living minds" (Eusebius, *The Proof of the Gospel*, Book I, ch. 8, p. 48).
[36] Eusebius, *The Proof of the Gospel*, Book III, ch. 2, p. 105.

with his face shining with glory; Jesus' face shone at the mount of Transfiguration. Moses cleansed a leper (Miriam); Jesus too cleansed a leper. Moses received the Torah written by the finger of God; Jesus did miracles by the "finger of God" (Mt 12:27). Moses established seventy men as leaders of the people; Jesus chose seventy of his disciples and sent them on mission. Moses sent twelve men to spy out the promised land; Jesus sent forth his twelve apostles. Moses condemned murder, adultery, theft, and lying; Jesus intensified each of these commandments. No one knew where Moses was buried; no one saw Jesus rise from the dead.

It follows that Jesus is the prophet like Moses promised in Deuteronomy 18:15 and 18:18. As Eusebius says, "If then no one but our Saviour can be shown to have resembled Moses in so many ways, surely it only remains for us to apply to Him, and to none other, the prophecy of Moses, in which he foretold that God would raise up one like unto himself."[37] In sum, Jesus is the New Moses.

4.3 The New Moses in the Gospel of Matthew and the Gospel of John

Let me now turn to the New Testament evidence for Jesus as a New Moses. To set forth this evidence, I will rely upon biblical scholars who have a mastery of typological allusions in the New Testament. The weight of my attention will be given to the Gospel of Matthew, but New Moses Christology also has a significant place in the Gospel of John, as we will see.[38]

In *The New Moses: A Matthean Typology*, Dale Allison observes that Matthew understands Israel's history to be guided by divine providence, so that "history becomes the arena of promise and

---

[37] Eusebius, *The Proof of the Gospel*, Book III, ch. 2, p. 108; translation slightly altered.
[38] See also the New Moses Christology argued for in D. P. Moessner, *Lord of the Banquet: The Literary and Theological Significance of the Lukan Travel Narrative*

fulfillment, type and antitype, prefiguration and manifestation."[39] At the heart of all history stands the Messiah in whom the meaning of history becomes apparent. Matthew considers everything in Israel's Scriptures to presage Jesus Christ. Of course, other figures in Scripture are also presented as a new Moses, especially Joshua, Elijah, Josiah, and Ezra. There are also passages in the Book of Ezekiel where the prophet Ezekiel appears as a new Moses. As Allison observes, Jon Levenson makes much of this connection in his *Theology of the Program of Restoration of Ezekiel 40–48*.[40] Ezekiel is a new Moses because Ezekiel gives cultic laws, which places him in a Mosaic role.

As Allison says, there seems to have been a broad expectation in Jesus' era that a Mosaic prophet would arrive and lead an eschatological deliverance of the people – even if the Qumran community expected a Mosaic prophet who would not be the Messiah. The hope for a coming Mosaic prophet and deliverer derived from Deuteronomy 18:15. There is evidence for the expectation of such a prophet in Josephus, who describes a few failed would-be prophets. The Gospel of John reports that after Jesus performed a feeding

---

(Minneapolis, MN: Fortress, 1989). Although Allison does not agree with Moessner's view of Luke 9–19, Allison demonstrates with ease that Luke's Gospel is replete with portraits of Jesus as a New Moses leading a new exodus. The Letter to the Hebrews depicts Jesus explicitly as the New Moses, as in Hebrews 3:2–3, 5–6 and 8:5–7. Paul does not offer a New Moses Christology, although he does conceive of the Christian life as a new exodus in 1 Corinthians 10. In fact, Paul at times presents himself as a new Moses, as for instance in Romans 9:2–3. Some Church Fathers, including Basil the Great, described the third-century Bishop Gregory Thaumaturgis ("Wonderworker") as a new Moses. Others linked Anthony the Desert Father to Moses; certainly in Athanasius's *Life of Anthony*, the holy hermit comes forth from his solitude on the mountain filled with the glory of divine wisdom. The fourth-century deacon Ephrem the Syrian received the same treatment in Jacob of Serug's panegyric to him, and Gregory of Nyssa's panegyric to his brother Basil also contains comparisons with Moses. Even Constantine, in Eusebius's hands, receives Mosaic colors.

[39] Allison, *The New Moses*, 288.
[40] See Jon D. Levenson, *Theology of the Program of Restoration of Ezekiel 40–48* (Missoula, MT: Scholars Press, 1976).

miracle, the people who experienced it said to each other, "This is indeed the prophet who is to come into the world!" (Jn 6:14). Allison demonstrates that typology in this period generally functioned through allusions rather than in a more explicit way, and he also demonstrates that a link with Moses was seen "to exalt a man and make him like the ideal king, savior, prophet, lawgiver, or intercessor."[41]

Allison's first case study is the infancy narrative, Matthew 1:18–2:23. These verses contain no mention of Moses. How then could there plausibly be a New Moses Christology here? Allison begins by noting the presence in Matthew 2:15 of Hosea 11:1, "Out of Egypt have I called my son," which Allison deems to be a new exodus motif. Jesus is presented as the new Israel (cf. Exodus 4:22) but also, like Moses, as a leader who is called out of Egypt. Matthew 2:19–21 echoes Exodus 4:19–20, with the infant Jesus being called back from exile to lead the new exodus.

Moreover, Josephus's *Antiquities* (2:210–16) relates the story that Moses' father Amram feared Pharaoh's command to the midwives to kill the Israelites' male infants. God appeared to Amram in a dream assuring him that Moses would live and be great. In Matthew 1:19–21, Joseph has a similar experience as Amram. Joseph learns from God in a dream that Jesus will be great and that he should not think that Mary has committed fornication. In Matthew 2:21, God commands Joseph to name his son "Jesus" ("God saves"), because "he will save his people from their sins." Similarly, Josephus's *Antiquities* (2:228) identifies the Egyptian name "Moses" as meaning "saved out of the water." Again, Josephus claims that the reason Pharaoh ordered the Israelite male infants to be killed is that he had come to learn that the future liberator of the Israelites had been born (*Antiquities* 2:205–09). This parallels Herod's learning from the Magi that the king of the Jews had been born. In *Antiquities* (2:206), Josephus reports that upon hearing about the

---

[41] Allison, *The New Moses*, 93.

birth of Israel's future liberator, Pharaoh was greatly fearful, just as Herod "was troubled" (Mt 2:3). The infant Moses is providentially preserved by God and eventually has to flee from Pharaoh; the infant Jesus is providentially preserved from Herod's murderous fear by God, who instructs Joseph in a dream, "Rise, take the child and his mother, and flee to Egypt" (Mt 2:13). Josephus also reports that Moses' mother Jochebed had no pain in childbirth, thus miraculously avoiding the curse of Genesis 3:16. Mary's childbearing similarly is miraculous.[42]

Allison argues that the story of the temptation of Jesus in Matthew 4:1–11 also presents Jesus as a New Moses. He considers that there was an original source for the temptation story, a source ("Q") that Matthew shared with Luke. In the original source, he believes, Jesus represents the people of Israel; Jesus succeeds where Israel, in Exodus 16–17 and 32, gave way to temptation. Allison thinks, however, that Matthew has "overlaid the existing Israel typology with specifically Mosaic motifs."[43] Specifically, he points to Matthew 4:2: "And he fasted forty days and forty nights." This detail connects Jesus with Moses in Exodus 24:18, as well as with Elijah (emulating Moses) in 1 Kings 19:8. Philo and Josephus both mention Moses' fasting for forty days and forty nights. In Allison's view, the addition of "forty nights" is what makes the Mosaic allusion evident, since the phrase "forty days and forty nights" is applied in Israel's Scriptures only to the fasting of Moses and Elijah.

Another passage from the temptation story that Allison finds redolent with Mosaic associations is Matthew 4:8: "[T]he devil took him to a very high mountain, and shown him all the kingdoms of the world and the glory of them." Moses, in Numbers 27 and Deuteronomy 32 and 34, is taken up Mount Pisgah (or Nebo or Abarim) by God and

---

[42] Allison relates the above details in *The New Moses*, 144–48. He also notes that later Rabbinic Jewish texts attribute further miracles to Jochebed's childbearing, including the notion that she was restored to virginal maidenhood.
[43] Allison, *The New Moses*, 166.

4.3 THE NEW MOSES IN THE GOSPEL OF MATTHEW

shown the promised land. Allison notes some verbal parallels that unite Matthew 4:8–9 and Deuteronomy 34:1–4, and he also points out that Matthew alone includes the detail "to a very high mountain." In the *Apocalypse of Abraham* 12–13, Abraham receives a vision not only of the promised land but of the entire cosmos, and this vision is followed by Abraham's being tempted by Satan (or Azazel). Although there are many points of difference between *Apocalypse of Abraham* 12–13 and Matthew 4, Allison suggests that their similarities indicate that a typological link to Moses has in both cases been developed. Allison adds that in Matthew 28, the risen Jesus obtains from God the very kingdom that he had refused when Satan offered it to him. In a somewhat similar fashion, Philo depicts Moses as giving up royal reign over Egypt (which Philo thinks Moses, having been raised by a princess, could have had), only to obtain a better reign over Israel from the hand of God.

Surely the most important instance of New Moses Christology in the Gospel of Matthew is the Sermon on the Mount. Allison begins his discussion of this passage by quoting the Congregation of the Doctrine of the Faith's (CDF)1986 "Instruction on Christian Freedom and Liberation," in which the CDF identifies Jesus as "the new Moses" due to his Sermon on the Mount.[44] As Allison says, many scholars have argued that Matthew's Gospel places Jesus on a mountain in order to draw a parallel with Moses giving the Torah from Mount Sinai. He notes that Luke locates Jesus' sermon on a plain, whereas Matthew deliberately moves it to a mountain. He also observes that the Greek phrase "went up on the mountain" (Mt 5:1) occurs twenty-four times in the LXX, almost always in reference to Moses. Jesus' sitting down on the mountain in order to teach has a parallel in Deuteronomy 9:9, where Moses recalls, "I remained on the mountain forty days and forty nights." The Hebrew word for "remained" often has the meaning "sit," and Rabbinic Jewish texts interpret it as "sit" in Deuteronomy 9:9. Matthew likely is doing

---

[44] Congregation of the Doctrine of the Faith, "Instruction on Christian Freedom and Liberation," March 22, 1986, §62, cited in Allison, *The New Moses*, 172.

the same. This would fit with Philo's claim that Moses sat beside God on Sinai. The scribes who write the law for forty days and forty nights in *4 Ezra* 14, similarly, are described as sitting – likely because Moses himself was thought to have done so at Sinai. In addition, the Sermon on the Mount concludes with the following statement: "When he came down from the mountain, great crowds followed him" (Mt 8:1). Allison shows that Exodus 34:29, in the LXX, uses almost this same language for Moses' descent from Sinai after receiving the Torah.

In Matthew 5:17–20, Jesus promises that he has not come to overturn the Mosaic Torah but has instead come to intensify the Torah. Whereas Moses forbids murder, for instance, Jesus forbids anger, which is the root of murder. Jesus has the authority to intensify the Torah because he is the Messianic New Moses, or, as Allison puts it, "the Moses-like Messiah who proclaims the eschatological will of God on a mountain typologically equated with Sinai."[45] In a number of late Second Temple texts (including from Qumran), the Messiah was expected to bring a divine teaching. As noted, many expected the Messiah to be a Moses-like prophet, in accord with Deuteronomy 18. The Messiah was expected to teach wisdom. Some Qumran documents, such as the *Temple Scroll*, appear to go so far as to make some changes to the Torah in light of the imminent kingdom.[46] In John 4:25, the Samaritan woman expresses the expectation that the Messiah, when he comes, "will show us all things." Paul speaks of a "law [or Torah] of the Messiah" (Gal 6:3). Thus, as a lawgiver, the Messiah was expected, in certain circles at least, to be a New Moses. It seems likely that Matthew represents such a perspective.

For Allison, the Sermon on the Mount's status as evidence of New Moses Christology is strengthened by the concluding portion,

---

[45] Allison, *The New Moses*, 185.
[46] Here Allison relies upon M. O. Wise, *A Critical Study of the Temple Scroll from Qumran Cave 11* (Chicago: Oriental Institute, 1990); Wise, "The Eschatological Vision of the Temple Scroll," *Journal of Near Eastern Studies* 49 (1990): 155–72.

4.3 THE NEW MOSES IN THE GOSPEL OF MATTHEW

Matthew 7:13-27. Allison shows that Matthew 7:13-14 describes the two ways, 7:15-23 warns against false prophets, and 7:24-27 compares the wise builder and the foolish builder. This pattern fits with that found in Deuteronomy 28-32. Allison argues that Matthew has shaped the material to reflect Deuteronomy. He observes that the transitional formula found in 7:28 – "And when Jesus finished" – appears four other times in Matthew's Gospel and reflects a formula found in Deuteronomy 31:1, 31:24, and 32:45 – "When Moses had finished."

Allison points out that during the time in which Israel was worshipping the Golden Calf, Moses was the sole representative of the true Israel, and "as with the first redeemer, so with the last: if Moses once constituted the people of God, the Mosaic Messiah did no less."[47] This is an important insight, insofar as it shows how Jesus' representation of sinners on the Cross fits with the New Moses theme.

Allison also shows that there is reason to think that the miracles presented immediately after the Sermon on the Mount – miracles that occupy Matthew 8-9 – extend the New Moses Christology. Although Allison remains hesitant about whether there really is a parallel here, there are some suggestive elements.[48] For instance, the ten plagues of Egypt are equaled in Matthew 8-9 by ten miracles. Jesus' healing of a leper parallels Moses' healing of a leper. Jesus' calming of the sea parallels Moses' ability to part the sea. Just as the plagues form three groups of three, so too with the miracles of Jesus in Matthew 8-9. Allison is made hesitant mainly by the fact that the tenth miracle (in Matthew 9:33) does not appear to be climactic, unlike the tenth plague.

More securely, Allison holds that Jesus' great thanksgiving in Matthew 11:25-30 – where Jesus thanks God for revealing his mysteries

---

[47] Allison, *The New Moses*, 199.
[48] Allison is here drawing upon B. W. Bacon, *Studies in Matthew* (New York: Henry Holt, 1930), 187-89.

to the humble, proclaims that "no one knows the Father except the Son and any one to whom the Son chooses to reveal him," and invites people to come to him for help in carrying their burdens – has Mosaic foundations. Specifically, Jesus is putting himself in the place of Moses, who knew God face to face (see Exodus 33:11–23, Numbers 12:1–8, and Deuteronomy 34:9–12). Jesus is thereby claiming the competence to lead the new exodus. Like Moses, Jesus is meek and humble and has a unique personal knowledge of God. To follow Jesus means to find spiritual rest, just as God promised Moses (Israel's representative) on the exodus, "My presence will go with you, and I will give you rest" (Exod 33:14). Jesus is a *New* Moses because he "knows the Father" far more intimately than Moses could. Jesus knows the entirety of revelation, or "all things" (Mt 11:27). This is much more than the biblical Moses knew, although the Moses of Jewish tradition – including Ezekiel the Tragedian's *Exagogue* as well as (seemingly to a lesser degree) *Jubilees* – does indeed see all things. Moreover, when Jesus exhorts his followers, "Take my yoke upon you" (Mt 11:29), there is an evident connection to the "yoke of wisdom" (Sir 6:30) or the "yoke" of the Torah (Jer 5:5).[49]

Allison gives other evidence for New Moses Christology in Matthew 11:25–30. He notes that the ordering of Matthew 11:27, beginning with "no one knows the Son except the Father" before moving to "no one knows the Father except the Son," seems strange until one recalls that in Exodus 33:12–13 God's knowledge of Moses is first affirmed, prior to Moses requesting to know God. Allison also remarks that 1 Corinthians 13:12, "For now we see in a mirror dimly, but then face to face," is in certain ways close to Matthew 11:27, which is notable given that Paul is here alluding to Moses in Numbers 12:8. Similarly, John 15:15, where Jesus calls his disciples "friends," likely alludes to Exodus 33:11, where God is depicted as speaking to Moses as to a friend. Allison adds that Jesus' command in Matthew 11:29, "learn from me," indicates that

---

[49] See Allison, *The New Moses*, 226.

4.3 THE NEW MOSES IN THE GOSPEL OF MATTHEW

Jesus is Torah or wisdom incarnate. As such, Jesus represents Moses, the lawgiver, most perfectly. In speaking of the Torah, first-century Jews often spoke simply of "Moses," and so Jesus is the New (and greater) Moses. Another factor is that the verb used in Matthew 11:27, "All things have been delivered [*paradidōmi*] to me by my Father," is used in certain contexts for the transmission of the law to Moses.

Allison finds possible New Moses Christology in Matthew 15:15–21's reference to the Servant of Isaiah 42, when combined with other clear or likely references to the Servant in Matthew 8:17, 17:5, 20:28, and 26:28. Moses is frequently labeled God's "servant," as, for example, in Numbers 12:7–8. Allison argues that the connection between Isaiah's "servant" and a new Moses may have been known to Matthew, since "Matt. 26:28 mixes allusions to Exod. 24:8 and Isa. 53:12. Here exodus and servant themes meet."[50] Jesus' pouring himself out as a self-sacrificial atonement offering (see Matthew 20:28 and 26:28) may recall Moses' offering of himself in Exodus 32:32 on behalf of the people. At the same time, Allison does not think demonstrative evidence is present with respect to whether Matthew intended to tie his Servant Christology to his New Moses Christology.

Similarly, Allison considers it possible that in Matthew's accounts of Jesus' feeding miracles (Matthew 14:31–21 and 15:29–39), Matthew intended to make a connection to the manna and to a new exodus. The second feeding miracle is reported by Matthew in a manner intended to link it to the Sermon on the Mount. Allison deems it likely that Matthew has the manna in view: "In Matthew's Jewish-Christian world the exodus from Egypt, the last supper, and the Messianic banquet were not three isolated events.... The exodus had been typologically recapitulated at the last supper ... and would again be typologically recapitulated at the consummation."[51]

---

[50] Allison, *The New Moses*, 234.
[51] Allison, *The New Moses*, 242.

CHRIST THE NEW MOSES: THE ESCHATOLOGICAL EXODUS

Allison has no doubt that the Transfiguration narrative of the Gospel of Mark aims to connect Jesus with Moses on Sinai. He shows this by listing the parallels between Mark 9:2–10 and Exodus 24 and 34. He remarks with regard to the Transfiguration narrative, "Matthew rescripted Mark in order to push thoughts towards Moses" – that is, even more toward Moses than is already found in Mark.[52] Allison emphasizes the connection to Moses' descent from Mount Sinai, when "Moses did not know that the skin of his face shone because he had been talking with God" (Exod 34:29) and when, as a result, Aaron and the other Israelites feared to come near him.

Allison sees New Moses Christology in three other places: Matthew 21:1–17 (Jesus' entrance into Jerusalem to the acclaim of the crowd), Matthew 26:17–30 (the Last Supper), and Matthew 28:16–20 (the encounter of the disciples with the risen Jesus). Briefly, let me explain Allison's reasons. In Matthew 21:5, Jesus – through a quotation from Zechariah – is described as humble or meek, an ascription that, as noted above, alludes to Moses. In Matthew 21:16, Jesus quotes Psalm 8:2, which both Wisdom of Solomon 10:21 and Rabbinic Judaism linked with Exodus 15:2 and Israel's song of praise for its deliverance. Matthew 21:15, in referring to the chief priests and scribes seeing "the wonderful things that he [Jesus] did," employs the same Greek terms as does LXX Deuteronomy 34:12's praise of "all the mighty power and all the great and terrible deeds which Moses wrought in the sight of all Israel." Allison even suggests a possible connection between Matthew 21:5, where Jesus rides into Jerusalem on two animals, and Moses' return to Egypt to deliver the people in LXX Exodus 4:20.

In Matthew 26:17–30, the evangelist presents Jesus' Last Supper as a Passover meal. This would connect it with Moses and the exodus. Jesus' reference to his "blood of the covenant" (Mt 26:28) echoes Exodus 24:8, where Moses sprinkled the people with the blood of the covenant. The phrase "for the forgiveness of sins" (Mt 26:28) likely also contains a link with Exodus 24:8, as becomes apparent

---

[52] Allison, *The New Moses*, 244.

4.3 THE NEW MOSES IN THE GOSPEL OF MATTHEW

when it is read in light of Hebrews 9:19-22, "where it is taken for granted that the blood Moses sprinkled was for the forgiveness of sins."[53] Matthew 26:19 parallels Exodus 12:28, not only in structure and in vocabulary but also in content, thereby strengthening the link between Jesus and Moses. The centerpiece of Allison's argument is that Matthew's Last Supper narrative follows the same approach taken by Hebrews 9 – thus making Jesus a New Moses.

Lastly, regarding Matthew's presentation of the risen Jesus in 28:16-20, Allison points out that such mountain scenes are typically Mosaic. He notes that Jesus' command to his disciples, "[teach] them to observe all that I have commanded you" (Mt 28:20), is a commissioning narrative of a kind that in Israel's Scriptures is consistently Mosaic.[54] Moreover, the relevant commissioning narratives in Israel's Scriptures involve Moses (or God) commissioning Joshua, just as Jesus is commissioning his disciples. A similar instance is found in *The Testament of Moses*, strengthening the case that the words employed by the evangelist in Matthew 28:20 are related to Deuteronomy 31:14-15 and Joshua 1:1-9. Allison adds some reasons for supposing that Matthew intentionally ended his gospel by highlighting Jesus as the New Moses: "Just as the lawgiver, at the close of his life, commissioned Joshua both to go into the land peopled by foreign nations and to observe all the commandments in the law, and then further promised his successor God's abiding presence, so similarly Jesus" commissioned his disciples, telling them to observe all his commandments and promising them his presence.[55]

Is Allison, then, implying that the theme of the New Moses is decisive for Matthew's presentation of Jesus? The answer is no. Allison himself calls for modesty: "The new Moses theme remains one of many things [in Matthew's Gospel], and not the most

---

[53] Allison, *The New Moses*, 258-59.
[54] See B. J. Hubbard, *The Matthean Redaction of a Primitive Apostolic Commissioning* (Missoula, MT: Society of Biblical Literature, 1974); cited in Allison, *The New Moses*, 263.
[55] Allison, *The New Moses*, 266.

important."⁵⁶ Besides, as Allison emphasizes, Matthew is not alone in presenting Jesus as the New Moses: The Gospel of John and the Letter to the Hebrews do so strongly, and the theme is not absent in the other Gospels, Acts, 1 Peter, Paul, and the Book of Revelation, at least through new exodus typology.

Allison's perspective is strengthened by recognition of a pattern that he briefly notes in his conclusion. Namely, the Gospel of Matthew mirrors Exodus's portrait of Moses by tracing Jesus through an infancy narrative (Exod 1:1–2:10), a crossing of water (Exod 14:10–31), a temptation in the wilderness (Exod 16:1–17:7), a mountain of lawgiving (Exod 19:1–23:33), a unique personal intimacy with God (Exod 33:1–23), and a transfiguration (Exod 34:29–35). Matthew also begins and ends his gospel with a New Moses reference, and he understands Jesus' self-sacrificial death and the Last Supper in light of Moses. Given all this, it may be that Allison actually understates his case. Of course, the Gospel of Matthew only explicitly mentions Moses seven times, and these references are not the significant ones for the Moses–Jesus relationship. An ancient writer did not need to make a typology explicit.

In his *Jesus as Israel*, Peter Leithart affirms that "Allison's thesis is compelling," but he believes it needs to be augmented and adjusted.⁵⁷ Leithart proposes that Matthew's New Moses Christology largely runs its course by the tenth chapter of Matthew's Gospel. Furthermore, he holds that even in the first chapters of Matthew's Gospel, Matthew's central concern is to present Jesus as the embodiment of Israel. As Leithart remarks, this need not be set in opposition to New Moses Christology, because Moses himself "is the representative Israel."⁵⁸ Creatively, Leithart argues that the

---

⁵⁶ Allison, *The New Moses*, 267.
⁵⁷ Peter J. Leithart, *The Gospel of Matthew through New Eyes*, vol. 1, *Jesus as Israel* (Monroe, LA: Athanasius Press, 2017), 10.
⁵⁸ Leithart, *Jesus as Israel*, 15n31, with reference to William F. Albright, *Matthew: A New Translation with Introduction and Commentary* (New York: Doubleday, 1971), 18.

4.3 THE NEW MOSES IN THE GOSPEL OF MATTHEW

Gospel of Matthew recapitulates the unfolding of Israel's history: Chapters 1–9 highlight Moses typology, 10–12 Joshua and David typology, 13 Solomon typology, 14–18 Elijah and Elisha typology, and 19–27 Jeremiah typology. The exodus and Torah are followed by the following events: the conquest of the land, the kingship and wisdom teaching, the formation of a faithful Israel in the midst of Israel, and the prophetic condemnation of Israel and its exile (with Jesus' Resurrection being his return from exile). With regard to chapters 8–9, where Allison proposed a connection to the Egyptian plagues, Leithart directs attention to the ten rebellions of Israel in the wilderness.[59]

Leithart offers helpful correctives to some interpretations that we found in Allison's work. Notably, he points out that the Sermon on the Mount does not simply have to do with intensifying the Torah by interiorizing it but, instead, involves numerous commandments regarding concrete external actions. Leithart and Allison agree that Jesus is not trying to overturn the Torah, although Leithart aptly comments that Jesus in numerous places amplifies the Torah in a way that stands as a corrective to the plain sense of the Torah.

---

[59] See Leithart, *Jesus as Israel*, 23–27. For the opposite perspective on Matthean typology, see Ben Witherington III, *Matthew* (Macon, GA: Smyth & Helwys, 2006), 69: "[I]t cannot be argued that Matthew or the First Evangelist makes much of Jesus being seen as Israel; rather he is seen as the King of the Jews and the Son of David, the one sent to free Israel, not to be Israel. Nor is there any sort of parallel with the story of Moses here [Mt 2:13–18], because Jesus is not said to be born in Egypt, and his family flees to Egypt." Similarly, when Witherington treats the Sermon on the Mount, he argues that we should simply read it as the wisdom teaching – in which law is included but not in an exclusive way – of the "great Davidic king" (Witherington, *Matthew*, 114). Even though Witherington wrote a decade after Allison, similar perspectives were well known to Allison. For a better recent approach, noting that for Matthew "Jesus is not simply Moses but one greater than Moses" and also arguing that "Matthew's story [in Mt 2:13–18] ... presents Jesus 'the Son of God' as the personification of Israel" – so that "Jesus-as-Israel is embarking on a new exodus," see Ian Boxall, *Discovering Matthew: Content, Interpretation, Reception* (Grand Rapids, MI: Eerdmans, 2014), 88.

For my purposes in this chapter, Leithart's affirmation that Matthew presents Jesus as the New Moses especially with regard to the Sermon on the Mount is significant. By contrast, Ulrich Luz holds that "the Moses typology is by no means the basic framework within which the Sermon on the Mount is to be interpreted."[60] With respect to the Sermon on the Mount, Luz does not think Matthew is presenting Jesus "programmatically as a second Moses," although he recognizes that Matthew is associating Jesus with Moses.[61] I think Luz is too strict with regard to what counts as a truly typological allusion, since he rules out all but the clearest. With Leithart and Allison, and against Luz, W. S. Baxter holds that Matthew's infancy narrative, the Sermon on the Mount, the Transfiguration, and the Last Supper show that for Matthew "Moses is a type of Christ."[62] For Baxter, however, the question is whether Matthew intentionally arranged his Gospel with the purpose of demonstrating that Jesus is the eschatological Moses. He argues that if Matthew had wanted to do this, then he would have explicitly made his case by openly comparing Jesus to Moses – as do the Gospel of John and Hebrews. For my purposes, it is not necessary to claim that Matthew built his Christology on the foundation of New Moses allusions.[63] Matthew may not intend to make the case that Jesus should be *primarily* understood as the New Moses, but neither does Matthew merely "color his gospel with Mosaic imagery."[64] There is a middle ground.

Let me add a few remarks on New Moses Christology in the Gospel of John before bringing this section to a close. Wayne

---

[60] Ulrich Luz, *Matthew 1–7: A Commentary*, trans. James E. Crouch, ed. Helmut Koester (Minneapolis, MN: Fortress, 2007), 182.

[61] Luz, *Matthew 1–7*, 182.

[62] W. S. Baxter, "Mosaic Imagery in the Gospel of Matthew," *Trinity Journal* 20 (1999): 69–83, at 80.

[63] Baxter is worried that typological allusions are not adequate for confidently drawing a "formal Christology" out of Matthew's Gospel (Baxter, "Mosaic Imagery in the Gospel of Matthew," 81).

[64] Baxter, "Mosaic Imagery in the Gospel of Matthew," 81.

4.3 THE NEW MOSES IN THE GOSPEL OF MATTHEW

Meeks's *The Prophet-King: Moses Traditions and the Johannine Christology* served as a valued source for Allison's work. Meeks's central argument is that John's references to Jesus the eschatological king are not simply an instance of New David Christology but rather should also be thought of in light of New Moses Christology. I am persuaded, with Allison, that Meeks is correct to posit the importance of Deuteronomy 18:18–22 for John 7. Jesus the Mosaic prophet-king has full knowledge of all reality, offers perfect intercession for Israel's sins, and is not conquered by death.[65] Yet, for Meeks, one has a New Moses Christology only when matters are made fully explicit. Since John does not do this, Meeks supposes that John does not intend "to depict Jesus as a 'new Moses.'"[66] I disagree with Meeks that a typology need be explicit. Likewise, the fact that John sees Jesus as greater than Moses certainly does not mean – as Meeks thinks it does – that Jesus is not a New Moses. On the contrary, it is precisely as the *New* Moses that "Jesus fulfills for the believer those functions elsewhere attributed to Moses" and "does this in a superior and exclusive way."[67]

Meeks shows that "John 17, which stands as a formal summary of Jesus' total mission, connects that mission in two important respects with the Sinai theophany, that is, with precisely the event that established Moses as Prophet and King of Israel."[68] Meeks thinks that Second Temple legends about Moses' ascent are connected in the Gospel of John with Jesus' Ascension. Nevertheless,

---

[65] For background see Wayne Meeks, *The Prophet-King* (Eugene, OR: Wipf and Stock, 2017), 156, 159–60. Meeks later observes, "In some circles of both Judaism and Samaritanism Moses was regarded as the prototypal king and prophet of Israel. The foundation of his prophetic-royal mission, in this view, was his enthronement in heaven (the Sinai theophany), where he received the Torah and, with or within it, all truth. From that moment he became God's emissary or agent ... and his vice-regent on earth" (Meeks, *The Prophet-King*, 286).
[66] Meeks, *The Prophet-King*, 319.
[67] Meeks, *The Prophet-King*, 319.
[68] Meeks, *The Prophet-King*, 291; cf. 304.

the latter (due to its claim that Jesus is enthroned on the Cross) is not strictly "dependent on the Moses traditions for its fundamental structure."[69] Whatever may be the case in this regard, Meeks reiterates that John's sense of Jesus as the Son sent by the Father flows from his understanding of Moses, God's prophetic agent.[70] He also observes that the Farewell Discourse, which concludes with John 17, reflects the closing chapters of Deuteronomy.[71] Similarly, just as Moses judges Israel by his Torah, Jesus judges Israel by his word. In Jewish tradition, Moses is also understood as Israel's shepherd (just as David is), and Meeks deems that the "Moses traditions did provide some of the material for the Good Shepherd symbolism."[72]

Francis Glasson's *Moses in the Fourth Gospel* details numerous typological connections between the Johannine Jesus and Moses, as for instance that "just as Moses when leaving the world appointed Joshua as shepherd (Num. 27.16–18) so Jesus appoints Peter as shepherd (John 21)."[73] Connections noted by Glasson include Moses' serving Joshua (a point found in Jewish traditions, not in Scripture) just as Jesus washed his disciples' feet; Moses' giving his glory and his Spirit to Joshua (Numbers 27:20; Deuteronomy 34:9); and Moses and Joshua acting as shepherd to the people (Numbers 27:17; Psalm 77:20). Both Moses and Jesus are murmured against, and both are threatened with stoning (see Exodus 17:4). Both are intercessors. Both experience their faces shining with glory. A number of new exodus elements, such as the new manna and the living water, are associated with Jesus. Glasson also argues that the Gospel of John presents Jesus as the fulfillment of the promise of a future prophet like Moses, found in Deuteronomy 18:15–18.[74]

---

[69] Meeks, *The Prophet-King*, 297.
[70] See Meeks, *The Prophet-King*, 305.
[71] See Meeks, *The Prophet-King*, 304n3.
[72] Meeks, *The Prophet-King*, 313.
[73] T. Francis Glasson, *Moses in the Fourth Gospel* (London: SCM Press, 1963), 84.
[74] See Glasson, *Moses in the Fourth Gospel*, 30.

In John 1:14–18, God reveals Jesus' glory to the disciples just as at Sinai God had revealed his glory to Moses: The disciples, not Jesus, stand here in the place of Moses.[75] Undoubtedly, Jesus is far greater than Moses. Jesus is the divine Word, and Moses a mere human. But still it is the case, as Craig Keener says, that "the briefest acquaintance with the biblical tradition could lead observers to suspect him [Jesus] as a sort of new Moses."[76] Keener grants that "Jesus is to some degree a new Moses in John."[77] So Jesus is indeed, and this fact – not by itself but in conjunction with the other ways in which the New Testament presents Jesus – should be important for Thomistic Christology.

4.4 Thomistic Christology and Christ the New Moses

Aquinas does not discuss Christ as the New Moses in the *Summa theologiae*. Nevertheless, his *Summa* includes an extensive discussion of the Old and New Laws, and he pays a good deal of attention to Moses. As Franklin Harkins says of Aquinas, "Moses stands as a seminal figure in his systematic works, appearing over 250 times in the *Summa theologiae* alone."[78] Aquinas treats Moses as a wise teacher who knows the divine mysteries, including the Christological and Trinitarian mysteries (for the latter, Genesis 1:1–3 has particular significance).[79] In Aquinas's view, Moses accommodated his teachings to his audience, so that his audience could receive, according to their more limited mode of understanding, what Moses

---

[75] See Craig S. Keener, *The Gospel of John: A Commentary*, vol. 1 (Grand Rapids, MI: Baker Academic, 2003), 405.
[76] Keener, *The Gospel of John*, vol. 1, 278.
[77] Keener, *The Gospel of John*, vol. 1, 291.
[78] Franklin T. Harkins, "*Primus Doctor Iudaeorum*: Moses as Theological Master in the *Summa Theologiae* of Thomas Aquinas," *The Thomist* 75 (2011): 65–94, at 66.
[79] Harkins points out, "In the opening chapter of Genesis, according to Thomas's reading, Moses clearly taught the Father, Son, and Holy Spirit as distinct divine persons" (Harkins, "*Primus Doctor Iudaeorum*," 74).

knew in a fuller way. Aquinas thinks that Moses' exalted knowledge comes from the grace of revelation: God spoke to Moses face to face, although Aquinas is unsure whether this actually entailed Moses seeing the divine essence.[80] Harkins sums up, "Moses, as human author of the Torah and teacher of Trinity, creation, and Christ, occupies a central position not only in the comprehensive theological enterprise of Thomas Aquinas, but also in the divinely ordained plan of *exitus-reditus* that the *Summa* aims to elucidate."[81]

Although the *Summa* does not contain explicit New Moses Christology but instead contains much about Moses himself, Aquinas's *Commentary on the Gospel of Matthew* does present Jesus as a New Moses at various places. Discussing Matthew 4:2 (Jesus' temptation in the desert), for instance, Aquinas points out that Jesus, Moses, and Elijah fasted for fifty days.[82] Similarly, commenting on Matthew 5:3 (the first beatitude) Aquinas states, "Hence just as Moses first set down the commandments, and afterwards said many things which were all referred back to the commandments given, so Christ in his teaching first sets forth these beatitudes, to which all the others are reduced."[83] Such comparisons indicate that Christ is like Moses and so in this sense a new Moses but not perhaps *the* New Moses. More suggestive with regard to the latter is Aquinas's remark on Matthew 11:11, where Aquinas identifies Abraham and Moses as "precursors

---

[80] On this topic, as Harkins shows, Aquinas takes different positions in his *Summa Theologiae*, trans. Fathers of the English Dominican Province (Westminster, MD: Christian Classics, 1981), I-II, q. 98, a. 3 and II-II, q. 174, a. 4.

[81] Harkins, "*Primus Doctor Iudaeorum*," 75–76. Harkins adds, "By teaching Christ figuratively, Moses fulfilled the teaching office for his Jewish pupils, whose nescience prevented them from comprehending divine truths explicitly" (Harkins, "*Primus Doctor Iudaeorum*," 87). For further background, see the chapter on the Mosaic law in my *Paul in the "Summa Theologiae"* (Washington, DC: Catholic University of America Press, 2014).

[82] See Thomas Aquinas, *Commentary on the Gospel of Matthew, Chapters 1–12*, trans. Jeremy Holmes and Beth Mortensen, ed. The Aquinas Institute (Lander, WY: The Aquinas Institute for the Study of Sacred Doctrine, 2013), §313, p. 102.

[83] Aquinas, *Commentary on the Gospel of Matthew, Chapters 1–12*, §411, p. 132.

4.4 THOMISTIC CHRISTOLOGY AND CHRIST THE NEW MOSES

of the Lord."[84] Likewise, when Aquinas treats the Sermon on the Mount, he gives five reasons why Jesus "opened his mouth and taught" the crowd only after ascending "the mountain" (Mt 5:1-2). The fifth reason is that a mountain is connected with the giving of the Torah.[85] Aquinas here implies that Jesus occupies the role of the New Moses, delivering divine teaching to the people from a mountain.

With respect to Matthew 17:3, Aquinas proposes that one reason why Moses appeared at Jesus' Transfiguration was to highlight Jesus' possession of the Mosaic attribute of meekness.[86] Aquinas does not state explicitly that Jesus is the New Moses, but his comparison implies it. Again, commenting on Matthew 27:45, he notes that just as Moses stretched out his hands with the result that the Lord brought the plague of darkness upon Egypt for three days (Exod 10:22), so also Jesus "spread out his hands on the cross, and a darkness was cast for three hours."[87] A remark in his treatise *On the Perfection of the Spiritual Life* also deserves mention here. Aquinas states that in Deuteronomy 5:1, where Moses acts in the role of a mediator between God and the people, Moses is "speaking as a type [figuram] of Our Lord" – with Christ as the fulfillment of this type, the one mediator and New Moses.[88]

Somewhat less along the lines of New Moses Christology, but still relevant, is an instance from his *Commentary on the Gospel of John*. In discussing John 3:14 – "And as Moses lifted up the serpent in the wilderness, so must the Son of man be lifted up" – Aquinas perceives

---

[84] Aquinas, *Commentary on the Gospel of Matthew*, Chapters 1–12, §917, p. 340.

[85] See Aquinas, *Commentary on the Gospel of Matthew*, Chapters 1–12, §399, p. 128.

[86] See Thomas Aquinas, *Commentary on the Gospel of Matthew*, Chapters 13–28, trans. Jeremy Holmes, ed. The Aquinas Institute (Lander, WY: The Aquinas Institute for the Study of Sacred Doctrine, 2013), §1428, p. 117.

[87] Aquinas, *Commentary on the Gospel of Matthew*, Chapters 13–28, §2380, p. 444.

[88] Thomas Aquinas, "On the Perfection of the Spiritual Life," in *St. Thomas Aquinas and the Mendicant Controversies: Three Translations*, trans. John Proctor, O.P., ed. Mark Johnson (Leesburg, VA: Alethes Press, 2007), 237–323, at 283.

that Moses' intercession with God to prevent the punishment of the people in Numbers 21 is paralleled by the intercessory and merciful role of Christ's Passion. But, while he compares the bronze serpent to Christ, Aquinas does not here compare Moses to Christ.[89]

In both his *Commentary on John* and his *Commentary on Matthew*, Aquinas makes clear that Jesus is indeed the prophet foretold in Deuteronomy 18:15, a prophet like Moses. Recall that although Deuteronomy 34:10 teaches that "there has not arisen a prophet since in Israel like Moses, whom the Lord knew face to face," Deuteronomy 18:15 promises a New Moses. Commenting on John 7:40, where in response to Jesus' words "some of the people said, 'This is really the prophet,'" Aquinas remarks: "They did not just call him a prophet, but the prophet, thinking that he was the one about whom Moses foretold: *the Lord your God will raise up a prophet for you from your brothers ... you will listen to him* (Deut 18:15).[90] Here it is clear that Jesus, as the promised Mosaic prophet, truly is *the* New Moses. Aquinas makes the same point in commenting on Matthew 13:57, where Jesus explains why he did not perform many miracles in his home town of Nazareth: "*[B]ut Jesus said to them: a prophet is not without honor, except in his own country*. The Lord calls himself a prophet; nor is this a marvel, since Moses also called him a prophet: *the Lord your God will raise up to you a prophet of your nation and of your brethren like unto me* (Deut 18:15)."[91] In other words, Jesus is the promised New Moses.

Overall, these texts make clear that Aquinas sees Moses as a central precursor of Jesus, and he suggests that Jesus' attributes and

---

[89] Thomas Aquinas, *Commentary on the Gospel of John: Chapters 1–5*, trans. Fabian Larcher, O.P., and James A. Weisheipl, O.P., ed. Daniel Keating and Matthew Levering (Washington, DC: Catholic University of America Press, 2010), §473, p. 178.

[90] Thomas Aquinas, *Commentary on the Gospel of John: Chapters 6–12*, trans. Fabian Larcher, O.P., and James A. Weisheipl, O.P., ed. Daniel Keating and Matthew Levering (Washington, DC: Catholic University of America Press, 2010), §1098, pp. 93–94.

[91] Aquinas, *Commentary on the Gospel of Matthew, Chapters 13–28*, §1212, p. 43. The text in italics was originally also in bold.

4.4 THOMISTIC CHRISTOLOGY AND CHRIST THE NEW MOSES

deeds often compare in a significant manner with those of Moses. At certain points, Aquinas is quite clear: Jesus is the New Moses. It will equally be clear that Aquinas does not particularly thematize or give a central role to New Moses Christology, even in the places where he most clearly brings it forward.

In my view, there are some places in the *secunda pars* and *tertia pars* of the *Summa theologiae* where Aquinas's Christology and his doctrines of the Old and New Laws and of grace open pathways for Thomistic Christology to amplify the New Moses theme. Servais Pinckaers has highlighted the importance of the Sermon on the Mount for Aquinas's moral theology.[92] This provides an opening for reflection on Christ the New Moses precisely in his teaching or *doctrina*. In III, q. 42, a. 1, on whether Christ should have taught not only Jews but also Gentiles, Aquinas affirms that "it was fitting that Christ's preaching, whether through Himself or through His apostles, should be directed at first to the Jews alone." An explicit New Moses Christology could expand upon the reasons that Aquinas gives in defense of this fittingness, given that Christ is the prophet like Moses foretold in Deuteronomy 18:15. In III, q. 42, a. 2, Aquinas asks whether Christ should have preached to his fellow Jews without offending them. It seems that the offense caused by *Moses'* words, and the resultant murmuring of the people against Moses, might shed further light upon why Christ preached as he did.

In Aquinas's *quaestio* on Christ's *doctrina*, he does not treat the Sermon on the Mount. Discussion of the Sermon and its eschatological beatitudes would place Christ's status as the New Moses front and center. Particularly important might be Matthew 7:13–27, where Jesus concludes his Sermon by echoing the two ways and the comparison between wise and foolish builders that we find in Moses' speech in Deuteronomy 28–32.

---

[92] See Servais Pinckaers, O.P., *The Sources of Christian Ethics*, trans. Mary Thomas Noble, O.P. (Washington, DC: Catholic University of America Press, 1995).

Aquinas's treatment of Christ's knowledge in III, question 9 could be another place for explicit recourse to New Moses Christology. As we saw, Allison compares Jesus' words about his unique knowledge of the Father with the statements about Moses' intimate knowledge of God found in Exodus 33:11–23, Numbers 12:1–8, and Deuteronomy 34:9–12. Aquinas thinks that Moses probably experienced a temporary vision of God's essence. This point provides an opportunity for presenting Christ as a New Moses in this regard, as do the Gospels.

Regarding the question of whether it was fitting that Christ be transfigured (III, q. 45, a. 1), the shining of Moses' face can easily be integrated into Aquinas's approach. The Transfiguration resonates with the theme of the eschatological new exodus. Aquinas observes that the fittingness of the Transfiguration has to do with Christ's desire to instruct his disciples about the road that they must follow, namely, one of suffering that leads to beatitude. Aquinas remarks, "Now in order that anyone go straight along a road, he must have some knowledge of the end: thus an archer will not shoot the arrow straight unless he first see the target.... Above all is this necessary when hard and rough is the road, heavy the going, but delightful the end."[93] At the Transfiguration, Christ gives a glimpse of the end (glory). New Moses Christology helps to locate the discussion of the Transfiguration firmly within the new exodus that is so central to the New Testament proclamation, given that the goal of the new exodus is everlasting glory.

As Brant Pitre and others have shown, in order to understand the New Testament's theology of the Cross and Resurrection, as well as the New Testament's Eucharistic theology, ecclesiology, and eschatology, it is important to appreciate the significance of the new exodus. Consider for instance Pitre's chapter on "The Paschal Tribulation, the Death of Jesus, and the New Exodus" in

---

[93] III, q. 45, a. 1.

4.4 THOMISTIC CHRISTOLOGY AND CHRIST THE NEW MOSES

his *Jesus, the Tribulation, and the End of the Exile: Restoration Eschatology and the Origin of the Atonement*.[94] In this chapter, Pitre describes Jesus as the Servant and the Shepherd Messiah. Above, we saw both the Servant and the Shepherd in Matthew's and John's New Moses Christology. There is also a notable parallel between Jesus' words at the Last Supper regarding the "blood of the covenant" (Mt 26:28) and Exodus 24:8, where Moses sprinkles the blood of the covenant upon the people during the exodus. In *Jesus and the Last Supper*, Pitre devotes a chapter to Jesus as the New Moses, with a focus on Jesus' feeding miracles, the "blood of the covenant," and the new bread of the presence. Pitre notes that "Jesus spoke and acted on occasion as if he were the long-awaited prophet like Moses (e.g., Matt 14:13–21; Mark 6:30–44; Luke 9:10–17; John 6:1–15; Matt 12:39–42; Luke 11:29–32; Mark 8:12, etc.)."[95] Furthermore, Pitre argues that Jesus instituted the "new bread and wine of the presence" in a manner that reveals him to be "modeling the various circles of his disciples on the priestly hierarchy of Mount Sinai."[96]

Thus, Christ as the New Moses could form part of the discussion of Christ's priesthood in III, question 22. Here Aquinas remarks that "as to others, one is a lawgiver, another is a priest, another is a king; but all these concur in Christ."[97] This is of course true, and its truth – along with its implications for the Eucharist and ecclesiology – is especially clear in light of Christ the New Moses. Similarly, New Moses Christology could be integrated into Aquinas's theology of the Eucharist, beginning with his discussion of the Old Testament "figures" of the Eucharist in III, q. 73, a. 6.

---

[94] Brant Pitre, *Jesus, the Tribulation, and the End of the Exile: Restoration Eschatology and the Origin of the Atonement* (Grand Rapids, MI: Baker Academic, 2005).
[95] Pitre, *Jesus and the Last Supper*, 139.
[96] Pitre, *Jesus and the Last Supper*, 141.
[97] III, q. 22, a. 1, ad 3.

Aquinas's treatment of the Mosaic Law is rich and detailed, as I have discussed elsewhere.[98] It inspires reflection on Christ as a lawgiver, even if the New Law that Christ gives is primarily the Holy Spirit rather than primarily specific teachings. Christ gives the Holy Spirit, just as Moses in a certain sense bestows the Spirit (as noted above). Christ also teaches "certain things that dispose us to receive the grace of the Holy Ghost, and pertaining to the use of that grace."[99] Attention to Christ as the New Moses can be a way of probing Aquinas's exposition of the continuities and notable differences between the Mosaic Law and the Law of Christ. In I-II, q. 108, aa. 1–4, Aquinas treats the precepts of the New Law in detail. Indebted to Augustine, Aquinas states that "the sermon, which Our Lord delivered on the mountain, contains the whole process of forming the life of a Christian."[100] This point is valuable indeed, and it has been developed recently by such theologians as Servais Pinckaers and William Mattison.[101]

Allison shows that Matthew's infancy narrative brims with allusions suggesting that Jesus is the New Moses. Thus, the theme of the New Moses could have a place within Aquinas's discussion in III, question 36 of the manifestation of Christ's birth. For example, the link to Pharaoh and the slaying of the newborn Israelite male children could be exploited in question 36, which inquires into whether Christ's birth was inappropriately made known, given that when Herod heard of it he slaughtered the infants in the region of Bethlehem.

Quite possibly, a whole question devoted to the new exodus – and thus in part to Christ the New Moses – might fit within the *tertia*

---

[98] See for example my "Aristotle and the Mosaic Law," in *Aristotle in Aquinas's Theology*, ed. Gilles Emery, O.P., and Matthew Levering (Oxford: Oxford University Press, 2015), 70–93; and my "Thomas Aquinas on Law and Love," *Angelicum* 94 (2017): 413–41.
[99] I-II, q. 106, a. 1.
[100] I-II, q. 108, a. 3.
[101] See William C. Mattison III, *The Sermon on the Mount and Moral Theology: A Virtue Perspective* (Cambridge: Cambridge University Press, 2017).

4.4 THOMISTIC CHRISTOLOGY AND CHRIST THE NEW MOSES

pars immediately after question 59. The eschatological new exodus offers an excellent way of transitioning from Christ to the sacraments, since this theme might strengthen the sense of the role of the sacraments within the inaugurated kingdom. Given that many of the great sacramental types are found in the exodus (the Passover lamb, the manna, the water from the Rock, the pillar of cloud, the crossing of the sea, and so on; see 1 Corinthians 10), the New Moses and new exodus themes form a natural connection between the *Summa*'s Christology and its sacramental theology. Equally, the New Moses and new exodus themes would fit into III, question 61 on the necessity of the sacraments, helping to show how "the state of the New Law is between the state of the Old Law, whose figures are fulfilled in the New, and the state of glory, in which all truth will be openly and perfected revealed."[102]

In the Christology of the *tertia pars*, there is not a question about Christ as a prophet, although there are questions about Christ's knowledge and about Christ's teaching. New Moses Christology might therefore envision a question on Christ as prophet next to the question on Christ as priest. Pitre comments in his chapter on Jesus as the New Moses, "If there is anything that is virtually uncontested in the highly contested world of Jesus scholarship, it is the conclusion that Jesus likely spoke and acted in ways that identified him as a prophet."[103] More specifically, Jesus likely saw himself as the prophet like Moses promised in Deuteronomy 18.[104] Aquinas certainly considered Jesus to be the promised prophet like Moses. Thus, a question in the *tertia pars* on Jesus as prophet would fit well with the theme of Christ the eschatological New Moses.

---

[102] III, q. 61, a. 4, ad 1.
[103] Pitre, *Jesus and the Last Supper*, 53.
[104] Pitre directs attention to Dale C. Allison, Jr., *Constructing Jesus: Memory, Imagination, and History* (Grand Rapids, MI: Baker Academic, 2010), 270–73; Craig S. Keener, *The Historical Jesus of the Gospels* (Grand Rapids, MI: Eerdmans, 2009); and Scot McKnight, *Jesus and His Death: Historiography, the Historical Jesus, and Atonement Theory* (Waco, TX: Baylor University Press, 2005), 197–200.

4.5 An Ontological Note

Ontologically, the concept of the "New Moses" especially involves the essence of the covenant: namely, law and grace. Exploring God's covenantal relationship with his people, Aquinas investigates God's working by law and grace. As an "extrinsic" principle moving his people to good and away from evil, God acts in a twofold way: He "instructs us by means of His law, and assists us by His grace."[105] At the core of God's covenantal relationship with Israel is the gift of divine law. According to Aquinas, law is a participation in God's eternal law or wisdom for human flourishing. The attainment of human beatitude requires not only law but also grace, because God calls us to a supernatural beatitude that is not possible to attain on the basis of human resources alone. Fallen humans need to be healed and elevated so as to live in accord with God's law of selfless love.

In Aquinas's view, as we have seen, the Mosaic Law contains both instruction in how to live as God's people and preparations for Jesus Christ and the Church. By faith in Christ as prefigured in the Mosaic Law, people under Israel's covenants can live in a state of grace, and thus already under the Law of Christ. In addition, in the moral teachings of the Mosaic Law, Aquinas finds the natural law spelled out. The natural law is also present in the Mosaic Law's teachings about acts of religion and in the Mosaic Law's teachings about political, judicial, and economic arrangements. The Mosaic Law cannot in itself accomplish the justification that the Law of Christ accomplishes. Nevertheless, the Mosaic Law "foreshadowed [its fulfillment] by certain ceremonial actions, and promised it in words."[106]

Aquinas considers grace itself to be a "law" insofar as grace interiorly regulates and rectifies action. The Law of Christ has two

---

[105] I-II, q. 90, Prologue; translation slightly altered.
[106] I-II, q. 107, a. 1.

elements: primarily the interior infusion of grace and secondarily the "teachings of faith, and those commandments which direct human affections and human actions."[107] Although God is the giver of both Laws, he gives the Mosaic Law by writing it "on tables of stone," which are carried to the people by Moses, and he gives the New Law in Christ who, by his Cross and Resurrection, accomplishes salvation.[108] The risen Christ, with the Father, pours out the Holy Spirit into human hearts.

The core of the covenant is found in the fact that "man is ordained to an end of eternal happiness which is unproportionate to man's natural faculty" and which is not accessible to sinners as such.[109] Graciously, God wills to enable human beings to share "more perfectly in the eternal law," which is his wisdom or wise plan for our fulfillment in beatitude.[110] God thereby makes covenant with his people and gives them divine law, first the Law of Moses and then, in the perfect fulfillment of the covenant, the Law of Christ. Christ's teaching of the beatitudes and his enactment of the new covenant make him the New Moses. He makes perfect charity possible for human beings.

Thus, Aquinas's theology already has much to offer to the investigation of the ontological reality enacted by Christ as the New Moses. But I hope to have shown that foregrounding the theme of the eschatological (New) Moses would enrich Thomistic Christology.

4.6 Conclusion

In his commentary on the Gospel of Matthew, composed in the midst of the Catholic Modernist controversy and the Church's

---

[107] I-II, q. 106, a. 2.
[108] I-II, q. 106, a. 2, ad 3.
[109] I-II, q. 91, a. 4.
[110] I-II, q. 91, a. 4, ad 1.

response to it, Marie-Joseph Lagrange raised the issue that too much attention to typology can undermine people's sense of the historicity of the biblical text.[111] As the Evangelical biblical scholar W. S. Baxter puts the concern: "A Christology based on allusion would seem more like an illusion."[112] Yet, there is no gainsaying – nor do Lagrange or Baxter disagree – that, in the words of Donald Senior, "it is likely that Matthew … intends to wrap Jesus in the mantle of Moses and the revelation on Sinai."[113]

Thomistic Christology should not back down from metaphysically realist dogmatic claims about Jesus Christ, the incarnate Lord. Equally, Thomistic Christology should also not neglect the fact that "Jesus was not doing away with that basic Jewish paradigm [i.e., the coming triumph of Israel's God in establishing his kingdom].... He was telling the story of Israel, giving it a dramatic new twist."[114] Thomistic Christology can employ the New Testament portrait of Christ the New Moses (and New Adam and New Isaac) to illuminate the truth of "Jesus' message that God is now fulfilling his purpose of the Messianic deliverance of Israel and, ultimately, of the world – the kingdom of God has come near."[115]

Matthias Joseph Scheeben points out that unlike the life of grace experienced by other humans, "Christ's humanity has the advantage" that qualitative divinization "*is due* to it in the strictest sense of the word and belongs to it as *an innate right*."[116] Jesus' intimacy

---

[111] See M.-J. Lagrange, O.P., *Evangile Selon Saint Matthieu*, 7th ed. (Paris: Gabalda, 1948), 82–83, cited in Allison, *The New Moses*, 267.
[112] Baxter, "Mosaic Imagery in the Gospel of Matthew," 81.
[113] Donald Senior, *Matthew* (Nashville, TN: Abingdon, 1998), 69.
[114] N. T. Wright, *Jesus and the Victory of God* (Minneapolis, MN: Fortress, 1996), 173.
[115] Eckhard J. Schnabel, *Jesus in Jerusalem: The Last Days* (Grand Rapids, MI: Eerdmans, 2018), 15.
[116] Matthias Joseph Scheeben, *Handbook of Catholic Dogmatics*, Book 5, *Soteriology*, Part 2, *The Work of Christ the Redeemer and the Role of His Virgin Mother*, trans. Michael J. Miller (Steubenville, OH: Emmaus Academic, 2021), 8.

4.6 CONCLUSION

with the Father through the Spirit was radical. He was never merely a sanctified man, as was Moses. Rather, Jesus is the Word incarnate, the source of the grace of the Holy Spirit in all others.

Moses was an ordinary man who, despite his extraordinary intimacy with God, sinned against God and was not allowed to enter into the promised land. Yet, describing Moses as an ordinary man does not exactly do him justice. After all, as the concluding sentence of Deuteronomy says, "there has not arisen a prophet since in Israel like Moses, whom the Lord knew face to face, none like him for all the signs and the wonders which the Lord sent him to do in the land of Egypt, to Pharaoh and to all his servants and to all his land, and for all the mighty power and all the great and terrible deeds which Moses wrought in the sight of all Israel" (Deut 34:10–12). With the possible exception of Abraham, Moses is the most extraordinary man described in Israel's Scriptures. Moses' intimacy with God, humility, courage, love for his people, intercessory urgency, deliverance of his people from slavery, reception of the law, covenant-making, and endurance of numerous trials over a forty-year exodus cause Moses to stand out among all other heroes of Israel. The Letter to the Hebrews praises Moses with the highest praise: "He considered abuse suffered for the Christ greater wealth than the treasures of Egypt" (Heb 11:26).

Thus, Christ's identity as the New Moses is a marker of Christ's eschatological vocation. In his commentary on the book of Exodus, Thomas Joseph White connects Moses' two visions on Mount Sinai in Exodus 24 with "the two deepest mysteries of revelation. Moses is invited to peer into the mystery of God, and he is instructed concerning the mystery of the ark and tabernacle. These two visions correspond to the mysteries of the Holy Trinity and the incarnation, respectively."[117] White deems that "Moses the prophet is

---

[117] Thomas Joseph White, O.P., *Exodus* (Grand Rapids, MI: Brazos, 2016), 223.

intimately associated with God."¹¹⁸ Since this is so, it was fitting that Jesus understood himself as the eschatological Moses, leading the new exodus of the people of God, and that the Gospels presented him as such. It is equally fitting that Thomistic Christology be richly informed by New Moses Christology.

[118] White, *Exodus*, 209.

5 | Christ the New Joshua

The Eschatological Promised Land

5.1 Introduction

In their commentary on the Gospel of Matthew, W. D. Davies and Dale Allison remark: "Why did Jesus submit to John's baptism? Matthew's answer – 'in order to fulfil all righteousness' (3.15) – has scarcely cancelled further discussion."[1] Among the contributors to such further discussion is David Friedrich Strauss, who in the mid-nineteenth century proposed that Jesus submitted to John's baptism because Jesus wanted to be forgiven his sins.[2] For their part, Allison and Davies suggest that Jesus may have sought from the baptism of John "a seal of divine protection ... from the imminent eschatological flood of fire."[3]

I contend that the significance of Jesus' baptism in the Jordan was indeed eschatological but not due to fear of a coming "flood of fire." Instead, Jesus intended to symbolize a central aspect of his mission: to usher God's people into the true Promised Land, the kingdom of God.[4] This kingdom has begun where Jesus is at the right hand of the Father, and Jesus calls his followers to join him in self-sacrificial

---

[1] W. D. Davies and Dale C. Allison, Jr., *A Critical and Exegetical Commentary on the Gospel according to Saint Matthew*, vol. 1, *Introduction and Commentary on Matthew I–VII* (New York: T&T Clark, 2004), 321.

[2] See David Friedrich Strauss, *The Life of Jesus Critically Examined*, 2nd ed., trans. George Eliot (New York: 1892).

[3] Davies and Allison, *Introduction and Commentary on Matthew I–VII*, 323.

[4] For various perspectives on the eschatological fulfillment of the land promise, see, for example, Patrick Schreiner, *The Body of Jesus: A Spatial Analysis of the Kingdom*

179

love – so as to join him in Resurrection life. Jesus is the New Joshua whose "crossing" of the Jordan at his baptism opens up the kingdom of God, to which Christ's people come to belong through faith and the sacrament of baptism instituted by Christ at his baptism.

Ultimately, the baptism that Jesus undergoes at the Jordan, and the sacrament of baptism to which he calls us, are inseparable from his dying and rising. At his baptism in the Jordan, his eschatological mission begins. This mission will lead him to the Cross – and the Resurrection. Christ's submersion in the Jordan leads into the true Promised Land. As Augustine says while arguing against Faustus the Manichean (who claimed that there is nothing in the Old Testament that "has to do with foretelling Christ"): "Let him see Jesus [i.e., Joshua of Nun and Jesus Christ] leading the people into the land of the promise."[5]

This chapter on the New Joshua will proceed in five steps. First, I examine the Letter to the Hebrews through the eyes of Richard Ounsworth's *Joshua Typology in the New Testament*, which argues that Hebrews frames Jesus' role in salvation history as (among other things) that of the New Joshua.[6] In light of the work of other

---

in Matthew (London: T&T Clark, 2016); Jonathan T. Pennington, *Heaven and Earth in the Gospel of Matthew* (Grand Rapids, MI: Baker Academic, 2009); and Brant Pitre, *Jesus and the Last Supper* (Grand Rapids, MI: Eerdmans, 2015), chapter 6. Some scholars hold that Jesus will "restore the Davidic kingdom and rule over the *house of Jacob*," with the result that "the Davidic kingdom will become a [worldwide] Davidic *empire*: the new international people that is formed in Acts and stands *with* (not instead of) Israel confesses a Davidic king" (Isaac W. Oliver, *Luke's Jewish Eschatology: The National Restoration of Israel in Luke-Acts* [Oxford: Oxford University Press, 2021], 146). See also my *Engaging the Doctrine of Israel: A Christian Israelology in Dialogue with Ongoing Judaism* (Eugene, OR: Cascade, 2021), chapter 6, as well as the background in David Frankel, *The Land of Canaan and the Destiny of Israel: Theologies of Territory in the Hebrew Bible* (Winona Lake, IN: Eisenbrauns, 2011); and Nili Wazana, *All the Boundaries of the Land: The Promised Land in Biblical Thought in Light of the Ancient Near East*, trans. Liat Qeren (Winona Lake, IN: Eisenbrauns, 2013).

[5] Augustine, *Answer to Faustus, a Manichean*, trans. Roland J. Teske, S.J., ed. Boniface Ramsey (Hyde Park, NY: New City Press, 2007), XII.31, p. 145.

[6] Richard Ounsworth, O.P., *Joshua Typology in the New Testament* (Tübingen: Mohr Siebeck, 2012).

scholars who favor or reject his perspective, I set forth Ounsworth's argument at length, since Hebrews is central to my case that the New Joshua theme pertains to New Testament Christology. Given that Ounsworth's focus is on Jesus as the New Joshua crossing into the true Promised Land, rather than on baptism, I then devote a second section to contemporary biblical scholarship and biblical theology on Jesus' baptism and the sacrament of baptism, in light of New Joshua Christology. Here my primary interlocutors are Colin Brown (who finds the New Joshua theme in the Gospels of Mark and Matthew), Joseph Ratzinger, Ronald Byars, and Kilian McDonnell.

As a third step, I turn to the Church Fathers, guided by Jean Daniélou. Origen is the central voice, but I examine other Church Fathers as well, such as Gregory of Nyssa. Origen sets the tone by connecting Jesus' baptism and the sacrament of baptism with Joshua's crossing the Jordan into the Promised Land and with believers crossing into the true Promised Land to dwell with the risen and ascended Christ. Fourth, in light of this background, I treat Thomas Aquinas's references to Jesus as the New Joshua. Aquinas recognizes the typological significance of Joshua's crossing into the Promised Land, and he considers it to be the main "type" of Jesus' baptism and of the sacrament of baptism. In his later work, he draws explicitly on Origen on this topic. He therefore has the beginnings of a New Joshua Christology that can be expanded today by Thomistic Christology. As a fifth and final step, I reflect upon certain ways that Aquinas's *sacra doctrina* already engages the eschatological reality of Jesus' crossing over and ours.

5.2 Jesus the New Joshua in the New Testament

Is there a New Testament basis for describing Jesus as the New Joshua? According to Zev Farber in his *Images of Joshua in the Bible and Their Reception*, the New Testament authors "took little or no interest in Joshua."⁷ Farber is aware of Bryan Whitfield's argument that the Letter to the Hebrews presents Jesus as the New Joshua, although Farber cites Whitfield's 2007 dissertation and his 2010 article rather than Whitfield's 2013 published book *Joshua Traditions and the Argument of Hebrews 3 and 4*. In Farber's view, Whitfield may be correct that the author of Hebrews draws upon Joshua the High Priest (Zechariah 3, as interpreted in Second Temple apocalyptic texts) in portraying Jesus. Regarding Joshua the successor of Moses, however, Farber concludes that the author of Hebrews "has a skeptical attitude ... and avoids referencing him positively."⁸

I am far more sympathetic to Whitfield's case regarding the "pioneer" Joshua (the successor of Moses) – especially with respect to Hebrews 3–4 – than is Farber. But I wish to focus here upon a book that neither Farber nor Whitfield cite, namely, Richard Ounsworth's *Joshua Typology in the New Testament*. As we will see, Ounsworth's claim that there is a New Testament basis for understanding Jesus Christ as leading Israel into the true Promised Land – and thus for understanding Jesus as the New Joshua – has strong grounds. It accords with the perspective of notable scholars such as Richard Hays and Thomas Schreiner, in addition to Whitfield.

⁷ Zev Farber, *Images of Joshua in the Bible and Their Reception* (Berlin: De Gruyter, 2016), 275.
⁸ Farber, *Images of Joshua in the Bible and Their Reception*, 283. Farber largely follows J. Cornelis de Vos's rejection of any significant connection, in J. Cornelis de Vos, "Josua und Jesus im Neuen Testament," in *The Book of Joshua*, ed. Ed. Noort (Leuven: Peeters, 2012), 523–40. See also Bryan J. Whitfield, "Joshua Traditions and the Argument of Hebrews 3 and 4," Ph.D. Dissertation, Emory University, 2007; Whitfield, "The Three Joshuas of Hebrews 3 and 4," *Perspectives in Religious Studies* 37 (2010): 21–35; Whitfield, *Joshua Traditions and the Argument of Hebrews 3 and 4* (Berlin: De Gruyter, 2013). In his 2013 book, Whitfield argues that from Zechariah 3, the author of Hebrews takes the priestly Joshua/Jesus, and from the Book of Joshua (along with Deuteronomy and, especially, Numbers 13–14) the author of Hebrews takes the "pioneer" Joshua. He concludes, "The author of Hebrews develops a complex understanding of Jesus that requires holding two images together: priest and pioneer" (*Joshua Traditions and the Argument of Hebrews 3 and 4*, 271). For his emphasis on the two Joshuas – Moses' successor and the priest in Zechariah 3 –

5.2 JESUS THE NEW JOSHUA IN THE NEW TESTAMENT

Ounsworth contends that the Letter to the Hebrews contains as a unifying theme "a typological relationship between Joshua the son of Nun and Jesus."[9] In Greek, the name for Joshua is the same as the name for Jesus: Ἰησοῦς. When in Hebrews 4:8 the author of the Letter to the Hebrews shows the insufficiency of Joshua's crossing into the Promised Land – "if Joshua had given them rest, God would not speak later of another day" – the name the author employs is Ἰησοῦς, the same as when the author speaks of Jesus. Both Jesus and Joshua/Jesus lead the people into the Promised Land, but only Jesus succeeds in doing so in a way that delivers the rest and flourishing that true restoration and covenant fulfillment require.

Ounsworth points out that the likely intended audience of Hebrews was quite attuned to Israel's salvation-history narratives. In this light, he interprets the "two controlling images" found in Hebrews: "[T]hat of Christ as High Priest entering the heavenly sanctuary, and that of the Christian community as the People of God on their pilgrimage to the Promised Land."[10] Both images involve crossing over into the divine realm, a realm of blessing, rest, and consummation.

Whitfield is especially indebted to James Rendel Harris, "The Sinless High Priest," *The Expository Times* 33 (1922): 217–18, whose insights are carried forward by F. C. Synge, *Hebrews and the Scriptures* (London: SPCK, 1959), 19–21. For additional noteworthy studies, see Stefan Koch, "Mose sagt zu 'Jesus' – Zur Wahrmehmung von Josua im Neuen Testament," in *The Book of Joshua*, ed. Ed Noort (Leuven: Leuven University Press, 2010), 541–54; and Andries van Aarde, "Jesus as Joshua: Moses en Dawidiese Messias in Matteus," *Scriptura* 84 (2003): 453–67.

[9] Ounsworth, *Joshua Typology in the New Testament*, 1. Ounsworth's book was published before Farber's and Whitfield's books. Admittedly, Ounsworth does not cite their dissertations or Whitfield's 2010 article (nor does he cite the articles by Vos or Koch).

[10] Ounsworth, *Joshua Typology in the New Testament*, 5; on the image of the heavenly sanctuary, see Ounsworth's chapter 5, especially 152–57, 160–65. For the efficacy of Christ's entrance into the heavenly sanctuary and his sacrifice, see Benjamin J. Ribbens, *Levitical Sacrifice and Heavenly Cult in Hebrews* (Berlin: De Gruyter, 2016), 236–40. From the perspective of historical-Jesus studies, Nicholas Perrin proposes that "Jesus' kingdom vision, like that of the prophets as a whole, revolved around the

No wonder, then, that Ounsworth is on the lookout for types drawn from Joshua and the crossing of the Jordan. Given that Joshua led the people into the Promised Land, it is reasonable to ask whether Christ, in his high-priestly entrance into the heavenly (Temple) sanctuary, acts as a New Joshua leading his people into a new Promised Land understood on the basis of the Temple imagery. There is no doubt about the typological relationship between the Temple and the heavenly sanctuary: Hebrews 8:5 confirms it. In Ounsworth's view, when Christ crosses through the curtain through his holy death in love for sinners, he arrives at the Promised Land toward which Joshua led the people.

Before proceeding with his case for Joshua typology in Hebrews, Ounsworth pauses to examine other instances of Joshua typology in biblical and patristic texts. He briefly mentions the proposal by Austin Farrer that Matthew's final chapters contain a mini-Book of Joshua, with Jerusalem being condemned instead of Jericho and with the twelve (or eleven) disciples gathering God's people into the true Promised Land under Christ's rule.[11] It is more likely that Jude 5 contains a reference to Joshua – with "Christ" or "Jesus" or "the Lord" (depending upon which textual variant one accepts) being linked to Joshua's role in saving the Israelites from Egyptian slavery and also in punishing them for their lack of faith.[12] Ounsworth identifies clear New Joshua typology in the Epistle of Barnabas, Justin Martyr, Tertullian, Aphraates, Ephrem the Syrian, and Origen. Origen and Aphraates explicitly connect their Joshua typology to Hebrews 4, notably to its reference to Joshua's failure to bring the

---

renewal of sacred space, populated by a new guild of priests, sustained by the Spirit and purged of idols" (Perrin, *Jesus the Priest* [Grand Rapids, MI: Baker Academic, 2018], 143).

[11] Ounsworth, *Joshua Typology in the New Testament*, 1–2, citing Austin Farrer, "On Dispensing with Q," in *Studies in the Gospels: Essays in Memory of R. H. Lightfoot*, ed. D. E. Nineham (Oxford: Blackwell, 1955), 55–88.

[12] Ounsworth, *Joshua Typology in the New Testament*, 10–13, in critical dialogue especially with Richard Bauckham.

people to the true Promised Land, by contrast to Jesus' attainment of that "rest" and his leading believers into that "rest."

Ounsworth then devotes a chapter to showing that Joshua is, in Hebrews 3–4, a type of Jesus Christ. He summarizes his argument thusly: "[A]s Joshua was able to succeed where Moses failed, in leading the People of Israel into the earthly Promised Land of Canaan, so Jesus has succeeded where Moses failed, in granting the People of God access to the heavenly rest of which the earthly Land was but a type or shadow."[13] I note that Ounsworth's perspective fits with Richard Hays's reading of the Matthean account of Jesus' baptism. According to Hays, "Jesus' acceptance of a baptism of repentance, performed at the Jordan River, is meant to signify his symbolic identification with sinful Israel (the people whom he will 'save from their sins'), and the figurative beginning of that new Israel's entry into the land of promise."[14] Since Jesus is the one not only representing all Israel but also leading all Israel into the true Promised Land (the kingdom of God), Jesus at the Jordan acts as the New Joshua.

Thomas Schreiner's position, too, is similar to Ounsworth's. Hebrews 4:8 makes clear that the author of Hebrews considers it important to register that "Jesus is better than Joshua, for Joshua did not give Israel a lasting and permanent rest."[15] Already in Hebrews 4, Jesus stands as a New or greater Joshua, given the fact that the two share a name and the fact that Jesus' goal is the

---

[13] Ounsworth, *Joshua Typology in the New Testament*, 55.

[14] Richard B. Hays, *Echoes of Scripture in the Gospels* (Waco, TX: Baylor University Press, 2016), 116. Hays goes on to say: "We have just been told in the preceding birth narratives that this Jesus is 'God's Son,' who takes on the role of God's 'son' Israel, called out of Egypt and out of exile; now, in a symbolically fraught act, he is to undergo repentance and, like Israel, pass through the waters. But before Jesus/Israel can enter the land, he must undergo a time of testing in the wilderness, just as unfaithful Israel had done once before – this time with dramatically different results" (ibid., 117).

[15] Thomas R. Schreiner, *The King in His Beauty: A Biblical Theology of the Old and New Testaments* (Grand Rapids, MI: Baker Academic, 2013), 586.

eschatological completion of the exodus journey to the Promised Land. Schreiner sums up the perspective of Hebrews regarding the exodus journey and its destination: "Israel's history from the time of Joshua until the writer's day demonstrates that any earthly rest is temporary. The possession of the land by one generation may be lost in the next. The only rest that is permanent, the only rest that will endure, is a heavenly rest."[16] The latter rest is what Jesus himself has achieved, according to Hebrews 1:3–4: "When he had made purification for sins, he sat down at the right hand of the Majesty on high." The Letter to the Hebrews devotes itself to showing how, through Jesus, the true Promised Land has been attained for all who are united to him, since he provides "direct access to God in the heavenly sanctuary."[17] This consummation is present even now. As Benjamin Ribbens says, "Perfection ... is about access to the divine presence, and the author clearly considers such access to be a present reality" due to Jesus' Cross and Resurrection.[18]

Ounsworth draws a connection between Psalm 95, as it is used in Hebrews 3–4, and Numbers 14. In Numbers 14, the people of Israel grumble against God and against Moses, and they begin to set in motion a plan to return to Egypt. As punishment, the people receive an extensive lengthening of their wandering in the desert (namely, for a period of forty years). In addition, God promises that no one currently above the age of nineteen will enter the Promised

---

[16] Schreiner, *The King in His Beauty*, 586.
[17] Ribbens, *Levitical Sacrifice and Heavenly Cult in Hebrews*, 215.
[18] Ribbens, *Levitical Sacrifice and Heavenly Cult in Hebrews*, 216. Ribbens adds, "The contrast is not that the old covenant *did not* perfect, whereas the new covenant *partially* or *will eventually* perfect; it is between what the old covenant sacrifice *did not do* and what Christ's sacrifice *does*" (216). See also Ounsworth, *Joshua Typology in the New Testament*, 132: "[T]he Yom Kippur typology is complemented by the theme of the inauguration of the sanctuary as the mark of the inauguration of a covenant, with Christ presented as inaugurating by his death a heavenly sanctuary and thus an eternal covenant." Ounsworth draws especially upon Paul Ellingworth, "Jesus and the Universe in Hebrews," *Evangelical Quarterly* 58 (1986): 337–54.

Land, with the exception of Joshua and Caleb. The latter two will enter the land because, when they spied out the land, they showed their trust in God's plan.

Ounsworth pays attention to Numbers 14 because he seeks to demonstrate that for the author of Hebrews, not only was Joshua superior to Moses with respect to the entry into the Land but also that Joshua's entry into the Land was "both comparable to and yet radically different from the entry of Jesus into heaven."[19] If the two entries are comparable in some way (even if Joshua's was lesser), then it makes sense to compare the leaders of the two entries and to describe the second leader as the New Joshua.

In defending the claim that Joshua 3–4 is related to Numbers 14, Ounsworth draws upon arguments made by Otfried Hofius and echoed in recent years by a number of exegetes.[20] The central point is that Joshua 3–4's numerous embedded citations of Psalm 95 have in view Numbers 14, so that the Book of Joshua's audience would "have before the eyes of their minds the absolute and fatal exclusion from the Promised Land of all those – every Israelite bar two, Joshua and Caleb – who refused to believe in the offer of entry into the Land made by God when they stood at the very threshold of that Land."[21] This point matters because Hebrews is exhorting its audience to follow Jesus/Joshua, and not to murmur or turn back. In addition, Hebrews is emphasizing that believers have received a promise. Just as God promised to effect the entry of the Israelites into the Promised Land, so also in Christ God has promised to effect the entry of Christ's followers into the true Promised Land. The people should seize upon God's promise and undertake the entry led by the New Joshua, rather than delaying and potentially having their entrance forbidden or further delayed.

---

[19] Ounsworth, *Joshua Typology in the New Testament*, 55.
[20] See Otfried Hofius, *Katapausis: Die Vorstellung vom endzeitlichen Ruheort im Hebräerbrief* (Tübingen: Mohr Siebeck, 1970).
[21] Ounsworth, *Joshua Typology in the New Testament*, 59.

Hebrews 4:3 cites Psalm 95:11, which Hebrews renders: "As I swore in my wrath, 'They shall never enter my rest.'" God swears this oath when the people, encamped at Kadesh-Barnea, deny God's ability to bring them into the Promised Land. At Kadesh-Barnea, just as the people were about to be led into the Land by God and Moses, God swears solemnly in response to the people's rebellion: "[N]one of the men who have seen my glory and my signs which I wrought in Egypt and in the wilderness, and yet have put me to the proof these ten times and have not hearkened to my voice, shall see the land which I swore to give to their fathers" (Num 14:22–23).[22] As noted above, this caused a delay of forty years before the people entered the Promised Land under Joshua.

Ounsworth emphasizes that Hebrews 4:2–3 has in view not merely a situation of "wandering towards a distant goal … but of *imminent* access to the promised inheritance."[23] This imminence does not mean a temporal timeframe (e.g., that the Parousia will take place within the next year), but it rather simply underscores that Hebrews's audience stands "on the threshold of the

---

[22] For further background, see Whitfield, *Joshua Traditions and the Argument of Hebrews 3 and 4*, 42–44, where he draws attention to Albert Vanhoye's "Longue marche ou accès tout proche? Le contexte biblique de Hébreux 3,7–4,11," *Biblica* 49 (1968): 9–26. Whitfield notes that Vanhoye "pushed past the explicit citation of Ps 95 to elucidate ways in which other Hebrew Bible texts and traditions shape Hebrews. In particular, he uncovered a number of additional contacts between Num 14 and Heb 3:1–4:11" (Whitfield, *Joshua Traditions and the Argument of Hebrews 3 and 4*, 43).

[23] Ounsworth, *Joshua Typology in the New Testament*, 60. Ounsworth grants, of course, that "it was at Meribah in the wilderness of Zin that Moses and Aaron are explicitly told (in Num 20) that they will not lead the people of Israel into the Promised Land, and not at Kadesh-Barnea. This chapter of Numbers, in which Joshua does not appear, seems to be a reprise of the first instance of wilderness murmurings related in Exodus 17 – certainly we learn that the events occur in the same place – and it is to this event, or perhaps pair of events, that the *Hebrew* text of Psalm 95 refers; whereas I have been eager to agree with Hofius and others that the Greek text of the Psalm more readily reads as relating to Numbers 14 and not to Numbers 20 or Exodus 17" (75). He points also to Deuteronomy 1:34–38.

5.2 JESUS THE NEW JOSHUA IN THE NEW TESTAMENT

[eschatological] Promised Land" and must now seek entry with full confidence in the New Joshua, without losing heart as did the Israelites under Moses.[24] Even now, believers are "entering into rest": as Hebrews 4:3 says in the present tense, "For we who have believed enter that rest."[25] Already, we can enter into the Promised Land with the New Joshua (by leading lives of faith, self-surrendering love, humility, mercy, and communion with the divine presence), even if we still await the glorious consummation of all things.

What differentiated Joshua and Caleb from the others who spied out the Land and instilled a spirit of fearfulness into the people? Ounsworth identifies two characteristics: a truthful assessment of reality and a firm belief in God's promise. For the wilderness generation, the result of disbelieving God's promise was that they never experienced its fulfillment. Joshua and Caleb were exceptional in their faith in God's promise, and so the fulfillment of God's original promise to the wilderness generation hinged upon them. Yet, Hebrews 4:4 makes clear that the "rest" which is the true Promised Land is nothing less than God's own Sabbath rest, far more than Joshua and Caleb expected or (in the Book of Joshua) received. As Ounsworth says, "Hebrews is making a contrast between something that Joshua *did* achieve and the rest of which the Psalm speaks [Ps 95:11], between possession of Canaan and true rest."[26] What Joshua achieved was not nothing, but it was as nothing compared to what God intended to give and what the New Joshua today gives. Psalm 95:7 exhorts, "O that today you would listen to his voice!"

---

[24] Ounsworth, *Joshua Typology in the New Testament*, 61.
[25] Ounsworth, *Joshua Typology in the New Testament*, 62.
[26] Ounsworth, *Joshua Typology in the New Testament*, 70. As Luke Timothy Johnson states, "the land itself is not the real promise! If the Jesus of the past [i.e., Joshua] had been able to provide that, then God would not have spoken about another day" (Johnson, *Hebrews: A Commentary* [Louisville, KY: John Knox Press, 2006], 128, cited in Ounsworth, *Joshua Typology in the New Testament*, 71).

This "today" has now made itself present in the New Joshua, Jesus, as Hebrews 4:7 indicates.[27]

Luke Timothy Johnson, Harold Attridge, and many other scholars have noted the typological significance in Hebrews 4 of the fact that the name Joshua and the name Jesus are both *Iēsous*. Attridge is aware that later Church Fathers developed an extensive Joshua–Jesus typology, but he considers that Hebrews does no more than suggest it.[28] With Ounsworth, however, I think the appearance of *Iēsous* in 4:8 would inevitably draw the intended audience's minds back to the beginning of the discourse: "Therefore, holy brethren, who share in a heavenly call, consider Jesus, the apostle and high priest of our confession" (Heb 3:1). Hebrews here argues that "Jesus has been counted worthy of as much more glory than Moses as the builder of a house has more honor than the house" (Heb 3:3). Hebrews 3:6 attributes Jesus' superiority over Moses to the superior faithfulness of Jesus: "Christ was faithful over God's house as a son."[29] The Old Testament texts about Joshua likewise highlight Joshua's superior faithfulness. Joshua is even more faithful than Moses, because God permits Joshua to lead the people into the

---

[27] Hebrews is well known for its distinctive contemporizing of citations from Israel's Scriptures, with effects that are especially prominent in Hebrews 3–4. Thus, for Hebrews, the words of the psalm are addressed directly by God to the Christians of Hebrews's day. For further discussion, see Simon Kistemaker, *The Psalm Citations in the Epistle to the Hebrews* (Amsterdam: Soest, 1961); Graham Hughes, *Hebrews and Hermeneutics: The Epistle to the Hebrews as a New Testament Example of Biblical Interpretation* (Cambridge: Cambridge University Press, 1979); and Susan E. Docherty, *The Use of the Old Testament in Hebrews: A Case Study in Early Jewish Bible Interpretation* (Tübingen: Mohr Siebeck, 2009).

[28] See Harold W. Attridge, *The Epistle to the Hebrews* (Philadelphia: Fortress Press, 1989); Attridge, "Let Us Strive to Enter That Rest: The Logic of Hebrews 4.1–11," *Harvard Theological Review* 73 (1980): 279–88.

[29] For discussion see Matthew C. Easter, *Faith and the Faithfulness of Jesus in Hebrews* (Cambridge: Cambridge University Press, 2014). Unfortunately, Easter does not appear to have been acquainted with Ounsworth's study, and Joshua is not mentioned at all.

5.2 JESUS THE NEW JOSHUA IN THE NEW TESTAMENT

Promised Land – which happens today in an eschatological way through Jesus.[30]

Drawing upon David Allen's work, Ounsworth suggests that Hebrews places Christ's followers in the position of the people of Israel in Deuteronomy. They are ready to enter into the Land – under the leadership of Joshua (Jesus).[31] In Deuteronomy, of course, Joshua remains subordinate to Moses, who is presented as uniquely blessed. Deuteronomy testifies that "there has not arisen a prophet since in Israel like Moses, whom the Lord knew face to face, none like him for all the signs and the wonders which the Lord sent him to do" (Deut 34:10–11). According to David Allen, the Moses–Joshua relationship in Deuteronomy reflects "a broader tension found in Deuteronomy between the imminent fulfillment of the covenant promises and the strongly implied inadequacy of that fulfillment."[32] In this sense, Deuteronomy invites a "new covenant" of the kind envisioned by Jeremiah. Given the tension in Deuteronomy regarding the imminent crossing over into the Promised Land, Hebrews can appeal to the existential situation of the Israelites to depict the existential situation of believers in Jesus. The difference is that "whereas Joshua took over from Moses to lead Israel into the earthly and, implicitly, insufficient fulfillment of the promises, the new Joshua, Son not of Nun but of God, ushers in a far more radically new era with a far more radical fulfillment."[33] The true successor of Moses is the New Joshua.

---

[30] Ounsworth explains further that the key Old Testament texts (Exodus 17, Numbers 14, Numbers 20, Deuteronomy 1:34–38) indicate that ultimately "Joshua's faith in God exceeded that of Moses and this was why he was qualified to do what Moses could not, completing the journey begun with the crossing of the Red Sea. Within the context of Heb 3.1–6, with its assertion that Jesus's faith is qualitatively superior to that of Moses, it is not too much to see great significance in the fact that his name is identical to that of the Joshua who succeeded, because of precisely this quality [faithfulness], where Moses failed" (Ounsworth, *Joshua Typology in the New Testament*, 76).

[31] See David M. Allen, *Deuteronomy and Exhortation in Hebrews: A Study in Narrative Re-presentation* (Tübingen: Mohr Siebeck, 2008).

[32] Ounsworth, *Joshua Typology in the New Testament*, 77.

[33] Ounsworth, *Joshua Typology in the New Testament*, 77.

Ounsworth proceeds to investigate the "rest" that Hebrews 4:8 has in view. He notes that the notion of "rest" – "eternal rest in heaven" – belongs to the "religious-historical background" of Hebrews rather than originating in Hebrews.[34] The new thing that Hebrews offers is simple: Jesus Christ has attained this "rest." Furthermore, Jesus' attainment of it will be the cause of all other people's entering into this "rest." Indeed, in fellowship with Jesus, we can today enter into his "rest" (see Hebrews 4:9). To do so, however, we must guard against the disobedience that caused the Israelites of Moses' generation to fail to be able to cross over the Jordan into the Land (see Hebrews 4:11).

In Psalm 95:11, "rest" meant the Promised Land, and this was extended to mean the place where God dwells – in an imperfect way the earthly Temple, in a perfect way the heavenly sanctuary (see Hebrews 8:1–2). "Rest" ultimately entails a condition of perfect peace. Ounsworth comments that in Hebrews 4, "the 'rest' that was denied to the People of Israel at Kadesh-Barnea is not only to be understood in primordial-cosmological terms, as a sharing in the eternal rest of God, but also in terms of the proleptic participation in and manifestation of that rest that is the Jewish Sabbath."[35] This is important because under Joshua, the people did enter the Land and observe the Sabbath in the Land (and in the Temple). It follows that there is "a positive relationship between that earthly entry and the entry into heavenly rest": Joshua is not nothing, even though the eschatological (New) Joshua fulfills that which Joshua strove to do.[36]

---

[34] Ounsworth, *Joshua Typology in the New Testament*, 78.

[35] Ounsworth, *Joshua Typology in the New Testament*, 83.

[36] Ounsworth, *Joshua Typology in the New Testament*, 85. Ounsworth adds a criticism of Hofius, whose perspective Ounsworth otherwise generally admires: "[W]hen he [Hofius] goes on to suggest that the Psalm [95] was understood to mean that, as a matter of historical fact, the wilderness generation were on the verge of entering heaven itself, he asserts something for which there is no evidence, and which entirely collapses the typological understanding of the Psalm" (85).

5.2 JESUS THE NEW JOSHUA IN THE NEW TESTAMENT

When Hebrews 4:9 states that "there remains a sabbath rest for the people of God," Ounsworth clarifies that σαββατισμός should be understood – as it was understood in late Second Temple Jewish eschatologies – in connection with an everlasting rest characterized by joy and celebration on the day of God's triumph.[37] Thus, the "sabbath rest" of Hebrews 4:9 should primarily be understood as the consummation described in Hebrews 12:22, with its portrait of the festivities enjoyed by the blessed angels and saints at "Mount Zion and ... the city of the living God, the heavenly Jerusalem."[38] In Hebrews 4:3–4, 9, however, none of this is set forth directly. Instead, what is described is God's Sabbath on the seventh day and the Israelites' participation in it on their weekly Sabbath. The Sabbath, the entry into the Land, and the Temple all have concrete reference in Jewish life that Hebrews does not abolish. Instead, Hebrews suggests that they "all ultimately point to the one reality which is now being made available," in and through the New Joshua, who is God's preexistent Son and who became "a merciful and faithful high priest in the service of God" (Heb 1:2 and 2:17), journeying through death so that we might sit down with him at the right hand of God.[39]

Ounsworth deems that, for Hebrews, Jesus-Joshua's "cosmic journey" is the "eschatological journey of which the Exodus is a type and shadow."[40] As Whitfield also emphasizes, Jesus is the "pioneer" (Heb 2:10) of this exodus-crossing into the eschatological Promised Land: "[T]he new and heavenly Joshua is now leading the

---

[37] Ounsworth, *Joshua Typology in the New Testament*, 87.
[38] For background to early Christian understanding of the angels (including the viewpoint of the Letter to the Hebrews), see Susan R. Garrett, *No Ordinary Angel: Celestial Spirits and Christian Claims about Jesus* (New Haven, CT: Yale University Press, 2008).
[39] Ounsworth, *Joshua Typology in the New Testament*, 88. For the significance of Jesus as high priest (in relation to Joshua 4:8), Ounsworth directs attention to Erich Grässer, *An die Hebräer*, vol. 1 (Zurich: Benziger, 1990), 214.
[40] Ounsworth, *Joshua Typology in the New Testament*, 89.

eschatological generation into the eternal resting place of God."[41] Only a New Joshua who is the Son, the very one "through whom" God "created the ages" (Heb 1:2), could lead believers into God's own Sabbath, the culmination of God's creative work. The New Joshua cannot be less than the incarnate Lord, the Creator, who alone can enable us to share in divine rest.[42]

Perhaps surprisingly, Ounsworth turns from Hebrews 4 to Hebrews 11 and contends that Joshua's *absence* in Hebrews 11 is supportive of his thesis that Jesus is the New Joshua in Hebrews. His argument is that just as Hebrews 3–4 recounts salvation history (the exodus journey) and includes a mention of *Iēsous* (4:8), so also Hebrews 11 recounts salvation history and sums it up with a mention of *Iēsous* "the pioneer and perfecter of our faith" (12:2). The Old Testament figures mentioned in Hebrews 11 are all figures who, unlike the wilderness generation, successfully crossed *by faith* into the true Promised Land, with *Jesus* as their leader. Jesus entered into the heavenly sanctuary by "[enduring] the cross, despising the shame," so that now he "is seated at the right hand of the throne of God" (Heb 12:2). In this high-priestly way, Jesus has accomplished the work of the New Joshua for all God's people. He is the faithful Lord. To live by faith is to journey toward the true Promised Land, trusting in God's promises, without cleaving to anything merely earthly.[43] The Old Testament figures were on this journey – Hebrews states that God "prepared for them a city" (11:16) – but

---

[41] Ounsworth, *Joshua Typology in the New Testament*, 90.
[42] As Ounsworth puts it, "because the eschatological fulfilment of the Promise is a participation in something primordial, it is Jesus who is qualified to lead those whose flesh and blood he shares into that fulfilment because he himself is primordial" (Ounsworth, *Joshua Typology in the New Testament*, 91).
[43] Thus "all the true descendants of Abraham – throughout the entirety of salvation history – are characterised by the recognition that their occupation of the Land of Canaan does not mean that they have truly received what was promised to their ancestors" (Ounsworth, *Joshua Typology in the New Testament*, 113). In this regard, he cites David Allen's argument that these Old Testament figures located themselves within Deuteronomy's existential situation: Allen, *Deuteronomy and Exhortation in Hebrews*, 76.

5.2 JESUS THE NEW JOSHUA IN THE NEW TESTAMENT

now that Christ has crossed over, believers have finally arrived in the eschatological Land, "the city of the living God, the heavenly Jerusalem" (12:22). In another sense, of course, believers still have to make the crossing insofar as they must "struggle against sin ... to the point of shedding [their] blood" (Heb 12:4).[44]

Ounsworth thinks Christ's status as the New Joshua is significant particularly with regard to "realized eschatology" (ascent), even though Hebrews also awaits Christ's coming in glory (descent and consummation).[45] The New Joshua, then, is the one who has brought the Old Testament heroes of Hebrews 11 into the true Land that they sought. Prior to his crossing into the heavenly sanctuary, the faithful were in the condition of the Israelites waiting to cross the Jordan; now that he has crossed, the faithful are in the condition of the generation that crossed with Joshua, having arrived at the *true* Land though not yet fully. The faithful must continue to struggle against sin and other problems, just as the people under Joshua endured many struggles in the land.

Ounsworth notes that the conquest of the Promised Land under Joshua's leadership receives appreciative attention from Hebrews.

---

[44] Ounsworth remarks: "[T]he certain hope of a heavenly inheritance is what makes it possible to endure the discomfort of any kind of alienation and estrangement from earthly society" (*Joshua Typology in the New Testament*, 115). With regard to Hebrews's depiction of believers as existentially similar to the journeying Israelites on the exodus, Ounsworth points appreciatively to Ernst Käsemann's *Das wandernde Gottesvolk: eine Untersuchung zum Hebräerbrief* (Göttingen: Vandenhoeck & Ruprecht, 1939), which appeared in English as *The Wandering People of God: An Investigation of the Letter to the Hebrews*, trans. R. A. Harrisville and I. L. Sandberg (Minneapolis, MN: Augsburg, 1984).

[45] See Ounsworth, *Joshua Typology in the New Testament*, 116; cf. 171: "[T]his eschatological tension reaches its climax almost at the end of Hebrews, at the point of its final rhetorical flourish. Hitherto, at least as far as the themes of entry and approach are concerned, matters have been quite clear: Jesus has entered, we are in the process of entering and approaching, but might yet fail to complete the journey. Now, as the epistle riches its climax [Hebrews 12], the tension is increased as the audience is taken higher up and further in." For the eschatological tension, see also Ounsworth's reflections on 186.

Indeed, it is difficult to read Hebrews 11:30 ("By faith the walls of Jericho fell down after they had been encircled for seven days") in anything but a positive way. This event happened under Joshua's leadership and implies that the crossing of the Jordan – without which there would have been no conquest of Jericho – was a laudable act of faith. Even so, believers must look to the New Joshua, who "stands in the role of the faithful spy," having by his Resurrection (and Ascension) arrived at the eschatological new creation, to which he calls us to cross over.[46] The task of conquering the true Promised Land, under the leadership of *Iēsous*, is ours.[47]

Ounsworth adds that we need not resolve every aspect of Hebrews's dense imagery into a well-ordered system. Some important points, however, can be made. It is clear that Christ's sacrificial death, through which he attains to the heavenly sanctuary and makes atonement there, "opens the way through the veil for those who follow him."[48] It is clear that the ascended Christ, at the right hand of the Father, manifests himself and his attainment of eschatological rest to believers. Hebrews 12:1–2 brings together the images of crossing into the Promised Land and entering into the heavenly sanctuary. It does so by urging believers to "run with perseverance ... looking to Jesus [*Iēsous*-Joshua]" and by describing Jesus' death and exaltation to God's "throne."[49] The exodus and

---

[46] Ounsworth, *Joshua Typology in the New Testament*, 124. Here Ounsworth could benefit from Whitfield's attention to Joshua the priest in the Book of Zechariah.

[47] See Ounsworth, *Joshua Typology in the New Testament*, 130. He goes on to add some other helpful elements, including the fact that Hebrews 5–6 "suggests that in order to continue in their journey towards the rest which is promised, unlike the Israelites of the wilderness generation, the audience must make a journey of intellectual growth, of which the goal is a full understanding of the priestly nature of Christ.... It is in this context that Hebrews first introduces the veil, and the notion that Jesus has passed beyond it in a high-priestly capacity" (138).

[48] Ounsworth, *Joshua Typology in the New Testament*, 161.

[49] As Ounsworth says: "Jesus's entry into heaven was foreshadowed both by the annual entry of the High Priest into the Holy of Holies and the one-off entry of Joshua *at the head of the People of Israel* into the Promised Land; Jesus's passing through death

Yom Kippur come together in Jesus, Ounsworth argues, because God's providence intended for them to do so. They also come together because Yom Kippur (the Day of Atonement) symbolically reenacts the inauguration and renewal of the covenant and points forward to its eschatological fulfillment, along lines paralleled by the Eucharist.[50]

Ounsworth concludes that Hebrews's New Joshua Christology teaches us that salvation comes about not by avoiding death but by crossing through death's deadly waters: "[W]e make the same journey that Christ has made. We who have not yet resisted to the shedding of our blood need have no fear of doing so, for as we look across that final crossing-place we see Jesus, our Joshua, beckoning to us from the opposite shore."[51] Joshua typology and high-priestly typology are joined here, just as Whitfield shows from his own angle. Jesus' death transforms death from being a barrier that separates mortal humans from the living God into being a portal to the life of God – the "rest" that is the true Promised Land.

5.3 Jesus' Baptism in the Jordan

Let me now briefly situate Ounsworth's reflections on Christ the New Joshua leading his people into the true Promised Land within the context of the baptism of Christ in the Jordan, understood as Christ's proleptic passing through the portal of death.

---

into the eternal rest of God was foreshadowed by the High Priest's passing beyond the veil and by Joshua's crossing of the Jordan" (Ounsworth, *Joshua Typology in the New Testament*, 168).

[50] A similar combination characterizes the Eucharistic liturgy, as "the cultic recapitulation of Christ's entry into heaven which also anticipates the believer's final entry into God's rest and the consummation of the world" (Ounsworth, *Joshua Typology in the New Testament*, 186).

[51] Ounsworth, *Joshua Typology in the New Testament*, 187.

James Dunn presents the baptism of Christ as "the beginning of a new epoch in salvation-history – the beginning, albeit in a restricted sense, of the End-time, the messianic age, the new covenant."[52] Christ's baptism inaugurated the kingdom, the Messianic age. But how precisely did Christ's baptism accomplish this, and how does it relate to our baptism? I find Colin Brown's answers to be particularly helpful. Brown directs attention to "the allusions contained in the Semitic forms *Yeshu* or *Yehoshua*, which connected him [Jesus] with the Joshua of the Hebrew Bible."[53] He links Jesus' Spirit-anointing at his baptism with Jesus' work as "the *new Joshua*, the shepherd of Israel" and, specifically in Mark's Gospel, with Jesus' journey to the Cross, which Brown describes as "a *second conquest*, led by a pacific 'Joshua.'"[54] Arguing that Matthew's Gospel contains not only a Moses typology but also a Joshua typology, Brown proposes that, having been anointed by the Spirit at his baptism in the Jordan, Jesus the New Joshua proceeds to pacify the "land" (God's people) "in a new conquest – not bloody like Joshua's – but one of peace to purify and heal Israel."[55]

Although most scholars do not make this connection to the New Joshua, scholars agree that in the Synoptic Gospels, Jesus' baptism in the Jordan inaugurates his Spirit-filled Messianic mission to establish the eschatological kingdom of God.[56] Summarizing

---

[52] James D. G. Dunn, *Baptism in the Holy Spirit: A Re-examination of the New Testament Teaching on the Gift of the Spirit in Relation to Pentecostalism Today* (Philadelphia: The Westminster Press, 1970), 24. Dunn suggests that the event initiates Jesus himself into the Messianic age by bestowing the Spirit upon him.

[53] Colin Brown, "With the Grain and against the Grain: A Strategy for Reading the Synoptic Gospels," in *The Handbook for the Study of the Historical Jesus*, vol. 1, ed. Tom Holmén and Stanley E. Porter, (Leiden: Brill, 2010), 619–48, at 624.

[54] Brown, "With the Grain and against the Grain," 628–29.

[55] Brown, "With the Grain and against the Grain," 638.

[56] Dunn remarks along lines that I find partly correct and partly mistaken: "Only with the descent of the Spirit does the new covenant and new epoch enter, and only thus does Jesus himself enter the new covenant and epoch. He enters as representative man – representing in himself Israel and even mankind. As such, this first baptism

twentieth-century German New Testament scholarship on this matter, Joseph Ratzinger observes, "The descent of the Holy Spirit upon Jesus, which concludes the baptismal scene, is to be understood as a kind of formal investiture with the messianic office."[57] This Messianic import fits with John the Baptist's promise that "he who is coming after me is mightier than I, whose sandals I am not worthy to carry; he will baptize you with the Holy Spirit and with fire" (Mt 3:11). The Messianic import allows us to assume that Jesus' baptism in the Jordan is connected with his ultimate Messianic action, his Pasch. Indeed, Ratzinger thinks that when we look at the baptism of Jesus from the perspective of the whole Gospel, it becomes evident that Jesus bore our sins "down into the depths of the Jordan. He inaugurated his public activity by stepping into the place of sinners. His inaugural gesture is an anticipation of the Cross."[58] On this view, Jesus' emerging from the water, when combined with the heavenly voice proclaiming "This is my beloved Son, with whom I am well pleased" (Mt 3:17), is "an anticipation of the Resurrection."[59] Although Ratzinger does not draw the connection, the entrance of the New Joshua into the true Promised Land, proleptically through the waters of the Jordan, seems to be expressed here.[60]

---

in the Spirit could well be taken as typical of all later Spirit-baptisms – the means by which God brings each to follow in Jesus' footsteps, Jesus as representative of the people ... is the first to enter the promise made to the people.... Jesus' entry into the new age and covenant is the type of every initiate's entry into the new age and covenant" (Dunn, *Baptism in the Holy Spirit*, 32).

[57] Joseph Ratzinger, *Jesus of Nazareth: From the Baptism in the Jordan to the Transfiguration*, trans. Adrian J. Walker (New York: Doubleday, 2007), 25.

[58] Ratzinger, *Jesus of Nazareth*, 18. See also (in a noticeably weaker form) Ronald P. Byars, *The Sacraments in Biblical Perspective: Interpretation* (Louisville, KY: John Knox Press, 2011), 39.

[59] Ratzinger, *Jesus of Nazareth*, 18.

[60] Ratzinger does identify the typological link to Joshua – via Elijah and Elisha – by attending to the Byzantine Liturgy's understanding of Christian baptism. Quoting Paul Evdokimov's *The Art of the Icon*, he states, "The troparia of the Byzantine Liturgy add yet another symbolic connection: 'The Jordan was turned back by Elisha's coat [2 Kgs 2:14], and the waters were divided leaving a dry path. This is

Emphasizing the theme of the New Joshua does not mean denying the presence of other typologies. Patrick Schreiner, in his commentary on Matthew's gospel, points out that the themes of the New Moses and the New Joshua are not in conflict (indeed, Joshua himself was a new Moses, and so any figure who is a new Moses is also in some sense a new Joshua). As Schreiner puts the matter, "Is Jesus's going through the water in his baptism a picture of Moses, Israel, Joshua, the new creation, or the kingdom? The answer is yes. These can all coalesce because Jesus is the gravitational force that pulls all things together."[61]

In *The Sacraments in Biblical Perspective*, Ronald Byars perceives the typological connection in Matthew's Gospel between Jesus' baptism and the exodus, but he does not mention Joshua. Later in his book, however, Byars attends to Joshua 3. He notes that in leading the Israelites across the Jordan, Joshua is as a new Moses, just as Elijah is when he strikes the River Jordan and crosses the river on dry land and just as Elisha is when he performs the same miracle using Elijah's cloak (2 Kgs 2:8, 13–14). In addition, Byars observes that the narrative of the crossing of the Jordan, inclusive of Joshua's command to the people to sanctify themselves prior to the crossing, has an eschatological resonance. But Byars does not develop this further, other than to recognize that "the sacrament of baptism also witnesses to an eschatological dimension" (see Ephesians 1:13–14; 2 Corinthians 1:22) and that "[b]aptism is a sanctification, of sorts, by which the church prepares for the ultimate christophany, the Parousia of the Lord."[62]

Let me mention one more scholarly study, Kilian McDonnell's *The Baptism of Jesus in the Jordan: The Trinitarian and Cosmic Order of Salvation*. Much of McDonnell's work reports upon the

---

a true image of Baptism by which we pass through life.'" See Ratzinger, *Jesus of Nazareth*, 19, citing Paul Evdokimov, *The Art of the Icon: A Theology of Beauty, Illustrated* (Redondo Beach, CA: Oakwood Publications, 1990), 296.

[61] Patrick Schreiner, *Matthew, Disciple and Scribe: The First Gospel and Its Portrait of Jesus* (Grand Rapids, MI: Baker Academic, 2019), 50.

[62] Byars, *The Sacraments in Biblical Perspective*, 107.

5.3 JESUS' BAPTISM IN THE JORDAN

rich perspective of the Church Fathers with regard to the baptism of Jesus. Regarding contemporary scholarship, he expresses surprise and dismay that "the baptism of Jesus has not prompted more serious scholarly attention."[63] On the basis of patristic texts, he argues that Christ's baptism in the Jordan "is the locus of the trinitarian knowledge of God" and extends to the Spirit's baptism of the whole cosmos in the new creation.[64] He underscores "[t]he centrality of Jesus' baptism for understanding of Christian baptism," in which the image of God is restored as the commencement of the "new age."[65]

Closer to my focus in this chapter, McDonnell notes that according to some Fathers, "What the passage through the Red Sea was for Israel, the passage through the Jordan was for Jesus."[66] But although he makes clear the specialness of the River Jordan, he does not present Jesus as leading the eschatological entrance into the true Promised Land at his baptism. He is aware that "[i]n his *Commentary on Joshua*, Origen, as Barnabas and Justin before him, sees Joshua as a type of Christ. In fact, Origen consistently speaks of either Joshua or Jesus, but he means Joshua/Jesus."[67] But McDonnell does not further develop this point.

I appreciate McDonnell's emphasis on the Trinitarian, cosmic, and divinizing dimensions of Christian baptism and of the baptism of Christ. With respect to divinization, he aptly recalls Galatians 3:27: "As many of you as were baptized into Christ have clothed yourselves with Christ."[68] Drawing upon the Church Fathers, he recognizes that, in an important sense, Christian "[e]schatology

---

[63] Kilian McDonnell, O.S.B., *The Baptism of Jesus in the Jordan: The Trinitarian and Cosmic Order of Salvation* (Collegeville, MN: Liturgical Press, 1996), ix. One of the few exceptions, in terms of monographs, is Daniel Vigne, *Christ au Jourdain. Le baptême de Jésus dans la tradition judéo-chrétienne* (Paris: Gabalda, 1992).
[64] McDonnell, *The Baptism of Jesus in the Jordan*, 49; cf. 243.
[65] McDonnell, *The Baptism of Jesus in the Jordan*, 70, 72.
[66] McDonnell, *The Baptism of Jesus in the Jordan*, 74.
[67] McDonnell, *The Baptism of Jesus in the Jordan*, 82.
[68] See McDonnell, *The Baptism of Jesus in the Jordan*, 136.

begins at the Jordan," and he links the River Jordan to the "cosmic river" or the Edenic river imagery that is central to Christian eschatology.[69] As McDonnell emphasizes, our baptism is connected with Jesus' death and Resurrection (see John 19:34, Mark 10:39, Romans 6:3-4, and so on) – and the same is true for Jesus' own baptism, which inaugurates his public mission as "the Lamb of God, who takes away the sin of the world" (Jn 1:29; cf. 1:32–34).[70]

Liturgically, the feast of Jesus' baptism is the oldest feast other than Easter.[71] McDonnell, therefore, is correct to highlight the baptism of Jesus. To my mind, his project would be enhanced by recalling that Christ came to inaugurate the Kingdom and to lead his people into that Kingdom – the eschatological Promised Land. Jesus, the New Joshua, began to accomplish this work at the River Jordan.

5.4 Patristic Approaches to the New Joshua

The next step is to investigate the Joshua typology of the Church Fathers. Some of the Fathers, especially Origen, identify Jesus as the New Joshua who leads his baptized people into the true Promised Land. This background receives careful attention in Jean Daniélou's *From Shadows to Reality: Studies in the Biblical Typology of the Fathers*. He devotes a full chapter to the typological connection between the sacrament of baptism and Joshua's crossing of the Jordan into the Promised Land.[72]

---

[69] McDonnell, *The Baptism of Jesus in the Jordan*, 148.

[70] In this regard, McDonnell urges that Jesus' baptism be given more prominence rather than crowded out by Jesus' death and Resurrection. McDonnell notes appreciatively that the baptism of Jesus does receive an important place in the *Catechism of the Catholic Church*.

[71] See McDonnell, *The Baptism of Jesus in the Jordan*, 246.

[72] Jean Daniélou, S.J., *From Shadows to Reality: Studies in the Biblical Typology of the Fathers*, trans. Wulstan Hibberd, O.S.B. (London: Burns & Oates, 1960). Daniélou

5.4 PATRISTIC APPROACHES TO THE NEW JOSHUA

As Daniélou shows, prior to Origen the typological connection made by Christian thinkers was generally between baptism and the crossing of the Red Sea. This connection comes from 1 Corinthians 10:1–2: "I want you to know, brethren, that our fathers were all under the cloud, and all passed through the sea, and all were baptized into Moses in the cloud and in the sea." For Paul, the miraculous, liberative, and life-saving crossing of the Red Sea is figurally an experience of baptism. The crossing of the Red Sea participates in baptism as a type, proleptically allowing faith-filled Israelites to enjoy its benefits – even if that generation of Israelites fell short because they sinned against the Lord and were not allowed to reach the Promised Land. Paul deems the Israelites' post–Red Sea sins to be a warning to the baptized Christian Corinthians. He exhorts, "Now these things happened to them [the Israelites] as a warning, but they were written down for our instruction, upon whom the end of the ages has come. Therefore let any one who thinks that he stands take heed lest he fall" (1 Cor 10:11–12).

The fact that the Israelites of Moses' generation (other than Joshua and Caleb) did not attain the goal of the exodus means that the liberative and life-saving crossing of the Red Sea is not quite a full parallel with baptism.[73] For baptism truly unites us to Christ's

---

draws upon other scholars of his day, including F. J. Dölger, "Die Durchzug durch den Jordan als Sinnbild der Christlichen Taufe," *Antike und Christentum* 2 (1930): 70–79; Per Lundberg, *La typologie baptismale dans l'ancienne Église* (Uppsala: Lundequist, 1942); and Edward J. Duncan, *Baptism in the Demonstrations of Aphraates, the Persian Sage* (Washington, DC: Catholic University of America Press, 1945). For more recent studies, see, for example, Robert L. Wilken, "The Interpretation of the Baptism of Jesus in the Later Fathers," *Studia Patristica* 11 (1972): 268–77; and Sebastian Brock, "The Baptism of Christ and Christian Baptism," in Brock, *The Luminous Eye: The Spiritual World Vision of Saint Ephrem the Syrian* (Rome: Centre for Indian and Inter-religious Studies, 1985), 70–76.

[73] The crossing of the Red Sea can nevertheless function as a symbol of the crossing into eternal life (the true Promised Land), as, for instance, it does at the conclusion of Bonaventure's *The Journey of the Mind to God*, trans. Philotheus Boehner, O.F.M., ed. Stephen F. Brown (Indianapolis, IN: Hackett, 1993), 37–38.

Cross and Resurrection, and thus truly unites us to the triumphant risen and ascended Lord at the right hand of the Father, where even now we dwell with Christ. The Letter to Colossians urges, "If then you have been raised with Christ, seek the things that are above, where Christ is, seated at the right hand of God.... For you have died, and your life is hidden with Christ in God" (Col 3:1, 3). This insistence that believers already have died with Christ and have been raised with Christ echoes comments that Paul makes in his letter to the Romans. There he asks rhetorically: "Do you not know that all of us who have been baptized into Christ Jesus were baptized into his death? We were buried therefore with him by baptism into death, so that as Christ was raised from the dead by the glory of the Father, we too might walk in newness of life" (Rom 6:3-4).

Thus, in a real though incomplete sense, baptized believers share in the "newness of life" enjoyed by the risen Christ. More than simply journeying toward the Promised Land, we are by baptism already *in* the Promised Land, the glorious new creation that has been inaugurated where Christ is at the right hand of the Father. Since we have crossed into the true Promised Land through the waters of baptism, there is a typological connection between what baptism accomplishes and the entrance into the Promised Land accomplished by Joshua's crossing of the Jordan.[74]

In his study of the patristic development of this typological connection, Daniélou focuses on Origen, while also drawing upon Justin Martyr, Cyril of Jerusalem, and Gregory of Nyssa.[75] According to Origen in his *Commentary on John* – indebted here to Philo's etymology – the word "Jordan" can be translated as "their

---

[74] For further discussion, see the forthcoming book of Isaac Augustine Morales, O.P., from Baker Academic, tentatively titled *The Fountain of Salvation: A Biblical Theology of Baptism*.

[75] See also Aidan Nichols, O.P., *Lovely, Like Jerusalem: The Fulfillment of the Old Testament in Christ and the Church* (San Francisco: Ignatius Press, 2007), 194-97.

descent."[76] In John 1 it is the divine Word, dwelling "in the bosom of the Father" (Jn 1:18), who "descends" in the sense of becoming flesh. Likewise, the Spirit descends and abides in Jesus (Jn 1:32). Christ, the incarnate Word, does not only "descend" but also is "lifted up" (Jn 3:14) on the Cross so that people may believe in him and thereby "have eternal life" (Jn 3:15).

For Origen, the Jordan's etymological meaning ("their descent") refers to Jesus: He is the one who descended from God. The Jordan is a type of Jesus Christ. The streams that come forth from this river are the apostles and prophets, the foundation of the Church of which Christ is the cornerstone. Origen states, "we must understand the Jordan to be [the] Word of God which became flesh and dwelt among us."[77] Jesus' baptism in the Jordan shows us that by being baptized in water, we will be baptized into Jesus Christ, into the incarnate divine Word. Origen adds that at his baptism, Jesus receives the Spirit and thus is now "able to baptize those who come to him with that very Spirit which remained."[78]

If Jesus typologically is the Jordan, how does this have anything to do with Joshua crossing the Jordan into the Promised Land? Origen knows that the Hebrew name "Jesus" (Yeshua) is a variant of "Joshua" (Yehoshua). Thus, he has no trouble holding that "Jesus [Joshua], who succeeded Moses, was a type of Jesus the Christ who succeeded the dispensation through the Law with the gospel proclamation."[79] On this view, Jesus Christ is the New Joshua because he succeeds Moses, by proclaiming the gospel. As John 1:17 observes: "For the law was given through Moses; grace and truth came through Jesus Christ." Jesus Christ, the New Joshua, leads the people into the true Promised Land, to dwell with God everlastingly

---

[76] Origen, *Commentary on the Gospel according to John: Books 1–10*, trans. Ronald E. Heine (Washington, DC: Catholic University of America Press, 1989), Book 6, 227.
[77] Origen, *Commentary on the Gospel according to John*, Book 6, 228.
[78] Origen, *Commentary on the Gospel according to John*, Book 6, 228.
[79] Origen, *Commentary on the Gospel according to John*, Book 6, 231.

in "grace and truth." To be baptized in the "Jordan" means to be baptized into Jesus Christ, the Word who descends so that we may ascend in the Spirit to eternal life with God. According to Origen, Jesus thereby leads the true crossing of the Jordan into the true Promised Land, through baptism.

But if Jesus is the New Joshua and baptism was typologically signified by Joshua's crossing of the Jordan, why didn't Paul say so? Origen does not doubt that the crossing of the Red Sea was a type of baptism. After all, Christ was present in that crossing as well. Paul teaches that the fleeing Israelites were being protected by "the Supernatural Rock ... and the Rock was Christ" (1 Cor 10:4). But the crossing of the Jordan led by Joshua was also a type of baptism. Origen thinks that Paul would have affirmed that the Israelites on the exodus "all passed through the Jordan, and all were baptized into Jesus in the Spirit and in the river."[80]

Indeed, Origen considers it reasonable to suppose that the people underwent two baptisms – just like there was a baptism given by John the Baptist that contrasts with the sacrament of baptism. The Israelites were "baptized into Moses" (1 Cor 10:2) in the crossing of the Red Sea, but they still needed to be baptized into Christ. Origen describes baptism into Moses as deficient in a certain way: "[T]heir baptism has a bitter and briny element, for they still fear their enemies and cry out to the Lord" in complaint.[81] He depicts the Jordan as much greater than the Red Sea. The Red Sea is rather salty whereas the Jordan is a "truly sweet and fresh river" that is superior to the Red Sea just as Jesus is superior to Moses.[82]

In Joshua 3, when the priests bearing the ark of the covenant enter the River Jordan, the river stops flowing and – as happened at the Red Sea – the people march across on dry ground. Joshua is thereby exalted, just as God had promised when he told Joshua, "Be strong

---

[80] Origen, *Commentary on the Gospel according to John*, Book 6, 230.
[81] Origen, *Commentary on the Gospel according to John*, Book 6, 231.
[82] Origen, *Commentary on the Gospel according to John*, Book 6, 231.

and of good courage; for you shall cause this people to inherit the land" (Jos 1:6). For Origen, when Joshua is exalted in the crossing of the Jordan, this means that Jesus (typologically signified by Joshua) is exalted. Once the people have crossed the Jordan, Joshua circumcises the whole nation of Israel, and God proclaims: "This day I have rolled away the reproach of Egypt from you" (Jos 5:9). They are now able to celebrate the Passover in a new way, freed entirely from Egypt and eating the food of the Promised Land. Origen sees all this as a description, typologically, of what Jesus Christ accomplishes. It is baptism into Jesus through crossing the Jordan that purifies the people. They now eat the life-giving Eucharist, a food better than the manna of the exodus, as "will be clear to the one who has perceived the true holy land and the Jerusalem above."[83]

Origen connects this point with John 6, where Jesus presents himself as the "bread of life" and the "living bread" (Jn 6:48, 51) who is greater than the manna.[84] He is the "bread" that descends or "comes down from heaven, that a man may eat of it and not die" (Jn 6:50). It is only after the crossing of the Jordan that the Israelites stop eating the manna. Having crossed the Jordan, they eat the food of the Promised Land – which Origen associates with the spiritual perfection of moving from the Law to the grace of Jesus Christ.

Origen also draws upon the narrative of Elijah and Elisha in 2 Kings. When Elijah is about to be taken up to heaven, Elisha travels with Elijah to the banks of the River Jordan. There Elijah performs a miraculous crossing of the Jordan that typologically reenacts the crossing of Joshua and the people into the Promised Land. The implication is that Elijah's crossing of the Jordan signifies his crossing over into heavenly dwelling with God. After Elijah strikes the River Jordan, "the water was parted to the one side and to the other, till the two of them could go over on dry ground" (2 Kgs 2:8). Origen interprets this event as indicative of baptism: Elijah and Elisha

---

[83] Origen, *Commentary on the Gospel according to John*, Book 6, 232.
[84] See Origen, *Commentary on the Gospel according to John*, Book 6, 232.

were, in this way, baptized into Christ (the River Jordan). Here Origen repeats his interpretation of the River Jordan as "a type of the Word who condescended to our descent."[85] Just as Moses struck the rock and life-giving water came out – "and the Rock was Christ" (1 Cor 10:4; see Exod 17:6 and Num 20:11) – so also Elijah strikes the Jordan River, and it too was Christ. The striking of Christ is not a physical attack, Origen suggests, but rather is a seeking to penetrate or understand the Word of God unto salvation.

Elisha's miraculous healing of Naaman the Syrian receives similar attention. When Naaman washes seven times in the Jordan, his leprosy clears up. Naaman, however, at first mocks Elisha's command. Prior to obeying Elisha's command, Naaman angrily says: "I thought that he [Elisha] would surely come out to me, and stand, and call on the name of the Lord his God, and wave his hand over the place, and cure the leper. Are not Abana and Pharpar, the rivers of Damascus, better than all the waters of Israel? Could I not wash in them, and be clean?" (2 Kgs 5:11–12). In Origen's interpretation, Naaman here has not realized the status of the River Jordan as a type of Christ. Just as non-Christians insult the saving power of Christ, so Naaman insults the power that Elisha ascribes to washing seven times in the Jordan. But just as Jesus heals lepers (see Mt 8:2–3), so also the Jordan can heal lepers. The Jordan typologically stands for baptism into Jesus. As Origen comments, the washing in the Jordan means washing "his soul with faith in Jesus."[86] No wonder, Origen adds, the exiled Israelites "sat down and wept" when they found themselves "by the waters of Babylon" (Ps 137:1). Having sinned, they yearned for the Jordan, the "saving river" Jesus Christ.[87]

Origen realizes that these typologies can seem fanciful to people. He argues, however, that God himself arranged for typological links within Scripture, so that we might better understand the revealed

---

[85] Origen, *Commentary on the Gospel according to John*, Book 6, 234.
[86] Origen, *Commentary on the Gospel according to John*, Book 6, 235.
[87] Origen, *Commentary on the Gospel according to John*, Book 6, 235.

mysteries of God. In his view, the typology of rivers can be seen in the prophetic books as well. When, in the book of Ezekiel, God describes the punishments that are going to come upon Egypt, rivers have an evident typological significance. Pharaoh lays claim to the Nile as though Pharaoh were its creator. Through Ezekiel, God compares Pharaoh to a sea dragon, and God promises Pharaoh: "I will cast you forth into the wilderness, you and all the fish of your streams" (Ezek 29:5). It is evident that this is imagery; the Nile is not the abode of a sea dragon. Typologically, however, the River Nile symbolizes the enemy of the River Jordan (Christ). Origen states: "[J]ust as the dragon is in the Egyptian river, so God is in the river which makes glad the city of God, for the Father is in the Son."[88] The point is that rivers in Scripture can and do have typological significance, standing for realities that transcend the earthly reality of (e.g.) the Nile River.

In sum: Jesus, the New Joshua, has crossed the Jordan at his baptism. We are to be baptized by sharing in the crossing of the New Joshua. Such baptism enables us to eat the heavenly life-giving food (the Eucharist, Christ himself) and to be taken up into God's embrace as was Elijah. The crossing of the Red Sea was a baptism into Moses, and it had as its goal the people's entrance into the Promised Land through the crossing of the Jordan. The New Joshua has definitively accomplished this crossing, and so we are now baptized into Christ.

When Origen takes up this same theme in his *Homilies on Joshua*, he proposes that the Israelites and the Egyptians at the Red Sea can be understood as types of two contrasting individuals: the righteous and the sinner. The sinner is easily caught up in the roiling waters of the Red Sea, symbolic of chaos and destruction. By contrast, for the righteous, the ark of God takes the lead, and the priests, following the ark, help to ensure that the people move safely and securely through the seas of this world.

---

[88] Origen, *Commentary on the Gospel according to John*, Book 6, 236.

Origen also refers again to the typology of baptism as found in the crossing of the Jordan. Everyone who has received the sacrament of baptism has "parted the waters of the Jordan" and crossed to the Promised Land.[89] Equally, everyone who has received baptism has received a passage – if taken – through any life-threatening difficulty. This requires, of course, "forsaking Egypt" (understood typologically as idolatry). It also requires learning the Law of God, which is the face of Moses that reveals the divine glory, in preparation for "the mystic font of baptism."[90] In baptism, the believer finds "the Jordan parted" and "enter[s] the land of promise," the Church or the inaugurated kingdom, where "Jesus receives you after Moses, and becomes for you the leader of a new way."[91]

Origen goes on to remark that just as Joshua was exalted in relation to the crossing of the Jordan, so Jesus was exalted at his baptism in the Jordan, which takes on its full meaning in light of "the exaltation of the cross."[92] The New Joshua leads us into the true Promised Land, and he is greatly exalted thereby. But we can turn away from him by sinning, cleaving to this world rather than cleaving, in purity of heart, to God and the world to come. Origen compares this situation to how the Jordan River divides into two parts: One flows on in sweetness, the other joins itself to the salty sea. The latter symbolizes the plight of sinners. They have abandoned the "one Lord, one faith, one baptism, one God and Father of us all" (Eph 4:5–6).[93]

In the same place, Origen comments upon the typologically rich date on which Joshua led the people across the Jordan. The date was

---

[89] Origen, *Homilies on Joshua*, trans. Barbara J. Bruce, ed. Cynthia White (Washington, DC: Catholic University of America Press, 2002), Homily 4, 51.
[90] Origen, *Homilies on Joshua*, Homily 4, 52–53.
[91] Origen, *Homilies on Joshua*, Homily 4, 53.
[92] Origen, *Homilies on Joshua*, Homily 4, 53.
[93] Interestingly, Kilian McDonnell, O.S.B., shows that it is Origen, rather than any earlier Father, "who introduces a substantial witness to the Pauline theology of Romans 6:4, a significant moment in the development of baptismal theology" (McDonnell, *The Baptism of Jesus in the Jordan*, 201).

5.4 PATRISTIC APPROACHES TO THE NEW JOSHUA

"the tenth day of the first month" (Jos 4:19), which is the date on which the lamb of sacrifice for Passover was supposed to be selected and inspected (Exod 12:3). God commanded Moses and Aaron to make the month on which the Passover took place to be the first month of the year. On the fourteenth day of the month the Passover lamb was to be killed and eaten in festal remembrance of the flight of the enslaved Israelites from Egypt (Exod 12:6). Jesus' death, too, takes place in relation to Passover; he is the fulfillment of the Paschal lamb, and his death is a sacrificial sin-offering.[94] On essentially the same date, Joshua crossed the Jordan, and Jesus prepared to cross over in death. Origen urges that we too should join ourselves to this saving "day" and "enter the land of promise" even now, living according to "the blessedness of perfection" in the spiritual life.[95] Origen concludes by reiterating Christ's identity as the New Joshua leading his baptismal people into the true Promised Land.

In a second homily on this topic in his *Homilies on Joshua*, Origen repeats what we found in his *Commentary on John*: The Israelites' crossing of the Red Sea was a baptism into Moses, while the Israelites' crossing of the Jordan was a baptism into Jesus.[96] The sacrament of baptism, for Christians, consists in a crossing of the Jordan into the Promised Land, an immersion into Jesus the New Joshua. In this crossing, we must hasten toward the Promised Land so as not to be waylaid by the pride and pomp of the world but rather to be configured to the humble and suffering Christ. We must hasten to obtain the virtues and to be strengthened by truth and sincerity.

Origen makes much of the fact that the crossing of the Jordan led directly into the conquest of Jericho. He interprets this conquest in terms not of literal warfare but of post-baptismal spiritual warfare against vices. The exaltation of Jesus the New Joshua (or of

---

[94] See Pitre, *Jesus and the Last Supper*.
[95] Origen, *Homilies on Joshua*, Homily 4, 57.
[96] Origen, *Homilies on Joshua*, Homily 5, 59–66.

Joshua/Jesus) takes place not through military might but through the revelation of Jesus' divinity. Joshua 4:14 says that on the day on which the Israelites passed over the Jordan, "the Lord exalted Joshua in the sight of all Israel; and they stood in awe of him, as they had stood in awe of Moses." Origen takes this statement to refer to Jesus: Prior to their baptism, they revered Moses, but now they worship Jesus. In a similar way, he interprets Joshua 5:2's reference to a second circumcision to be, in the spiritual sense, a reference to the dual circumcision of the heart by the Law and by the gospel. It is the gospel that takes away "the reproach of Egypt" (Jos 5:9) from the Israelites. The gospel's "circumcision" is baptism, as Origen goes on to say.

Throughout this discussion, "Joshua" is consistently "Jesus" for Origen. For those who cross the Jordan with Joshua/Jesus through baptism, the danger consists in falling back into sin. Origen mentions here Paul's manifold warnings to the Corinthian Christians. He places emphasis on Paul's description of the Christian as "a temple of the Holy Spirit" (1 Cor 6:19) and of the Church as the "body" of Christ (Col 1:24). Even after crossing the Jordan, it remains possible to return to the "reproach of Egypt." Baptism, the crossing of the Jordan, and Christ as the New Joshua who leads us through the waters of the Jordan (empowered by his Cross and Resurrection) to the Promised Land are intertwined in Origen's exegesis.

According to Daniélou, in linking the crossing of the Jordan with the sacrament of baptism – and in relegating the crossing of the Red Sea to a "baptism into Moses" – Origen knew that he was innovating. Daniélou notes, however, that Origen was not innovating in applying the already "traditional idea that Joshua is a type of Christ."[97] Justin Martyr connects Moses with the Law and Joshua with the gospel. In his *Dialogue with Trypho*, Justin Martyr states that "[t]he people found seventy willows and twelve springs after

---

[97] Daniélou, *From Shadows to Reality*, 263.

5.4 PATRISTIC APPROACHES TO THE NEW JOSHUA

crossing the Jordan," and for Justin this is a symbolic suggestion that crossing the Jordan (baptism) has led them into the fullness of life.[98]

It could be, then, that Origen is drawing upon Justin Martyr. Certainly, in his reflections on the River Jordan and Naaman the Syrian, Origen is indebted to "a traditional theme of early baptismal catechetical courses."[99] For my purposes here, however, the key is the typological link that Origen makes between Joshua and Jesus the New Joshua, so that the crossing of the Jordan into the Promised Land typologically signifies the sacrament of baptism and the regeneration that baptism accomplishes. The Jordan itself, furthermore, is a type of Christ (the Word's "descent"), and so "the baptismal waters represent Christ himself in whom the baptized is washed."[100] This connects Christ's baptism in the Jordan with our baptism into Christ in multiple ways. As Daniélou remarks, "Joshua crossing the Jordan, with the dove of the Spirit resting on him, is a type of the humanity of Jesus assumed by the Word and dwelt in by the Holy Spirit: the theme of Joshua and that of Baptism harmonize to form a great theological symbol."[101]

After Origen, Daniélou observes, the crossing of the Red Sea remains a type of Christian baptism (rather than merely of "baptism into Moses"). Nevertheless, some of Origen's suggestions regarding baptism and the New Joshua are taken up by later Fathers. For example, in his *Catechetical Lectures*, Cyril of Jerusalem refers to Elijah having "crossed the Jordan" as a preparation for being taken up into heaven.[102] Cyril also depicts a sea dragon in the

---

[98] Justin Martyr, "Dialogue with Trypho," in *The Apostolic Fathers, Justin Martyr, Irenaeus*, ed. Alexander Roberts and James Donaldson, vol. 1 of Ante-Nicene Fathers Series (Peabody, MA: Hendrickson, 1995), 194–270, at 242 (ch. 86).
[99] Daniélou, *From Shadows to Reality*, 266–67. He names Tertullian, Didymus of Alexandria, and Ambrose.
[100] Daniélou, *From Shadows to Reality*, 268.
[101] Daniélou, *From Shadows to Reality*, 269.
[102] Cyril of Jerusalem, *Catechetical Lectures*, III.5, trans. Edward Hamilton Gifford, in *Cyril of Jerusalem, Gregory Nazianzen*, vol. 7 of Nicene and Post-Nicene Fathers, Second Series, ed. Philip Schaff and Henry Wace (Peabody, MA: Hendrickson, 1995), 1–157, at 15.

Jordan (drawing upon Job 40:23) that Christ, in his baptism, conquers – perhaps similar to the dragon in the Nile depicted typologically in Ezekiel, to which Origen refers.[103] Somewhat more to the point, Cyril argues that Moses gave his successor the name "Jesus" ("Joshua"), since Jesus the New Joshua was to become Israel's King. Cyril adds: "And Jesus [Joshua] the son of Nave was in many things a type of Him [Christ]. For when he [Joshua] began to rule over the people, he began from Jordan, whence Christ also, after He was baptized, began to preach the gospel."[104] Christ's baptism at the Jordan is here linked with Joshua's crossing of the Jordan, and it establishes Christ as the New Joshua and thus the rightful ruler of his people (and, as the *New* Joshua, the ruler not only of the twelve tribes but of the whole world, to which the risen Christ sends the eleven remaining disciples in Matthew 28:19).

Similarly, according to Gregory of Nyssa, it is manifest that the Old Testament "everywhere prefigured the likeness of our regeneration," including the sacrament of baptism.[105] He gives various examples of salvific water, including the crossing of the Red Sea, which signifies a flight from sin and a purification unto salvation. Much like Origen, he moves from the Red Sea to Joshua's crossing of the Jordan. He observes that the people of Israel "did not enter the land of promise until it had first been brought, with Joshua for its guide and the pilot of its life, to the passage of the Jordan."[106] Crossing over the Jordan entails entering into the Promised Land, which Gregory associates with entering into the new covenant in Christ through baptism.

Gregory thinks that by commanding the Israelites to collect twelve stones from the River Jordan during the crossing (see Joshua 4:3),

---

[103] Cyril of Jerusalem, *Catechetical Lectures*, III.11, p. 17.
[104] Cyril of Jerusalem, *Catechetical Lectures*, X.11, p. 60.
[105] Gregory of Nyssa, "On the Baptism of Christ," in *Gregory of Nyssa: Dogmatic Treatises, Etc.*, trans. William Moore and Henry Austin Wilson, vol. 5 of Nicene and Post-Nicene Fathers, Second Series, ed. Philip Schaff and Henry Wace (Peabody, MA: Hendrickson, 1995), 518–24, at 521.
[106] Gregory of Nyssa, "On the Baptism of Christ," 522.

Joshua is anticipating Christ's establishment of the Church upon the twelve disciples. To cross over the Jordan thus symbolizes our baptismal entrance into the Church, the true Promised Land. Gregory also gives special significance to the Jordan in connection with Elisha's miracle of cleansing Naaman the Syrian. For Gregory, the mode by which Naaman is healed signifies the power of baptism, and the River Jordan stands as the fount of all baptismal water. He states, "For Jordan alone of rivers, receiving in itself the first-fruits of sanctification and benediction, conveyed in its channel to the whole world, as it were from some fount in the type afforded by itself, the grace of Baptism."[107] The Jordan has a major place in the history of salvation. Not only do Joshua and the Israelites cross it but also Elijah crosses it, and John the Baptist, fulfilling the role of Elijah, dwells near it. Most notably, John the Baptist baptizes Jesus in the Jordan. Gregory concludes: "For as great Lebanon presents a sufficient cause of wonder in the very trees which it brings forth and nourishes, so is the Jordan glorified by regenerating men and planting them in the Paradise of God."[108]

Thus for Gregory, as for Origen, the sacrament of baptism is grounded in the Jordan and in the baptism of Jesus. Baptism enables us to cross over to the Promised Land, the "Paradise of God." We do this by becoming true disciples of Christ in his Church and thereby becoming the bride of Christ, rejoicing in the eschatological marriage of God and creation.

5.5 Aquinas's Contributions

In the seventh volume of *The Glory of the Lord: A Theological Aesthetics*, Hans Urs von Balthasar remarks with respect to Jesus'

---

[107] Gregory of Nyssa, "On the Baptism of Christ," 522.
[108] Gregory of Nyssa, "On the Baptism of Christ," 523.

baptism: "The profound immersion at the Baptism into salvation history, which was itself actually moving towards this point, is, with the narrative of the childhood of Jesus, an allusive recapitulation of the chief stages of this salvation history."[109] He argues that the temptation in the wilderness that comes after Jesus' baptism in the Jordan is a parallel to Israel's existential stance on the exodus, during which Israel stands alone in the presence of God, in a condition of temptation and in constant need of grace. In this context, Balthasar deems Jesus to be both "the new Moses" and "the new Israel," but he does not mention Joshua.[110] He connects Jesus' "fulfil[ling] all righteousness" (Mt 3:15) at Jesus' baptism with God's will "to lead Jesus, as the author of the salvation of all God's sons, to perfection through the Passion (Heb 2.10)."[111] While Balthasar grasps the connection of Jesus' baptism to his Passion, he does not comment upon its connection to the crossing over to the Promised Land.

By comparison, when Aquinas turns to Jesus' baptism in III, q. 39, he notes (in an objection to his own view) that if Jesus intended to connect his own baptism with the sacrament of baptism, then Jesus should have traveled to the Red Sea to be baptized, since Paul specially links the crossing of the Red Sea to the sacrament of baptism. Against this view, Aquinas argues that the crossing of the Jordan under the leadership of Joshua signifies baptism more fully than does the crossing of the Red Sea. He explains that Jesus chose to be baptized in the River Jordan because of Joshua's crossing over the Jordan into the Promised Land. Aquinas comments, "The crossing of the Red Sea foreshadowed baptism in this – that baptism takes away sin: whereas the crossing of the Jordan foreshadows

---

[109] Hans Urs von Balthasar, *The Glory of the Lord: A Theological Aesthetics*, vol. 7, *Theology: The New Covenant*, trans. Brian McNeil, C.R.V., ed. John Riches (San Francisco: Ignatius Press, 1989), 69–70.

[110] Balthasar, *The Glory of the Lord*, 68.

[111] Balthasar, *The Glory of the Lord*, 315–16.

it in this – that it opens the gate to the heavenly kingdom: and this is the principal effect of baptism, and accomplished through Christ alone."[112] This is a New Joshua Christology.

According to Aquinas, Christ instituted the sacrament of baptism at his baptism by John at the Jordan. Emphasizing how fitting this location is, he again observes, "It was through the river Jordan that the children of Israel entered into the land of promise. Now, this is the prerogative of Christ's baptism over all other baptisms: that it is the entrance to the kingdom of God, which is signified by the land of promise."[113] By being baptized in the Jordan, Christ revealed and instituted the sacrament of baptism as a crossing over into the true Promised Land. Aquinas explains that the sacrament of baptism accomplishes this crossing over by the divine power of the Trinity, by our faith in the Trinity and in Christ, and by the removal of the debt of original sin that impeded communion with God.

For the baptized, access to the divine ("heavenly") life is immediately granted. The baptized stand with the crucified, risen, and ascended Christ, sharing in the love and joy of Christ's kingdom. But, at the same time, the full consummation of the crossing over into the kingdom awaits Christ's coming in glory. For now, the baptized person "needs to pray continually, in order to enter heaven: for though sins are remitted through baptism, there still remain the fomes of sin assailing us from within, and the world and the devils assailing us from without."[114] Aquinas thinks this latter point is why the evangelist Luke mentions that Jesus, just prior to the theophany and just after his baptism, "was praying" (Lk 3:21).

In his discussion of Christ's baptism, Aquinas remarks that "Christ, when He had sanctified baptism [by sanctifying the waters

---

[112] Thomas Aquinas, *Summa Theologiae*, trans. Fathers of the English Dominican Province (Westminster, MD: Christian Classics, 1981), III, q. 39, a. 4, ad 1.
[113] III, q. 39, a. 4.
[114] III, q. 39, a. 5.

of the Jordan], saw that heaven was opened to men."[115] Access to the eschatological kingdom of God had arrived. But if "Christ's Passion is ... the cause of our reconciliation to God,"[116] then how can Christ's baptism already mark the inauguration of the kingdom of God? Indeed, Aquinas holds that only when the redemptive "cost of Christ's blood" had been paid out of love did anyone "enter the kingdom of heaven by obtaining everlasting beatitude."[117] Aquinas's position is that the sacrament of baptism was instituted at the moment of Christ's baptism, and this sacrament opens up the kingdom of God. But the sacrament of baptism derives its spiritual power or efficacy from the Cross of Christ, not from Christ's baptism.[118]

Aquinas also thinks that Christ's Ascension plays a role in opening up the kingdom of God to believers. When Christ in his glorified

---

[115] III, q. 39, a. 5, ad 2. Aquinas takes this point from a patristic debate over whether the opening of the heaven (reported by all the Synoptics) was seen corporeally or spiritually by Jesus. Jerome and Chrysostom, among other Fathers, think it was a spiritual vision similar to what Ezekiel experienced (Ezek 1:1). Some Fathers argue to the contrary that Jesus was surrounded by a bright light and all could see it.

[116] III, q. 49, a. 4.

[117] III, q. 49, a. 5, ad 1.

[118] See III, q. 49, a. 5, ad 3. In the third edition of their *On the Sacraments in General: On Baptism, Confirmation, Eucharist, Penance and Anointing*, the neo-scholastic Jesuit theologians Joseph A. de Aldama, Severino Gonzalez, Francis A. P. Sola, and Joseph F. Sagüés take up the question of when Christ instituted the sacrament of baptism. They note that according to Francisco Suárez and others, Aquinas's position is not to be understood as indicating that the sacrament of baptism was actually instituted at his baptism by John; rather Aquinas means only to say that the form was present (the Trinity) and the matter was present (the water), thus foreshadowing the sacrament. See Joseph A. de Aldama, S.J., Severino Gonzalez, S.J., Francis A. P. Sola, S.J., and Joseph F. Sagüés, S.J., *On the Sacraments in General. On Baptism, Confirmation, Eucharist, Penance and Anointing*, 3rd (Latin) ed., trans. Kenneth Baker, S.J. (n.p.: Keep the Faith, 2015), 132, citing Francisco Suárez's *De Sacramentis*, d. 19, s. 2, n. 4. Aquinas holds this view in his *Commentary on the Sentences: Book IV, Distinctions 1–13*, trans. Beth Mortensen (Green Bay, WI: Aquinas Institute, 2017), d. 3, q. 1, a. 5, response to qla. 2 (p. 146). See also *Summa theologiae* III, q. 66, a. 2, where by contrast Aquinas states that "baptism received this power [to confer grace] when Christ was baptized. Consequently Baptism was truly instituted then, if we consider it as a sacrament."

5.5 AQUINAS'S CONTRIBUTIONS

humanity ascended to the Father, the bodily entrance of humans into the kingdom began.[119] Now that Christ is there, we have the hope of joining him fully there, through the charity given us by the Holy Spirit. In this regard Aquinas cites Micah 2:13, "He who opens the breach will go up before them; they will break through and pass the gate, going out by it. Their king will pass on before them, the Lord at their head."[120]

In responding to the question of whether Christ opened the gates of heaven (the kingdom of God) by his Passion, Aquinas cites a passage from Hebrews that is also treated by Ounsworth: "We have confidence to enter the sanctuary [the eschatological Temple, the kingdom of God] by the blood of Jesus, by the new and living way which he opened for us through the curtain, that is, through his flesh" (Heb 10:19–20).[121] Christ opened this way for us by his death on the Cross. But we are incorporated into his saving death through baptism, as Romans 6:3 says: "[A]ll of us who were baptized into Christ Jesus were baptized into his death." Aquinas cites the latter passage in a reply to an objection where he is discussing the heavens being opened at Christ's baptism in the Jordan.[122] Christ's institution of the sacrament of baptism at the Jordan is the institution of a saving sacrament whose power depends upon Christ's Cross. Because of this connection of baptism to the power of the Cross, the heavens open when Christ receives baptism. Aquinas explains that the events that surround Christ's baptism are figures of what the sacrament accomplishes in us.[123]

Discussing Christ's miracles, Aquinas argues that it would not have been fitting for Christ, like Moses, Joshua, and Elijah, to perform a miracle of dividing the waters, because Christ came not to divide but "to restore all things to a state of peace and calm."[124] In

---

[119] See III, q. 49, a. 5, ad 4.
[120] Cited in III, q. 57, a. 1, ad 3.
[121] Cited in III, q. 49, a. 5, *sed contra*.
[122] See III, q. 39, a. 5, ad 3.
[123] See III, q. 39, a. 8.
[124] III, q. 44, a. 4, ad 3.

his *Commentary on Hebrews*, Aquinas does not draw an explicit connection between Joshua's miraculous crossing of the Jordan and Christ's crossing into the true Promised Land, but he does observe that Hebrews 4:8, in accord with Psalm 95, intends to show that the "rest" sought by Israel was not the "rest" for which we must seek. The rest sought by the Israelites under Joshua was temporal and earthly, whereas the rest sought by Christians – and delivered by Jesus Christ – is "a spiritual rest," of which the rest sought by Israel in the Promised Land was "a sign."[125]

In his *Commentary on the Gospel of Matthew*, Aquinas explains Jesus' name by remarking that "there have been others who were also called Jesus, like Jesus the son of Nave [Joshua the son of Nun]" – and he then observes that this Joshua prefigured Jesus Christ.[126] Moreover, Joshua prefigured Jesus in exactly the way that Ounsworth supposes. Aquinas states, "Jesus [Joshua] led the people of Israel into the land of the promise; but this Jesus, i.e., our Savior, led us not into a fleshly land, but into a heavenly land. *For we have him as the author and finisher in his blood* (Heb 12:2)."[127] Aquinas highlights the eschatological value of New Joshua Christology.

Commenting on Matthew's account of Jesus' baptism by John (Mt 3:13–17), Aquinas picks up on Origen's etymology of "Jordan" as meaning "descent."[128] Given this etymology, Aquinas deems the River Jordan to be a symbol of humility. Not only does Jesus embody humility but also humility is required for the baptized to be able to receive the grace given by the sacrament. The meaning of "descent" and the connection of this meaning to humility are

---

[125] Thomas Aquinas, *Commentary on the Letter of Saint Paul to the Hebrews*, trans. Fabian Larcher, O.P., ed. J. Mortensen and E. Alarcón (Lander, WY: The Aquinas Institute for the Study of Sacred Doctrine, 2012), §207, p. 96.

[126] Thomas Aquinas, *Commentary on the Gospel of Matthew*, Chapters 1–12, trans. Jeremy Holmes and Beth Mortensen, ed. The Aquinas Institute (Lander, WY: The Aquinas Institute for the Study of Sacred Doctrine, 2013), §18, p. 6.

[127] Aquinas, *Commentary on the Gospel of Matthew*, §18, p. 7.

[128] Aquinas, *Commentary on the Gospel of Matthew*, §290, p. 94.

5.5 AQUINAS'S CONTRIBUTIONS

attributed by Aquinas in his *Catena Aurea* to a ninth-century monk of Auxerre, Remigius.[129] Aquinas adds that "Scripture tells of many wonders wrought at various times in this river"; for instance, "as Elijah divided the waters of old, so Christ the Lord wrought in the same Jordan the separation of sin."[130] He also remarks that according to (Pseudo-)Chrysostom, the opening of the heavens (Mt 3:16) signifies the opening of the gate of heaven or the opening of the heavenly kingdom of God, accomplished by the sacrament of baptism.

Again in his *Commentary on the Gospel of Matthew*, Aquinas observes that the baptized – having been united to Christ (Galatians 3:27) – "gain a heavenly inheritance" as noted in 1 Peter 1:3–4, so that it is no longer the case that "heaven [is] closed to the human race by sin."[131] When he turns to the temptation of Jesus in the wilderness in Matthew 4:1–11, he mentions the crossing of the Jordan into the Promised Land. He notes that the Israelites on the exodus pointed forward to the sacrament of baptism when, "after the crossing of the Red Sea, which was a figure of baptism, [they] came into the land of promise through the desert and the wilderness."[132] Although he mentions the entrance into the Promised Land, he mentions only the crossing of the Red Sea under Moses and not the crossing of the Jordan under Joshua that he had mentioned earlier.

In his *Commentary on the Gospel of John*, he not only attributes the etymology of "Jordan" ("their descent") to Origen – again demonstrating his knowledge of Origen's Joshua-rich

---

[129] Thomas Aquinas, *Catena Aurea: Commentary on the Four Gospels Collected out of the Works of the Fathers*, vol. 1, Part 1, *St. Matthew*, trans. John Henry Newman (Albany, NY: Preserving Christian Publications, 1995), 108.

[130] Aquinas, *Catena Aurea*, vol. 1, Part 1, 108.

[131] Aquinas, *Commentary on the Gospel of Matthew*, §§297–98, p. 96. Notably, in his commentary, Aquinas holds that the vision that Jesus saw of the Spirit descending in the form of a dove was seen by the bystanders as well, rather than solely by Jesus.

[132] Aquinas, *Commentary on the Gospel of Matthew*, §309, pp. 100–01.

commentary – but also observes that the River Jordan has importance for understanding the sacrament of baptism because "it is the border line between those who received their inheritance from Moses on one side of the Jordan, and those who received it from Joshua on the other side."[133] The former are Jews (inheritors of Moses), the latter are Christian Jews and Christian Gentiles (inheritors of Joshua). The connection between Joshua and Jesus the New Joshua is clear. Those who receive baptism enter the true Promised Land under the New Joshua. As Aquinas says, "For just as the Jews had to cross the Jordan to enter the Promised Land, so one must pass through baptism to enter into the heavenly land."[134] The baptism of Jesus in the Jordan shows that the crossing led by Joshua signifies the baptismal Jordan-crossing of Jesus, by which Jesus institutes the sacrament of baptism and leads his people into the eschatological kingdom of God.

I note that Jesus' role as the New Joshua, leading his people into the true Promised Land, could be integrated into what Aquinas says about Christ as Head of the Church in III, question 8. Even more, Jesus' role as the New Joshua could receive a separate article in question 39 on Jesus' baptism in the Jordan, or at least articles 1 and 3 provide room for this theme. In addition, Aquinas's reflections on Jesus' death in question 50 naturally leads to reflection upon the parallel between crossing the Jordan and crossing into the true Promised Land, perhaps especially in article 6 on how Christ's death (his being dead) conduced to our salvation. The same point holds for Aquinas's reflections on Christ's burial in question 51, since the crossing of the Jordan and Jesus' baptism in the Jordan are symbolic of a burial. Aquinas's question on Christ's Ascension (question 57) might be another place for further consideration of the eschatological New Joshua and the new exodus.

---

[133] Thomas Aquinas, *Commentary on the Gospel of John:* Chapters 1–5, trans. Fabian Larcher, O.P., and James A. Weisheipl, O.P., ed. Daniel Keating and Matthew Levering (Washington, DC: Catholic University of America Press, 2010), §252, p. 102.

[134] Aquinas, *Commentary on the Gospel of John:*, §252, p. 102.

5.6 An Ontological Note

Ontologically, the concept of the "New Joshua" has especially to do with the resurrected body and the glorified subject (individual and communal) in eternal life, because the eschatological Joshua leads us into the true Promised Land where we will dwell forever (and perfectly) with God. Christ is the eschatological Joshua because he has the power to lead all human beings to eternal life. Aquinas states that Christ, "by coming sacramentally into man, causes the life of grace, according to John 1:17."[135] This life of grace is the condition of the new exodus, although Aquinas does not describe it as such. Christ crosses over the "Jordan" of death by his Passion, and the sacraments unite us to the power of his Passion.

Not only baptism but also the Eucharist has an important role to play. Aquinas remarks that the Eucharist inaugurates our eternal life, insofar as it "cause[s] the attaining of eternal life" and is a foretaste of the heavenly banquet or of "the refreshment of spiritual food" that will characterize eternal life.[136] Our journey to eternal life receives powerful assistance from the Eucharist. Aquinas describes the Eucharist as "spiritual food and spiritual medicine" that strengthens our spiritual life, which is precisely what the new exodus journey requires.[137]

In response to the question of when the fullness of the Promised Land will be reached by Christ's members, Aquinas observes that Christ deliberately did not reveal when the end will come.[138] When it does happen, it will come suddenly and all at once. In Aquinas's view, all will die, all will be burned to ashes in an eschatological fiery purification of the cosmos, and all shall rise. Our risen bodies will be translucent to our charity, and we will see the

---

[135] III, q. 79, a. 1; translation slightly altered.
[136] III, q. 79, a. 2.
[137] III, q. 79, a. 6.
[138] See Suppl., q. 77, a. 3.

divine essence. In eternal life, when we see bodies, we "will see so great a glory of God in bodies, especially in the glorified bodies and most of all in the body of Christ."[139] Our degree of blessedness will depend upon our degree of charity, and the whole Church will be God's bride, brought into "Christ's dwelling" and rejoicing in his spiritual gifts.[140]

Thus, Aquinas has much to offer to our reflection on the ontological realities that are the new exodus and its terminus in the true Promised Land, brought about by the New Joshua. Contemporary Thomistic Christology would be wise to make even more central these New Joshua themes, especially with respect to life in Christ, the sacraments, and eternal life.

5.7 Conclusion

Ounsworth, Origen, and Aquinas are in agreement about the central points regarding Christ the New Joshua. Ounsworth adds a notable element to the discussion by arguing that much of Hebrews is shaped around the New Joshua motif, with Christ entering into the heavenly sanctuary – the true Promised Land and Sabbath "rest" – and calling all people to be united with him there. Origen and Aquinas focus attention especially on Christ's baptism in the Jordan. For Aquinas in question 39 of the *tertia pars*, as we saw, Joshua's crossing of the Jordan foreshadows the sacrament of baptism (instituted by Christ at his baptism in the Jordan). Christ the New Joshua has led the way across the waters of death and to the kingdom of the Father, where God's people dwell with God. Aquinas states that Christ chose to be baptized in the Jordan because "it was through the river Jordan that the children of Israel entered into the land of promise," and Christ's baptism institutes the sacrament

---

[139] Suppl., q. 92, a. 2.
[140] Suppl., q. 95, a. 1, *sed contra*.

of baptism by which Christians cross over into the true Promised Land, the kingdom of God.[141] The ascended Christ has completed the new exodus and enables us to join him.

In his biblical commentaries, Aquinas is explicit in presenting Christ as the New Joshua who has accomplished the entrance into the true Promised Land, in fulfillment of the exodus. In his *Commentary on Hebrews*, Aquinas notes that the "rest" (Heb 4:8) that Christ provides is "a spiritual rest," symbolized by the rest that Israel sought in crossing the Jordan into the Promised Land.[142] In his *Commentary on the Gospel of Matthew*, Aquinas notes that Joshua (or "Jesus the son of Nave") prefigures Jesus Christ.[143] Along lines that are fully seconded by Ounsworth, Aquinas states, "Jesus [i.e., Joshua] led the people of Israel into the land of the promise; but this Jesus, i.e., our Savior, led us not into a fleshly land, but into a heavenly land."[144] As we observed, in his *Commentary on John*, Aquinas connects this new exodus with Jesus' baptism in the Jordan, insofar as Jesus there instituted the sacrament of baptism. Thus, not only the entrance into the Promised Land but also the Jordan River unites Joshua and Jesus.[145]

The New Joshua Christology to which Ounsworth has made a major contribution is, therefore, richly present in Aquinas's writings, both in the *tertia pars* and in his biblical commentaries. My suggestion is that it could be even more explicit in the *tertia pars*, given the biblical centrality of the theme of the new exodus to the Promised Land. In relation to Christ's Paschal mystery, Christ's baptism in the Jordan deserves more attention, as Kilian McDonnell shows. Christ's baptism helps us to understand our baptism, that is, our place in the crossing into the true Promised Land that

---

[141] III, q. 39, a. 4.
[142] Aquinas, *Commentary on the Letter of Saint Paul to the Hebrews*, §207, p. 96.
[143] Aquinas, *Commentary on the Gospel of Matthew*, §18, p. 6.
[144] Aquinas, *Commentary on the Gospel of Matthew*, §18, p. 7.
[145] Aquinas, *Commentary on the Gospel of John*, §252, p. 102.

has been accomplished by the New Joshua. These themes presently receive too little attention in Thomistic Christology.

It is worth noting that New Joshua Christology continues today to be of importance in the interpretation of Jesus' baptism in the Jordan. According to the interpretation offered by the *Catechism of the Catholic Church*, Jesus' baptism in the Jordan begins his public life and signals his "acceptance and inauguration of his mission as God's suffering Servant."[146] The *Catechism* takes up the theme of the New Joshua in discussing the sacrament of baptism, when it describes the Easter Vigil's rite for the Blessing of the Water. Among the liturgical figures of baptism are the Spirit's "moving over the face of the waters" at the dawn of creation (Gen 1:2), Noah's ark, and the crossing of the Red Sea. To these figures, the *Catechism* adds the "the crossing of the Jordan River by which the People of God received the gift of the land promised to Abraham's descendants."[147] The Promised Land that Joshua entered was, as the *Catechism* says, "an image of eternal life."[148] Christ the New Joshua leads us into the eschatological inheritance of the people of God.

Indeed, we are truly "heirs of God and fellow heirs with Christ, provided we suffer with him in order that we may also be glorified with him" (Rom 8:17). We must cross the Jordan with Christ the New Joshua, dying and rising with him in baptism and living even now in union with him through the Eucharist. Empowered by the grace of the Holy Spirit, we today journey together with the New Joshua on the new exodus into the fullness of the Promised Land. Christ has entered into the eschatological Land of everlasting love, to which he calls us. These themes, well known to Aquinas, deserve to be amplified in Thomistic Christology.

---

[146] *Catechism of the Catholic Church*, 2nd ed. (Vatican City: Libreria Editrice Vaticana, 1997), §536.

[147] *Catechism of the Catholic Church*, §1222.

[148] *Catechism of the Catholic Church*, §1222.

6 | Christ the New David

The Eschatological Kingdom

6.1 Introduction

The Gospel of Matthew opens with these words: "The book of the genealogy of Jesus Christ, the son of David, the son of Abraham" (Mt 1:1). When Jesus, son of Abraham and son of David, enters triumphantly into Jerusalem on Palm Sunday, the crowd acclaims him as the Messiah: "Hosanna to the Son of David!" (Mt 21:9). In Gospel of Mark, the acclamation invokes the eschatological Davidic kingdom: "Blessed is he who comes in the name of the Lord! Blessed is the kingdom of our father David that is coming!" (Mk 11:9–10). Similarly, in the Gospel of Luke, the angel Gabriel tells Mary at the annunciation that her son "will be great, and will be called the Son of the Most High; and the Lord God will give to him the throne of his father David, and he will reign over the house of Jacob for ever; and of his kingdom there will be no end" (Lk 1:32–33). According to the Gospel of John, Jesus will be the "King of Israel" (Jn 1:49), in such a way that he will stand as the ladder between heaven and earth, and believers "will see heaven opened, and the angels of God ascending and descending upon the Son of man" (Jn 1:51).

Thus, the Gospels make clear that while Jesus is in the long-awaited Davidic king, his rule far exceeds the earthly kingship that David possessed. No wonder that Jesus says in the Gospel of John, "My kingship is not of this world" (Jn 18:36). No wonder, too, that he speaks of his eschatological kingdom as something far greater and more mysterious than a mere extension of the Davidic kingdom, as when he says, "Then the righteous will shine like the sun in the kingdom of their Father" (Mt 13:43), or when he identifies status in the kingdom as being based upon humility: "Whoever humbles himself like this child, he is the greatest in the kingdom of heaven" (Mt 18:4). Likewise, the transcendent character of the New David's kingdom is clear when Paul says that "flesh and blood cannot inherit the kingdom of God," insofar as the citizens of the Son of David's everlasting kingdom will bear glorified bodies in the image of Jesus' glorified body (1 Cor 15:50).

In light of the above, the first section of this chapter will provide an extensive survey of recent biblical scholarship about the theme of the New David in the Gospels. In the second section of the chapter, then, I take up the reflections on the New David offered by Irenaeus, Augustine, and Thomas Aquinas. To what degree are their understandings of Christ set forth within the framework of the eschatological David? Is N. T. Wright correct when he complains, "The gospels were all about God becoming king, but the creeds [and thus classical Christologies] are focused on Jesus being God"?[1] In the final section, I address certain ways in which Aquinas's *sacra doctrina* probes into the saving realities under discussion in this chapter.

6.2 The New David in Contemporary Biblical Scholarship

6.2.1 Luke-Acts

Let me begin with Yuzuru Miura's study *David in Luke-Acts*. Drawing upon 1–2 Samuel, 1–2 Kings, and 1–2 Chronicles, Miura attends to the events of David's life: his being chosen by God, his military valor, his bringing the ark to Jerusalem, his reception of a covenant, his sins, and so on. Miura then explores prophetic texts, arguing

---

[1] N. T. Wright, *How God Became King: The Forgotten Story of the Gospels* (New York: HarperCollins, 2012), 20.

6.2 NEW DAVID IN CONTEMPORARY BIBLICAL SCHOLARSHIP

that preexilic texts such as Hosea 3:5, Amos 9:11, and Isaiah 9–11 contain a portrait of a future Davidic king restoring the long-lost United Kingdom, whereas postexilic texts such as Isaiah 55, Jeremiah 23, and Ezekiel 34 and 37 point forward to a Davidic king who either leads the people back from exile or, as a righteous "new David," establishes a unified kingdom.[2] The prophets envision a typological relationship between David and the Messiah that is, at least in some cases, clearly a genealogical relationship as well.

Miura examines Second Temple texts that provide background for interpreting the New Testament, beginning with Sirach's presentation of the "historical" David. David is the ideal Israelite, a powerful warrior and a man of prayer and praise who adorned the Israelite worship service and who received the divine forgiveness of his sins. Psalms of Solomon 17 calls upon God to raise up a son of David as king and urges God to remember the covenant that he made, in which he swore that the Davidic kingship would never fail. Psalms of Solomon anticipates that this Davidic king will be righteous, wise, Spirit-filled, God-fearing, a restorer of Israel, a ruler over the nations, and a royal shepherd.

Like Psalms of Solomon, the Qumran documents look back to David's life and look forward to an eschatological Davidic king. This future David will do such things as compose a perfect number of Psalms ($150 \times 24 = 3600$), serve as a model for Israel in the "eschatological war," restore Israel, rebuild the Temple, and reign

---

[2] See Yuzuru Miura, *David in Luke-Acts* (Tübingen: Mohr Siebeck, 2007), 31. See also Mark Strauss, *The Davidic Messiah in Luke-Acts: The Promise and Its Fulfillment in Lukan Christology* (Sheffield: Sheffield Academic Press, 1995). Miura regularly cites and engages with Strauss's work, which he admires and incorporates into his own study. For further background, see, for example, H. G. M. Williamson, "Davidic Kingship in Isaiah," in *The Oxford Handbook of Isaiah*, ed. Lena-Sofia Tiemeyer (Oxford: Oxford University Press, 2020), 280–92, which draws upon Williamson's *Variations on a Theme: King, Messiah and Servant in the Book of Isaiah* (Carlisle, UK: Paternoster, 1998); and chapter 3 of Isaac W. Oliver, *Luke's Jewish Eschatology: The National Restoration of Israel in Luke-Acts* (Oxford: Oxford University Press, 2021).

forever.³ Some of Qumran's texts that appear to refer to the eschatological Messiah are only partially preserved, but many other texts make clear that a righteous Messianic "branch" of David will lead Israel in triumphant eschatological warfare. In addition, the Qumran documents recall David's life, presenting him as a man of piety who obtained forgiveness for his sins due to his repentance. Miura observes that for the Qumran documents "all ideal aspects of the life of the historical David would be those of the Davidic Messiah in a more idealized way."⁴

Philo and Josephus avoid the Messianic dimension of the Davidic tradition. Philo appreciates David as a prophet and as the inspired author of the Psalms, but he thinks the Messiah will be a Mosaic figure. For Josephus, the Davidic covenant was fulfilled by the building of the Temple. Perhaps for political reasons, Josephus ignores the promise that a Davidic king would reign in Jerusalem forever.

Turning to the New Testament, Miura begins with the Book of Acts. David appears in Acts 2 as the psalmist who is possessed of prophetic knowledge about Jesus (specifically about his Resurrection and Ascension). The key argument in Acts 2 is that "Jesus is *the Davidic Messiah* whom Jews have expected, correcting another kind of Jewish Davidic eschatological/messianic expectation of *David redivivus*."⁵ Miura identifies in Acts 2 a threefold typology between David and the New David, rooted in three aspects of David's life: David's righteous suffering (as expressed in the Psalm), David's hope for God's deliverance (in the midst of fleeing from Saul), and David's hope for enthronement. These three elements are correlated with Jesus' crucifixion, Resurrection, and Ascension.

Other quotations from David the prophetic psalmist play a role in the early chapters of Acts. For example, Acts 1 quotes Psalms 68 and 108 (LXX) as prophetic speech expressing Jesus' judgment

---

³ Miura, *David in Luke-Acts*, 73.
⁴ Miura, *David in Luke-Acts*, 88.
⁵ Miura, *David in Luke-Acts*, 149.

6.2 NEW DAVID IN CONTEMPORARY BIBLICAL SCHOLARSHIP

against Judas. In Acts 4, the disciples quote Psalm 2:1–2, interpreted as a prophetic description of the conspiracy (involving the Gentile and Jewish leaders) to kill Jesus. Acts 4 offers the following parallels between David and Jesus: Both have Gentile and Jewish adversaries; both are righteous sufferers; both have a kingdom; both are anointed (David by Samuel, Jesus at his baptism); both are proclaimed "son" of God (Psalm 2:7; Luke 3:22); both have their status as king confirmed by enthronement; both have their kingdom made firm sometime after its establishment (in Solomon's day for David; at his Second Coming for Jesus). Miura sums up: "[W]e see the complete picture of the ideal king David in Samuel (as chosen, pious, triumphant [warrior], and righteous king) in Luke's presentation of Jesus."[6]

Miura next examines the later chapters of Acts. In Stephen's speech in Acts 7, Stephen presents David as the Temple builder, in accordance with the Chronicler's depiction of David as the one who prepared for the Temple to be built. Paul's speech in Acts 13 presents David as a righteous king, chosen by God, by quoting Psalm 88:21 and 1 Samuel 13:14. An important element here, Miura suggests, is that the "historical David" in the Psalms suffers for his people. In Acts 13, Paul is also drawing upon the Isaianic New Exodus and proposing that "the new [much more glorious] Davidic kingdom is now rebuilt, and the new deliverer from captivity to the kingdom is the Davidic Messiah/ the Isaianic Servant, Jesus."[7] In his speech in Acts 15, James quotes Amos 9 in order to refer to the Messianic restoration of the Davidic kingdom, into which the Gentiles are now to be incorporated.

In the Gospel of Luke, David is mentioned in chapters 1–3, 6, 18, and 20. On the one hand, Luke frequently describes Jesus as the "son of David" in a genealogical descent. On the other hand, in the same places Luke also describes Jesus as having more than the

[6] Miura, *David in Luke-Acts*, 174.
[7] Miura, *David in Luke-Acts*, 186.

231

father–son relationship to God that God had promised in 2 Samuel 7. Jesus is conceived by the Holy Spirit and is called "Son of God" and "Lord."

Miura attends to the presence of Davidic themes in Mary's Magnificat and Zechariah's song of praise. Zechariah announces that God "has raised up a horn of salvation for us in the house of his servant David" (Lk 1:69). Zechariah rejoices that the Davidic Messiah will accomplish what God "spoke by the mouth of his holy prophets from of old, that we should be saved from our enemies, and from the hand of all who hate us; ... that we, being delivered from the hand of our enemies, might serve him without fear" (Lk 1:71, 74). Luke holds that Jesus, as the suffering Messiah ("the righteous (sufferer) king"), has brought spiritual deliverance; it is only in his second coming, described in imagery of a victorious warrior, that Jesus will bring political deliverance.[8] Even so, Luke 1–2 presents Jesus as a righteous warrior accomplishing deliverance, in accord with 1–2 Samuel's portrait of David. Jesus is also presented as chosen and pious, just as David was. Miura comments that Luke 1–2 fulfills "the typological character of Samuel's Davidic messianic expectation: Jesus is the *ideal* chosen, pious, triumphant (warrior), and righteous king."[9]

Intriguingly, Luke in his genealogy does not trace Jesus' ancestry along the Davidic royal line. Instead, he asserts that Jesus descends from David through David's son Nathan (2 Samuel 5:14), rather than through Solomon or the line of kings descending from Solomon. Miura notes that there is a Targum that associates Nathan (David's son) with the prophet Nathan who played a significant role in correcting David after he sinned with Bathsheba. Perhaps, then, Luke is accentuating Jesus' prophetic status, in addition to his royal Messianic status. Luke also thereby distinguishes Jesus, the Davidic Messiah, from the kings who ruled in Jerusalem.

---

[8] Miura, *David in Luke-Acts*, 208.
[9] Miura, *David in Luke-Acts*, 211.

6.2 NEW DAVID IN CONTEMPORARY BIBLICAL SCHOLARSHIP

Miura has much to say about potential Davidic resonances in Luke 6, particularly with respect to connecting Jesus' community with David's community and emphasizing Jesus' identity as a "righteous sufferer" like David.[10] He underscores the connection of Jesus the Davidic Messiah with the new exodus, conceived along both Isaianic and Deuteronomic lines. In Luke 20, the identification of the Davidic Messiah as κύριος indicates Jesus' divine Sonship; Jesus is able to heal by the divine power.[11] Jesus is both Messiah and Lord, son of David and Son of God; the one cannot be understood without the other.

Miura's findings accord with the perspective much more briefly taken by Wright in his *The New Testament and the People of God*. Wright summarizes his viewpoint: "Luke's Davidic theme is indeed typological – Jesus really is seen as the 'true David' – but this is neither random nor arbitrary: it is held firmly *within a historical scheme*.... Luke is telling the story of Jesus as the fulfilment, the completion, of the story of David and his kingdom."[12] The parallels include the context of rejoicing (Hannah's song, Mary's and Zechariah's songs); judgment (upon Eli and Shiloh, upon Jerusalem and the Temple); anointing (by the prophet Samuel, by John the Baptist); possession of the Spirit (see 1 Samuel 16:13); being the son of the divine Father (see 2 Samuel 7:14); single-handed combat with a fierce enemy (Goliath, Satan); an ambiguous reception (enthusiastic welcome from some, rejection and persecution by others); and wandering with a group of followers under threat of death.

Like Miura, Wright also draws attention to Luke's identification of Jesus as the Davidic Messiah and as the Lord. Luke's account of Jesus' death contains the good thief's prayer, "Jesus, remember me

---

[10] Miura, *David in Luke-Acts*, 220.

[11] See also C. Kavin Rowe, *Early Narrative Christology: The Lord in the Gospel of Luke* (Berlin: De Gruyter, 2006).

[12] N. T. Wright, *The New Testament and the People of God* (Minneapolis, MN: Fortress, 1992), 381.

when you come into your kingly power" (Lk 23:42), and the inscription "This is the King of the Jews." Luke's account of Jesus' Resurrection appearances shows the risen Jesus opening the Scriptures to demonstrate that it was "necessary that the Christ should suffer these things and enter into his glory" (Lk 24:26). According to Wright, then, Acts tells the story of the spread of Jesus' Davidic kingdom to Rome and the ends of the earth: "[T]he true Davidic kingdom has been established, and the nations will become subject to it."[13]

6.2.2 The Gospel of John

David is mentioned only once in the Gospel of John. However, in *David in the Fourth Gospel: The Johannine Reception of the Psalms*, Margaret Daly-Denton has demonstrated that Davidic echoes are found throughout John's account of Jesus' public ministry and also that John's Passion narrative contains extensive "intertextual reference to 2 Sam 15–18," in which Absalom attempts to replace his father as king.[14] Daly-Denton shows that the New David theme likewise appears in John's depiction of Jesus' relation to John the Baptist and in John's presentation of Jesus as the good shepherd.

John is not the only evangelist to draw a connection between Jesus' Passion and David's betrayal by his son Absalom. In Matthew 27:5 ("And throwing down the pieces of silver in the temple, he [Judas] departed; and he went and hanged himself"), Daly-Denton finds an allusion to 2 Samuel 17:23: "When Ahithophel saw that his counsel was not followed, he saddled his donkey, and went off

---

[13] Wright, *The New Testament and the People of God*, 380–81. Isaac Oliver comments, "For Luke, Jesus's resurrection does not simply fulfill a prophecy David pronounced long ago in Scripture. The resurrection of Jesus confirms that he is the legitimate heir to David's throne.... With Jesus's heavenly ascension and exaltation, which closely follow his resurrection, David's throne has been restored. In the heavens above, Jesus reigns as the new Davidic king" (Oliver, *Luke's Jewish Eschatology*, 63).

[14] Margaret Daly-Denton, *David in the Fourth Gospel: The Johannine Reception of the Psalms* (Leiden: Brill, 2000), 302.

6.2 NEW DAVID IN CONTEMPORARY BIBLICAL SCHOLARSHIP

home to his own city. And he set his house in order, and hanged himself; and he died."[15] Just as David is betrayed by a confidant in his close circle, so is Jesus. Ahithophel advises seizing David by night (2 Samuel 17:1) and predicts that, if his counsel is followed, all of David's supporters "will flee" (2 Sam 17:2). Judas advises that Jesus be seized at night, and Jesus' disciples do indeed flee. David's faithful servants profess loyalty to him as he walks toward the Mount of Olives; Jesus' disciples, having heard Jesus' prediction that they will abandon him, profess their loyalty to Jesus as they walk toward the Mount of Olives (2 Sam 15; Mt 26:30–35). We read that "David went up the ascent of the Mount of Olives, weeping as he went, barefoot and with his head covered; and all the people who were with him covered their heads, and they went up, weeping as they went" (2 Sam 15:30). Jesus, on the Mount of Olives on the night of his arrest, proclaims, "My soul is very sorrowful, even to death" (Mt 26:37). These links are noted by Daly-Denton. Given these links, it is likely that Matthew's (and Mark's) quotation of Zechariah 13:7 – "I will strike the shepherd, and the sheep of the flock will be scattered" (Mt 26:31) – serves as an intentional echo of 2 Samuel 17:2, "I will strike down the king only" and "all the people who are with him will flee."[16]

Daly-Denton shows that John's Gospel connects the narrative of Jesus' Passion with 2 Samuel 15. Just after the close of Jesus' Farewell Discourse, we read: "When Jesus had spoken these words, he went forth with his disciples across the Kidron valley, where there was a garden, which he and his disciples entered" (Jn 18:1). This has a parallel in 2 Samuel 15:23, when David and his followers are beginning their flight from Jerusalem. The narrator tells us: "And all the country wept aloud as all the people passed by, and the king

---

[15] See Daly-Denton, *David in the Fourth Gospel*, 290.
[16] See Daly-Denton, *David in the Fourth Gospel*, 291. For further insights, see Charlene McAfee Moss, *The Zechariah Tradition and the Gospel of Matthew* (Berlin: De Gruyter, 2008), chapter 8.

CHRIST THE NEW DAVID: THE ESCHATOLOGICAL KINGDOM

crossed the brook Kidron, and all the people passed on toward the wilderness." There may also be a link to the Mount of Olives, which is across the Kidron from Jerusalem. Zechariah 14:4 gives Messianic significance to the Mount of Olives: "On that day his [the Lord's] feet shall stand on the Mount of Olives which lies before Jerusalem on the east; and the Mount of Olives shall be split in two from east to west by a very wide valley."

Connections to 2 Samuel 15–17 are present much earlier in John's Gospel. Thus, in John 12:26, having announced that his "hour" has come (Jn 12:23), Jesus tells his disciples, "If any one serves me, he must follow me; and where I am, there shall my servant be also." David's faithful follower Ittai the Gittite, undeterred by Absalom's seeming triumph, remains with David and employs very similar words when he tells David: "As the Lord lives, and as my lord the king lives, wherever my lord the king shall be, whether for death or for life, there also will your servant be" (2 Sam 15:21). As Daly-Denton comments, the true king (Jesus the New David) will be rejected just as King David was. Just as the people should stand with David, so the people should stand with Jesus.

Another connection to 2 Samuel 15–17 in John's Gospel comes when the high priest Caiaphas proposes to the gathered Pharisees that "it is expedient for you that one man should die for the people" so that "the whole nation should not perish" (Jn 11:50). This statement echoes the words of Ahithophel among the plotters against David, when Ahithophel urges Absalom's followers to "seek the life of only one man [David], and all the people will be at peace" (2 Sam 17:3). The opponents of the true king imagine that by killing the king, they will serve the peace of the land, whereas the opposite is true. The true king will triumph through his suffering.

In addition, Ahithophel's counsel that only the king be killed fits with Jesus' statement to those who have come to arrest him: "I am he; so, if you seek me, let these men go" (Jn 18:8). Even Peter, who cuts off the ear of the high priest's slave, avoids arrest. Jesus' opponents appear to have taken to heart the counsel that Ahithophel gave

6.2 NEW DAVID IN CONTEMPORARY BIBLICAL SCHOLARSHIP

to David's opponents, thereby indicating that Jesus is indeed the New David and his opponents are (like Ahithophel and his associates) the enemies of the true king of Israel.[17] However, Daly-Denton points out that Jesus, unlike David, is not portrayed in the Gospel of John as discouraged or unable to control the situation; indeed the opposite is the case. Jesus' disciples do not flee in the Gospel of John, but instead Jesus is led away by the soldiers only after he has secured good treatment for his disciples. In Daly-Denton's view, John 18 correlates with 2 Samuel 15:25–27, where David shows his firm trust in God's plan by telling his priestly allies Abiathar and Zadok to return to Jerusalem. Just as David says, "let him [God] do to me what seems good to him" (2 Sam 15:26), so also Jesus in the Gospel of John says such things as "My food is to do the will of him who sent me, and to accomplish his work" (Jn 4:34).

Daly-Denton also identifies connections between David as shepherd in 1 Samuel and Jesus as shepherd in the Gospel of John. When God commands the prophet Samuel to go to the house of Jesse to anoint a new king, all Jesse's sons but one are shown to Samuel. Jesse tells Samuel, "There remains yet the youngest, but behold, he is keeping the sheep" (1 Sam 16:11). Shortly afterward, King Saul himself sends messengers to Jesse with the request: "Send me David your son, who is with the sheep" (1 Sam 16:19). David is the shepherd-king, who uses his experience as a shepherd to defeat the mighty Philistine Goliath. David appeals to his experience as a shepherd: "Your servant used to keep sheep for his father; and when there came a lion, or a bear, and took a lamb from the flock, I went after him and struck him and delivered it out of his mouth" (1 Sam 17:34–35). Later, when he is on the run from Saul – and when an enraged Saul has seen fit to slaughter eighty-five priests – David tells the priest Abiathar (who has escaped from the slaughter), "Stay

---

[17] See Daly-Denton, *David in the Fourth Gospel*, 296. Daly-Denton credits this link to Raymond E. Brown, S.S., *The Death of the Messiah*, vol. 1 (Garden City, NY: Doubleday, 1994), 291.

with me, fear not; for he that seeks my life seeks your life; with me you shall be in safekeeping" (1 Sam 22:23). Jesus similarly protects his disciples from the soldiers who in John 18:8–9 come to arrest Jesus. There is a clear reference to Jesus as shepherd in John 18:9: "This was to fulfil the word which he had spoken, 'Of those whom you gave me I lost not one.'"

Daly-Denton compares Absalom's and Judas's dishonest plots against the true king. Recall Absalom's deception: "[A]t the end of four years Absalom said to the king, 'Please let me go and pay my vow, which I have vowed to the Lord, in Hebron'" (2 Sam 15:7). Likewise, Judas is not honest about his intentions. The fact that Jesus does not act against Judas and does not resist the soldiers who come to arrest him leads Daly-Denton to a further comparison with David: "Peter's attempt to defend Jesus with his sword recalls the request of Abishai to David to be allowed to cut off Shimei's head (2 Sam 16:9). Neither Jesus nor David allows violent reprisals. Each entrusts himself to God."[18]

Jesus warns his disciples that his opponents will be their opponents. In a manner that parallels David's remark "he that seeks my life seeks your life," Jesus tells his disciples: "If the world hates you, know that it has hated me before it hated you.... Remember the word that I said to you, 'A servant is not greater than his master.' If they persecuted me, they will persecute you" (Jn 15:18, 20). The disciples can expect to be hated and persecuted. It seems to me that Daly-Denton is correct that this is an echo of 1 Samuel 22:23, along lines that underscore Jesus' righteous suffering.

During the Passion narrative, John repeatedly hammers home the point that Jesus is the king of Israel. Pilate's very first question is: "Are you the King of the Jews?" (Jn 18:33). When Jesus explains his kingship to Pilate ("my kingship is not from the world" [Jn 18:36]), Pilate's response is simply to repeat his original question: "So you are a king?" (Jn 18:37). Pilate asks the people if they want

---

[18] Daly-Denton, *David in the Fourth Gospel*, 298.

6.2 NEW DAVID IN CONTEMPORARY BIBLICAL SCHOLARSHIP

him to release "the King of the Jews" (Jn 18:39). The soldiers prepare Jesus for crucifixion by giving him a crown of thorns and a purple robe while mocking him: "Hail, King of the Jews!" (Jn 19:3). When Pilate attempts to release him, the people respond by arguing that Jesus has claimed to be a king and has thereby made himself into a threat to the Romans. They warn Pilate that he himself will come under Roman reprisal unless he sets himself against Jesus: "If you release this man, you are not Caesar's friend; every one who makes himself a king sets himself against Caesar" (Jn 19:12). Finally, when Pilate judges Jesus at Gabbatha, he emphasizes that Jesus is Israel's king: "Here is your King! ... Shall I crucify your King?" (Jn 19:14–15). The people, caught up in the moment, affirm: "We have no king but Caesar" (Jn 19:15). Jesus' cross bears the title, "Jesus of Nazareth, the King of the Jews" (Jn 19:19). Despite requests, Pilate refuses to change this inscription to "This man said, 'I am King of the Jews'" (Jn 19:21). The connections here to David's royal status are evident.

Drawing upon the work of such scholars as Eduardo Huerta and Raymond Brown, Daly-Denton also observes that the events surrounding Jesus' burial provide further evidence that Jesus is the New David. In John's Gospel, we find the following detail: "Nicodemus ... came bringing a mixture of myrrh and aloes, about a hundred pounds' weight" (Jn 19:39). Clearly, this is an extraordinary amount of perfume, suitable for royalty. Unlike regular people, kings were anointed with a great amount of perfume and were buried in gardens. According to Huerta, Jesus' death – as the death of the true Davidic king, the New David – is presented as a royal enthronement in the Gospel of John, while Jesus' burial is a royal burial.[19] We read that "in the place where he was crucified there was a garden, and in the garden a new tomb where no one had ever been

---

[19] See Daly-Denton, *David in the Fourth Gospel*, 299, citing Eduardo Huerta, "La realeza de Jesús en el cuarto evangelio," *Teología y Vida* 32 (1991): 213–20. See also Raymond E. Brown, S.S., *The Death of the Messiah*, vol. 2 (Garden City, NY: Doubleday, 1994), 1268–70.

laid" (Jn 19:41). The description of a new tomb in a "garden" has royal, Davidic overtones. 2 Kings 21:18 reports that King Manasseh "was buried in the garden of his house, in the garden of Uzza," and Manasseh's son King Amon, father of the good King Josiah, was later buried in this same place (2 Kings 21:26). Nehemiah 3:15, describing the rebuilding of the walls of Jerusalem after the exile, speaks of "the king's garden," and the Septuagint version of this verse identifies this garden as containing David's tomb.

When, immediately after the Farewell Discourse, Jesus leads his disciples across the Kidron valley, the evangelist notes that Jesus enters into "a garden" (Jn 18:1). It is in this garden that the soldiers arrest him. Thus the garden of his arrest leads to the garden where he is crucified and where he is buried. Indebted to Nicolas Wyatt, Daly-Denton argues that the garden references in the Gospel of John "are redolent of the Davidic palace and temple complex on Mount Sion on which Jewish tradition super-imposes a whole range of images."[20]

Jon Levenson devotes a good bit of attention to showing the connections between the Garden of Eden and the Temple Mount or Mount Zion. As Levenson remarks, Ezekiel 28:13–14 implicitly links "Eden, the garden of God" and "the holy mountain of God."[21] One of the rivers that flows forth from Eden, the River Gihon (Gen 2:13), has the same name as "a spring on the eastern side of the City of David which served as the principal source of water for Jerusalem."[22] In 1 Kings 1, David commands that Nathan the prophet and Zadok the priest take Solomon to the Gihon River in order to anoint him king over Israel. On the basis of this text and others like it, Levenson deems that "it is reasonable to assume that some

---

[20] Daly-Denton, *David in the Fourth Gospel*, 301, citing Nicolas Wyatt, "Supposing Him to Be the Gardener (John 20, 15): A Study of the Paradise Motif in John," *Zeitschrift für die neutestamentliche Wissenschaft* 81 (1990): 21–38.

[21] See Jon D. Levenson, *Sinai and Zion: An Entry into the Jewish Bible* (San Francisco: Harper & Row, 1985), 128.

[22] Levenson, *Sinai and Zion*, 130.

6.2 NEW DAVID IN CONTEMPORARY BIBLICAL SCHOLARSHIP

in Israel saw in Zion the cosmic mountain which is also the primal paradise called the Garden of Eden. The sacramental spring which is the source of Jerusalem's miraculous waterworks was conceived as the cosmic stream which issues from that mountain."[23] The "garden" is Mount Zion, and the "garden" is also the New Eden, the place where the New David will be enthroned and glorified, bringing about the kingdom of God and eternal life.

Daly-Denton also points to 1 Chronicles 17:13, where God says of Solomon, "I will be his father, and he shall be my son; I will not take my merciful love from him." The Gospel of John presents Jesus as this true Davidic son. When Jesus goes to the Cross, he does so in full assurance of the Father's love, knowing that he will be vindicated. Thus, in the Farewell Discourse, Jesus tells his disciples: "I do as the Father has commanded me, so that the world may know that I love the Father" (Jn 14:31).

For a Gospel that mentions David by name only once, then, the Gospel of John is filled with allusions that show that Jesus is the New David. Daly-Denton provides other examples in addition to the main ones noted above. For example, the persecuted David dwells in the wilderness with his followers, and so also, in a sense, does Jesus when he is under mortal threat from the Jewish leaders. Both David (in 1 Samuel 30:6) and Jesus are threatened with stoning. Both David and Jesus feed admiring crowds in connection with ritual and enthronement events. John the Baptist is presented as a light preparing the way for Jesus, just as Samuel in Jewish tradition was thought to be a light preparing the way for David. David, as ruler and judge, "dawns ... like the morning light" in Israel (2 Sam 23:4), while Jesus is "the true light that enlightens every man" (Jn 1:9). In 2 Samuel 7, God promises that David's throne will be everlasting, and the Gospel of John depicts Jesus as preexistent and everlasting.

The remainder of Daly-Denton's book focuses on the Gospel of John's use of Davidic themes from the Psalms. One such instance

---

[23] Levenson, *Sinai and Zion*, 131.

consists in the psalmist's portrait of the Davidic shepherd (e.g., Psalms 23 and 95). Other psalms are quoted in the Gospel of John to express both righteous suffering and everlasting reward. Of the Gospel of John's explicit scriptural quotations, three-fourths come from the Psalms, which the evangelist likely assumed to have been composed by David. In the period in which the evangelist wrote, as in Jesus' lifetime as well, "The ascription of psalms to David led naturally to the association of particular psalms with incidents in his career."[24]

Daly-Denton also directs attention to Isaiah 55, in which God invites all peoples to "come to the waters" and to "eat what is good" (Isa 55:1–2), and in which God's "steadfast, merciful love for David" will make David a witness to all peoples and "a leader and commander for the peoples" (Isa 55:3–4). As Daly-Denton says, in this passage "the eternal covenant promise is being interpreted in a new non-dynastic sense as a privilege granted by God through David to the entire nation and through the nation to the world."[25] The Gospel of John similarly portrays Jesus as a witness to truth to all nations (Jn 18:37). Daly-Denton argues that John reads Isaiah 55 through the lens of Psalm 18 (which is found in 2 Samuel 22), in which the psalmist – David – praises God for making him "the head of the nations" (Ps 18:43). Thus, New David Christology is present in myriad ways throughout the Gospel of John.[26]

---

[24] Daly-Denton, *David in the Fourth Gospel*, 82.
[25] Daly-Denton, *David in the Fourth Gospel*, 86.
[26] See also Joshua W. Jipp, *The Messianic Theology of the New Testament* (Grand Rapids, MI: Eerdmans, 2020), chapter 4. Jipp maintains, "one of the primary purposes of John's Gospel is to elicit faith in Jesus as the messianic king and to clarify the very meaning of this confession. The Gospel invites the reader, then, to join Philip, Andrew, Nicodemus, the Samaritan woman, and many other Johannine characters in this quest for the Messiah and the meaning of his kingdom and kingship" (146–47). See also Jörg Frey, *The Glory of the Crucified One: Christology and Theology in the Gospel of John*, trans. Wayne Coppins and Christoph Heilig (Waco, TX: Baylor University Press, 2018); Martin Hengel, "The Kingdom of Christ in John," in Hengel, *Studies in Early Christology* (Edinburgh: T&T Clark, 1995), 333–58.

6.2 NEW DAVID IN CONTEMPORARY BIBLICAL SCHOLARSHIP

6.2.3 The Gospel of Mark

Briefly, let me make a few remarks about the New David in the Gospel of Mark, drawing upon Bernardo Cho's *Royal Messianism and the Jerusalem Priesthood in the Gospel of Mark*.[27] Cho begins his book with a scene noted above: the anointing of Solomon as king in the Kidron valley (1 Kings 1:32–40). Solomon rides to his anointing on "King David's mule" (1 Kgs 1:38). Similarly Jesus rides triumphantly into Jerusalem, as the anointed Messiah, and the joyful people greet him as the one who brings "the kingdom of our father David that is coming!" (Mk 11:10).

Cho points out that according to the prophecy of Zechariah, the eschatological Davidic king would ride into Jerusalem and bring about world peace and the completion of the Second Temple. Zechariah, however, envisions this Davidic king as accompanied by a priest. The contrast with Jesus is significant, since the Gospel of Mark (like the other Gospels) portrays Jesus as highly critical of the Temple priests. According to Cho, the evangelist Mark explains the destruction of the Temple as rooted in the fact that the priests rejected Jesus as royal Messiah.[28]

In Psalm 2:7–8, God tells his anointed, "You are my son, today I have begotten you. Ask of me, and I will make the nations your

---

[27] Bernardo Cho, *Royal Messianism and the Jerusalem Priesthood in the Gospel of Mark* (London: T&T Clark, 2019). In the same year, Max Botner published *Jesus Christ as the Son of David in the Gospel of Mark* (Cambridge: Cambridge University Press, 2019). Although I focus on Cho's book in this section, Botner's book is equally pertinent. Much like Cho, Botner demonstrates that "the extent to which Markan messiah language resources Davidic traditions is more expansive than has typically been realized" (193). Not surprisingly, "The points at which Mark tends to draw n Davidic scriptural traditions revolve around the motifs of persecution and suffering, on the one hand, and the motifs of vindication and exaltation, on the other"; however, Botner adds that "these foci inform Mark's selection and refraction of iconic moments in David's life not only in the passion narrative, but also in the early stages of Jesus's messianic career" (193–94).

[28] See Cho, *Royal Messianism and the Jerusalem Priesthood in the Gospel of Mark*, 205.

heritage, and the ends of the earth your possession." In Mark 1:11, at Jesus' baptism, the first part of Psalm 2:7 appears: "You are my beloved Son; with you I am well pleased." From the very outset of Mark's Gospel, Jesus is identified as the "Christ" (Mk 1:1). Mark's understanding of the kingdom inaugurated by Jesus fits with the dominion promised in Psalm 2. Cho also notes the significance of Mark 9, where Jesus first predicts that "there are some standing here who will not taste death before they see the kingdom of God come with power" (Mk 9:1) and then receives the Father's blessing at his Transfiguration, "This is my beloved Son; listen to him" (Mk 9:7).

Since Mark employs the phrase "Son of David" only twice, some commentators argue that Mark's Jesus distances himself from this title and its implications. They cite Mark 12:35-37, where Jesus urges that David (in Psalm 110:1) calls the Messiah "Lord," with the implication that the Messiah cannot also be David's son. Paul Achtemeier, among others, denies that for Mark the Messiah descends from David.[29] In the Gospel of Mark, Jesus never calls himself the Son of David.

In response, Cho points especially to Mark 10:46-52.[30] Here a blind beggar, Bartimaeus, begs for mercy and healing from Jesus as the "Son of David" (Mk 10:47-48). Jesus responds positively to Bartimaeus's words. Cho observes that the location of this interchange has importance, because it comes right before Jesus enters into Jerusalem on Palm Sunday. Bartimaeus, blind though he is, perceives what the Jewish leaders will ultimately not perceive: Jesus is the Davidic Messiah. Although this has not been proclaimed earlier in the Gospel, its proclamation now shows the meaning of Jesus' triumphant entry into Jerusalem. The crowd that greets Jesus

---

[29] Paul Achtemeier, "'And He Followed Him': Miracles and Discipleship in Mark 10:46-52," *Semeia* 11 (1978): 115-45, at 130.

[30] Although I am here tracking Cho's response, see also the excellent treatment of Mark on Jesus' Davidic descent, in Timothy C. Gray, *The Temple in the Gospel of Mark: A Study in Its Narrative Role* (Tübingen: Mohr Siebeck, 2008), 79-90.

6.2 NEW DAVID IN CONTEMPORARY BIBLICAL SCHOLARSHIP

recognizes him rightly: He is the one bringing the "kingdom of our father David" (Mk 11:10), since he is the Davidic king, the New David. He is indeed the "Christ," just as Peter confesses in response to Jesus' question on the way to Caesarea Philippi (Mk 8:29).

In Mark 11:9, the crowd greeting Jesus' triumphant entry quotes Psalm 118:26, "Blessed be he who enters in the name of the Lord!" This verse of Psalm 118 refers to the Davidic king's entrance into the Temple. The same Psalm contains the statement "The stone which the builders rejected has become the cornerstone" (Ps 118:22). In Mark 12:10, Jesus identifies himself as that "cornerstone." He does so in a parable that describes the tenants' killing of the heir, thereby identifying himself as uniquely Son of God and, at the same time, as the Son of David whose entrance into the Temple is celebrated by Psalm 118. When the Jewish leaders reject him, they bring disaster upon the Temple but they do not overthrow the ultimate triumph, through suffering, of the New David.

Zechariah 9:9 speaks of the triumphant Davidic king, the Messiah, entering Jerusalem "humble and riding on a donkey." Jesus, by his own careful plan, rides into Jerusalem on Palm Sunday on a young donkey. As Cho says, this fact "highlights the event as symbolizing the coming of the eschatological king to Zion" and indicates Jesus' royal Davidic status.[31] It is no wonder, therefore, that Mark, like the other Gospels, accentuates Jesus' royal status in his Passion narrative. Pilate twice seeks to release "the King of the Jews"; the soldiers mock him as "King of the Jews" and place a crown of thorns and purple robe upon him; his cross bears the inscription "The King of the Jews"; and the priests and scribes revile him as "the Christ, the King of Israel" (Mk 15:9, 12, 18, 26, 32). In these ways, Mark makes clear the importance of the fact that Jesus is the Messianic Davidic king.

Discussing Mark 12:37, where (as noted) Jesus seems to argue that the Messiah cannot be the "son" of David because he is David's

---

[31] Cho, *Royal Messianism and the Jerusalem Priesthood in the Gospel of Mark*, 96.

Lord, Cho argues that the best translation of the Greek text of Mark 12:37 is: "[H]ow, or in what sense, is the messiah David's son?" The answer is that as David's Lord, the Messiah or son of David does not need to resort to violence in order to overthrow his enemies. Cho notes that Mark's emphasis on the cross "undermines the nationalistic overtones of Davidic sonship" while depending upon God to put Jesus' enemies under his feet, in accord with Psalm 110:1 (cited by Jesus in Mark 12:36), "The Lord said to my lord: 'Sit at my right hand, till I make your enemies your footstool.'"[32]

6.2.4 Further Reflections on the New David

In *The Messianic Theology of the New Testament*, Joshua Jipp proposes that "Jesus's messianic kingship is something of a root metaphor, a primary designation and driving image for making sense of NT Christology.... [N]ot only do the major NT compositions presuppose Jesus as the Davidic messianic king but they are also creative expansions upon the earliest Christian confession that Jesus is the Messiah of God."[33] What does he mean by "creative expansions"? And what does centering Christology in the fact that Jesus is "the Davidic messianic king" entail?

For one thing, we should recognize that Jesus' saving work consists above all in "the inauguration of the saving reign of the

---

[32] Cho, *Royal Messianism and the Jerusalem Priesthood in the Gospel of Mark*, 102. Cho concludes, "The close identification of the messiahship of Jesus with his fate on the cross is highly significant, considering that nowhere in the late Second Temple period can one find the idea of violent suffering as a necessity for the career of the messiah" (104).

[33] Jipp, *The Messianic Theology of the New Testament*, 3. I note that the dominant form of Messianic hope in the first-century Jewish world was Davidic, as is pointed out by Brant Pitre, Michael P. Barber, and John A. Kincaid, *Paul, a New Covenant Jew: Rethinking Pauline Theology* (Grand Rapids, MI: Eerdmans, 2019), 96–97. See also John P. Meier, "From Elijah-Like Prophet to Royal Davidic Messiah," in *Jesus: A Colloquium in the Holy Land*, ed. Doris Donnelly (New York: Continuum, 2001), 45–83.

6.2 NEW DAVID IN CONTEMPORARY BIBLICAL SCHOLARSHIP

messianic king."[34] It is necessary to give a central place to Jesus' apocalyptic eschatology, his expectation and proclamation of the imminent arrival (in some form) of the kingdom of God. Commenting upon Joseph Ratzinger/Pope Benedict XVI's first volume of *Jesus of Nazareth*, Richard Hays urges theologians to "take seriously Jesus' identification with – and redefinition of – Israel's national hope, his formation of a countercultural Israel symbolized by the Twelve, and his orientation toward future eschatological judgment and vindication in the resurrection of the dead."[35] A New David Christology can help theologians place all these elements at the center, as they are in the New Testament itself.

Figures such as Athanasius, Anselm, and Aquinas do not place Jesus' status as the Davidic king at the center of their Christologies in an explicit way. In Aquinas's *tertia pars*, he includes questions on the fittingness of the Incarnation, the mode of union of the two natures, Christ's grace and knowledge and defects, Christ's unity of being and of will/operation, Christ's subjection to the Father, Christ's prayer and priesthood, Christ's adoption and predestination, Christ as the Mediator, Christ's conception and nativity, Christ's manifestation and circumcision, Christ's baptism and manner of life, Christ's temptation, Christ's teaching and miracles, Christ's Transfiguration and Passion, Christ's death and burial and descent into hell, Christ's Resurrection and Ascension, and Christ as judge. None of this excludes his status as Davidic Messianic king, by any means, but neither does Aquinas give this element direct attention. The questions in the *tertia pars* reflect the main emphases of the Church Fathers (East and West) and of the earlier medieval theologians.

As Jipp shows, in some streams of historical-critical scholarship, "Jewish messianic traditions and texts have been minimized or seen

---

[34] Jipp, *The Messianic Theology of the New Testament*, 6.
[35] Richard B. Hays, *Reading with the Grain of Scripture* (Grand Rapids, MI: Eerdmans, 2020), 129–30.

as somewhat insignificant for NT Christology."³⁶ Jipp points to the influence of Wilhelm Bousset's 1913 *Kyrios Christos: A History of the Belief in Christ from the Beginning of Christianity to Irenaeus*, which argued that the Palestinian Jewish notions of a nationalistic David-figure were of little interest and gave way quickly to a more profound, spiritualized, Hellenistic understanding of a heavenly, transcendent figure, an exalted Lord.³⁷ Almost no scholars accept this view today, but its influence was large. In addition, other scholars argued that Jesus never claimed to be the Davidic Messiah. On this view, his disciples proclaimed him to have become the Messiah at the moment when he was exalted to the right hand of the Father. Martin Hengel and others have debunked this viewpoint.³⁸ By contrast, a third group of scholars have gone to the other extreme, exaggerating the place and consistency of Davidic Messianism in postexilic prophecy and Second Temple Judaism. Here the work of Matthew Novenson is helpful in showing the distinctiveness and diversity of Second Temple Jewish Messianic ideas.³⁹ Finally, a fourth group of scholars have sought, for theopolitical reasons such as feminist concerns or the critique of empire, to avoid or minimize talk about kings.

Jipp approvingly cites Matthew Bates's position that "the gospel is the full narrative of what God has done in the person of the messianic king" and that "the Paul gospel climaxes in God's enthronement of the messianic king."⁴⁰ Similarly, Scott Hahn's

---

³⁶ Jipp, *The Messianic Theology of the New Testament*, 7.

³⁷ See Wilhelm Bousset's *Kyrios Christos: A History of the Belief in Christ from the Beginning of Christianity to Irenaeus*, trans. John E. Steely (Nashville, TN: Abingdon, 1970).

³⁸ See Martin Hengel, "Jesus, the Messiah of Israel," in his *Studies in Early Christology* (Edinburgh: T&T Clark, 1995), 1–72.

³⁹ See Matthew V. Novenson, *The Grammar of Messianism: An Ancient Jewish Political Idiom and Its Users* (Oxford: Oxford University Press, 2017).

⁴⁰ Novenson, *The Grammar of Messianism*, 13–14, citing Matthew W. Bates, *Salvation by Allegiance Alone: Rethinking Faith, Works, and the Gospel of Jesus the King* (Grand Rapids, MI: Baker Academic, 2017), chapters 2–3.

6.2 NEW DAVID IN CONTEMPORARY BIBLICAL SCHOLARSHIP

Kinship by Covenant makes much of Jesus' status as the Davidic king who came to restore and transform the kingdom of David, reuniting Samaria and Judah within the new Eucharistic, apostolic, and pneumatic Davidic kingdom that is the Church, with Christ reigning at the right hand of the Father (rather than in the city of Jerusalem) and spreading his kingdom worldwide by the power of the Holy Spirit.[41] For his part, Richard Bauckham has demonstrated that central to the Book of Revelation is the "image of Jesus as a conquering Davidic Messiah whose triumph takes place through his sacrificial death."[42]

Christ the New David thus plays a decisive role in the entirety of the New Testament. Jipp thinks that the exalted view of Jesus, his inclusion in God's throne and his being worshiped, derives in part from the early Christians' perception of Jesus as the Messianic Davidic king. Among the psalms understood to be about the Davidic king and used in New Testament to ground a "high" Christology, Jipp identifies Psalms 2, 3, 19, 22, 45, 62, 89, 90, and 110. In the Psalms, we find that the Davidic king receives a share in God's throne and God's rule and God's glory, and is called God's anointed, the Son of God, God's firstborn son, and the Lord.[43] According to Sean McDonough, furthermore, the claim that Christ is Creator arose from early Christian reflection upon his Messianic Lordship, in light of Psalm 89:27's statement that the

---

[41] See Scott W. Hahn, *Kinship by Covenant: A Canonical Approach to the Fulfillment of God's Saving Promises* (New Haven, CT: Yale University Press, 2009), 218–37; for background in the prophets and Second Temple literature, see 202–12.

[42] Jipp, *The Messianic Theology of the New Testament*, 14, citing Richard Bauckham, *The Climax of Prophecy: Studies on the Book of Revelation* (London: T&T Clark, 1993).

[43] See Jipp, *The Messianic Theology of the New Testament*, 342. See also Sam Janse, *"You Are My Son": The Reception History of Psalm 2 in Early Judaism and the Early Church* (Leuven: Peeters, 2009), as well as James H. Charlesworth, "From Jewish Messianology to Christian Christology: Some Caveats and Perspectives," in *Judaisms and Their Messiahs at the Turn of the Christian Era*, ed. Jacob Neusner, William S. Green, and Ernest S. Frerichs (Cambridge: Cambridge University Press, 1987), 225–64.

Davidic Messiah will be "the first-born, the highest of the kings of the earth."[44]

Although Jipp's discussion of Paul is extensive, it is nicely summed up by Jipp's contention that the Pauline "gospel is centered upon the resurrection of the offspring of David and his installation in heaven as the powerful Son of God.... Paul's frequent application of Davidic psalms to articulate the identity and activity of Jesus only makes sense on the assumption that he is the Davidic Messiah," the "apocalyptic messianic king."[45] Among the psalms that Paul employs as a Davidic "prophetic sourcebook" for Jesus the New David, Jipp names Psalm 44, 69, and 115. An example of Paul's method is "Romans 15:1-12, where Paul portrays Christ as the messianic king by placing portions of two Davidic psalms on the lips of Jesus."[46] In making this connection, Jipp is especially indebted to Wright, who shows how powerfully Psalm 2 (along with 2 Samuel 7:12-14) echoes in Romans 1:3-4 and who makes the point that

---

[44] Sean M. McDonough, *Christ as Creator: Origins of a New Testament Doctrine* (Oxford: Oxford University Press, 2009), 65-68, cited in Jipp, *The Messianic Theology of the New Testament*, 343.

[45] Jipp, *The Messianic Theology of the New Testament*, 319. For a contrasting view, see Andrew Chester, "Christ of Paul," in *Redemption and Resistance: The Messianic Hopes of Jews and Christians in Antiquity*, ed. Markus Bockmuehl and James Carleton Paget (London: T&T Clark, 2009), 109-21.

[46] Jipp, *The Messianic Theology of the New Testament*, 156. Jipp further comments: "That Paul sees his task as situated within the fulfillment of the scriptural promises that look forward to a coming Davidic king who would receive the obedience of the nations is further indicated by the catena of scriptural quotations in Romans 15:9-12, quotations which are best taken as the enthroned Lord's celebration of his eschatological receipt of his royal inheritance and entrance into his rule over the nations" (162). Jipp argues, too, that there is an *inclusio* here, between Romans 1:3-4 and 15:9-12. He draws upon Don Garlington, "Israel's Triumphant King: Romans 1:5 and the Scriptures of Israel," in *Jesus and Paul: Global Perspectives in Honour of James D. G. Dunn for His 70th Birthday*, ed. B. J. Oropeza, C. K. Robertson, and Douglas C. Mohrmann (London: T&T Clark, 2010), 173-83; J. R. Daniel Kirk, *Unlocking Romans: Resurrection and the Justification of God* (Grand Rapids, MI: Eerdmans, 2008), 51-53; and Donald Dale Walker, *Paul's Offer of Leniency (2 Cor 10:1): Populist Ideology and Rhetoric in a Pauline Letter Fragment* (Tübingen: Mohr Siebeck, 2002), 172-73.

6.2 NEW DAVID IN CONTEMPORARY BIBLICAL SCHOLARSHIP

Romans 15:1–13 is "the carefully designed goal of the entire theological argument [of Romans]," whose purpose is to reveal the "Davidic Messiah whose resurrection established him as the true world ruler, accomplishing the creator's purpose for the whole creation" by overcoming sin and death.[47]

Jipp is equally clear about the important place of the theme of the Davidic Messiah – the New David – in the Gospel of Matthew. As he shows, "Jesus's identity as 'the Son of David' and God's 'Messiah' within the Gospel of Matthew is indisputable."[48] Even as an infant Jesus is identified as "king of the Jews" by the Magi (Mt 2:2). Jesus' baptism bears the marks of a Messianic anointing and commission. In the Gospel of Matthew, the New David establishes his followers as the eschatological (Messianically reconfigured) Temple, who continue the ministry of the Messiah by teaching, judging, and forgiving sins as royal priests and stewards of the New David's royal-priestly house. At the end of the Gospel, Matthew draws upon Daniel 7:13–14 and (likely) Psalm 2:8 to depict Jesus as the enthroned New David with a worldwide kingdom. Earlier in his Gospel, Matthew presents Jesus as the "messianic shepherd," as, for example, in Matthew 9–10 and 18.[49] Jesus has compassion upon the crowds who come to hear his preaching of the kingdom, because they are "harassed and helpless, like sheep without a shepherd" (Mt 9:36).

---

[47] N. T. Wright, *Paul and the Faithfulness of God*, vol. 2 (Minneapolis, MN: Fortress, 2013), 819–20. See also Matthew Scott, *The Hermeneutics of Christological Psalmody in Paul: An Intertextual Enquiry* (Cambridge: Cambridge University Press, 2014), chapters 3 and 4. Scott seeks "to build a cumulative case, based in part on observed patterns of metalepsis, for a radical discontinuity between Christ and David in the discursive hands of Paul" (131). For example, Scott notes in that in Romans 15:9 Paul "evokes the warrior-king not least to overturn the discourse of violence" (132). Christ's status as the New David includes, in various ways, a "radical discontinuity" between Christ and David.

[48] Jipp, *The Messianic Theology of the New Testament*, 21. For further background, see Joel Willitts, *Matthew's Messianic Shepherd-King: In Search of "The Lost Sheep of the House of Israel"* (Berlin: De Gruyter, 2007), especially chapter 2.

[49] Jipp, *The Messianic Theology of the New Testament*, 54.

In a lengthy monograph, Young Chae examines the place of the shepherd image in Matthew's Gospel. He shows that "Matthew's presentation of Jesus in his narrative is a result of his intense dialogue with the Davidic Shepherd tradition (esp. Mic 2–5; Zech 9–14; and Ezek 34–37)."[50] According to Ezekiel 34–37, as Chae observes, Israel's rulers will be replaced, eschatologically, by "YHWH's appointed new David."[51] YHWH is and always has been the Shepherd of Israel, but the new David will be appointed by God to serve not merely as an extension of the Davidic monarchy but as the eschatological shepherd who will heal and restore God's people by establishing them in justice and by leading them along the path of righteousness. Chae demonstrates that Matthew's Christology follows the pattern set by Ezekiel, for whom "Davidic expectation merges with the shepherd image.... The eschatological Shepherd will rescue, heal, feed, pour out his Spirit upon, and raise up his people from the grave."[52] Jesus is this eschatological shepherd, and as such he is the New David who, through his teachings and actions, enables the people to follow God's will.[53] Moreover, Jesus is not only the Davidic shepherd (appointed by God) but also the "divine eschatological shepherd" promised in Ezekiel.[54]

The Davidic king who conquers through suffering rather than through power accords with the Book of Revelation, despite its images of military conquest. Jipp notes that in the Book of Revelation, "Jesus is the conquering, triumphant Davidic Messiah, but

---

[50] Young S. Chae, *Jesus as the Eschatological Davidic Shepherd: Studies in the Old Testament, Second Temple Judaism, and in the Gospel of Matthew* (Tübingen: Mohr Siebeck, 2006), 5. See also Moss, *The Zechariah Tradition and the Gospel of Matthew*; John Paul Heil, "Ezekiel 34 and the Narrative Strategy of the Shepherd and Sheep Metaphor in Matthew," *Catholic Biblical Quarterly* 55 (1993): 698–708.

[51] Chae, *Jesus as the Eschatological Davidic Shepherd*, 272.

[52] Chae, *Jesus as the Eschatological Davidic Shepherd*, 277.

[53] Chae, *Jesus as the Eschatological Davidic Shepherd*, 277.

[54] Chae, *Jesus as the Eschatological Davidic Shepherd*, 277. See also Francis Martin, "The Image of Shepherd in the Gospel of Saint Matthew," *Science et Esprit* 27 (1975): 261–301.

this military battle and act of conquering has taken place through the highly paradoxical sacrificial death of Jesus the slaughtered Lamb."⁵⁵ The New David is not rightly understood if measured by nationalistic, militaristic royal ideology – present among Israelites as among all nations. It is through self-sacrificial love, even unto death, that the *New* David conquers, and his conquest is over sin and death, for the purpose of establishing a truly "priestly and royal people for God."⁵⁶

6.3 Irenaeus, Augustine, and Aquinas on the New David

What happened to this emphasis on the eschatological Davidic king after the New Testament period? Since my ultimate purpose is to get to Aquinas, I do not have space to survey all the Church Fathers. As preparation for discussing Aquinas's position, I will examine two particularly notable figures: Irenaeus and Augustine.⁵⁷

6.3.1 *Irenaeus*

In an essay on "Messianic Christology in Paul and Irenaeus," Jipp observes that "Irenaeus is a witness to Jewish messianism in his reading of scripture, articulation of the identity of Jesus as the Son of God, and the accomplishment of humanity's salvation in their

---

⁵⁵ Jipp, *The Messianic Theology of the New Testament*, 294.
⁵⁶ Jipp, *The Messianic Theology of the New Testament*, 295.
⁵⁷ See also Ambrose's treatises "A Defense of the Prophet David" and "The Second Defense of David," in Ambrose, *Treatises on Noah and David*, trans. Brian P. Dunkle, S.J. (Washington, DC: Catholic University of America Press, 2020), 105–51 and 152–94. At some length, Ambrose addresses the fact that David was an adulterer and a murderer, highlighting the difference between David and Christ. Ambrose seeks to explain how such a flagrant sinner as David could have been chosen not only to hymn prophetically about the future Christ in the Psalms but also in his own person to prefigure Christ.

becoming sons of God."[58] He points especially to Book III of *Against Heresies*. Irenaeus thinks that David, in the Psalms, prophesies what will happen to the New David. According to Irenaeus, David (the psalmist) prophesies Christ's virgin birth and Resurrection when David says, "Truth has sprung out of the earth [RSV: Righteousness will spring out of the ground]" (Ps 85:11).[59] Irenaeus argues for a divine Christology on the ground of Psalm 110:1, cited repeatedly in the New Testament, including by Jesus. Here David the psalmist states, "The Lord says to my lord: 'Sit at my right hand, till I make your enemies your footstool.'" Irenaeus quotes this text as an indication that the New David is in fact the divine Lord, as the "Son who has received dominion from His Father over all creation"; when the Father speaks to the Son, both are "truly Lord."[60] Irenaeus also quotes Psalm 45:6–7 to show that the Son, the "anointed" one (the Messiah), is divine. The passage reads in the RSV: "Your divine throne endures for ever and ever. Your royal scepter is a scepter of equity; you love righteousness and hate wickedness. Therefore God, your God, has anointed you" (Ps 45:6–7).[61]

Likewise, Psalm 50, attributed to David, proclaims: "The Mighty One, God the Lord, speaks and summons the earth … Our God comes, he does not keep silence" (Ps 50: 1, 3). In the Septuagint version used by Irenaeus, the verb is past tense in verse one ("has spoken and has called") and future in verse three ("shall come"). The one who has spoken and who will come is the New David, the Son who came and spoke as the Messiah. It is the divine Messiah who has summoned all nations to union with himself. Irenaeus backs

---

[58] Joshua W. Jipp, "Messiah Christology in Paul and Irenaeus," in *Irenaeus and Paul*, ed. Todd D. Still and David E. Wilhite (London: T&T Clark, 2020), 81–88, at 81.
[59] See Irenaeus, "Against Heresies," Book III, chapter 5, in *The Apostolic Fathers, Justin Martyr, Irenaeus*, vol. 1 of Ante-Nicene Fathers Series, ed. Alexander Roberts and James Donaldson, (Peabody, MA: Hendrickson, 1995), 315–567, at 417.
[60] Irenaeus, "Against Heresies," Book III, chapter 6, 418.
[61] I cite the RSV, which is based upon the Hebrew Masoretic text, because it reflects the standard contemporary Psalter to which modern readers have access.

6.3 IRENAEUS, AUGUSTINE, AND AQUINAS ON THE NEW DAVID

up the Davidic psalm with Isaiah 65:1, which in his version reads, "I have openly appeared to those who seek me not" (RSV: "I was ready to be found by those who did not seek me"). This, too, seems to Irenaeus to be a clear reference to the divine Messiah, since it is in Christ Jesus that God manifests himself to a world caught up in idolatry. Irenaeus reads Isaiah 43:10 in a similar way. In the Gospel of John, precisely such language as that of Isaiah 43:10 is placed in the mouth of the divine Son, Jesus Christ. Irenaeus thinks Moses, as the author of the Torah, also prophesied the divine Messiah. In Exodus 3:8, God tells Moses at the burning bush, "I have come down to deliver them [i.e., the people of Israel]." When does God more evidently "come down" for the purpose of delivering his people than when he takes flesh in Jesus Christ?

Irenaeus notes that Christ is the divine son called forth out of Egypt (Mt 3:15). Christ is "Emmanuel" or "God with us" (Mt 1:23). In this regard, Irenaeus quotes Psalm 132:11, with its reference to the Davidic covenant of 2 Samuel 7: "The Lord swore to David a sure oath from which he will not turn back: One of the sons of your body I will set on your throne."[62] Irenaeus understands David the psalmist to be prophetically pointing forward – like the Davidic covenant itself – to a Davidic king who will not simply be a mere extension of the Davidic line but rather will be the divine Messiah. It is through this category of the divine Messiah, drawn in significant part from Old Testament texts, that Irenaeus identifies Jesus. He sees Jesus as the eschatological king restoring his people and inaugurating his worldwide kingdom. Along these lines Irenaeus quotes Psalm 76:1: "In Judah God is known, his name is great in Israel. His abode has been established in Salem, his dwelling place in Zion." This verse indicates a prophetic witness to the divine Messiah, as do the words of the prophet Balaam (during the Israelites' exodus wanderings), "a star shall come forth out of Jacob, and a scepter shall rise out of Israel" (Num 24:17). Irenaeus comments that the Magi saw this

---

[62] See Irenaeus, "Against Heresies," Book III, ch. 9, p. 422.

"star" and they came to the infant Jesus, to whom they gave three gifts: myrrh as a sign of his death, gold because he is the everlasting and universal king, and frankincense because he is God and worthy of worship.

In underscoring that the Word became flesh, Irenaeus recalls another Messianic or proto-Messianic text, Isaiah 11. Jesus does not bear the Word extrinsically; rather Jesus *is* the Word incarnate. Irenaeus considers this extraordinary reality to be prophesied in Isaiah 11, which announces in verses 1–2: "There shall come forth a shoot from the stump of Jesse, and a branch shall grow out of his roots. And the Spirit of the Lord shall rest upon him." This is the royal Messiah, the New David; he will judge "with righteousness" and "with equity," ruling the entire earth (Isa 11:4). Irenaeus pairs this passage from Isaiah 11 with Isaiah 61:1–2, "The Spirit of the Lord God is upon me, because the Lord has anointed me to bring good tidings to the afflicted;… to proclaim the year of the Lord's favor, and the day of vengeance of our God; to comfort all who mourn." In the Gospel of Luke, Jesus reads this passage in the synagogue at Nazareth and declares himself to be its fulfillment (Lk 4:16–21). Irenaeus lays stress upon Jesus' status as the divine Davidic Messiah: "[T]he Word was man from the root of Jesse."[63]

Irenaeus also recalls the angel Gabriel's words (cited above) to Mary about the One who is to be her Son: "He will be great, and will be called the Son of the Most High; and the Lord God will give to him the throne of his father David, and he will reign over the house of Jacob for ever; and of his kingdom there will be no end" (Lk 1:32–33). He employs this central passage of New David Christology in order to indicate Jesus' divinity and to emphasize that Jesus is the same Lord who, in the Old Testament, promised salvation to his people. No merely human king – no mere extension of the Davidic line – could reign forever. Christ is the one who fulfills Zechariah's prophecy in Luke 1:78–79. Christ is the dawn, the light, who gives hope and

---

[63] Irenaeus, "Against Heresies," Book III, ch. 9, p. 423.

6.3 IRENAEUS, AUGUSTINE, AND AQUINAS ON THE NEW DAVID

peace to those who live in the midst of sin and death. Irenaeus highlights Zechariah's proclamation of the New David: "Blessed be the Lord God of Israel, for he has visited and redeemed his people, and has raised up a horn of salvation for us in the house of his servant David, as he spoke by the mouth of his holy prophets from of old, that we should be saved from our enemies" (Lk 1:69–71).[64]

In highlighting Jesus' status as the New David, the divine Davidic king who fulfills God's covenantal promises, Irenaeus is polemicizing against Gnostic Christians who imagine that the salvation delivered by Jesus has nothing to do with the Old Testament witness. When the angel tells the shepherds "Be not afraid; for behold, I bring you good news of a great joy which will come to all the people; for to you is born this day in the city of David a Savior, who is Christ the Lord" (Lk 2:10–11), the Gnostics supposed that the angels came from Ogdoad and revealed to the shepherds the coming descent of "Christ" into this world at the baptism of Jesus. Irenaeus counters by strongly insisting upon Jesus as the royal Messiah descended from David.[65]

---

[64] It is interesting that, as Per Beskow points out, the early Church Fathers did not generally make use of the royal Messianic overtones of "shepherd" in the New Testament, although Clement and Origen so. However, as Beskow states, "In Hellenistic syncretism 'shepherd' is an epithet constantly used of Hermes-Logos, and Christian preachers were able to link 'shepherd' and Logos as a title for Christ" (Beskow, *Rex Gloriae: The Kingship of Christ in the Early Church*, trans. Eric J. Sharpe [Eugene, OR: Wipf and Stock, 2014], 89). Beskow further remarks, "Theologians in the highly Hellenized milieu of Alexandria did not think in terms of eschatology.... The distinction between Christ the Teacher and Christ the King should not however lead us to a one-sided estimation of the Alexandrian theologians' image of Christ. Clement and Origen also played a considerable part in spreading the concept of the Kingship of Christ, as it began to make its mark on the young Byzantine Empire.... We find a Hellenistic ideal of Kingship, taken over from Philo" (212–13).

[65] Oddly, Origen suggests that Christ not only became a human being but also became an angel: see Origen, *Homilies on the Psalms: Codex Monacensis Graecus 314*, trans. Joseph W. Trigg (Washington, DC: Catholic University of America Press, 2020), 45. For discussion, see Joseph W. Trigg, "The Angel of Great Counsel: Christ and the Angelic Hierarchy in Origen's Theology," *Journal of Theological Studies* 42 (1991): 33–51.

CHRIST THE NEW DAVID: THE ESCHATOLOGICAL KINGDOM

As Irenaeus asks rhetorically regarding Luke 2:11, "why did [the angels] add, 'in the city of David,' if they did not proclaim the glad tidings of the fulfilment of God's promise made to David, that from the fruit of his body there should be an eternal king?"[66] The covenant with David made by God in 2 Samuel 7 thus has a central importance. If Christ is the Davidic king, then Christ is not some kind of spirit-avatar whose mission is separate from Israel's Scriptures. According to Luke, Simeon had received a promise from God that he would not die before he saw the Messiah in the flesh. When he sees the baby Jesus, Simeon rejoices that God's covenantal preparation of the salvation of all peoples is being fulfilled in Jesus. The prophetess Anna has the same reaction, speaking about the baby Jesus "to all who were looking for the redemption of Jerusalem" (Lk 2:38) – that is, to all who were looking for the coming of the New David. Jipp remarks that with regard to Jesus' baptism – which the Gnostics interpret as the coming of the "Christ" – Irenaeus defends Jesus' Spirit-anointing by invoking "[Isaiah] 11:1–4 which foretells of a ruler from the line of David whose rule with be empowered by the Spirit of God."[67] Even more than I have done, Jipp shows that Irenaeus "read[s] Israel's scriptures through a messianic paradigm."[68]

6.3.2 Augustine

Although I will concentrate especially on Augustine's *Exposition of the Psalms*, let me begin with his account of David in Book XVII of his *City of God*. Augustine is particularly interested in the meaning of the Davidic covenant in 2 Samuel 7:8–16. Recall that God promises David, "When you days are fulfilled and you lie down with your fathers, I will raise up your offspring after you, who shall come forth

---

[66] Irenaeus, "Against Heresies," Book III, chapter 10, 425.
[67] Jipp, "Messiah Christology in Paul and Irenaeus," 83.
[68] Jipp, "Messiah Christology in Paul and Irenaeus," 85.

6.3 IRENAEUS, AUGUSTINE, AND AQUINAS ON THE NEW DAVID

from your body, and I will establish his kingdom. He shall build a house for my name, and I will establish the throne of his kingdom for ever. I will be his father, and he shall be my son" (2 Sam 7:12–14). Solomon, David's son, did indeed have his kingdom established, and he also built a Temple for God. But Solomon's throne was not established forever; the Davidic line was cut off, in terms of reigning in Jerusalem, by the Babylonians in 586 BC. Having made the covenant, why did God allow the reign of David's descendants to break off?

In response, Augustine argues that even if "a partial reflection of the future reality was shown even in Solomon, in that he did build the Temple," the true future reality nevertheless was Christ and his kingdom.[69] Christ is in the line of David, and his kingdom will endure forever. Augustine considers it significant that a psalm (attributed to Solomon) begs God regarding the king: "May he have dominion from sea to sea, and from the River to the ends of the earth!" (Ps 72:8). This worldwide kingdom goes far beyond "the limits bounding Solomon's kingdom."[70] Thus, the psalmist must have had something in mind other than Solomon's kingdom. In Christ Jesus, says Augustine, the psalmist's words are fulfilled. Augustine also argues that the Davidic covenant's terms cannot refer to Solomon because David was not yet dead when Solomon became king. For Augustine, the "offspring" to which 2 Samuel 7:12 refers, who becomes king after David's death and whose reign has no end, can only be Jesus. Jesus builds God a "house" (2 Sam 7:13) – not the kind that corrodes over time, as every earthly temple does, but rather the "house" that is the Church of faithful believers in Christ.

Augustine is aware that 2 Samuel 7 has parallels in both 1 Chronicles 17 and Psalm 89. In Psalm 89, God promises David that he

---

[69] Augustine, *City of God*, trans. Henry Bettenson (London: Penguin, 1984), Book XVII, ch. 8, p. 735.

[70] Augustine, *City of God*, Book XVII, chapter 8, 735.

(David) will be "the first born, the highest of the kings of the earth," and also that David's line will be established "for ever" (Ps 89:27–28). In the same psalm, however, the Davidic psalmist complains that God has not kept his covenant: "You have renounced the covenant with your servant; you have defiled his crown in the dust" (Ps 89:39). Therefore, Augustine argues that the promises recorded in the psalm must be interpreted as prophetic, just as the Davidic covenant is prophetic. The psalm's promises should be "referred to the Lord Jesus, under the name of David because of the 'form of a servant' which that same mediator took from the virgin, from the line of David."[71]

In *City of God*, then, Augustine's main question has to do with why the Davidic covenant means more than, on the surface, it may seem to mean. David himself, in 2 Samuel 7, interprets the covenant as being about the perpetual royal rule and flourishing of his line in Jerusalem, beginning with one of his sons. David says to God in response to God's covenantal promises: "And now, O Lord God, you are God, and your words are true, and you have promised this good thing to your servant; now therefore may it please you to bless the house of your servant, that it may continue for ever before you" (2 Sam 7:28–29). Such a blessing seems to require the Davidic line to continue reigning over Jerusalem forever. But Augustine, joined by the New Testament, knows that historically this did not happen. Augustine strives to show that Christ the New David is the true fulfillment of the covenant, not a second-best outcome of the covenantal promises.

Psalm 3, attributed to David during his flight from Absalom, describes David's righteous suffering and his trust in God. Augustine reads this psalm as a prophecy of Christ. Verse five particularly impresses him with regard to Christ's righteous suffering: "I lie down and sleep; I wake again, for the Lord sustains me" (Augustine's version is even more clearly Christological: "I have fallen asleep and

---

[71] Augustine, *City of God*, XVII, chapter 9, 737.

6.3 IRENAEUS, AUGUSTINE, AND AQUINAS ON THE NEW DAVID

have taken my rest, and I have risen up, because the Lord will uphold me"). These words, says Augustine, are "more in keeping with our Lord's passion and resurrection than with the account which history gives of David's flight before the face of his own rebel son."[72] Augustine adds, furthermore, that just as David fled from his enemies (Absalom and his followers), so also Christ "fled" – though only in the spiritual sense, by removing the interior indwelling of the Word from Judas so that the devil could take mastery of Judas. Just as David loved Absalom and wished to have died in his place, so also Jesus loved Judas and did in fact die in his place, though Judas rejected him. Much as I noted in the Gospels' typological use of 2 Samuel, Augustine takes every verse of this psalm and applies it to the New David in some way. Even so, Augustine does not neglect the historical David entirely.

In his exposition of another psalm significant for Christology (due in part to its being applied to Christ by Hebrews 1:8–9), namely Psalm 45, Augustine argues that it is about the divine "Son, our King."[73] He reflects upon the eternal generation of the Word, on the supposition that Psalm 45:1, "I address my verses to the king" (in his version: "I tell my works to the King"), may refer to the Father's speaking his entire being in generating the Son. Commenting on his version of Psalm 45:5, he suggests that "Ride forth victoriously and seize your kingdom" may be applied to what Christ has accomplished: "Do we not see this fulfilled already? It has undeniably taken place. Look round at the whole world: he has ridden forth victoriously and seized his kingdom, for all nations are his subjects."[74] Augustine insists that Christ in fact has inaugurated his kingdom, and he argues that the kingdom is the Church or, more specifically,

---

[72] Augustine, *On the Psalms*, vol. 1, *Psalms 1–29*, trans. Scholastica Hebgin and Felicitas Corrigan (Westminster, MD: Newman Press, 1960), 30.

[73] Augustine, *Expositions of the Psalms*, vol. 2, *33–50*, trans. Maria Boulding, O.S.B., ed. John E. Rotelle, O.S.A. (Hyde Park, NY: New City Press, 2000), 285.

[74] Augustine, *Expositions of the Psalms*, vol. 2, 292.

those persons who have true faith and charity and therefore are members of the Church not only externally but also internally. Christ reigns in his members through love, and his members spread his reign and perform kingdom-acts by love. We are conquered by Christ the king when we desist from our pride and, in faith and love, become subject to his rule. When Christ the king conquers us, says Augustine, what has happened is that "Christ's enemy was slain so that Christ's disciple might be raised to life."[75]

Commenting on Psalm 45:6, "Your divine throne endures for ever and ever," Augustine briefly mentions the earthly Davidic kingdom. He does so, however, only to dismiss it: "The throne that stood in the Jewish kingdom stood for a time only, as befitted those who were under the law, but not those under grace. Then he came to deliver those who were under the law, and establish them under the reign of grace."[76] He does not hesitate to reflect upon Christ the king in this context. Christ, "our ruler," stands as "sovereign over those who have been made straight."[77] Christ reigns through justice, and his reign is utterly opposed to sin. The next clause of Psalm 45:6 reads: "Your royal scepter is a scepter of equity." On this text, Augustine comments: "Draw near to this scepter and let Christ be your king, allow this scepter to rule you."[78] To belong to Christ's kingdom is to love and do justice. When we hate justice, we have rejected Christ's reign, since it is by the grace of Christ that our wills are enabled to do good in a full sense.

In the above examples, Augustine has not lost a sense of the inaugurated Messianic kingdom. He sees this kingdom as both individual and corporate (ecclesial). He certainly identifies Christ as a king, though not in anything like the normal earthly sense, since Christ reigns by love rather than power. We reign with Christ and are members of his kingdom when we truly love. This happens only

---

[75] Augustine, *Expositions of the Psalms*, vol. 2, 293.
[76] Augustine, *Expositions of the Psalms*, vol. 2, 294.
[77] Augustine, *Expositions of the Psalms*, vol. 2, 294.
[78] Augustine, *Expositions of the Psalms*, vol. 2, 295.

6.3 IRENAEUS, AUGUSTINE, AND AQUINAS ON THE NEW DAVID

through the grace of the Holy Spirit that Christ pours out in inaugurating his kingdom. Yet, although Augustine retains a sense of Christ the king and of his kingdom, it is generally fair to say that he does not unfold his Christology in relation to David.

Something of an exception, however, is his commentary on Psalm 110 (in his numbering, Psalm 109). In a verse quoted by Jesus in all the Synoptic Gospels in reference to his status as Lord, and quoted elsewhere in the New Testament in reference to his Ascension to the Father's right hand, this psalm of David states, "The Lord says to my lord: 'Sit at my right hand, till I make your enemies your footstool'" (Ps 110:1). Augustine explains that when Jesus brings forward this verse in Matthew 22:45, the question Jesus poses is, how can the Messiah be the son of David if the Messiah is David's Lord? It might seem the answer is that Christ is solely the Lord of David. But this would be to contradict the Gospel, since Matthew's Gospel begins by announcing that Jesus Christ is "the son of David" (Mt 1:1). Likewise, the blind men whom Jesus healed in Matthew 20 recognize Jesus as the son of David.

Augustine argues that what is at issue here is the distinction between Jesus' divine and human natures. In his humanity, he is the son of David. Drawing upon Philippians 2, Augustine comments that in the form of a servant, Christ is David's son, but in the form of God, he is David's Lord – or, as the Gospel of Matthew goes on to say, quoting Isaiah 7:14, he is "Emmanuel" (Mt 1:23). Returning to the psalm, Augustine makes much of David's authorship. How does David know that the Messiah, his son and Lord, will sit at the right hand of God and receive royal dominion over the whole world? Augustine reasons that David learns this in a spiritual vision. When he learned this, David must have rejoiced, since he was to be "honored by his son's birth and set free by his son's lordship."[79]

---

[79] Augustine, *Expositions of the Psalms*, vol. 5, 99–120, trans. Maria Boulding, O.S.B., ed. Boniface Ramsey (Hyde Park, NY: New City Press, 2003), 268.

CHRIST THE NEW DAVID: THE ESCHATOLOGICAL KINGDOM

In his interpretation of Psalm 110, Augustine goes on to insist that Christ's enemies are even now, as verse one indicates, "being put under his feet while he sits enthroned at the Father's right hand."[80] This is happening because the Lord "sends forth" his "mighty scepter" (Ps 110:2), which Augustine interprets as Christ's kingdom. The "rule" that Christ enjoys is one of mercy and love, and his "foes" are those who continue to live in their sins (whether they are nominally or heretically Christian or are non-Christians). Augustine thinks that the kingdom of God comes in our midst when we contemplate "the Word through whom all things were made," who is Truth incarnate as Love, and for this purpose "we need great purity, perfect purity of heart, and this can be gained only through faith."[81]

Augustine is well versed in David's story, as one would expect. In his exposition of Psalm 52 (or 51 in his Bible), he begins by reflecting upon the psalm's title, which explains that David wrote it when Doeg the Edomite told Saul about David's visit to the priestly house of Ahimelech (see 1 Samuel 22:9). Augustine observes that God chose Saul as king in order to teach the people a lesson about hardness of heart, whereas God chose David as king in order to prepare for the New David. Augustine states, "in David God was foreshadowing a reign of eternal salvation, and he had chosen David to abide for ever in his posterity."[82]

From eternity, God chose and predestined David to ascend to the throne of a united Israel, but before doing so David had to undergo persecution from his enemies (specifically Saul). David can therefore be seen as prefiguring Christ through his righteous suffering, with Saul taking the place of Judas. Without rejecting this link, Augustine suggests instead that the point is that David could not

---

[80] Augustine, *Expositions of the Psalms*, vol. 5, 271.
[81] Augustine, *Expositions of the Psalms*, vol. 5, 274.
[82] Augustine, *Expositions of the Psalms*, vol. 3, 51–72, trans. Maria Boulding, O.S.B., ed. John E. Rotelle, O.S.A. (Hyde Park, NY: New City Press, 2001), 13.

6.3 IRENAEUS, AUGUSTINE, AND AQUINAS ON THE NEW DAVID

rule over his kingdom until God "had freed him from his persecutors."[83] Christ, even on the Cross, was already the "king of the Jews" (Mt 27:37). By contrast, we, his followers, must be freed from our persecutors – namely sin and death – before we can fully reign with Christ. In this regard David prefigures Christ's Body, rather than prefiguring Christ the Head. Augustine grants, of course, that Christ "our head willed to reign in heaven only after he had completed his travail on earth, and willed only by way of suffering to raise to glory the body he had received below."[84] But Christ was never *not* king, whereas David's righteous suffering preceded his royal reign. Augustine emphasizes that our true enemy is death, since it is death that threatens to obliterate the meaning of every human life. Christ's great royal conquest, therefore, was his conquest of death.

Augustine also comments on David's actions at the priestly house of Ahimelech, where he and his men ate the bread of the presence, which only priests could lawfully eat (see Mt 12:4). David was both king and priest, just as Jesus is both king and priest, and just as all who belong to Christ's Body are royal priests. For his part, Doeg betrayed David just as Judas betrayed Jesus. Here Augustine draws a connection to the Church and its opponents: "[A]s we recognize the kingly and priestly body today, ... so we shall recognize the body that is opposed to the king and priest still."[85] Doeg represents the earthly kingdom or city, and David represents the heavenly kingdom or city (the Church).

At present, says Augustine, the two kingdoms are intermingled in the world. It happens that people who belong to the heavenly kingdom are pressed into service of various kinds by the earthly kingdom. Likewise, people who actually belong to the earthly kingdom may work for the heavenly kingdom, as when bad bishops preach

---

[83] Augustine, *Expositions of the Psalms*, vol. 3, 13.
[84] Augustine, *Expositions of the Psalms*, vol. 3, 13.
[85] Augustine, *Expositions of the Psalms*, vol. 3, 15.

the gospel. Augustine observes, "What they say belongs to David, what they do, to Doeg."[86] Augustine also finds spiritual meaning in a typo in the psalm's title in his version, which replaced "Ahimelech" with "Abimelech." David sojourned with the Philistine king Abimelech for a period during Saul's persecution of David. During this time, David lived with the Gentiles rather than with the Jews. Augustine connects this with the fact that faith in Christ moved from the Jews to the Gentiles when the apostles focused their attention upon the Gentiles. When Christ lived with the Jews, he was persecuted and killed. David symbolizes this experience, insofar as when he lived in Saul's court he was persecuted. David was not killed, but he nevertheless symbolizes righteous suffering and willingness to die. David was a figure of Christ, and God allowed David to live in order to symbolize Resurrection.

Augustine, therefore, does not fail to treat David's typological prefiguring of Christ the New David. Nor does Augustine fail to attend to Christ the king or to the inauguration (and visibility) of Christ's kingdom, as well as to what this kingdom requires of Christ's members. In general, however, Augustine does not devote much attention to examining the attributes of Christ through the lens of David. When he does so, furthermore, he often appeals to etymologies or to the spiritual sense, rather than exploiting the connections made in the New Testament's literal sense. Without exaggerating his lack of interest in David, it is true that he offers relatively little in the way of a New David Christology.

6.3.3 Aquinas

Does Aquinas do more in this regard? By my count, 1 Samuel does not appear much in the *Summa theologiae*. In the *secunda pars*, for instance, it appears 26 times, whereas the Psalms appear 319 times.

---

[86] Augustine, *Expositions of the Psalms*, vol. 3, 16.

6.3 IRENAEUS, AUGUSTINE, AND AQUINAS ON THE NEW DAVID

The books of Genesis, Exodus, Leviticus, and Deuteronomy each appear over a hundred times. 2 Samuel appears only ten times in the *secunda pars*, and 2 Samuel 7 and 1 Chronicles 17 (which describe the Davidic covenant) never appear. What about the *tertia pars*? Again 2 Samuel 7 and 1 Chronicles 17 are missing. In Aquinas's treatment of Christ's sitting at the Father's right hand and Christ's judiciary power – which is arguably the closest Aquinas comes in the *Summa* to a question devoted to Christ's kingship – Aquinas does not cite any Davidic text.

Yet, quotations from 1–2 Samuel are not entirely absent in the *tertia pars*: They appear eight times. Notably, 1 Samuel 15 – where King Saul sins against God, setting in motion God's anointing (through the prophet Samuel) of David to be king in 1 Samuel 16 – appears twice in Aquinas's discussion of Christ's grace of headship and once in Aquinas's question on Christ's Passion. This is significant since Christ is king precisely through his Cross and since Christ is king as Head of his Body the Church. The actual citations of 1 Samuel 15 do little work, but, as I have shown elsewhere, Aquinas's scriptural citations generally function in a cumulative fashion, establishing a scriptural framework that undergirds his theological arguments.[87]

In the first article of his discussion of Christ's Headship, Aquinas quotes the words of Samuel in 1 Kings 15:17: "Though you [Saul] are little in your own eyes, are you not the head of the tribes of Israel? The Lord anointed you king over Israel."[88] This biblical quotation supports Aquinas's contention that reign is marked by three elements: order or hierarchy, perfection, and power. (Specifically, the quotation of 1 Kings 15:17 has to do with the power that is associated with reign.) Aquinas argues that all three elements "belong

---

[87] See my *Paul in the "Summa Theologiae"* (Washington, DC: Catholic University of America Press, 2014).

[88] See Thomas Aquinas, *Summa theologiae*, trans. Fathers of the English Dominican Province (Westminster, MD: Christian Classics, 1981), III, q. 8, a. 1.

spiritually to Christ."[89] This is a helpful reflection upon the analogy between human rule and Christ's reign as Head of his Body the Church, but it does not involve the positing of a Davidic Christology. Similarly, when in the sixth article of this same question on Christ's grace of headship Aquinas again cites 1 Samuel 15:17 (now in an objection), it serves the purpose of addressing why, if Saul (or a pope) is head of Israel or of the Church, Christ's Body does not have two Heads. Aquinas goes on to demonstrate that Christ is the sole Head of his Body the Church, but he does so without further recourse to David.

In question 22 on Christ's priesthood, Aquinas answers an objection in article 1 by pointing out that Christ can be prophet, priest, and king. Although he affirms that Christ is Head and that Christ sits at the right hand of the Father with full judiciary power, he does not discuss Christ's kingship per se.[90] He does not cite any Davidic

---

[89] III, q. 8, a. 1.

[90] In the *Commentary on the Sentences*, Book IV, dist. 49, q. 1, a. 2, response to qla. 5, Aquinas comments regarding the kingdom of God: "men are said to be 'in the kingdom of God' when they are perfectly subject to his providence.... For this reason 'kingdom of God' is said antonomastically, in two ways: at times to mean the congregation of those who walk by faith, and in this way the church militant is called the kingdom of God; at other times to mean the company of those who are already established in the end, and in this way the church triumphant is called the kingdom of God. And according to this latter meaning, to be in the kingdom of God is the same thing as beatitude" (Aquinas, *Commentary on the Sentences: Book IV, Distinctions 43–50*, trans. Beth Mortensen, Peter Kwasniewski, and Dylan Schrader [Green Bay, WI: Aquinas Institute, 2018], 383). Commenting on Matthew 3:11, Aquinas states that the "kingdom is Christ" (§275), and commenting on Matthew 3:2, he affirms that "the kingdom of heaven is taken in four ways in the Scriptures. For sometimes Christ himself dwelling in us through grace is called the kingdom of heaven.... Second, the sacred Scriptures are called the kingdom of God.... And this is called a kingdom because its law leads to a kingdom. Third, the present Church militant is called the kingdom of heaven.... And it is called the kingdom of heaven because it is established after the manner of the heavenly Church. Fourth, the heavenly court is called the kingdom of heaven" (§250): see Thomas Aquinas, *Commentary on the Gospel of Matthew, Chapters 1–12*, trans. Jeremy Holmes and Beth Mortensen, ed. The Aquinas Institute (Lander, WY: The Aquinas Institute for the Study of Sacred Doctrine, 2013), 80–81, 89.

6.3 IRENAEUS, AUGUSTINE, AND AQUINAS ON THE NEW DAVID

texts here but instead quotes Isaiah 33:22, which proclaims that "the Lord is our king" and which does not mention a Davidic king at all – though Isaiah 33:17 does contain the beautiful promise "Your eyes will see the king in his beauty."

First Samuel 15:22 appears in Aquinas's question on whether Christ died out of obedience to the Father. In this verse, Samuel announces that because of Saul's disobedience, God has rejected him from being king over Israel. The true king of Israel will be marked by obedience – and 1 Samuel 16 proceeds to depict young David in these terms. One can see here the foundations of a New David Christology with respect to Christ's Passion, but Aquinas does not develop it further in any explicit way. Still, the fact that the treatments of Christ's Headship and Christ's Passion (and perhaps, implicitly, Christ's priesthood) contain allusions or references to Davidic kingship indicate that Aquinas has some appreciation for David's typological place.

Asking whether Christ's crucifiers committed the most grievous sin – despite the fact that Christ died willingly – Aquinas makes reference to David's recognition that killing the king of Israel (Saul) merited the death penalty even if, as was the case, Saul requested to be slain by his armor-bearer rather than be killed by enemy soldiers.[91] In discussing whether Christ's Passion reconciles us to God, Aquinas makes reference to David's words when Saul was pursuing David with the intention of killing him. David tells Saul that if it is truly God who wants David dead, then David will earnestly make an atonement offering (1 Sam 26:19).[92] Lastly, while inquiring whether Christ was baptized by John at a fitting age, Aquinas makes reference to the fact that David began to reign at the same age – thirty years old, according to 2 Samuel 5:4.[93]

In addition, at various points in the Christology of the *tertia pars*, Aquinas describes Christ by reference to what David prophetically

---

[91] See III, q. 47, a. 6, citing 2 Samuel 1:5–14.
[92] See III, q. 49, a. 4.
[93] See III, q. 39, a. 3.

CHRIST THE NEW DAVID: THE ESCHATOLOGICAL KINGDOM

says in the Psalms. For example, in investigating why the Son of God assumed a human nature subject to defects (to which Adam's body, prior to the fall, was not subject), Aquinas remarks that it was proper that Christ in his human nature suffer and be tempted due to infirmities. Only because Christ assumed human nature in its weakened condition can he heal and redeem it from within. Here Aquinas cites David's prophetic vision of the coming Christ: "I lift up my eyes to the hills. From where does my help come? My help comes from the Lord, who made heaven and earth" (Ps 121:1–2).[94] Similarly, in an objection in article 1 of question 15, on whether Christ was subject to sin, Aquinas quotes Psalm 22:1, a Davidic psalm that Christ himself, by proclaiming it on the Cross, reveals to be words spoken by David on the New David's behalf: "My God, my God, why have you forsaken me?"[95]

Aquinas strengthens the *tertia pars*'s claim to a New David Christology through his remarks upon question 35, article 7, which treats why Christ was born in Bethlehem. The objections inquire into why Christ was not born in Jerusalem, Nazareth, or Rome. After quoting Micah 5:2 – "But you, O Bethlehem Ephrathah, who are little to be among the clans of Judah, from you shall come forth for me one who is to be ruler in Israel, whose origin is from of old, from ancient days" (cf. Mt 2:6; Jn 7:42) – Aquinas responds that God had promised David that the Messiah would come from David's descendants. Aquinas quotes a phrase in David's prophetic oracle that describes David as "the anointed of the God of Jacob" (2 Sam 23:1 RSV). In Aquinas's Parisian Vulgate, this verse portrays David as "the man to whom it was appointed concerning the Christ

---

[94] III, q. 14, a. 1, *sed contra*. Aquinas's version (Psalm 120 in the Vulgate) takes away the rhetorical question, so that Aquinas need only quote Psalm 120:1: "I have lifted up my eyes to the mountains, from whence help shall come to me."

[95] III, q. 15, a. 1, obj. 1; the objection draws its strength from the fact that in the Vulgate version, the verse continues as "Far from my salvation are the words of my sins" whereas in the RSV the verse continues as "Why are you so far from helping me, from the words of my groaning?"

6.3 IRENAEUS, AUGUSTINE, AND AQUINAS ON THE NEW DAVID

of the God of Jacob." Although Aquinas is employing a misleading translation, two points stand out that can be justified on the basis of other biblical texts. First, Aquinas perceives David to be a prophet, and, second, he holds that David received a promise about the coming Davidic Messiah. Aquinas goes on to say that Christ was born in Bethlehem, the city in which David was born, in order to show that God's promise to David was being fulfilled. Aquinas does not use the phrase "New David," but it is clear that this is what Jesus is, symbolized by his being born in the same city in which David was born.

Responding to the objection that Christ should have been born in Jerusalem, Aquinas further strengthens his portrait of Christ as the New David. He deems it appropriate that Christ follow David's trajectory. Born in Bethlehem, David reigned in Jerusalem. In accordance with this pattern, Christ the New David is born in Bethlehem and reigns in Jerusalem.

Yet, there is a further problem caused by the Book of Acts, which traces a movement from Jerusalem to Rome. If Christ's birth in Bethlehem and death in Jerusalem are intended to signify Christ's identity as the promised New David, why did the Church not extend this Davidic symbolism by establishing Jerusalem as its papal court? Aquinas answers that the New David establishes a worldwide kingdom by his Cross, Resurrection, and Ascension to the right hand of the Father. It is therefore necessary to signify the scope of the Christ's kingdom by "set[ting] up the head of His Church in Rome itself, which was the head of the world, in sign of His complete victory, in order that from that city the faith might spread throughout the world."[96] Aquinas here applies to Rome the words sung by the inhabitants of Judah on the day of God's eschatological victory. Rome is the "lofty city" that is now trampled by "the steps of the needy" (Isa 26:5–6), that is to say by the apostles and the followers of Christ. This is the work of the New David, conquering the world

[96] III, q. 35, a. 7, ad 3.

on behalf of the poor and needy – namely, on behalf of all those who are in need of divine mercy.

Aquinas augments his portrait of Christ as the New David when he discusses the slaughter of the infant male children in the region of Bethlehem by Herod (Mt 2:16). Herod committed this gruesome act, according to the Gospel of Matthew, because he feared that the Messiah might grow up to overthrow his dynastic rule. In an objection, Aquinas raises the idea that God should never have allowed the Magi or anyone else to know that the Messiah had been born, given that this knowledge resulted in such a terrible slaughter. In response to this objection, Aquinas reasons that not only was Christ's judicial power thereby foreshadowed – since the infant Christ could already terrify a powerful king – but also Christ's overthrow of the kingdoms of this world was foreshadowed, given that Herod and Satan were already trembling. This overthrow, however, does not take place by the establishment of another earthly kingdom. Drawing upon Leo the Great and John Chrysostom, Aquinas observes that a mere earthly kingdom is not enough for Christ (the *New* David), since Christ wills to reign by love rather than by the normal earthly modes.[97]

Further additions to the portrait of Christ the Messianic Davidic king are provided in the eighth article of question 36. Discussing the fittingness of the visit of the Magi to the infant Christ, Aquinas remarks in the objections that it might seem odd for Gentiles to come pay homage to the king of the Jews, not least when Herod was already reigning over the Jewish people and when the infant Jesus was in a manger rather than seated upon a throne. In response, Aquinas emphasizes that Christ (the New David) reigns over the entire earth, Jews and Gentiles. Indebted to Augustine and Chrysostom, he notes that the Magi foreshadow the conversion of the Gentiles. Through the Magi, furthermore, the birth of the New David, the rightful king, is proclaimed in Jerusalem. The Magi also

---

[97] See III, q. 36, a. 2, ad 3.

6.3 IRENAEUS, AUGUSTINE, AND AQUINAS ON THE NEW DAVID

teach what should be offered to Christ the king: gold signifying wisdom, incense signifying fervor of prayer, and myrrh signifying mortification of the flesh and repentance for sin. The New David desires from us these things – wisdom, prayer, and repentance – for the upbuilding of his kingdom.

Aquinas also discusses why Christ took flesh from within the line of David. Here he addresses problems arising from the contrasting genealogies found in Matthew and Luke. Matthew's genealogy runs through Joseph, but Matthew makes clear that Joseph was not the father, since Mary conceived virginally (Mt 1:18). If Joseph was only an adoptive father and yet it was through Joseph that Jesus was descended from David, then Jesus would have been in the line of David only by adoption, not by blood. In a strict sense, he would therefore not be "descended from David according to the flesh" (Rom 1:3). Another problem becomes apparent in Luke. Elizabeth, Mary's cousin, is described by Luke as "of the daughters of Aaron" (Lk 1:5). This seems to imply that Mary too is from the line of Aaron, which would mean that neither Mary nor Jesus is from the line of David. Aaron belonged to the tribe of Levi, whereas David belonged to the tribe of Judah. If Jesus is a Levite, then he is not a son of David. Another problem is that Matthew traces Jesus' genealogy through King Jechoniah (also called Jehoiachin and Coniah), but in Jeremiah 22:30 we read an ominous prophecy about Jechoniah: "Write this man down as childless, a man who shall not succeed in his days; for none of his offspring shall succeed in sitting on the throne of David, and ruling again in Jerusalem."

Aquinas replies to all this by pointing out that the Gospel is clear that Jesus cannot be understood otherwise than as descended from Abraham and David (see Matthew 1:1). Regarding Christ's descent from David according to the flesh, this is important because God swore to David, as reported in Psalm 132:11, that "one of the sons of your body I will set on your throne." Aquinas chooses to quote this prophetic psalm rather than 2 Samuel 7. Given God's oath to David, the Jewish people were expecting a Messianic Davidic king, and for this reason they greeted Jesus joyfully on Palm Sunday as royalty: "Hosanna to the Son of David!" (Mt 21:9). In Aquinas's view, it is necessary that Jesus be king, priest, and prophet. David was both prophet and king, while Abraham was a priest, and David's status is another reason for Christ's descent from David.

Aquinas also thinks the Son of God became incarnate from the seed of David because David manifests divine election, just as Abraham manifests the privileges given to the Jewish people. Aquinas quotes 1 Samuel 13:14, where the prophet Samuel tells Saul: "But now your kingdom shall not continue; the Lord has sought out a man after his own heart; and the Lord has appointed him to be prince over his people, because you have not kept what the Lord commanded you."[98] The New David, Jesus Christ, is most fully a man after God's own heart, and he is the king not only over the Jewish people but also over the elect Gentiles.

To answer the objections named above regarding the genealogies of Jesus, Aquinas relies upon Augustine, Jerome, and Gregory of Nazianzus. Quoting their viewpoints, he states that Mary was of the same tribe and Davidic family as Joseph, either through her father or through her mother. Likewise, either Mary's father married a woman of the tribe of Aaron or else her cousin Elizabeth's father married a woman of the family of David. Lastly, although none of Jechoniah's descendants reigned as earthly kings in Jerusalem, Jechoniah had children and descendants, including Christ, whose kingdom is not a mere extension of David's and thus does not fall under the ban described by the prophet Isaiah.

Aquinas also reflects upon Christ as the Davidic king, the Son of David, outside the pages of the *Summa theologiae*. Let me offer a few examples. In his *De regno, ad regem Cypri*, Aquinas pauses in his discussion of politics to observe that a good king is worthy of a great reward. He cites Zechariah 12:8, where the prophet proclaims: "On that [eschatological] day the Lord will put a shield about the

---

[98] III, q. 31, a. 2.

6.3 IRENAEUS, AUGUSTINE, AND AQUINAS ON THE NEW DAVID

inhabitants of Jerusalem so that the feeblest among them on that day shall be like David, and the house of David shall be like God, like the angel of the Lord, at their head." Although it is David's entire "house" that will "be like God," Aquinas focuses on David: "The house of David will be as the house of God, because just as he carried out the work of God among the people by ruling faithfully, so in his reward he will adhere more closely to God."[99] In the background here is Aquinas's awareness that the Son of David is indeed the everlastingly exalted head of all nations, as the incarnate Lord.

Similarly, in his Academic Sermon "Osanna Filio David," Aquinas calls to mind the prophecy in Jeremiah 23 about salvation coming through a future Davidic king. Aquinas's Vulgate version of Jeremiah 23:5 states, "In those days I will save Judah and I will raise for David a just shoot," whereas the RSV says essentially the same thing in verses 5 and 6: "I will raise up for David a righteous Branch.... In his days Judah will be saved." Aquinas argues that the crowds greeting Jesus on Palm Sunday understood that the Savior would be a divine Davidic king, and thus (in my phrase) the New David. The crowds on Palm Sunday combine these elements when they greet Jesus, "Hosanna to the Son of David! Blessed is he who comes in the name of the Lord!"

In this sermon, Aquinas then proceeds to unfold a New David Christology by exploring how David "bears the image of Christ."[100] David does so in three ways: royal dominion, victorious warfare, and grace. Regarding royal dominion, David was not the first king of Israel, but he was the first king whom God accepted. David, the divinely approved king of Israel, is therefore the image of Christ who, as Mary learns from the angel Gabriel, receives from God "the

---

[99] Thomas Aquinas, *On Kingship: To the King of Cyprus*, trans. Gerald B. Phelan, trans. rev. I. T. Eschmann, O.P. (Toronto: Pontifical Institute of Mediaevel Studies, 1949), ch. 9, §74, p. 43. For historical-critical reflection, see Robert L. Foster, *The Theology of the Books of Haggai and Zechariah* (Cambridge: Cambridge University Press, 2021), 178.

[100] Thomas Aquinas, *The Academic Sermons*, trans. Mark-Robin Hoogland, C.P. (Washington, DC: Catholic University of America Press, 2010), 58.

throne of his father David" (Lk 1:32). Regarding warfare, David credits God for his military successes (see Psalm 144:1), while Christ defeats the demons and triumphantly leads to safety those whom the demons had defeated. Lastly, regarding grace, David is praised by God as "a man after his [God's] own heart" (1 Sam 13:14), while God says of Christ, "This is my beloved Son, with whom I am well pleased." David's justice, charity, peace, meekness, and humility appear in various psalms, as Aquinas points out. Christ's graced person and victorious work are thus well explicated by the Davidic typology.

In another Academic Sermon, "Ecce Rex Tuus," Aquinas discusses Jesus as the Davidic Messiah, with attention to Zechariah 9:9 and Matthew 21:5.[101] He again quotes Jeremiah 23:5 about the coming of the Davidic king, and he again mentions Christ's conquest of the demons. He notes that Christ alone is king; Christ has no competitors. In this regard he cites Ezekiel 37:22, which says of the eschatologically restored kingdom of Israel "one king shall be king over them all." Christ is the supreme lawgiver, able even to change the law given by God. Aquinas quotes Isaiah 33:22, as he did in the question on Christ's priesthood in the *Summa theologiae*. Christ has absolute authority, as can be seen from John 5:22 and Matthew 28:18. Christ's dominion is worldwide, as we learn of God's "son" in Psalm 2:8, where God says, "I will make the nations your heritage, and the ends of the earth your possession." Christ is just and righteous, using his power for the purpose of service and salvation, as shown in Matthew 20:28 and elsewhere.[102] Beyond his choice of biblical citations, Aquinas does not explicitly compare Christ to

---

[101] For historical-critical reflections on Zechariah 9:9's function in Matthew 21:5, see Moss, *The Zechariah Tradition and the Gospel of Matthew*, chapter 3. As she says: "As he enters Jerusalem, having descended the Mount of Olives (see Matt. 21.1; cf. Zech 14:4–5), the Matthean Jesus is portrayed as a royal figure. The image of Jesus as Davidic *king*, which first appeared in the Infancy Narrative, is suddenly reintroduced by means of the Zechariah fulfillment citation" (62).

[102] See Aquinas, *The Academic Sermons*, 70.

6.3 IRENAEUS, AUGUSTINE, AND AQUINAS ON THE NEW DAVID

David in this sermon, which goes on to expound Christ's kingship and its benefits.

In Aquinas's biblical commentaries, some further developments along the lines of New David Christology can be found. For example, in commenting on John's account of the soldiers' mocking of Jesus – "Hail, King of the Jews!" (Jn 19:3) – Aquinas compares this to the greeting of royal personages found in the narratives about David. Specifically, he notes that Hushai the Archite greets Absalom after the latter has captured Jerusalem: "Long live the king!" (2 Sam 16:16).[103] In fact, Hushai is there on behalf of David; the true king whom Hushai hopes will live long is David. There is a play on words also in the soldiers' mockery, since Jesus is in fact the true king who will not succumb to their military power but will rise again. (Aquinas does not bring out all these elements explicitly but instead simply juxtaposes the soldiers' mockery and Hushai's greeting.) Aquinas also frequently quotes Davidic psalms in discussing the further iterations of "the king of the Jews" in John's Passion narrative.

Often, the biblical commentaries quote verses that we have seen Aquinas quote in the *Summa*. For instance, in commenting on John 7:42 – where, as noted above, John reports that some Jews doubted that Jesus was the Messiah because they thought Jesus was from Galilee – Aquinas quotes Jeremiah 23:5, 2 Samuel 23:1, and Micah 5:2. Likewise, in commenting on Matthew 1:1's reference to "Jesus Christ, the son of David, the son of Abraham," Aquinas states (just as we have seen above) that these designations show that Jesus was priest, prophet, and king. As Aquinas says, had Matthew's Gospel "named only Abraham, it would not have indicated that Christ was

---

[103] See Thomas Aquinas, *Commentary on the Gospel of John: Chapters 13–21*, trans. Fabian Larcher, O.P., and James A. Weisheipl, O.P., ed. Daniel Keating and Matthew Levering (Washington, DC: Catholic University of America Press, 2010), §2377, p. 227.

a king; while if David alone had been named, it would not have shown the priestly dignity in Christ."[104] Indebted to Ambrose, Aquinas goes on to propose that Matthew 1:1 names David first because David had a greater dignity, insofar as God promised that the Messiah (the Head) would come forth from him, whereas God promised Abraham that all peoples (the Members) would be blessed in his seed. In defense of this claim, Aquinas quotes Psalm 132:11, which he quoted above in a similar context.

Aquinas's unfinished *Commentary on the Psalms* also contains multiple Davidic themes, as one would expect. In commenting on Psalm 2, for instance, Aquinas remarks with regard to the Psalm's title that David is a fitting type of Jesus, because "David is said to be brave in battle, and Christ, the power of God [1 Cor 1:24]."[105] In Aquinas's view, the Psalm can be read in the literal sense as being about David's kingdom, but it can also be read in the literal sense as being spoken by Christ. When Psalm 2:2 refers to the rulers plotting "against the Lord and his anointed," Aquinas argues that in the mystical sense, "these words were said under the likeness of David concerning Christ." Likewise, when Psalm 2:6 states that the king has been established in Zion, Aquinas holds that in the mystical sense, this is a reference to Christ, whose royal domain is the whole universe. At various points in the New Testament, Psalm 2:7 is applied to Christ, and Aquinas notes that verse 7 specifically pertains to Christ's eternal generation as the divine Son.

Aquinas, therefore, appreciates Christ's status as the eschatological Davidic king. Yet, Christ the New David needs to be added more fully to Thomistic Christology. Let me refer to the framework of the *tertia pars* as a way of offering some suggestions. When treating the fittingness of the Incarnation, God's history with Israel could

---

[104] Aquinas, *Commentary on the Gospel of Matthew*, Chapters 1–12, §20, p. 7.
[105] I have taken this translation from the Latin–English text of Aquinas's *Commentary on the Psalms* found at https://isidore.co/aquinas/PsalmsAquinas/ThoPs2.htm, accessed August 17, 2021.

6.3 IRENAEUS, AUGUSTINE, AND AQUINAS ON THE NEW DAVID

be further integrated – for example with respect to the timing of the Incarnation in question 1, article 5. Reference to David could assist in showing how "man was to be liberated in such a manner that he might be humbled and see how he stood in need of a deliverer."[106] Reference to David could also assist in showing precisely what kind of liberation and deliverance Christ brings. In question 1, article 2, Aquinas asks whether it was "necessary for the reparation of the human race that the Word of God should become incarnate." Has Christ actually repaired the human race? A great deal depends upon what we think that the Messiah should have accomplished for us. Here reflection upon New David Christology can make a contribution, since, unlike David, the Messiah chooses not to be a mere earthly political ruler.

When treating the mode of union in question 2 of the *tertia pars*, Aquinas drives the discussion forward through reflection upon the conciliar teachings. With regard to such questions as whether "the union of the Word Incarnate took place in the nature,"[107] I think attention to the scriptural language about the Messianic Davidic king could assist in further grounding the conciliar teachings in God's saving purposes, since both the humanity and divinity of Jesus are a part of the biblical teaching about the eschatological David.

When discussing Christ's grace and virtue (question 7), I suggest that the New David theme of the righteousness and piety of David might be helpful. Similarly, when discussing Christ's "gratuitous graces,"[108] David's role as a prophet might make a contribution. Aquinas already briefly includes David in his discussion of Christ's Headship, but the latter could be connected even more firmly with Christ's Davidic kingship. The fact that Christ now reigns as the Messianic New David in the Church (and world) and the manner in which Christ reigns have a natural place early in the *tertia*

---

[106] III, q. 1, a. 5.
[107] III, q. 2, a. 1.
[108] III, q. 7, a. 7.

pars, either in the question on Christ's Headship or in a question on Christ as king, just as Aquinas devotes a separate question to Christ's priesthood. Christ as the eschatological Davidic shepherd could likewise receive explicit attention in probing what it means for us to reign in Christ and for Christ to reign in us. The relationship of Christ's kingship to earthly royal rule, and of Christ's kingship to political and economic programs, might here be specified. Precisely in his suffering, Christ is a righteous Davidic warrior, a conqueror.

Christ's status as the New David is deeply related to his Cross, Resurrection, and Ascension, as well as to his sitting at the right hand of the Father and judiciary power. Thus, a deeper integration of the New David theme into the discussions found in questions 46–59 could be fruitful. As already noted, more attention could be given to Christ's reigning (and judging) as the New David here and now, and not solely at the final judgment. In Aquinas's discussion of "redemption" in question 48, article 4 – or else in a separate article – the *Christus Victor* motif could be developed along New David lines. Question 49, on the effects of Christ's Passion, offers room for further reflection on the inauguration of the New David's eschatological kingdom. Also, the New David framework could be drawn upon in question 49, article 2's discussion of Christ's deliverance of the human race from the power of Satan. Question 47, article 2's discussion of Christ's obedience could be linked to the righteous suffering and obedience of David in 1 Samuel, 1 Chronicles, and the Psalms.

Question 24's discussion of Christ's predestination could also be brought explicitly into the New David framework, since a central theme of New David Christology, as Aquinas recognizes, is David's election or chosenness. Aquinas does quote Romans 1:3–4, which is a New David text. These verses describe "the gospel concerning his Son, who was descended from David according to the flesh and designated Son of God in power according to the Spirit of holiness by his resurrection from the dead." Aquinas quotes this text in order to make the point that God eternally predestined Christ *in his human nature* to be the incarnate Son of God. He explains that these verses "give us to understand that in respect of His being of the seed of David according to the flesh, He was predestinated the Son of God in power."[109] To this Davidic element drawn from Romans 1, a fuller New David portrait could be added. This would enrich our appreciation for how David is a representative figure and how the New David's election, as the election of a righteous sufferer and pious man who trusts in God, is the exemplar of ours.

6.4 An Ontological Note

Ontologically, the concept of the "New David" especially involves Christ's Headship of grace and the mystical body or kingdom of grace. The biblical portrait of Christ as inaugurating a kingdom is not a mere metaphor, even though this kingdom is not a mere earthly kingdom. Just as Scripture says, Christ truly reigns here and now. Christ reigns through his love and by the power of his salvific suffering. The royal path by which we here and now participate in Christ's reign is not this-worldly exaltation but self-sacrificial service in love. The reign of God is an eternal reign of self-surrendering love, in which we are called to share.

It may seem counterfactual (at least in the short run), but those who put their trust in earthly power have chosen a flimsy and foolish path. Recall the vision of the Seer in the Book of Revelation, describing those who choose the City of Man (selfish self-love) rather than the City of God (selfless love, Christ's kingdom). The former path is shown to be "drunk with the blood of the saints and the blood of the martyrs of Jesus" (Rev 17:6). In the end, "the kings of the earth, who committed fornication and were wanton with her, will weep and wail over her [the City of Man] when they see the smoke of her burning" (Rev 18:9).

---

[109] III, q. 24, a. 1, ad 2.

Aquinas affirms that "Christ is the Head of the Church by His own power and authority" and that "Christ is the Head of all who pertain to the Church in every place and time."[110] In the inaugurated kingdom, the Church or mystical body, Christ the New David rules here and now by love, by the grace of the Holy Spirit that configures all Christ's members to himself. Indeed, Christ "loves us and has freed us from our sins by his blood and made us a kingdom, priests to his God and Father" (Rev 1:5–6). According to Aquinas, Christ rules by leading his people to obey God's law of love, whereas Satan abuses all rule by seeking "to lead man [away] from obeying the divine precept."[111] Christ's royal work is his headship of grace, as he pours out the Spirit.

Aquinas holds that "in the same way and by the same eternal act God predestinated us and Christ."[112] Yet, in this eternal plan of grace, Jesus is chosen or predestined by God to be not an adopted son but rather the "natural Son of God."[113] He is the king because he is the source of all grace, as the incarnate Son. As Aquinas says, "being established in His heavenly seat as God and Lord," Christ "send[s] down gifts upon men, according to Eph. 4:10."[114]

Thus, Aquinas has a keen sense of the realities that pertain to the theme of Christ the eschatological David. Aquinas provides profound insight into Christ's rule over the universal kingdom of God as the source of the grace of the Holy Spirit. He makes clear that this reign of justice, mercy, and love, for which Jesus was chosen from all eternity and which Jesus consummated on the Cross and now enacts at the right hand of the Father, is the real meaning and purpose of human history. Thomistic Christology can accentuate this teaching and make the connections more explicit, along the biblical path of the New David.

---

[110] III, q. 8, a. 6.
[111] III, q. 8, a. 7; translation slightly altered.
[112] III, q. 24, a. 3.
[113] III, q. 24, a. 3.
[114] III, q. 57, a. 6; translation slightly altered.

6.5 Conclusion

The New Testament's Christology is a New David Christology in multiple ways. Jesus' humanity and divinity are perceived through the lens of his status as Messiah and through texts from Israel's Scriptures that prepare for the Messianic Davidic king. Indeed, the typological theme of the New David penetrates into every aspect of New Testament Christology. As the eschatological Davidic king, the eschatological shepherd, Christ "procures a kingdom for himself through his unfailing faithfulness and testimony to truth, which results in his death."[115] Christ is the eschatological king because by his Cross, he establishes justice through true love and true worship. He liberates all who have faith in him from sin and death. He now reigns at the right hand of the Father, sending forth his Holy Spirit to unite people to his salvific Cross and Resurrection and enabling people to live in truth and love rather than "in deception, manipulation, and violence."[116] Now that the Messianic Davidic kingdom has been inaugurated, believers have our "primary identity as citizens of the kingdom of God and subjects of Christ's kingship," insofar as we live by the law of love through the grace of Christ.[117]

Miura, Cho, Daly-Denton, Chae, and Jipp display the value of exegetical reflection upon Jesus' Messianic Davidic kingship. Davidic psalms, 1–2 Samuel, 1 Chronicles, and the prophetic texts that treat the figure of David contribute to New Testament Christology. Jesus proclaimed himself to be the Messianic Davidic king, the son of David and the Lord of David. His identity as Mediator,

---

[115] Jipp, *The Messianic Theology of the New Testament*, 394. Jipp is here describing the Messianic theology of the Book of Revelation, but this aspect applies across the New Testament.
[116] Jipp, *The Messianic Theology of the New Testament*, 395.
[117] Jipp, *The Messianic Theology of the New Testament*, 395.

Priest, God's predestined one, and Savior – and as the one who is fully human and fully divine – comes to be known in light of his Messianic Davidic kingship and his kingdom purposes.

I hope to have demonstrated that Wright exaggerates when he suggests that the Church Fathers and their medieval successors forgot about the Messianic Davidic king and the inauguration of the kingdom. Nevertheless, Wright has a point. Even though the eschatological king was not forgotten, theologians devoted much time and energy to other topics and did so in ways that rendered the Davidic context much less central.

The enthronement of the New David, in his Cross, Resurrection, and Ascension, merits emphasis in Thomistic Christology. As Aquinas recognizes, David suffered grave persecution before reigning as king. In his *Perfection in Death: The Christological Dimension of Courage in Aquinas*, Patrick Clark has observed that for Paul and Aquinas, "the limited suffering we experience now is well worth the eternal glory and exalted dignity that God's grace bestows upon us in Christ," if we endure these sufferings in love and obedience.[118] The framework offered by New David Christology will help to hold together suffering and enthronement, along with the good of prayerful communion with the God who, in Christ, pours out his grace to configure us to his love. A Thomistic Christology enriched by further reflection on Christ the eschatological New David will appreciate ever more surely the truth that, as Scot McKnight says, "the cross was the crown" for Jesus Christ, just as it is for us today.[119]

---

[118] Patrick M. Clark, *Perfection in Death: The Christological Dimension of Courage in Aquinas* (Washington, DC: Catholic University of America Press, 2015), 237.

[119] Scot McKnight, *The King Jesus Gospel: The Original Good News Revisited* (Grand Rapids, MI: Zondervan Academic, 2011), 151.

Conclusion

Thomistic theologians naturally tend to focus on the themes explicitly treated by Thomas Aquinas in the *Summa theologiae*. The benefits of this focus appear in mid-twentieth century works such as those by Réginald Garrigou-Lagrange and Bernard Lonergan and in the recent Thomistic Christological works by Thomas Joseph White, Simon Gaine, Adonis Vidu, Dominic Legge, and many others. Recent Thomists have offered much insight into such themes as Christ's human perfection under grace, Christ's divine Sonship, and the atonement as Christ's loving self-offering to the Father.

Nevertheless, I have argued in this book that contemporary Thomistic Christology requires augmenting in light of the eschatological insights of New Testament scholarship. In 1981 Stanley Hauerwas observed, "It has become a commonplace that one of the great contributions of [historical-]critical scholarship has been a renewed sense of the significance of the Kingdom of God in Jesus' preaching and ministry."[1] Hauerwas describes the Kingdom of God as grounded in the claim that God, in Christ, is the Lord of history and of creation. He quotes Origen to the effect that "Jesus is the *autobasileia* – the Kingdom in person."[2] In the four decades since Hauerwas wrote these lines, New Testament scholarship has traveled even farther in this direction. Contemporary New Testament scholarship gives extensive attention to Christ as proclaiming and

---

[1] Stanley Hauerwas, *A Community of Character: Toward a Constructive Christian Social Ethic* (Notre Dame: University of Notre Dame Press, 1981), 44.
[2] Hauerwas, *A Community of Character*, 45.

CONCLUSION

inaugurating the Kingdom of God by undergoing the eschatological tribulation on behalf of his people, leading a new exodus, and standing as the perfect priest-king.

Although Aquinas infrequently discusses the Kingdom of God, Origen was an important contributor to Aquinas's understanding of Jesus. To say the least, Origen had a keen sense for the New Testament's use of Old Testament typologies in portraying Jesus Christ. As we have seen, Aquinas's biblical commentaries attend to these typologies, and the typologies are also present in his systematic works. Aquinas values the way in which Christ recapitulates and fulfills the salvation history of the Old Testament. Piotr Roszak expresses Aquinas's perspective when he says that Sacred Scripture is anchored "in the unique relationship of unity guaranteed by Christ."[3] For Christians, it is necessary to appreciate that "[t]he meaning of the Old Testament Scriptures" is "inherently christological," even though other meanings are present as well.[4]

In this light, I have proposed a typological path for enriching the eschatological dimension of Thomistic Christology. Put simply, it behooves contemporary Thomistic Christology to take advantage of the insights of Aquinas, the Church Fathers, and modern biblical scholarship into Jesus Christ as the New Adam, New Isaac, New Moses, New Joshua, and New David. These typologies are not mere metaphors, since divine providence was preparing for Jesus Christ

---

[3] Piotr Roszak, "Exegesis and Contemplation: The Literal and Spiritual Sense of Scripture in Aquinas' Biblical Commentaries," *Espíritu* 65 (2016): 481–504, at 482.

[4] Hans Boersma, *Five Things Theologians Wish Biblical Scholars Knew* (Downers Grove, IL: IVP Academic, 2021), 20. See also my "Mystagogy and Aquinas's *Commentary on Isaiah*: Initiating God's People into Christ," in *Initiation and Mystagogy in Thomas Aquinas: Scriptural, Systematic, Sacramental and Moral, and Pastoral Perspectives*, ed. Henk Schoot, Jacco Verburgt, and Jörgen Vijgen (Leuven: Peeters, 2019), 17–40. Along lines befitting the present volume, Boersma argues that "it is the church's task to safeguard and pass on the truth of the Scriptures so that they may continue in their role of assisting people in safely crossing the Jordan River into the Promised Land" (Boersma, *Five Things Theologians Wish Biblical Scholars Knew*, 138).

in every aspect of Israel's history, including the history of Israel's composition of the Scriptures.[5] The scriptural imagination that illuminates the eschatological figure of Jesus is not mere imagination. The incarnate Lord, Jesus, really is the head of the human race, the perfect priest and sacrifice, the perfect lawgiver, the perfect leader of the people into the true Promised Land, and the perfect king – even though he is not these things in the same way that the Old Testament figures were. Retrieving the typological Christology that is present in Aquinas's work shows his awareness of the importance of "the symbols and stories of the Old Testament" for knowing the incarnate Lord who is the Messiah of Israel, the giver of the New Law of the grace of the Holy Spirit, and the Savior of the world by his Cross, Resurrection, and Ascension.[6]

It should go without saying that for Aquinas, dogmatic loci such as the Incarnation and Cross are inseparable from the Jesus of Nazareth whose identity was forged in his particular Jewish context. This fact means that the Jewish expectations that framed his coming into the world are important for appreciating his cosmic significance. He is the one in whom "all things hold together" precisely as the eschatological prophet inaugurating the Kingdom of God, the leader of the new exodus restoring God's people Israel, and the priestly and sacrificial embodiment of God's Temple. These dimensions of Jesus Christ's identity receive intensive typological portraiture in the New Testament.

---

[5] Boersma observes, "Divine providence has implications both for our understanding of what Scripture is and for how we are supposed to read it. For Origen, providence implies that God uses human words to make known his will so as to lead us to salvation. This in turn suggests a close link between Scripture's words, on the one hand, and its providential ground and salvific end, on the other hand. God's actions in history, as well as the words that Scripture uses to describe them, participate, according to Origen, in God's providential, salvific plan in Christ" (Boersma, *Five Things Theologians Wish Biblical Scholars Knew*, 71).

[6] See Paul Murray, O.P., *Aquinas at Prayer: The Bible, Mysticism and Poetry* (London: Bloomsbury, 2013), 216.

CONCLUSION

Christ's self-understanding as an eschatological prophet inaugurating God's kingdom is often explored today by biblical scholars. For example, Dale Allison observes that "Jesus himself is, in the canonical Gospels, the eschatological king, or destined to be such."[7] Jesus announced an "imminent universal judgment" with himself at the very center of the eschatological drama.[8] Jesus considered himself able to reveal the divine meaning of the Torah and to bring to fulfillment the teachings of Israel's prophets. Focusing on the Gospel of John, Benjamin Reynolds states that Jesus is "the Revealer par excellence," and he concludes that "[t]he 'apocalyptic' Gospel claims the authority of Moses and other heroes of Israel as evidence that Jesus and the revelation he brings ultimately comes from God."[9] According to N. T. Wright, indebted (in his own way) to Albert Schweitzer, Jesus appears to have believed that God "would act through the suffering of a particular individual in whom Israel's sufferings were focused; that this suffering would carry redemptive significance; *and that this individual would be himself.*"[10] Allison affirms that from the perspective of Paul, we are now living in the time of the "eschatological woe" inaugurated by Jesus, with Jesus' Resurrection being the first fruits of an ongoing "eschatological harvest."[11]

[7] Dale C. Allison, Jr., *Constructing Jesus: Memory, Imagination, and History* (Grand Rapids, MI: Baker Academic, 2010), 245. Allison adds: "No follower of Jesus, to our knowledge, ever called Paul divine or reckoned him a god. Christians did, however, say astounding things about Jesus, and that from the very beginning. The differing evaluations, I submit, had something to do with who those two people actually were. We should hold a funeral for the view that Jesus entertained no exalted thoughts about himself" (304).

[8] Allison, *Constructing Jesus*, 55.

[9] Benjamin E. Reynolds, *John among the Apocalypses: Jewish Apocalyptic Tradition and the "Apocalyptic" Gospel* (Oxford: Oxford University Press, 2020), 208.

[10] N. T. Wright, *Jesus and the Victory of God* (Minneapolis, MN: Fortress, 1996), 593.

[11] Allison, *Constructing Jesus*, 63. See also Brant Pitre, *Jesus, the Tribulation, and the End of the Exile: Restoration Eschatology and the Origin of the Atonement* (Grand Rapids, MI: Baker Academic, 2005), 511–15.

Biblical scholars have likewise rediscovered the importance of the theme of the "new exodus" in the eschatologies of Second Temple Judaism and the New Testament. The widespread expectation – fulfilled in a surprising way by Jesus and the Church – was for "the restoration of Israel in a New Exodus," as Brant Pitre maintains.[12] Like Pitre, Scot McKnight connects Jesus' actions at the Last Supper with the exodus narrative. McKnight argues, "In stating that the bread was his body and the wine his blood, Jesus suggested that he was the Passover victim whose blood would protect his followers from the imminent judgment of God."[13] As the New Passover Lamb, Jesus triggers a salvific new exodus. Rodrigo Morales (now Isaac Augustine Morales, O.P.) has shown that the early Christian emphasis on "the eschatological outpouring of the Spirit" is linked to prophetic texts that describe "a new creation and/or a new exodus."[14] Likewise, Michael Morales finds that Jesus' journey to the "Father's house" (Jn 14:2) through his death and Resurrection "*is the new exodus*" and Jesus is "the true Passover lamb."[15] In a similar vein, connecting the new exodus theme (and the outpouring of the Spirit) with the eschatology of Zechariah 9–14 – an influence on many New Testament texts – Kelly Liebengood observes that the travails of Christ's followers "are likened to a second exodus journey," which commences after the salvific death of the Good Shepherd.[16]

---

[12] Pitre, *Jesus, the Tribulation, and the End of the Exile*, 259. Without using the phrase "new exodus," Allison seconds E. P. Sanders's view that many of Jesus' contemporaries fervently hoped for "the restoration of the tribes of Israel; the conversion, destruction, or subjugation of the Gentiles; the renewal of Jerusalem, including a new or rebuilt temple; and the purification of God's people and their worship" (Allison, *Constructing Jesus*, 76).

[13] Scot McKnight, *Jesus and His Death: Historiography, the Historical Jesus, and Atonement Theory* (Waco, TX: Baylor University Press, 2005), 339.

[14] Rodrigo J. Morales, *The Spirit and the Restoration of Israel: New Exodus and New Creation Motifs in Galatians* (Tübingen: Mohr Siebeck, 2010), 13.

[15] L. Michael Morales, *Who Shall Ascend the Mountain of the Lord? A Biblical Theology of the Book of Leviticus* (Downers Grove, IL: IVP Academic, 2015), 265, 277.

[16] Kelly D. Liebengood, *The Eschatology of 1 Peter: Considering the Influence of Zechariah 9–14* (Cambridge: Cambridge University Press, 2014), 217. Liebengood

In addition, many recent exegetical studies have reflected upon the relation of Christ to the Temple, showing that in the view of the evangelists, "The eschatological tribulation begun in Jesus' passion and death sets in motion the tribulation that will bring about the end of the temple and eventually of the world."[17] Drawing together Markan eschatology and the Temple, Timothy Gray states, "Mark suggests that Jesus [by his death and Resurrection] will usher in a new temple, the eschatological temple identified with the Kingdom of God and Mount Zion."[18] Indeed, "God's new eschatological Temple" or new creation will have Jesus Christ as its cornerstone, since the eschatological Temple will be the "body" of Christ comprised of all the members united to their head.[19] Wright argues similarly, "Jesus saw himself, and perhaps his followers with him, as the new Temple."[20] Various New Testament texts offer their own distinctive perspectives on this reality, such as, for instance, the Letter to the Hebrews's argument that Christ's sacrificial death, offered cultically in the heavenly sanctuary, achieved once and for all the purposes of the Temple: "atonement, forgiveness, purification, sanctification, perfection, redemption, the removal of sins, the non-remembrance of sins, and the purification of the conscience."[21]

---

specifically has 1 Peter in view. See also David W. Pao, *Acts and the Isaianic New Exodus* (Grand Rapids, MI: Baker Academic, 2002).

[17] Timothy C. Gray, *The Temple in the Gospel of Mark: A Study in Its Narrative Role* (Tübingen: Mohr Siebeck, 2008), 155. In this passage, Gray specifically has the Gospel of Mark in view.

[18] Gray, *The Temple in the Gospel of Mark*, 197.

[19] Gray, *The Temple in the Gospel of Mark*, 200.

[20] Wright, *Jesus and the Victory of God*, 426. See also Nicholas Perrin, *Jesus the Temple* (Grand Rapids, MI: Baker Academic, 2010), 12: "Jesus of Nazareth saw himself and his movement as nothing less than the decisive embodiment of Yahweh's eschatological temple." Of course, there are dissenting voices: see, for example, Simon J. Joseph, *Jesus and the Temple: The Crucifixion in Its Jewish Context* (Cambridge: Cambridge University Press, 2016).

[21] Benjamin J. Ribbens, *Levitical Sacrifice and Heavenly Cult in Hebrews* (Berlin: De Gruyter, 2016), 239.

For contemporary Thomistic Christology, the typologies regarding Adam, Isaac, Moses, Joshua, and David constitute a promising path for integrating the above exegetical and eschatological insights. However, one might still ask: Why not simply integrate the insights without recourse to the typologies, especially given the perennial concern – grounded though it is in a failure to appreciate the providential preparation in Israel's life and Scriptures for the coming of the incarnate Lord – that the presence of typology implies something other than a historical reality? A concise answer to this question is one to which Aquinas often appeals in the *sed contra* of the articles of the *tertia pars*: "The authority of Scripture suffices."[22] Thomistic Christology should follow the lead of the New Testament itself in portraying Jesus in a typological (and therefore eschatological) fashion. Attuned to the whole of Israel's Scriptures, the New Testament consistently deems it important to unite "Jesus's ministry with Israel's history and the promises that those very literary contexts evoke."[23]

What the New Testament does, Thomistic Christology today should do. Given the status of Jesus as Israel's Messiah and the divine Son, it is only reasonable to affirm that God would make providential use of the central figures of Israel's Scriptures to illuminate, in an enduringly instructive way, the eschatological fulfillment brought by Jesus. Consider the example of the New Isaac. According to Aquinas, "Isaac was a type of Christ, being himself offered in sacrifice."[24] The Jewish exegete Jon Levenson has shown how central is the theme of Christ the New Isaac in the New Testament. Levenson points out, "Given the threefold equation of the

---

[22] Thomas Aquinas, *Summa Theologiae*, trans. Fathers of the English Dominican Province (Westminster, MD: Christian Classics, 1981), III, q. 31, a. 3, *sed contra*.

[23] Craig S. Keener, *Spirit Hermeneutics: Reading Scripture in Light of Pentecost* (Grand Rapids, MI: Eerdmans, 2016), 242. Keener is referring here specifically to the Gospel of Matthew.

[24] II-II, q. 85, a. 1, ad 2.

CONCLUSION

Paschal lamb, the beloved son, and Jesus that we found lurking beneath the surface of the Gospel of John, we should not be surprised to find Paul identifying his Christ not only with the Passover offering but also with Isaac, the beloved son par excellence of the Hebrew Bible."[25] Although Levenson does not consider Jesus to have been Israel's Messiah, he recognizes the significance of typology, not only with respect to the New Isaac but also with respect to the New David. He concludes, "Much early christology is ... best understood as a midrashic recombination of biblical verses associated with Isaac, the beloved son of Abraham, with the suffering servant in Isaiah who went, Isaac-like, unprotesting to his slaughter, and with another miraculous son the son of David, the future messianic king whom the people Israel awaited."[26]

I believe that New Testament Christology is best understood not simply as a midrash on Israel's Scriptures but rather as arising from Christ's words and deeds, including his Cross, Resurrection, Ascension, and pouring out of the Spirit. But Christ's words and deeds fulfilled and perfected the missions of the central figures of Israel's Scriptures, including Adam, Isaac, Moses, Joshua, and David. It should not surprise us, therefore, that Jesus Christ is ultimately only intelligible through "the ongoing arc of the story told by Israel's Scripture, as it is filtered through the prism of the fourfold Gospel" in a typological manner, under the providence of God.[27] As the New

---

[25] Jon D. Levenson, *The Death and Resurrection of the Beloved Son: The Transformation of Child Sacrifice in Judaism and Christianity* (New Haven, CT: Yale University Press, 1993), 210. Levenson is not enthusiastic about this identification, though he notes that "[i]n the hands of Paul ... the identification of Jesus and Isaac assumed an especially forceful and far-reaching statement" (218). He adds that for Paul, Isaac is a type of Christ but even more a type of the Church (see 213).

[26] Levenson, *The Death and Resurrection of the Beloved Son*, 218. For various Jewish readings of Isaiah 53, see Antti Laato, "Isaiah in Ancient, Medieval, and Modern Jewish Traditions," in *The Oxford Handbook of Isaiah*, ed. Lena-Sofia Tiemeyer (Oxford: Oxford University Press, 2020), 507–30, at 517–21.

[27] Richard B. Hays, *Echoes of Scripture in the Gospels* (Waco, TX: Baylor University Press, 2016), 366.

Adam, Jesus is the universal Savior and the incarnate Lord establishing the new creation. Jesus is the beloved Son and true sacrificial Lamb, fulfilling the sacrificial cult of the Temple and unleashing the divine presence as the New Isaac. Jesus is the one giving the new Law, establishing the new covenant, and leading the new exodus to the true Promised Land through his teaching, miracles, and Paschal mystery, as the New Moses and New Joshua. Jesus is the eschatological king inaugurating God's kingdom, as the New David.

Here we may heed Maximus the Confessor, who remarks that Jesus, the divine Son, has "perfectly become the New Adam, while bearing in himself the first Adam."[28] The New Adam is not a generic human being, though he bears "Adam" in himself. Rather, the New Adam is a Jew. When "the Word became flesh and dwelt among us" (Jn 1:14), he did so as a member of God's people Israel. As shown by Israel's Torah, Temple cult, and Scriptures, the people of Israel yearned to be in full communion with the all-holy God, but they needed a Redeemer, as do we. The deacon Stephen is not being too harsh, biblically speaking, when he states of Moses: "Our fathers refused to obey him, but thrust him aside, and in their hearts they turned to Egypt" (Acts 7:39). In small and large ways, our own hearts still turn to "Egypt" – namely, to that which leads away from God. We need a New Adam who founds the human race anew as its head in the order of grace. We need a New Isaac who offers himself sacrificially to God, putting his obedience in the place of our disobedience. We need a New Moses to mediate a new and perfect covenant marked by the law of love, freeing us from slavery to sin and death. We need a New Joshua to lead us into a Promised Land constituted by everlasting communion with God and each other. We need a New David who will truly establish justice, which the first David could not do even in his own heart, let alone for his whole kingdom.

---

[28] Maximus the Confessor, *On the Cosmic Mystery of Jesus Christ: Selected Writings from St. Maximus the Confessor*, trans. Paul M. Blowers and Robert L. Wilken (Crestwood, NY: St. Vladimir's Seminary Press, 2003), 80–81.

CONCLUSION

The incarnate Lord, Jesus Christ, eschatologically accomplished the work of these central figures of Israel's Scriptures. He understood himself in light of these central figures, or more accurately, he interpreted these figures in light of himself. Contemporary Thomistic Christology should incorporate this crucial dimension of New Testament Christology, by drawing more deeply upon the Old Testament connections found in the New Testament's portraits of Jesus. In this book, I have offered a proposal for how to undertake this task in a manner that I think Aquinas himself would have recognized and appreciated. In Aquinas's own texts, Thomists have available superb resources for articulating a Christology that is instructed by typological connections to Israel's fathers in faith and charged with eschatological import. Aquinas did not have access to what Scot McKnight praises as "the most important contribution made by those in biblical studies" today, namely, "Jewish and Greco-Roman contextual studies" that assist in retrieving Jesus' historical context.[29] But Aquinas, like the Fathers, had in his possession the typological keys employed by the New Testament itself.

Thomistic Christology can make use of these keys today in order to incorporate the insights of biblical scholars into Jesus' eschatological identity and mission. By uniting the two Testaments in a powerful portrait of the incarnate Lord, this reconfiguring will redound to the benefit of all Christians. For as Jesus says in his parable of the rich man and Lazarus, "If they do not hear Moses and the prophets, neither will they be convinced if some one should rise from the dead" (Lk 16:31).

---

[29] Scot McKnight, *Five Things Biblical Scholars Wish Theologians Knew* (Downers Grove, IL: IVP Academic, 2021), 23. McKnight offers a valuable "integrative model" (33) that affirms the authority of Scripture without falling into Biblicism.

Bibliography

Achtemeier, Paul. "'And He Followed Him': Miracles and Discipleship in Mark 10:46–52." *Semeia* 11, no. 1 (1978): 115–45.
Albert the Great. *On the Body of the Lord*. Translated by Albert Marie Surmanski, O.P. Washington, DC: Catholic University of America Press, 2017.
Albright, William F. *Matthew: A New Translation with Introduction and Commentary*. New York: Doubleday, 1971.
Alfeyev, Hilarion. *Orthodox Christianity*. Vol. 2, *Doctrine and Teaching of the Orthodox Church*. Translated by Andrew Smith. Yonkers, NY: St. Vladimir's Seminary Press, 2012.
Allen, David M. *Deuteronomy and Exhortation in Hebrews: A Study in Narrative Re-presentation*. Tübingen: Mohr Siebeck, 2008.
Allen, R. Michael. *The Christ's Faith: A Dogmatic Account*. London: Continuum, 2009.
Allison, Jr., Dale C. *Constructing Jesus: Memory, Imagination, and History*. Grand Rapids, MI: Baker Academic, 2010.
Allison, Jr., Dale C. *The New Moses: A Matthean Typology*. Minneapolis, MN: Fortress, 1993.
Ambrose. *On Abraham*. Translated by Theodosia Tomkinson. Etna, CA: Center for Traditional Orthodox Studies, 2000.
Ambrose. *Seven Exegetical Works*. Translated by Michael P. McHugh. Washington, DC: Catholic University of America Press, 1972.
Ambrose. *Treatises on Noah and David*. Translated by Brian P. Dunkle, S.J. Washington, DC: Catholic University of America Press, 2020.
Anatolios, Khaled. *Deification through the Cross: An Eastern Christian Theology of Salvation*. Grand Rapids, MI: Eerdmans, 2020.
Anatolios, Khaled. *Retrieving Nicaea: The Development and Meaning of Trinitarian Doctrine*. Grand Rapids, MI: Baker Academic, 2011.

Aquinas, Thomas. *The Academic Sermons*. Translated by Mark-Robin Hoogland, C.P. Washington, DC: Catholic University of America Press, 2010.

Aquinas, Thomas. *Catena Aurea: Commentary on the Four Gospels Collected out of the Works of the Fathers*. Translated by John Henry Newman. Albany, NY: Preserving Christian Publications, 1995.

Aquinas, Thomas. *Commentary on Saint Paul's Epistle to the Ephesians*. Translated by Matthew L. Lamb. Albany, NY: Magi Books, 1966.

Aquinas, Thomas. *Commentary on the Book of Job*. Translated by Brian Thomas Becket Mullady. Lander, WY: The Aquinas Institute for the Study of Sacred Doctrine, 2016.

Aquinas, Thomas. *Commentary on the Gospel of John: Chapters 1–5*. Translated by Fabian Larcher, O.P., and James A. Weisheipl, O.P. Edited by Daniel Keating and Matthew Levering. Washington, DC: Catholic University of America Press, 2010.

Aquinas, Thomas. *Commentary on the Gospel of John: Chapters 6–12*. Translated by Fabian Larcher, O.P., and James A. Weisheipl, O.P. Edited by Daniel Keating and Matthew Levering. Washington, DC: Catholic University of America Press, 2010.

Aquinas, Thomas. *Commentary on the Gospel of John: Chapters 13–21*. Translated by Fabian Larcher, O.P., and James A. Weisheipl, O.P. Edited by Daniel Keating and Matthew Levering. Washington, DC: Catholic University of America Press, 2010.

Aquinas, Thomas. *Commentary on the Gospel of Matthew: Chapters 1–12*. Translated by Jeremy Holmes and Beth Mortensen. Edited by The Aquinas Institute. Lander, WY: The Aquinas Institute for the Study of Sacred Doctrine, 2013.

Aquinas, Thomas. *Commentary on the Gospel of Matthew: Chapters 13–28*. Translated by Jeremy Holmes. Lander, WY: The Aquinas Institute for the Study of Sacred Doctrine, 2013.

Aquinas, Thomas. *Commentary on the Letters of Saint Paul to the Corinthians*. Translated by Fabian Larcher, O.P., Beth Mortensen, and Daniel Keating. Edited by John Mortensen and Enrique Alarcón. Lander, WY: The Aquinas Institute for the Study of Sacred Doctrine, 2012.

Aquinas, Thomas. *Commentary on the Letter of Saint Paul to the Hebrews*. Translated by Fabian Larcher, O.P. Edited by John Mortensen and

Enrique Alarcón. Lander, WY: The Aquinas Institute for the Study of Sacred Doctrine, 2012.

Aquinas, Thomas. *Commentary on the Letter of Saint Paul to the Romans.* Translated by Fabian Larcher, O.P. Edited by John Mortensen and Enrique Alarcón. Lander, WY: The Aquinas Institute for the Study of Sacred Doctrine, 2012.

Aquinas, Thomas. *Commentary on the Letters of Saint Paul to the Galatians and Ephesians.* Translated by Fabian Larcher, O.P., and Matthew L. Lamb. Edited by John Mortensen and Enrique Alarcón. Lander, WY: The Aquinas Institute for the Study of Sacred Doctrine, 2012.

Aquinas, Thomas. *Commentary on the Letters of Saint Paul to the Philippians, Colossians, Thessalonians, Timothy, Titus, and Philemon.* Translated by Fabian Larcher, O.P. Edited by John Mortensen and Enrique Alarcón. Lander, WY: The Aquinas Institute for the Study of Sacred Doctrine, 2012.

Aquinas, Thomas. *Commentary on the Sentences: Book IV, Distinctions 1–13.* Translated by Beth Mortensen. Green Bay, WI: Aquinas Institute, 2017.

Aquinas, Thomas. *Commentary on the Sentences: Book IV, Distinctions 43–50.* Translated by Beth Mortensen, Peter Kwasniewski, and Dylan Schrader. Green Bay, WI: Aquinas Institute, 2018.

Aquinas, Thomas. *Light of Faith: The Compendium of Theology.* Translated by Cyril Vollert, S.J. Manchester, NH: Sophia Institute Press, 1993.

Aquinas, Thomas. *On Kingship: To the King of Cyprus.* Translated by Gerald B. Phelan, translation revised by I. T. Eschmann, O.P. Toronto: Pontifical Institute of Mediaeval Studies, 1949.

Aquinas, Thomas. "On the Perfection of the Spiritual Life." In *St. Thomas Aquinas and the Mendicant Controversies: Three Translations*, translated by John Proctor, O.P., edited by Mark Johnson, 237–323. Leesburg, VA: Alethes Press, 2007.

Aquinas, Thomas. *Summa Theologiae [Theologica].* Translated by Fathers of the English Dominican Province. 5 vols. Westminster, MD: Christian Classics, 1981.

Arnold, Bill T. *Genesis.* Cambridge: Cambridge University Press, 2008.

Attridge, Harold W. *The Epistle to the Hebrews.* Philadelphia: Fortress Press, 1989.

BIBLIOGRAPHY

Attridge, Harold W. "Let Us Strive to Enter That Rest: The Logic of Hebrews 4.1–11." *Harvard Theological Review* 73, no. 1 (1980): 279–88.

Augustine. *Answer to Faustus, a Manichean*. Translated by Ronald J. Teske, S. J. Edited by Boniface Ramsey. Hyde Park, NY: New City Press, 2007.

Augustine. *Augustine: Sermon on the Mount, Harmony of the Gospels, Homilies on the Gospels*. Vol. 6 of Nicene and Post-Nicene Fathers, First Series. Edited by Philip Schaff. Peabody, MA: Hendrickson, 1995.

Augustine. *City of God*. Translated by Henry Bettenson. London: Penguin, 1984.

Augustine. *Expositions of the Psalms*. Vol. 2, *33–50*. Translated by Maria Boulding, O.S.B. Edited by John E. Rotelle, O.S.A. Hyde Park, NY: New City Press, 2000.

Augustine. *Expositions of the Psalms*. Vol. 3, *51–72*. Translated by Maria Boulding, O.S.B. Edited by John E. Rotelle, O. S. A. Hyde Park, NY: New City Press, 2001.

Augustine. *Expositions of the Psalms*. Vol. 5, *99–120*. Translated by Maria Boulding, O.S.B. Edited by Boniface Ramsey. Hyde Park, NY: New City Press, 2003.

Augustine. *In Evangelium Ioannis tractatus centum viginti quatuor*. PL 35. www.augustinus.it/latino/commento_vsg/index2.htm

Augustine. *On the Psalms*. Vol. 1, *Psalms 1–29*. Translated by Scholastica Hebgin and Felicitas Corrigan. Westminster, MD: Newman Press, 1960.

Augustine. *The Trinity*. Translated by Edmund Hill, O.P. Edited by John E. Rotelle, O.S.A. Brooklyn, NY: New City Press, 1991.

Ayres, Lewis. "'There's Fire in That Rain': On Reading the Letter and Reading Allegorically." In *Heaven on Earth? Theological Interpretation in Ecumenical Dialogue*, edited by Hans Boersma and Matthew Levering, 33–52. Oxford: Wiley-Blackwell, 2013.

Bacon, B. W. *Studies in Matthew*. New York: Henry Holt, 1930.

Balberg, Mira. *Blood for Thought: The Reinvention of Sacrifice in Early Rabbinic Literature*. Oakland, CA: University of California Press, 2017.

Balthasar, Hans Urs von. *Cosmic Liturgy: The Universe according to Maximus the Confessor*. Translated by Brian E. Daley, S.J. San Francisco: Ignatius Press, 2003.

BIBLIOGRAPHY

Balthasar, Hans Urs von. *The Glory of the Lord: A Theological Aesthetics*. Vol. 7, *Theology: The New Covenant*. Translated by Brian McNeil, C.R.V. Edited by John Riches. San Francisco: Ignatius Press, 1989.

Balthasar, Hans Urs von. *Love Alone Is Credible*. Translated by D. C. Schindler. San Francisco: Ignatius Press, 2004.

Balthasar, Hans Urs von. *Theo-Drama: Theological Dramatic Theory*. Vol. 3, *The Dramatis Personae: The Person in Christ*. Translated by Graham Harrison. San Francisco: Ignatius Press, 1992.

Balthasar, Hans Urs von. *Theo-Drama: Theological Dramatic Theory*. Vol. 4, *The Action*. Translated by Graham Harrison. San Francisco: Ignatius Press, 1994.

Barber, Michael Patrick. "Jesus as the Davidic Temple Builder and Peter's Priestly Role in Matthew 16:16–19." *Journal of Biblical Literature* 132, no. 4 (2013): 935–53.

Barnes, Corey L. "Aristotle in the *Summa Theologiae*'s Christology." In *Aristotle in Aquinas's Theology*, edited by Gilles Emery, O.P., and Matthew Levering, 186–204. Oxford: Oxford University Press, 2015.

Barnes, Corey L. *Christ's Two Wills in Scholastic Thought: The Christology of Aquinas and Its Historical Contexts*. Toronto: Pontifical Institute of Mediaeval Studies, 2012.

Barnes, Michel René. "Irenaeus's Trinitarian Theology." *Nova et Vetera* 7, no. 1 (2009): 67–106.

Barrett, Matthew. *Canon, Covenant and Christology: Rethinking Jesus and the Scriptures of Israel*. Downers Grove, IL: IVP Academic, 2020.

Barth, Karl. *Church Dogmatics*. Vol. 1, *The Doctrine of the Word of God*, Part 1. 2nd ed. Translated by G. W. Bromiley. Edited by G. W. Bromiley and T. F. Torrance. Edinburgh: T&T Clark, 1975.

Barth, Karl. *Church Dogmatics*. Vol. 1, *The Doctrine of the Word of God*, Part 2. Translated by G. T. Thomson and Harold Knight. Edited by G. W. Bromiley and T. F. Torrance. Edinburgh: T&T Clark, 1956.

Barth, Karl. *Church Dogmatics*. Vol. 4, *The Doctrine of Reconciliation*, Part 1. Translated by G. W. Bromiley. Edited by G. W. Bromiley and T. F. Torrance. Edinburgh: T&T Clark, 1956.

Bates, Matthew W. *The Hermeneutics of the Apostolic Proclamation: The Center of Paul's Method of Scriptural Interpretation*. Waco, TX: Baylor University Press, 2012.

BIBLIOGRAPHY

Bates, Matthew W. *Salvation by Allegiance Alone: Rethinking Faith, Works, and the Gospel of Jesus the King*. Grand Rapids, MI: Baker Academic, 2017.

Bauckham, Richard. *The Climax of Prophecy: Studies on the Book of Revelation*. London: T&T Clark, 1993.

Bauckham, Richard. *Gospel of Glory: Major Themes in Johannine Theology*. Grand Rapids, MI: Baker Academic, 2015.

Bauerschmidt, Frederick Christian. *Julian of Norwich and the Mystical Body Politic of Christ*. Notre Dame: University of Notre Dame Press, 1999.

Baxter, W. S. "Mosaic Imagery in the Gospel of Matthew." *Trinity Journal* 20, no. 1 (1999): 69–83.

Beale, G. K. *A New Testament Biblical Theology: The Unfolding of the Old Testament in the New*. Grand Rapids, MI: Baker Academic, 2011.

Behr, John. *Asceticism and Anthropology in Irenaeus and Clement*. Oxford: Oxford University Press, 2000.

Behr, John. *The Mystery of Christ: Life in Death*. Crestwood, NY: St. Vladimir's Seminary Press, 2006.

Bellamah, Timothy, O.P. "*Tunc scimus cum causas cognoscimus*: Some Medieval Endeavors to Know Scripture in Its Causes." In *Theology Needs Philosophy: Acting against Reason Is Contrary to Human Nature*, edited by Matthew L. Lamb, 154–72. Washington, DC: Catholic University of America Press, 2016.

Benedict XVI. "The Catholic Priesthood." In *From the Depths of Our Hearts: Priesthood, Celibacy and the Crisis of the Catholic Church*, translated by Michael J. Miller. Edited by Nicholas Diat, 23–60. San Francisco: Ignatius Press, 2020.

Beskow, Per. *Rex Gloriae: The Kingship of Christ in the Early Church*. Translated by Eric J. Sharpe. Eugene, OR: Wipf and Stock, 2014.

Biffi, Inos. *I misteri di Cristo in Tommaso d'Aquino*. Milan: Jaca Book, 2014.

Blackwell, Ben C. *Christosis: Pauline Soteriology in Light of Deification in Irenaeus and Cyril of Alexandria*. Tübingen: Mohr Siebeck, 2011.

Boersma, Hans. *Five Things Theologians Wish Biblical Scholars Knew*. Downers Grove, IL: IVP Academic, 2021.

Boersma, Hans. *Heavenly Participation: The Weaving of a Sacramental Tapestry*. Grand Rapids, MI: Eerdmans, 2011.

Boersma, Hans. *Sacramental Preaching: Sermons on the Hidden Presence of Christ*. Grand Rapids, MI: Baker Academic, 2016.

Bonaventure. *The Journey of the Mind to God*. Translated by Philotheus Boehner, O.F.M. Edited by Stephen F. Brown. Indianapolis, IN: Hackett, 1993.

Bonino, Serge-Thomas, O.P. *Reading the Song of Songs with St. Thomas Aquinas*. Translated by Andrew Levering with Matthew Levering. Washington, DC: Catholic University of America Press, forthcoming.

Bonino, Serge-Thomas, O.P. *Saint Thomas d'Aquin, lecteur du Cantique des cantiques*. Paris: Cerf, 2019.

Botner, Max. *Jesus Christ as the Son of David in the Gospel of Mark*. Cambridge: Cambridge University Press, 2019.

Bousset, Wilhelm. *Kyrios Christos: A History of the Belief in Christ from the Beginnings of Christianity to Irenaeus*. Translated by John E. Steely. Nashville, TN: Abingdon Press, 1970.

Bouyer, Louis. *The Seat of Wisdom: An Essay on the Place of the Virgin Mary in Christian Theology*. Translated by A. V. Littledale. London: Darton, Longman & Todd, 1960.

Boxall, Ian. *Discovering Matthew: Content, Interpretation, Reception*. Grand Rapids, MI: Eerdmans, 2014.

Bray, Gerald L. "Overview of 15:45–50." In *1–2 Corinthians*, edited by Gerald L. Bray and Thomas C. Oden. Ancient Christian Commentary on Scripture Series. Downers Grove, IL: IVP Academic, 1999.

Briggman, Anthony. *God and Christ in Irenaeus*. Oxford: Oxford University Press, 2019.

Brock, Sebastian. *The Luminous Eye: The Spiritual World Vision of Saint Ephrem the Syrian*. Rome: Centre for Indian and Inter-religious Studies, 1985.

Brosend II, William F. *James and Jude*. Cambridge: Cambridge University Press, 2004.

Brown, Colin. "With the Grain and against the Grain: A Strategy for Reading the Synoptic Gospels." In *The Handbook for the Study of the Historical Jesus*, vol. 1, edited by Tom Holmén and Stanley E. Porter, 619–48. Leiden: Brill, 2010.

Brown, Joshua R. *Balthasar in Light of Early Confucianism*. Notre Dame: University of Notre Dame Press, 2020.

Brown, Raymond E., S.S. *The Death of the Messiah*. 2 vols. Garden City, NY: Doubleday, 1994.
Brueggemann, Walter. *Genesis*. Atlanta, GA: John Knox Press, 1982.
Byars, Ronald P. *The Sacraments in Biblical Perspective: Interpretation*. Louisville, KY: John Knox Press, 2011.
Byers, Andrew J. *Ecclesiology and Theosis in the Gospel of John*. Cambridge: Cambridge University Press, 2017.
Byrne, Brendan, S.J. *Romans*. Collegeville, MN: Liturgical Press, 1996.
Caspi, Mishael Maswari, and Sascha Benjamin Cohen. *The Binding (Aqedah) and Its Transformations in Judaism and Islam: The Lambs of God*. Lewiston, NY: Mellen Biblical Press, 1995.
Catechism of the Catholic Church. 2nd ed. Vatican City: Libreria Editrice Vaticana, 1997.
Cessario, Romanus, O.P. *Christian Satisfaction in Aquinas: Towards a Personalist Understanding*. Washington, DC: University Press of America, 1982.
Cessario, Romanus, O.P., and Cajetan Cuddy, O.P. *Thomas and the Thomists: The Achievement of Thomas Aquinas and His Interpreters*. Minneapolis, MN: Fortress, 2017.
Chae, Young S. *Jesus as the Eschatological Davidic Shepherd: Studies in the Old Testament, Second Temple Judaism, and in the Gospel of Matthew*. Tübingen: Mohr Siebeck, 2006.
Charlesworth, James H. "From Jewish Messianology to Christian Christology: Some Caveats and Perspectives." In *Judaisms and Their Messiahs at the Turn of the Christian Era*, edited by Jacob Neusner, William S. Green, and Ernest S. Frerichs, 225–64. Cambridge: Cambridge University Press, 1987.
Chester, Andrew. "Christ of Paul." In *Redemption and Resistance: The Messianic Hopes of Jews and Christians in Antiquity*, edited by Markus Bockmuehl and James Carleton Paget, 109–21. London: T&T Clark, 2009.
Cho, Bernardo. *Royal Messianism and the Jerusalem Priesthood in the Gospel of Mark*. London: T&T Clark, 2019.
Chou, Abner. *The Hermeneutics of the Biblical Writers: Learning to Interpret Scripture from the Prophets and Apostles*. Grand Rapids, MI: Kregel Academic, 2018.
Clark, Patrick. *Perfection in Death: The Christological Dimension of Courage in Aquinas*. Washington, DC: Catholic University of America Press, 2015.

Colish, Marcia. *Ambrose's Patriarchs: Ethics for the Common Man*. Notre Dame: University of Notre Dame Press, 2005.

Colón-Emeric, Edgardo. *Wesley, Aquinas, and Christian Perfection: An Ecumenical Dialogue*. Waco, TX: Baylor University Press, 2009.

Congregation of the Doctrine of the Faith. "Instruction on Christian Freedom and Liberation." March 22, 1986.

Cross, Richard. *The Metaphysics of the Incarnation: Thomas Aquinas to Duns Scotus*. Oxford: Oxford University Press, 2002.

Crowe, Brandon D. *The Last Adam: A Theology of the Obedient Life of Jesus in the Gospels*. Grand Rapids, MI: Baker Academic, 2017.

Cruz, Luis M. "*Christus, novissimus Adam*. La relación Cristo-Adán en los Comentarios de Santo Tomás de Aquino a las epístolas paulinas." *Revista española de teología* 76, no. 1 (2016): 25–107.

Cyril of Alexandria. *Commentary on John*. Vol. 1. Ancient Christian Texts. Translated by David R. Maxwell. Edited by Joel C. Elowsky. Downers Grove, IL: IVP Academic, 2013.

Cyril of Alexandria. *Glaphyra on the Pentateuch*. Vol. 1, *Genesis*. Translated by Nicholas P. Lunn. Washington, DC: Catholic University of America Press, 2018.

Cyril of Jerusalem, *Catechetical Lectures*. Translated by Edward Hamilton Gifford. In *Cyril of Jerusalem, Gregory Nazianzen*, 1–157. Vol. 7 of *Nicene and Post-Nicene Fathers*, Second Series. Edited by Philip Schaff and Henry Wace. Peabody, MA: Hendrickson, 1995.

Daguet, François. *Théologie Du Dessein Divin Chez Thomas d'Aquin. Finis Omnium Ecclesia*. Paris: J. Vrin, 2003.

Dahan, Gilbert. "Thomas Aquinas: Exegesis and Hermeneutics." In *Reading Sacred Scripture with Thomas Aquinas: Hermeneutical Tools, Theological Questions and New Perspectives*, edited by Piotr Roszak and Jörgen Vijgen, 45–70. Turnhout: Brepols, 2015.

Daly-Denton, Margaret. *David in the Fourth Gospel: The Johannine Reception of the Psalms*. Leiden: Brill, 2000.

Daniélou, Jean, S.J. *From Shadows to Reality: Studies in the Biblical Typology of the Fathers*. Translated by Wulstan Hibberd, O.S.B. London: Burns & Oates, 1960.

Daniélou, Jean, S.J. *The Lord of History: Reflections on the Inner Meaning of History*. Translated by Nigel Abercrombie. Chicago: Henry Regnery, 1958.

Dauphinais, Michael, and Matthew Levering, eds. *Reading John with St. Thomas Aquinas: Theological Exegesis and Speculative Theology*. Washington, DC: Catholic University of America Press, 2004.

Dauphinais, Michael, Barry David, and Matthew Levering, eds. *Aquinas the Augustinian*. Washington, DC: Catholic University of America Press, 2007.

Dauphinais, Michael, Andrew Hofer, O.P., and Roger W. Nutt, eds. *Thomas Aquinas and the Crisis of Christology*. Ave Maria, FL: Sapientia Press, 2021.

Dauphinais, Michael, Andrew Hofer, O.P., and Roger W. Nutt, eds. *Thomas Aquinas and the Greek Fathers*. Ave Maria, FL: Sapientia Press, 2019.

Davies, W.D., and Dale C. Allison, Jr. *A Critical and Exegetical Commentary on the Gospel according to Saint Matthew*. 3 vols. New York: T&T Clark, 2004.

Dawkins, Richard. *The God Delusion*. Boston: Houghton Mifflin, 2006.

de Aldama, Joseph A., S.J., Severino Gonzalez, S.J., Francis A. P. Sola, S.J., and Joseph F. Sagüés, S.J. *On the Sacraments in General: On Baptism, Confirmation, Eucharist, Penance and Anointing*. 3rd (Latin) ed. Translated by Kenneth Baker, S.J. n.p.: Keep the Faith, 2015.

Delaney, Carol. *Abraham on Trial: The Social Legacy of Biblical Myth*. Princeton, NJ: Princeton University Press, 1998.

de Lange, Nicholas. *Origen and the Jews: Studies in Jewish-Christian Relations in Third-Century Palestine*. Cambridge: Cambridge University Press, 1976.

de Lubac, Henri, S.J. *Medieval Exegesis*. Vol. 1, The Four Senses of Scripture. Translated by Mark Sebanc. Grand Rapids, MI: Eerdmans, 1998.

de Lubac, Henri, S.J. "'Typologie' et Allégorisme." *Recherches de Science Religieuse* 34 (1947): 180–226.

de Vos, J. Cornelis. "Josua und Jesus im Neuen Testament." In *The Book of Joshua*, edited by Ed Noort, 523–40. Leuven: Peeters, 2012.

Di Noia, J. Augustine, O.P. "Christ Brings Freedom from Sin and Death: The Commentary of St. Thomas Aquinas on Romans 5:12–21." *The Thomist* 73, no. 3 (2009): 381–98.

Docherty, Susan E. *The Use of the Old Testament in Hebrews: A Case Study in Early Jewish Bible Interpretation*. Tübingen: Mohr Siebeck, 2009.

Dölger, F. J. "Die Durchzug durch den Jordan als Sinnbild der Christlichen Taufe." *Antike und Christentum* 2, no. 1 (1930): 70–79.

Duby, Steven J. *God in Himself: Scripture, Metaphysics, and the Task of Christian Theology.* Downers Grove, IL: IVP Academic, 2019.

Duncan, Edward J. *Baptism in the Demonstrations of Aphraates, the Persian Sage.* Washington, DC: Catholic University of America Press, 1945.

Dunn, James D. G. *Baptism in the Holy Spirit: A Re-examination of the New Testament Teaching on the Gift of the Spirit in Relation to Pentecostalism Today.* Philadelphia: The Westminster Press, 1970.

Dunn, James D. G. *Jesus Remembered.* Grand Rapids, MI: Eerdmans, 2019.

Dunn, James D. G. *The Theology of Paul the Apostle.* Grand Rapids, MI: Eerdmans, 1998.

Durand, Emmanuel, O.P. *Évangile et Providence: Une théologie de l'action de Dieu.* Paris: Cerf, 2014.

Durand, Emmanuel, O.P. *L'Offre universelle du salut en Christ.* Paris: Cerf, 2012.

Dvořáček, Jiri. *The Son of David in Matthew's Gospel in the Light of the Solomon as Exorcist Tradition.* Tübingen: Mohr Siebeck, 2016.

Dy-Liacco, Veronica Chiari A. "The Jewish Tradition of the Divine Presence, Sacrifice, and Substitutive Suffering: The Background to a Catholic Understanding." *Communio* 47, no. 1 (2020): 155–89.

Easter, Matthew C. *Faith and the Faithfulness of Jesus in Hebrews.* Cambridge: Cambridge University Press, 2014.

Elders, Leo J., S.V.D. *Thomas Aquinas and His Predecessors: The Philosophers and the Church Fathers in His Works.* Washington, DC: Catholic University of America Press, 2018.

Ellingworth, Paul. "Jesus and the Universe in Hebrews." *Evangelical Quarterly* 58, no. 4 (1986): 337–54.

Elowsky, Joel C., and Thomas C. Oden, eds. *John 11–21.* Ancient Christian Commentary on Scripture. Downers Grove, IL: IVP Academic, 2007.

Emery, Gilles, O.P. "Foreword." In Dominic Legge, O.P., *The Trinitarian Christology of St Thomas Aquinas*, v–viii. Oxford: Oxford University Press, 2017.

Emery, Gilles, O.P. "Kenosis, Christ, and the Trinity in Thomas Aquinas." *Nova et Vetera* 17, no. 3 (2019): 839–69.

Emery, Gilles, O.P. "The Personal Mode of Trinitarian Action in Saint Thomas Aquinas." *The Thomist* 69, no. 1 (2005): 31–77.

Emery, Gilles, O.P. "*Theologia and Dispensatio*: The Centrality of the Divine Missions in St. Thomas's Trinitarian Theology." *The Thomist* 74, no. 4 (2010): 515–61.

Eusebius. *The Proof of the Gospel*. Translated by W. J. Ferrar. Eugene, OR: Wipf and Stock, 2001.

Evdokimov, Paul. *The Art of the Icon: A Theology of Beauty, Illustrated*. Redondo Beach, CA: Oakwood Publications, 1990.

Farber, Zev. *Images of Joshua in the Bible and Their Reception*. Berlin: De Gruyter, 2016.

Farrer, Austin. "On Dispensing with Q." In *Studies in the Gospels: Essays in Memory of R. H. Lightfoot*, edited by D. E. Nineham, 55–88. Oxford: Blackwell, 1955.

Fee, Gordon D. *Pauline Christology: An Exegetical-Theological Study*. Peabody, MA: Hendrickson, 2007.

Fishbane, Michael. *Biblical Interpretation in Ancient Israel*. Oxford: Oxford University Press, 1985.

Fisk, Bruce N. "Offering Isaac Again and Again: Pseudo-Philo's Use of the Aqedah as Intertext." *Catholic Biblical Quarterly* 62, no. 3 (2000): 481–507.

Fitzmyer, Joseph A., S.J. *First Corinthians: A New Translation with Introduction and Commentary*. New Haven, CT: Yale University Press, 2008.

Fitzmyer, Joseph A., S.J. *The Gospel according to Luke I–IX*. Garden City, NY: Doubleday, 1982.

Flannery, Austin, O.P., ed. *Vatican Council II*. Vol. 1, The Conciliar and Post Conciliar Documents. Rev. ed. Northport, NY: Costello, 1996.

Foster, Robert L. *The Theology of the Books of Haggai and Zechariah*. Cambridge: Cambridge University Press, 2021.

Frankel, David. *The Land of Canaan and the Destiny of Israel: Theologies of Territory in the Hebrew Bible*. Winona Lake, IN: Eisenbrauns, 2011.

Frey, Jörg. *The Glory of the Crucified One: Christology and Theology in the Gospel of John*. Translated by Wayne Coppins and Christoph Heilig. Waco, TX: Baylor University Press, 2018.

Gagliardi, Mauro. *Truth Is a Synthesis: Catholic Dogmatic Theology*. Steubenville, OH: Emmaus Academic, 2020.

Gaine, Simon Francis, O.P. *Did the Saviour See the Father? Christ, Salvation, and the Vision of God*. London: Bloomsbury, 2015.

Garlington, Don. "Israel's Triumphant King: Romans 1:5 and the Scriptures of Israel." In *Jesus and Paul: Global Perspectives in Honour of James D. G. Dunn for His 70th Birthday*, edited by B. J. Oropeza, C. K. Robertson, and Douglas C. Mohrmann, 173–83. London: T&T Clark, 2010.

Garrett, Susan R. *No Ordinary Angel: Celestial Spirits and Christian Claims about Jesus*. New Haven, CT: Yale University Press, 2008.

Garrigou-Lagrange, Réginald. *Christ the Savior: A Commentary on the Third Part of St. Thomas' Theological Summa*. Translated by Dom Bede Rose, O.S.B. St. Louis, MO: Herder, 1957.

Garrigues, Jean-Miguel. "The 'Natural Grace' of Christ in St. Thomas." In *Surnaturel: A Controversy at the Heart of Twentieth-Century Thomistic Thought*, edited by Serge-Thomas Bonino, O.P., translated by Robert Williams, translation revised by Matthew Levering, 103–15. Ave Maria, FL: Sapientia Press, 2009.

Gathercole, Simon J. *The Pre-existent Son: Recovering the Christologies of Matthew, Mark and Luke*. Grand Rapids, MI: Eerdmans, 2007.

Geffré, Claude. *The Risk of Interpretation: On Being Faithful to the Christian Tradition in a Non-Christian Age*. Translated by David Smith. New York: Paulist Press, 1987.

Gerhardsson, Birgir. "Sacrificial Service and Atonement in the Gospel of Matthew." In *Reconciliation and Hope: New Testament Essays on Atonement and Eschatology Presented to L. L. Morris on His 60th Birthday*, edited by Robert Banks, 25–35. Grand Rapids, MI: Eerdmans, 1974.

Glasson, T. Francis. *Moses in the Fourth Gospel*. London: SCM Press, 1963.

Gondreau, Paul. "The Humanity of Christ, the Incarnate Word." In *The Theology of Thomas Aquinas*, edited by Rik Van Nieuwenhove and Joseph Wawrykow, 252–76. Notre Dame: University of Notre Dame Press, 2005.

Gondreau, Paul. *The Passions of Christ's Soul in the Theology of St. Thomas Aquinas*. Providence, RI: Cluny, 2018.

Gorman, Michael. *Aquinas on the Metaphysics of the Hypostatic Union*. Cambridge: Cambridge University Press, 2017.

Gorman, Michael J. *The Death of the Messiah and the Birth of the New Covenant: A (Not So) New Model of the Atonement*. Eugene, OR: Cascade, 2014.

Grässer, Erich. *An Die Hebräer*. Vol. 1. Zurich: Benziger, 1990.
Gray, Timothy C. *The Temple in the Gospel of Mark: A Study in Its Narrative Role*. Tübingen: Mohr Siebeck, 2008.
Gregory of Nyssa. *Gregory of Nyssa: Dogmatic Treatises, Etc*. Vol. 5 of Nicene and Post-Nicene Fathers, Second Series. Translated by William Moore and Henry Austin Wilson. Edited by Philip Schaff and Henry Wace. Peabody, MA: Hendrickson, 1995.
Hahn, Scott W. *Kinship by Covenant: A Canonical Approach to the Fulfillment of God's Saving Promises*. New Haven, CT: Yale University Press, 2009.
Harkins, Franklin T. "*Primus Doctor Iudaeorum*: Moses as Theological Master in the *Summa Theologiae* of Thomas Aquinas." *The Thomist* 75, no. 1 (2011): 65–94.
Harkins, Franklin T. *Thomas Aquinas: The Basics*. London: Routledge, 2021.
Harris, James Rendel. "The Sinless High Priest." *The Expository Times* 33, no. 5 (1922): 217–18.
Hauerwas, Stanley. *A Community of Character: Toward a Constructive Christian Social Ethic*. Notre Dame: University of Notre Dame Press, 1981.
Hauerwas, Stanley. *Matthew*. Grand Rapids, MI: Brazos, 2006.
Hays, Richard B. *The Conversion of the Imagination: Paul as Interpreter of Israel's Scripture*. Grand Rapids, MI: Eerdmans, 2005.
Hays, Richard B. *Echoes of Scripture in the Gospels*. Waco, TX: Baylor University Press, 2016.
Hays, Richard B. *First Corinthians*. Louisville, KY: John Knox Press, 1997.
Hays, Richard B. *Reading Backwards: Figural Christology and the Fourfold Gospel Witness*. Waco, TX: Baylor University Press, 2014.
Hays, Richard B. *Reading with the Grain of Scripture*. Grand Rapids, MI: Eerdmans, 2020.
Healy, Mary. *Hebrews*. Grand Rapids, MI: Baker Academic, 2016.
Heil, John Paul. "Ezekiel 34 and the Narrative Strategy of the Shepherd and Sheep Metaphor in Matthew." *Catholic Biblical Quarterly* 55, no. 4 (1993): 698–708.
Hengel, Martin. *Studies in Early Christology*. Edinburgh: T&T Clark, 1995.
Hofius, Otfried. *Katapausis: Die Vorstellung vom endzeitlichen Ruheort im Hebräerbrief*. Tübingen: Mohr Siebeck, 1970.

Holmes, Jeremy. "Participation and the Meaning of Scripture." In *Reading Sacred Scripture with Thomas Aquinas: Hermeneutical Tools, Theological Questions and New Perspectives*, edited by Piotr Roszak and Jörgen Vijgen, 91–113. Turnhout: Brepols, 2015.

Hooker, Morna D. *Not Ashamed of the Gospel: New Testament Interpretations of the Death of Christ*. Grand Rapids, MI: Eerdmans, 1994.

Horton, Jr., Fred L. *The Melchizedek Tradition: A Critical Examination of the Sources to the Fifth Century A.D. and in the Epistle to the Hebrews*. Cambridge: Cambridge University Press, 1976.

Hoskins, Paul M. *Jesus as the Fulfillment of the Temple in the Gospel of John*. Eugene, OR: Wipf and Stock, 2007.

Houck, Daniel W. *Aquinas, Original Sin, and the Challenge of Evolution*. Cambridge: Cambridge University Press, 2020.

Huerta, Eduardo. "La realeza de Jesús en el cuarto evangelio." *Teología y Vida* 32, no. 3 (1991): 213–20.

Hugenberger, Gordon Paul. "The Servant of the Lord in the 'Servant Songs' of Isaiah: A Second Moses Figure." In *The Lord's Anointed: Interpretation of Old Testament Messianic Texts*, edited by P. E. Satterthwaite, R. S. Hess, and G. J. Wenham, 105–40. Grand Rapids, MI: Baker Academic, 1995.

Hughes, Graham. *Hebrews and Hermeneutics: The Epistle to the Hebrews as a New Testament Example of Biblical Interpretation*. Cambridge: Cambridge University Press, 1979.

Huizenga, Leroy A. *Loosing the Lion: Proclaiming the Gospel of Mark*. Steubenville, OH: Emmaus Road, 2017.

Huizenga, Leroy A. *The New Isaac: Tradition and Intertextuality in the Gospel of Matthew*. Leiden: Brill, 2009.

Hurtado, Larry W. *Lord Jesus Christ: Devotion to Jesus in Earliest Christianity*. Grand Rapids, MI: Eerdmans, 2003.

Irenaeus. "Against Heresies." In *The Apostolic Fathers, Justin Martyr, Irenaeus*. Vol. 1 of Ante-Nicene Fathers Series, edited by Alexander Roberts and James Donaldson, 315–567. Peabody, MA: Hendrickson, 1995.

Janse, Sam. *"You Are My Son": The Reception History of Psalm 2 in Early Judaism and the Early Church*. Leuven: Peeters, 2009.

Jipp, Joshua W. "Messiah Christology in Paul and Irenaeus." In *Irenaeus and Paul*, edited by Todd D. Still and David E. Wilhite, 81–88. London: T&T Clark, 2020.

Jipp, Joshua W. *The Messianic Theology of the New Testament*. Grand Rapids, MI: Eerdmans, 2020.

Johnson, Luke Timothy. *Hebrews: A Commentary*. Louisville, KY: John Knox Press, 2006.

Jones, David Albert. *Approaching the End: A Theological Exploration of Death and Dying*. Oxford: Oxford University Press, 2007.

Joseph, Simon J. *Jesus and the Temple: The Crucifixion in Its Jewish Context*. Cambridge: Cambridge University Press, 2016.

Julian of Norwich. *Showings*. Translated by Edmund Colledge, O.S.A., and James Walsh, S.J. Mahwah, NJ: Paulist Press, 1978.

Justin Martyr. "Dialogue with Trypho." In *The Apostolic Fathers, Justin Martyr, Irenaeus*, edited by Alexander Roberts and James Donaldson, 194–270. Vol. 1 of Ante-Nicene Fathers Series. Peabody, MA: Hendrickson, 1995.

Kant, Immanuel. "The Conflict of the Faculties." In *Religion and Rational Theology*, translated by Mary J. Gregor and Robert Anchor, edited by Allen W. Wood, 233–328. Cambridge: Cambridge University Press, 1996.

Käsemann, Ernst. *The Wandering People of God: An Investigation of the Letter to the Hebrews*. Translated by R. A. Harrisville and I. L. Sandberg. Minneapolis, MN: Augsburg, 1984.

Keating, Daniel. "The Baptism of Jesus in Cyril of Alexandria: The Re-creation of the Human Race." *Pro Ecclesia* 8, no. 2 (1999): 201–22.

Keener, Craig S. *The Gospel of John: A Commentary*. 2 vols. Grand Rapids, MI: Baker Academic, 2003.

Keener, Craig S. *The Historical Jesus of the Gospels*. Grand Rapids, MI: Eerdmans, 2009.

Keener, Craig S. *Spirit Hermeneutics: Reading Scripture in Light of Pentecost*. Grand Rapids, MI: Eerdmans, 2016.

Kessler, Edward. *Bound by the Bible: Jews, Christians and the Sacrifice of Isaac*. Cambridge: Cambridge University Press, 2004.

Kirk, J. R. Daniel. *Unlocking Romans: Resurrection and the Justification of God*. Grand Rapids, MI: Eerdmans, 2008.

Kistemaker, Simon. *The Psalm Citations in the Epistle to the Hebrews*. Amsterdam: Soest, 1961.

Klawans, Jonathan. *Purity, Sacrifice, and the Temple: Symbolism and Supersessionism in the Study of Ancient Judaism*. Oxford: Oxford University Press, 2006.

Knasas, John F. X. "Suffering and the 'Thomistic Philosopher': A Line of Thought Instigated by Job Commentary." In *Reading Job with St. Thomas Aquinas*, edited by Matthew Levering, Piotr Roszak, and Jörgen Vijgen, 185–219. Washington, DC: Catholic University of America Press, 2020.

Koch, Stefan. "Mose Sagt Zu 'Jesus' – Zur Wahrmehmung von Josua im Neuen Testament." In *The Book of Joshua*, edited by Ed Noort, 541–54. Leuven: Peeters, 2012.

Kromholtz, Bryan, O.P. "The Spirit of the Letter: St. Thomas's Interpretation of Scripture in His Reading of Job's Eschatology." In *Reading Job with St. Thomas Aquinas*, edited by Matthew Levering, Piotr Roszak, and Jörgen Vijgen, 364–83. Washington, DC: Catholic University of America Press, 2020.

Kugel, James L. *The Bible as It Was*. Cambridge: Harvard University Press, 1997.

Laato, Antti. "Isaiah in Ancient, Medieval, and Modern Jewish Traditions." In *The Oxford Handbook of Isaiah*, edited by Lena-Sofia Tiemeyer, 507–30. Oxford: Oxford University Press, 2020.

Lagrange, Marie-Joseph, O.P. *Evangile Selon Saint Matthieu*. 7th ed. Paris: Gabalda, 1948.

Lanier, Gregory R. *Old Testament Conceptual Metaphors and the Christology of Luke's Gospel*. London: T&T Clark, 2018.

Le Donne, Anthony. *The Historiographical Jesus: Memory, Typology, and the Son of David*. Waco, TX: Baylor University Press, 2009.

Legge, Dominic, O.P. *The Trinitarian Christology of St Thomas Aquinas*. Oxford: Oxford University Press, 2017.

Leithart, Peter J. *The Gospel of Matthew through New Eyes*. Vol. 1, *Jesus as Israel*. Monroe, LA: Athanasius Press, 2017.

Levenson, Jon D. *The Death and Resurrection of the Beloved Son: The Transformation of Child Sacrifice in Judaism and Christianity*. New Haven, CT: Yale University Press, 1993.

Levenson, Jon D. *Inheriting Abraham: The Legacy of the Patriarch in Judaism, Christianity, and Islam*. Princeton, NJ: Princeton University Press, 2014.

Levenson, Jon D. *Sinai and Zion: An Entry into the Jewish Bible*. San Francisco: Harper & Row, 1985.

Levenson, Jon D. *Theology of the Program of Restoration of Ezekiel 40–48*. Missoula, MT: Scholars Press, 1976.

Levering, Matthew. "Aquinas on Romans 8: Predestination in Context." In *Reading Romans with St. Thomas Aquinas*, edited by Matthew Levering and Michael Dauphinais, 196–215. Washington, DC: Catholic University of America Press, 2012.

Levering, Matthew. *Aquinas's Eschatological Ethics and the Virtue of Temperance*. Notre Dame: University of Notre Dame Press, 2019.

Levering, Matthew. "Aristotle and the Mosaic Law." In *Aristotle in Aquinas's Theology*, edited by Gilles Emery, O.P. and Matthew Levering, 70–93. Oxford: Oxford University Press, 2015.

Levering, Matthew. *Christ's Fulfillment of Torah and Temple: Salvation according to Thomas Aquinas*. Notre Dame: University of Notre Dame Press, 2002.

Levering, Matthew. *Did Jesus Rise from the Dead? Historical and Theological Reflections*. Oxford: Oxford University Press, 2019.

Levering, Matthew. *Engaging the Doctrine of Israel: A Christian Israelology in Dialogue with Ongoing Judaism*. Eugene, OR: Cascade, 2021.

Levering, Matthew. "God and Natural Law: Reflections on Genesis 22." *Modern Theology* 24, no. 2 (2008): 151–77.

Levering, Matthew. *Jesus and the Demise of Death: Resurrection, Afterlife, and the Fate of the Christian*. Waco, TX: Baylor University Press, 2012.

Levering, Matthew. "Mystagogy and Aquinas's *Commentary on Isaiah*: Initiating God's People into Christ." In *Initiation and Mystagogy in Thomas Aquinas: Scriptural, Systematic, Sacramental and Moral, and Pastoral Perspectives*, edited by Henk Schoot, Jacco Verburgt, and Jörgen Vijgen, 17–40. Leuven: Peeters, 2019.

Levering, Matthew. *Participatory Biblical Exegesis: A Theology of Biblical Interpretation*. Notre Dame: University of Notre Dame Press, 2008.

Levering, Matthew. *Paul in the "Summa Theologiae."* Washington, DC: Catholic University of America Press, 2014.

Levering, Matthew. *Proofs of God: Classical Arguments from Tertullian to Barth*. Grand Rapids, MI: Baker Academic, 2016.

Levering, Matthew. *Sacrifice and Community: Jewish Offering and Christian Eucharist*. Oxford: Blackwell, 2005.

Levering, Matthew. "Thomas Aquinas on Law and Love." *Angelicum* 94, no. 2 (2017): 413–41.

Levering, Matthew, and Marcus Plested, eds. *The Oxford Handbook of the Reception of Aquinas*. Oxford: Oxford University Press, 2021.

Levine, Baruch. *In the Presence of the Lord: A Study of Cult and Some Cultic Terms in Ancient Israel*. Leiden: Brill, 1974.

Liebengood, Kelly D. *The Eschatology of 1 Peter: Considering the Influence of Zechariah 9-14*. Cambridge: Cambridge University Press, 2014.

Lohfink, Gerhard. *The Forty Parables of Jesus*. Translated by Linda M. Maloney. Collegeville, MN: Liturgical Press Academic, 2021.

Loiseau, Stéphane. *De l'écoute à la parole. La lecture biblique dans la doctrine sacrée selon Thomas d'Aquin*. Paris: Cerf, 2017.

Lombardo, Nicholas E., O.P. *The Father's Will: Christ's Crucifixion and the Goodness of God*. Oxford: Oxford University Press, 2013.

Lonergan, Bernard, S.J. *The Incarnate Word*. Translated by Charles Hefling, Jr. Edited by Robert M. Doran and Jeremy D. Wilkins. Toronto: University of Toronto Press, 2016.

Lonergan, Bernard, S.J. *The Triune God: Systematics*. Toronto: University of Toronto Press, 2007.

Lundberg, Per. *La Typologie Baptismale Dans l'Ancienne Église*. Uppsala: Lundequist, 1942.

Luz, Ulrich. *Matthew 1-7: A Commentary*. Translated by James E. Crouch. Edited by Helmut Koester. Minneapolis, MN: Fortress, 2007.

Maimonides, Moses. *The Guide for the Perplexed*. Translated by M. Friedländer. Rev. ed. London: Routledge & Kegan Paul, 1904.

Mansini, Guy, O.S.B. "Christology in Context: Review Essay of Thomas Joseph White, O.P., *The Incarnate Lord*." *Nova et Vetera* 14, no. 4 (2016): 1271-91.

Marcus, Joel. "Son of Man as Son of Adam." *Revue Biblique* 110, no. 1 (2003): 38-61.

Marcus, Joel. "Son of Man as Son of Adam. Part II: Exegesis." *Revue Biblique* 110, no. 3 (2003): 370-86.

Marshall, Bruce D. "The Dereliction of Christ and the Impassibility of God." In *Divine Impassibility and the Mystery of Human Suffering*, edited by James F. Keating and Thomas Joseph White, O.P., 246-98. Grand Rapids, MI: Eerdmans, 2009.

Marshall, Bruce D. "God Almighty in the Flesh: Christology and the Crisis of Faith." In *Thomas Aquinas and the Crisis of Christology*, edited by

Michael Dauphinais, Andrew Hofer, O.P., and Roger W. Nutt, 345–67. Ave Maria, FL: Sapientia Press, 2021.

Martin, Francis. "The Image of Shepherd in the Gospel of Saint Matthew." *Science et Esprit* 27, no. 3 (1975): 261–301.

Martin, Francis. *Sacred Scripture: The Disclosure of the Word*. Naples, FL: Sapientia Press, 2006.

Mattison III, William C. *The Sermon on the Mount and Moral Theology: A Virtue Perspective*. Cambridge: Cambridge University Press, 2017.

Maximus the Confessor. *On the Cosmic Mystery of Jesus Christ: Selected Writings from St. Maximus the Confessor*. Translated by Paul M. Blowers and Robert L. Wilken. Crestwood, NY: St. Vladimir's Seminary Press, 2003.

McDonnell, Kilian, O.S.B. *The Baptism of Jesus in the Jordan: The Trinitarian and Cosmic Order of Salvation*. Collegeville, MN: Liturgical Press, 1996.

McDonough, Sean M. *Christ as Creator: Origins of a New Testament Doctrine*. Oxford: Oxford University Press, 2009.

McGinn, Bernard. *Thomas Aquinas's "Summa Theologiae": A Biography*. Princeton, NJ: Princeton University Press, 2014.

McKnight, Scot. *Five Things Biblical Scholars Wish Theologians Knew*. Downers Grove, IL: IVP Academic, 2021.

McKnight, Scot. *Jesus and His Death: Historiography, the Historical Jesus, and Atonement Theory*. Waco, TX: Baylor University Press, 2005.

McKnight, Scot. *The King Jesus Gospel: The Original Good News Revisited*. Grand Rapids, MI: Zondervan Academic, 2011.

McNall, Joshua M. *The Mosaic of Atonement: An Integrated Approach to Christ's Work*. Grand Rapids, MI: Zondervan Academic, 2019.

Meeks, Wayne. *The Prophet-King*. Eugene, OR: Wipf and Stock, 2017.

Meier, John P. "From Elijah-Like Prophet to Royal Davidic Messiah." In *Jesus: A Colloquium in the Holy Land*, edited by Doris Donnelly, 45–83. New York: Continuum, 2001.

Meier, John P. *A Marginal Jew: Rethinking the Historical Jesus*. Vol. 1, The Roots of the Problem and the Person. New York: Doubleday, 1991.

Meiers, Anna Elisabeth. *Eschatos Adam: Zentrale Aspekte der Christologie bei Joseph Ratzinger/Benedikt XVI*. Regensburg: Friedrich Pustet, 2019.

Melito of Sardis. *On Pascha: With the Fragments of Melito and Other Material Related to the Quartodecimans*. Translated by Alistair Stewart-Sykes. 2nd ed. Yonkers, NY: St. Vladimir's Seminary Press, 2016.

Merton, Thomas. *The New Man*. New York: Farrar, Straus and Giroux, 1961.
Meyer, Ben F. "Appointed Deed, Appointed Doer: Jesus and the Scriptures." In *Authenticating the Activities of Jesus*, ed. Bruce Chilton and Craig A. Evans, 155–76. Leiden: Brill, 1999.
Mittleman, Alan L. *Does Judaism Condone Violence? Holiness and Ethics in the Jewish Tradition*. Princeton, NJ: Princeton University Press, 2018.
Miura, Yuzuru. *David in Luke-Acts*. Tübingen: Mohr Siebeck, 2007.
Moberly, R. W. L. *The Bible, Theology, and Faith: A Study of Abraham and Jesus*. Cambridge: Cambridge University Press, 2000.
Moberly, R. W. L. "Living Dangerously: Genesis 22 and the Quest for Good Biblical Interpretation." In *The Art of Reading Scripture*, edited by Ellen F. Davis and Richard B. Hays, 181–97. Grand Rapids, MI: Eerdmans, 2003.
Moberly, R. W. L. *The Old Testament of the Old Testament: Patriarchal Narratives and Mosaic Yahwism*. Minneapolis, MN: Augsburg Fortress, 1992.
Moessner, David P. *Lord of the Banquet: The Literary and Theological Significance of the Lukan Travel Narrative*. Minneapolis, MN: Fortress, 1989.
Morales, L. Michael. *Who Shall Ascend the Mountain of the Lord? A Biblical Theology of the Book of Leviticus*. Downers Grove, IL: IVP Academic, 2015.
Morales, Rodrigo J. *The Spirit and the Restoration of Israel: New Exodus and New Creation Motifs in Galatians*. Tübingen: Mohr Siebeck, 2010.
Morgan, Robert. "Christology through Scriptural Interpretation through New Testament Theology." In *Christology and Scripture: Interdisciplinary Perspectives*, edited by Andrew T. Lincoln and Angus Paddison, 58–83. London: T&T Clark, 2007.
Morgan, Teresa. *Roman Faith and Christian Faith: Pistis and Fides in the Early Roman Empire and Early Churches*. Oxford: Oxford University Press, 2015.
Moss, Charlene McAfee. *The Zechariah Tradition and the Gospel of Matthew*. Berlin: De Gruyter, 2008.
Murray, Paul, O.P. *Aquinas at Prayer: The Bible, Mysticism and Poetry*. London: Bloomsbury, 2013.
Nachmanides (Rambam). *Commentary on the Torah: Genesis*. Edited by Charles B. Chavel. New York: Shiloh, 1999.

Newman, Judith H. *Before the Bible: The Liturgical Body and the Formation of Scriptures in Early Judaism*. Oxford: Oxford University Press, 2018.

Nichols, Aidan, O.P. *Deep Mysteries: God, Christ and Ourselves*. Lanham, MD: Lexington Books, 2019.

Nichols, Aidan, O.P. *Discovering Aquinas: An Introduction to His Life, Work and Influence*. London: Darton, Longman & Todd, 2002.

Nichols, Aidan, O.P. *Lovely, Like Jerusalem: The Fulfillment of the Old Testament in Christ and the Church*. San Francisco: Ignatius Press, 2007.

Nichols, Aidan, O.P. "St. Thomas Aquinas on the Passion of Christ: A Reading of *Summa Theologiae* IIIa, q. 46." *Scottish Journal of Theology* 43, no. 4 (1990): 447–59.

Nicolas, Jean-Hervé, O.P. *Synthèse Dogmatique. De la Trinité à la Trinité*. Paris: Beauchesne, 1985.

Nicolas, Marie-Joseph, O.P. "La théologie du Christ nouvel dans saint Thomas d'Aquin." *Bulletin de la Société française d'études mariales* 13 (1955): 1–13.

Nielsen, Jan Tjeerd. *Adam and Christ in the Theology of Irenaeus of Lyons: An Examination of the Function of the Adam-Christ Typology in the "Adversus Haereses" of Irenaeus, of Irenaeus, against the Background of the Gnosticism of His Time*. Assen: Van Gorcum, 1968.

Novenson, Matthew V. *The Grammar of Messianism: An Ancient Jewish Political Idiom and Its Users*. Oxford: Oxford University Press, 2017.

Nutt, Roger W. "From Eternal Sonship to Adoptive Filiation: St. Thomas on the Predestination of Christ." In *Thomism and Predestination: Principles and Disputations*, edited by Steven A. Long, Roger W. Nutt, and Thomas Joseph White, O.P., 77–93. Ave Maria, FL: Sapientia Press, 2016.

Nutt, Roger, and Michael Dauphinais, eds. *Thomas Aquinas, Biblical Theologian*. Steubenville, OH: Emmaus Academic, 2021.

Oliver, Isaac W. *Luke's Jewish Eschatology: The National Restoration of Israel in Luke-Acts*. Oxford: Oxford University Press, 2021.

Olivi, Peter John. "Romans 5." In *The Letter to the Romans*, translated and edited by Ian Christopher Levy, Philip D. W. Krey, and Thomas Ryan, The Bible in Medieval Tradition Series, 134–43. Grand Rapids, MI: Eerdmans, 2013.

Origen. *Commentary on the Epistle to the Romans: Books 1–5*. Translated by Thomas P. Scheck. Washington, DC: Catholic University of America Press, 2001.

Origen. *Commentary on the Epistle to the Romans: Books 6–10*. Translated by Thomas P. Scheck. Washington, DC: Catholic University of America Press, 2002.

Origen. *Commentary on the Gospel according to John, Books 1–10*. Translated by Ronald E. Heine. Washington, DC: Catholic University of America Press, 1989.

Origen. *Homilies on Genesis and Exodus*. Translated by Ronald E. Heine. Washington, DC: Catholic University of America Press, 1982.

Origen. *Homilies on Joshua*. Translated by Barbara J. Bruce. Edited by Cynthia White. Washington, DC: Catholic University of America Press, 2002.

Origen. *Homilies on the Psalms: Codex Monacensis Graecus 314*. Translated by Joseph W. Trigg. Washington, DC: Catholic University of America Press, 2020.

Origen. *Treatise on the Passover and Dialogue of Origen with Heraclides and His Fellow Bishops on the Father, the Son, and the Soul*. Translated by Robert J. Daly, S.J. New York: Paulist Press, 1992.

Ounsworth, Richard, O.P. *Joshua Typology in the New Testament*. Tübingen: Mohr Siebeck, 2012.

Paluch, Michał, O.P. *La Profondeur de l'amour divin. Évolution de la doctrine de la predestination dans l'oeuvre de saint Thomas d'Aquin*. Paris: J. Vrin, 2004.

Pannenberg, Wolfhart. *Systematic Theology*. Vol. 1. Translated by G. W. Bromiley. Grand Rapids, MI: Eerdmans, 1991.

Pao, David W. *Acts and the Isaianic New Exodus*. Grand Rapids, MI: Baker Academic, 2002.

Pawl, Timothy. *In Defense of Conciliar Christology: A Philosophical Essay*. Oxford: Oxford University Press, 2016.

Pawl, Timothy. *In Defense of Extended Conciliar Christology: A Philosophical Essay*. Oxford: Oxford University Press, 2019.

Pennington, Jonathan T. *Heaven and Earth in the Gospel of Matthew*. Grand Rapids, MI: Baker Academic, 2009.

Perrin, Nicholas. *Jesus the Priest*. Grand Rapids, MI: Baker Academic, 2018.

Perrin, Nicholas. *Jesus the Temple*. Grand Rapids, MI: Baker Academic, 2010.
Philo. *The Works of Philo: Complete and Unabridged*. Translated by C. D. Yonge. Rev. ed. Peabody, MA: Hendrickson, 1993.
Pinckaers, Servais, O.P. *The Sources of Christian Ethics*. Translated by Mary Thomas Noble, O.P. Washington, DC: Catholic University of America Press, 1995.
Pitre, Brant. *The Case for Jesus: The Biblical and Historical Evidence for Christ*. New York: Image, 2016.
Pitre, Brant. "Excursus: N. T. Wright and 'the End of the Exile.'" In *Jesus, the Tribulation, and the End of the Exile: Restoration Eschatology and the Origin of the Atonement*, 31–40. Grand Rapids, MI: Baker Academic, 2005.
Pitre, Brant. *Jesus and the Last Supper*. Grand Rapids, MI: Eerdmans, 2015.
Pitre, Brant. *Jesus the Bridegroom: The Greatest Love Story Ever Told*. New York: Random House, 2014.
Pitre, Brant. *Jesus, the Tribulation, and the End of the Exile: Restoration Eschatology and the Origin of the Atonement*. Grand Rapids, MI: Baker Academic, 2005.
Pitre, Brant, Michael P. Barber, and John A. Kincaid. *Paul, a New Covenant Jew: Rethinking Pauline Theology*. Grand Rapids, MI: Eerdmans, 2019.
Pius XII. Encyclical Letter *Humani Generis*. August 12, 1950.
Plested, Marcus. *Orthodox Readings of Aquinas*. Oxford: Oxford University Press, 2012.
Plumer, Eric. "Introduction." In *Augustine's Commentary on Galatians: Introduction, Text, Translation, and Notes*, translated by Eric Plumer, 1–121. Oxford: Oxford University Press, 2003.
Presley, Stephen O. "The Use of Paul in Irenaeus's Christology." In *Irenaeus and Paul*, edited by Todd D. Still and David E. Wilhite, 65–80. London: T&T Clark, 2020.
Prinzivalli, Emanuela. "Adam and the Soul of Christ in Origen's *Commentary on Genesis*: A Possible Reconstruction." *Adamantius* 23, no. 1 (2017): 119–29.
Pulse, Jeffrey. *Figuring Resurrection: Joseph as a Death and Resurrection Figure in the Old Testament and Second Temple Judaism*. Bellingham, WA: Lexham, 2021.
Radner, Ephraim. *Time and the Word: Figural Reading of the Christian Scriptures*. Grand Rapids, MI: Eerdmans, 2016.

Rahner, Karl. "Christology Today?" In *Theological Investigations*, vol. 17, translated by Margaret Kohl, 24–38. London: Darton, Longman & Todd, 1981.

Raith II, Charles. *Aquinas and Calvin on Romans: God's Justification and Our Participation*. Oxford: Oxford University Press, 2014.

Ratzinger, Joseph. *Daughter Zion: Meditations on the Church's Marian Belief*. Translated by John M. McDermott, S.J. San Francisco: Ignatius Press, 1983.

Ratzinger, Joseph. *Introduction to Christianity*. Translated by J. R. Foster. San Francisco: Ignatius Press, 2004.

Ratzinger, Joseph. *Jesus of Nazareth: From the Baptism in the Jordan to the Transfiguration*. Translated by Adrian J. Walker. New York: Doubleday, 2007.

Regev, Eyal. *The Temple in Early Christianity: Experiencing the Sacred*. New Haven, CT: Yale University Press, 2019.

Reno, R. R. *Genesis*. Grand Rapids, MI: Brazos, 2010.

Reynolds, Benjamin E. *John among the Apocalypses: Jewish Apocalyptic Tradition and the "Apocalyptic" Gospel*. Oxford: Oxford University Press, 2020.

Ribbens, Benjamin J. *Levitical Sacrifice and Heavenly Cult in Hebrews*. Berlin: De Gruyter, 2016.

Rice, Peter H. *Behold, Your House Is Left to You: The Theological and Narrative Place of the Jerusalem Temple in Luke's Gospel*. Eugene, OR: Pickwick, 2016.

Riches, Aaron. *Ecce Homo: On the Divine Unity of Christ*. Grand Rapids, MI: Eerdmans, 2016.

Rogers, Jr., Eugene F. *Blood Theology: Seeing Red in Body- and God-Talk*. Cambridge: Cambridge University Press, 2021.

Rosenberg, Randall S. "Being-toward-a-Death-Transformed: Aquinas on the Naturalness and Unnaturalness of Human Death." *Angelicum* 83, no. 4 (2006): 747–66.

Rosenberg, Roy A. "Jesus, Isaac, and the 'Suffering Servant.'" *Journal of Biblical Literature* 84, no. 4 (1965): 381–88.

Roszak, Piotr. "Exegesis and Contemplation: The Literal and Spiritual Sense of Scripture in Aquinas' Biblical Commentaries." *Studium* 65 (2016): 481–504.

Roszak, Piotr, and Jörgen Vijgen. "Introduction." In *Towards a Biblical Thomism: Thomas Aquinas and the Renewal of Biblical Theology*, edited by Piotr Roszak and Jörgen Vijgen, 11–20. Pamplona: EUNSA, 2018.

Roszak, Piotr, and Jörgen Vijgen, eds. *Reading the Church Fathers with St. Thomas Aquinas: Historical and Systematical Perspectives*. Turnhout: Brepols, 2021.

Roszak, Piotr, and Jörgen Vijgen, eds. *Towards a Biblical Thomism: Thomas Aquinas and the Renewal of Biblical Theology*. Turnhout: Brepols, 2015.

Rowe, C. Kavin. *Early Narrative Christology: The Lord in the Gospel of Luke*. Berlin: De Gruyter, 2006.

Ruello, Francis. *La christologie de Thomas d'Aquin*. Paris: Beauchesne, 1987.

Sanders, E. P. *The Historical Figure of Jesus*. London: Penguin, 1993.

Sanders, E. P. *Jesus and Judaism*. Minneapolis, MN: Fortress, 1985.

Sasson, Jack M. "The Servant's Tale: How Rebekah Found a Spouse." *Journal of Near Eastern Studies* 65, no. 4 (2006): 241–65.

Scheeben, Matthias Joseph. *Handbook of Catholic Dogmatics*. Book 5, Soteriology. Part 1, The Person of Christ the Redeemer. Translated by Michael J. Miller. Steubenville, OH: Emmaus Academic, 2020.

Scheeben, Matthias Joseph. *Handbook of Catholic Dogmatics*. Book 5, Soteriology. Part 2, The Work of Christ the Redeemer and the Role of His Virgin Mother. Translated by Michael J. Miller. Steubenville, OH: Emmaus Academic, 2021.

Schnabel, Eckhard J. *Jesus in Jerusalem: The Last Days*. Grand Rapids, MI: Eerdmans, 2018.

Schoenfeld, Devorah. *Isaac on Jewish and Christian Altars: Polemic and Exegesis in Rashi and the Glossa Ordinaria*. New York: Fordham University Press, 2013.

Schreiner, Patrick. *The Body of Jesus: A Spatial Analysis of the Kingdom in Matthew*. London: T&T Clark, 2016.

Schreiner, Patrick. *Matthew, Disciple and Scribe: The First Gospel and Its Portrait of Jesus*. Grand Rapids, MI: Baker Academic, 2019.

Schreiner, Thomas R. *The King in His Beauty: A Biblical Theology of the Old and New Testaments*. Grand Rapids, MI: Baker Academic, 2013.

Scott, Matthew. *The Hermeneutics of Christological Psalmody in Paul: An Intertextual Enquiry*. Cambridge: Cambridge University Press, 2014.

Scroggs, Robin. *The Last Adam: A Study in Pauline Anthropology.* Philadelphia: Fortress Press, 1966.
Seitz, Christopher R. *Figured Out: Typology and Providence in Christian Scripture.* Louisville, KY: John Knox Press, 2001.
Senior, Donald. *Matthew.* Nashville, TN: Abingdon Press, 1998.
Sherwood, Yvonne. "Binding-Unbinding: Divided Responses of Judaism, Christianity, and Islam to the 'Sacrifice' of Abraham's Beloved Son." *Journal of the American Academy of Religion* 72, no. 4 (2004): 821–61.
Siker, Jeffrey S. *Sin in the New Testament.* Oxford: Oxford University Press, 2020.
Sobrino, Jon, S.J. *Christ the Liberator: A View from the Victims.* Translated by Paul Burns. Maryknoll, NY: Orbis, 2001.
Sobrino, Jon, S.J. *Jesus the Liberator: A Historical-Theological Reading of Jesus of Nazareth.* Translated by Paul Burns and Francis McDonagh. Maryknoll, NY: Orbis, 1993.
Sonderegger, Katherine. "Christ as Infinite and Finite: Rowan Williams' *Christ the Heart of Creation.*" *Pro Ecclesia* 30, no. 1 (2021): 98–113.
Spezzano, Daria. *The Glory of God's Grace: Deification according to St. Thomas Aquinas.* Ave Maria, FL: Sapientia Press, 2015.
Stewart-Sykes, Alistair. "Melito's Anti-Judaism." *Journal of Early Christian Studies* 5, no. 2 (1997): 271–83.
Strauss, David Friedrich. *The Life of Jesus Critically Examined.* 2nd ed. Translated by George Eliot. New York: Macmillan & Co., 1892.
Strauss, Mark. *The Davidic Messiah in Luke-Acts: The Promise and Its Fulfilment in Lukan Christology.* Sheffield: Sheffield Academic Press, 1995.
Stump, Eleonore. *Aquinas.* London: Routledge, 2003.
Stump, Eleonore. *Atonement.* Oxford: Oxford University Press, 2018.
Svensson, Manfred, and David VanDrunen, eds. *Aquinas among the Protestants.* Oxford: Wiley-Blackwell, 2017.
Swain, Scott R. "The Radiance of the Father's Glory: Eternal Generation, the Divine Names, and Biblical Interpretation." In *Retrieving Eternal Generation,* edited by Fred Sanders and Scott R. Swain, 29–43. Grand Rapids, MI: Zondervan Academic, 2017.
Swetnam, James, S.J. "Isaac as Promise: A Study of the Symbolism in Hebrews 11,19." *Melita Theologica* 55, no. 1 (2004): 65–74.

Swetnam, James, S.J. *Jesus and Isaac: A Study of the Epistle to the Hebrews in the Light of Aqedah.* Rome: Pontifical Biblical Institute, 1981.

Synge, F. C. *Hebrews and the Scriptures.* London: SPCK, 1959.

Thompson, Marianne Meye. *Colossians and Philemon.* Grand Rapids, MI: Eerdmans, 2005.

Torrell, Jean-Pierre, O.P. *Christ and Spirituality in St. Thomas Aquinas.* Translated by Bernhard Blankenhorn, O.P. Washington, DC: Catholic University of America Press, 2011.

Torrell, Jean-Pierre, O.P. *Jésus le Christ chez saint Thomas d'Aquin. Texte de la tertia pars (ST IIIa) traduit et commenté, accompagné de données historiques et doctrinales et de cinquante textes choisis.* Paris: Cerf, 2008.

Torrell, Jean-Pierre, O.P. *Le Christ en ses mystères: La Vie et l'oeuvre de Jésus selon saint Thomas d'Aquin.* 2 vols. Paris: Desclée, 1999.

Torrell, Jean-Pierre, O.P. *Saint Thomas Aquinas.* Vol. 1, The Person and His Work. Translated by Robert Royal. Washington, DC: Catholic University of America Press, 1996.

Torrell, Jean-Pierre, O.P. *Saint Thomas Aquinas.* Vol. 2, *Spiritual Master.* Translated by Robert Royal. Washington, DC: Catholic University of America Press, 2003.

Trigg, Joseph W. "The Angel of Great Counsel: Christ and the Angelic Hierarchy in Origen's Theology." *Journal of Theological Studies* 42, no. 1 (1991): 33–51.

Troeltsch, Ernst. "Historical and Dogmatic Method in Theology." In *Religion in History*, translated by James Luther Adams and Walter Bense, 11–33. Minneapolis, MN: Fortress, 1991.

Tück, Jan-Heiner. *A Gift of Presence: The Theology and Poetry of the Eucharist in Thomas Aquinas.* Translated by Scott G. Hefelfinger. Washington, DC: Catholic University of America Press, 2018.

Turner, Denys. "The Human Person." In *The Cambridge Companion to the "Summa Theologiae,"* edited by Philip McCosker and Denys Turner, 168–80. Cambridge: Cambridge University Press, 2016.

Turner, Denys. *Julian of Norwich, Theologian.* New Haven, CT: Yale University Press, 2011.

Turner, Denys. *Thomas Aquinas: A Portrait.* New Haven, CT: Yale University Press, 2013.

Van Aarde, Andries. "Jesus as Joshua, Moses en Dawidiese Messias in Matteus." *Scriptura* 84, no. 1 (2003): 453–67.

Van Wart, T. Adam. "Aquinas's Eschatological Historiography: Job, Providence, and the Multiple Senses of the Historical Event." *Pro Ecclesia* 30, no. 1 (2021): 32–50.

Vanhoye, Albert, S.J. "Longue marche ou accès tout proche? Le contexte biblique de Hébreux 3,7–4,11." *Biblica* 49, no. 1 (1968): 9–26.

Venard, Olivier-Thomas, O.P. *La langue de l'ineffable. Essai sur le fondement théologique de la métaphysique.* Geneva: Ad Solem, 2004.

Venard, Olivier-Thomas, O.P. *Littérature et théologie. Une saison en enfer.* Geneva: Ad Solem, 2002.

Venard, Olivier-Thomas, O.P. *Pagina sacra. Le passage de l'Écriture sainte à l'écriture théologique.* Paris: Cerf, 2009.

Venard, Olivier-Thomas, O.P. *A Poetic Christ: Thomist Reflections on Scripture, Language and Reality.* Translated by Kenneth Oakes and Francesca Aran Murphy. London: T&T Clark, 2019.

Vial de Amesti, Catalina. "La muerte según los comentarios de santo Tomás a las cartas de san Pablo." *Forum: Supplement to Acta Philosophica* 5, no. 1 (2019): 339–51.

Vidu, Adonis. *The Same God Who Works All Things: Inseparable Operations in Trinitarian Theology.* Grand Rapids, MI: Eerdmans, 2021.

Vigne, Daniel. *Christ au Jourdain: Le baptême de Jésus dans la tradition judéo-chrétienne.* Paris: Gabalda, 1992.

Walker, Donald Dale. *Paul's Offer of Leniency (2 Cor 10:1): Populist Ideology and Rhetoric in a Pauline Letter Fragment.* Tübingen: Mohr Siebeck, 2002.

Walkey, Jeffrey M. "'Putting on' the Lord Jesus Christ: Thomistic Reflections on Kenosis and the Christ Hymn as a Model for Mystagogical Formation." In *Initiation and Mystagogy in Thomas Aquinas: Scriptural, Systematic, Sacramental and Moral, and Pastoral Perspectives*, edited by Henk Schoot, Jacco Verburgt, and Jörgen Vijgen, 61–82. Leuven: Peeters, 2019.

Watson, Francis. *Text and Truth: Redefining Biblical Theology.* Grand Rapids, MI: Eerdmans, 1997.

Wazana, Nili. *All the Boundaries of the Land: The Promised Land in Biblical Thought in Light of the Ancient Near East.* Translated by Liat Qeren. Winona Lake, IN: Eisenbrauns, 2013.

Weinandy, Thomas G., O.F.M. Cap. *Does God Change? The Word's Becoming in the Incarnation*. Still River, MA: St. Bede's Publications, 1985.
Weinandy, Thomas G., O.F.M. Cap. *Does God Suffer?* Notre Dame: University of Notre Dame Press, 2000.
Weinandy, Thomas G., O.F.M. Cap. *Jesus: Essays in Christology*. Ave Maria, FL: Sapientia Press, 2014.
White, Thomas Joseph, O.P. *Exodus*. Grand Rapids, MI: Brazos, 2016.
White, Thomas Joseph, O.P. *The Incarnate Lord: A Thomistic Study in Christology*. Washington, DC: Catholic University of America Press, 2015.
White, Thomas Joseph, O.P. "Introduction: The *Analogia Entis* Controversy and Its Contemporary Significance." In *The Analogy of Being: Invention of the Antichrist or the Wisdom of God?* edited by Thomas Joseph White, O.P., 1–31. Grand Rapids, MI: Eerdmans, 2011.
White, Thomas Joseph, O.P. "The Precarity of Wisdom: Modern Dominican Theology, Perspectivalism, and the Tasks of Reconstruction." In *Ressourcement Thomism: Sacred Doctrine, the Sacraments, and the Moral Life. Essays in Honor of Romanus Cessario, O.P.*, edited by Reinhard Hütter and Matthew Levering, 92–123. Washington, DC: Catholic University of America Press, 2010.
White, Thomas Joseph, O.P. *Wisdom in the Face of Modernity: A Study in Thomistic Natural Theology*. 2nd ed. Ave Maria, FL: Sapientia Press, 2016.
Whitfield, Bryan J. "Joshua Traditions and the Argument of Hebrews 3 and 4." Ph.D. Dissertation, Emory University, 2007.
Whitfield, Bryan J. *Joshua Traditions and the Argument of Hebrews 3 and 4*. Berlin: De Gruyter, 2013.
Whitfield, Bryan J. "The Three Joshuas of Hebrews 3 and 4." *Perspectives in Religious Studies* 37, no. 1 (2010): 21–35.
Wilken, Robert L. "The Interpretation of the Baptism of Jesus in the Later Fathers." *Studia Patristica* 11, no. 1 (1972): 268–77.
Wilken, Robert L. *Judaism and the Early Christian Mind: A Study of Cyril of Alexandria's Exegesis and Theology*. New Haven, CT: Yale University Press, 1971.
Wilken, Robert L. "Origen, Augustine, and Thomas: Interpreters of the Letter to the Romans." In *Reading Romans with St. Thomas Aquinas*, edited by Matthew Levering and Michael Dauphinais, 288–301. Washington, DC: Catholic University of America Press, 2012.

Wilken, Robert L. "St. Cyril of Alexandria: The Mystery of Christ in the Bible." *Pro Ecclesia* 4, no. 4 (1995): 454–78.

Wilkins, Jeremy D. *Before Truth: Lonergan, Aquinas, and the Problem of Wisdom*. Washington, DC: Catholic University of America Press, 2018.

Williams, A. N. *The Ground of Union: Deification in Aquinas and Palamas*. Oxford: Oxford University Press, 1999.

Williams, Rowan. *Christ the Heart of Creation*. London: Bloomsbury, 2018.

Williamson, H. G. M. "Davidic Kingship in Isaiah." In *The Oxford Handbook of Isaiah*, edited by Lena-Sofia Tiemeyer, 280–92. Oxford: Oxford University Press, 2020.

Williamson, H. G. M. *Variations on a Theme: King, Messiah and Servant in the Book of Isaiah*. Carlisle, UK: Paternoster, 1998.

Willitts, Joel. *Matthew's Messianic Shepherd-King: In Search of "The Lost Sheep of the House of Israel."* Berlin: De Gruyter, 2007.

Wise, Michael Owen. *A Critical Study of the Temple Scroll from Qumran Cave 11*. Chicago: Oriental Institute, 1990.

Wise, Michael Owen. "The Eschatological Vision of the Temple Scroll." *Journal of Near Eastern Studies* 49, no. 2 (1990): 155–72.

Witherington III, Ben. *The Christology of Jesus*. Minneapolis, MN: Fortress, 1990.

Witherington III, Ben. *John's Wisdom: A Commentary on the Fourth Gospel*. Louisville, KY: John Knox Press, 1995.

Witherington III, Ben. *Matthew*. Macon, GA: Smyth & Helwys, 2006.

Wolter, Michael. *The Gospel according to Luke*. Vol. 1, *Luke 1–9:50*. Translated by Wayne Coppins and Christoph Heilig. Waco, TX: Baylor University Press, 2016.

Wright, N. T. "Adam, Israel and the Messiah." In *The Climax of the Covenant: Christ and the Law in Pauline Theology*, 18–40. Minneapolis, MN: Fortress, 1992.

Wright, N. T. *History and Eschatology: Jesus and the Promise of Natural Theology*. Waco, TX: Baylor University Press, 2019.

Wright, N. T. *How God Became King: The Forgotten Story of the Gospels*. New York: HarperCollins, 2012.

Wright, N. T. *Jesus and the Victory of God*. Minneapolis, MN: Fortress, 1996.

Wright, N. T. "The Letter to the Romans." In *The New Interpreter's Bible*, vol. 10, edited by Leander E. Keck, 395–770. Nashville, TN: Abingdon Press, 2002.

Wright, N. T. *The New Testament and the People of God*. Minneapolis, MN: Fortress, 1992.

Wright, N. T. *Paul and the Faithfulness of God*. Vol. 2, Parts III and IV. Minneapolis, MN: Fortress, 2013.

Wyatt, Nicolas. "'Supposing Him to Be the Gardener' (John 20, 15): A Study of the Paradise Motif in John." *Zeitschrift für die neutestamentliche Wissenschaft* 81, no. 1 (1990): 21–38.

Index

4 Maccabees, 116

Abraham, 9, 14, 76, 106–12, 114, 115, 120–24, 126–34, 153, 166, 177, 194, 226, 273, 274, 277, 278
Absalom, 234, 236, 238, 260, 261, 277
Akedah, 105–108, 110, 114–19, 122–24, 126, 129, 130, 133–38
allegorical sense, 18
Allen, David, 191, 194
Allen, Michael, 34
Allison, Dale, 22–23, 122, 141, 149–163, 170, 172–73, 176, 179, 288–89
Ambrose, 91, 123, 213, 253, 278
Anatolios, Khaled, 7, 40–42, 47
Annunciation, 27, 227
Anselm, 28, 29, 247
Aristotle, 27, 61
Ascension, 23, 50, 163, 196, 218, 222, 230, 234, 247, 263, 271, 280, 284, 287, 292
atonement, 4, 35, 38, 42, 43, 94, 116, 123, 136, 137, 157, 196, 197, 269, 285, 290
Augustine, 66, 80–82, 91, 96, 107, 123, 124, 144–47, 172, 180, 228, 253, 258–66, 272, 274

baptism, 16, 23, 84, 120, 143, 179, 180, 181, 185, 197–226, 231, 244, 247, 251, 257, 258
Barnes, Corey, 27, 33, 34
Barth, Karl, 26–28, 35, 48–51
Baxter, W. S., 162, 176
beatific vision, 46, 47
Behr, John, 73, 104
Bellamah, Timothy, 5, 13
Beskow, Per, 257

Bethlehem, 172, 270–72
Biblical Thomism, ix, 21
biblical typologies, 1, 6, 19
Blessed Virgin Mary, 2, 27, 70, 82, 92, 113, 120, 151, 152, 227, 232, 233, 256, 260, 273–75
Boersma, Hans, 19, 59, 286, 287
Bonino, Serge-Thomas, 21
Botner, Max, 243
Brown, Colin, 181, 198
Brueggemann, Walter, 111, 112
Byars, Ronald, 181, 200
Byzantine Liturgy, 41, 199

Cessario, Romanus, 5, 30
charity, 39, 136–38, 175, 219, 223, 224, 262, 276
Cho, Bernardo, 243–46, 283
Christus Victor, 116, 280
Chrysostom, John, 130, 218, 272
Church Fathers, 2–4, 6, 9, 12, 25, 59, 60, 62, 64, 72, 80, 82, 108, 122, 123, 147, 150, 181, 190, 201, 202, 247, 253, 257, 284, 286
circumcision, 142, 212, 247
Clement, 257
consciousness, 50–52, 54
Council of Chalcedon, 47, 49, 64
Council of Ephesus, 47, 64, 74
covenant, 11, 13, 14, 19, 111, 113, 116, 118, 138, 158, 171, 174, 175, 177, 183, 186, 191, 197, 199, 206, 228, 229, 230, 242, 255, 258–60, 267, 285, 293
  new covenant, 11, 17, 147, 148, 175, 186, 191, 198, 214, 293

327

INDEX

Crowe, Brandon, 71, 72
crucifixion, 40, 82, 85, 89, 104, 120, 134, 136, 138, 230, 239
Cuddy, Cajetan, 5
Cyril of Alexandria, 62, 64, 69, 73, 74, 123, 128, 129
Cyril of Jerusalem, 80, 204, 213, 214

Daguet, François, 85
Daly-Denton, Margaret, 234–42, 283
Daniélou, Jean, 19, 20, 181, 202–204, 212, 213
deification, 87, 101
disobedience, 66, 67, 72–74, 86–88, 94–96, 101, 124, 192, 269, 293
divine nature, 36, 48, 50, 61, 65, 85, 88, 91, 97, 131
divinization, 176, 201
Duby, Steven, 35
Durand, Emmanuel, 46

Easter, 202
Easter Vigil. *See* Easter
Elijah (prophet), 10, 150, 152, 161, 166, 199, 200, 207–209, 213, 215, 219, 221
Elisha (prophet), 161, 199, 200, 207, 208, 215
Emmanuel, 255, 263
eternal life, 77, 81, 84, 85, 87–89, 93–95, 97, 113, 124, 137, 146, 203, 205, 206, 223, 224, 226, 241
Eucharist, 39, 84, 118, 129, 171, 197, 207, 209, 223, 226
Eusebius of Caesarea, 141, 147–50
exile, 5, 6, 72, 151, 161, 185, 229, 240
exodus, 5, 6, 11, 14, 15, 16, 23, 59, 115, 139, 140, 142, 150, 151, 156–58, 160, 161, 164, 170–73, 177, 178, 186, 193–96, 200, 203, 206, 207, 216, 221–26, 231, 233, 255, 286–89, 293

Farber, Zev, 181, 182
Farewell Discourse, 164, 235, 240, 241
First Council of Constantinople, 55, 64

Gaine, Simon Francis, 45, 46, 285
Garden of Eden, 75, 240, 241
Garrett, Susan, 25

Garrigou-Lagrange, Réginald, 62, 64, 74, 82, 83, 285
Geffré, Claude, 55
genealogy, 69–73, 119, 227, 232, 273
Gentiles, 143, 169, 222, 231, 266, 272, 274, 289
Gethsemane, 72, 122
Glasson, Francis, 164
Gondreau, Paul, 7, 33
Gorman, Michael, 11, 32, 33
grace, 4, 39, 43, 44, 49, 51, 58, 62, 63, 68, 76, 77, 83–85, 87, 90, 93, 94, 97–101, 115, 136, 166, 169, 172, 174–77, 205, 206, 207, 215, 216, 218, 220, 223, 226, 247, 262, 263, 267, 268, 275, 276, 279, 281–85, 287, 293
Greek Fathers, 47, 134
Gregory of Nazianzus, 274
Gregory of Nyssa, 150, 181, 204, 214

Harkins, Franklin, 18, 165, 166
Hauerwas, Stanley, 119, 285
Hays, Richard, 3, 14, 15, 22, 70, 79, 81, 139, 140, 182, 185, 247
Head of Christ/Christ's Headship, 4, 6, 16, 24, 84, 85, 98–100, 102, 265, 267–69, 275, 278–82, 287, 290
Head of the Church, 99, 222, 282
heavenly kingdom, 217, 221, 265
Herod, 151, 152, 172, 272
historical criticism, 16
Hofius, Otfried, 187, 188, 192
Huizenga, Leroy, 17, 105, 108, 113–22
human nature, 36–39, 47–52, 56, 61, 65, 68, 80, 85, 88, 90, 92, 95, 97, 99, 100, 107, 131, 263, 270, 280
Humani Generis, 20
humility, 86, 87, 94, 177, 189, 220, 228, 276
Hurtado, Larry, 91, 92
Hushai the Archite, 277
hypostatic union, 29, 34, 39, 47–49, 58, 62, 98

inaugurated eschatology, 14, 25
Incarnation, 22, 28, 30–35, 38, 39, 40, 42, 44, 45, 49, 57, 61, 63, 65, 66, 67, 73, 77, 79, 80, 82, 83, 85, 87, 88, 90, 91, 96, 97, 177, 247, 278, 279, 287

Irenaeus, 2, 69, 72, 73, 228, 248, 253–58

Jacob, 109–111, 115, 180, 227, 255, 256, 270, 271
Jericho, 184, 196, 211
Jerome, 25, 75, 218, 274
Jerusalem, 24, 25, 38, 138, 158, 184, 193, 195, 207, 227, 228, 230, 232, 233, 235–37, 240, 241, 243–45, 249, 258, 259, 260, 270–77, 289
Jipp, Joshua, 15, 242, 246–54, 258, 283
John Duns Scotus, 36, 37
John the Baptist, 79, 120, 131, 199, 206, 215, 233, 234, 241
Jordan River, 11, 16, 179, 180, 181, 184, 185, 192, 195–202, 204–26, 286
Josephus, 114, 150–52, 230
Judah, 15, 249, 255, 270, 271, 273, 275
Judas, 121, 231, 234, 235, 238, 261, 264, 265
Julian of Norwich, 101–103
justification, 67, 85, 101, 174
Justin Martyr, 184, 201, 204, 212, 213

Kadesh-Barnea, 188, 192
Keener, Craig, 75, 165, 291
Kidron valley, 235, 236, 240, 243
kingdom of God, 3–5, 9, 11, 16, 22, 23, 59, 86, 100, 176, 179, 180, 185, 198, 217–19, 222, 224, 225, 228, 241, 244, 247, 264, 268, 282, 283, 285–87, 290
kingdom of heaven, 148, 218, 228, 268

Lamb of God, 113, 126, 131, 133, 142, 202
Last Supper, 23, 140, 157, 158, 159, 160, 162, 171, 289
Lauda Sion, 129
law, 4, 8, 11, 13, 17, 18, 72, 87, 141–45, 147, 148, 150, 154, 157, 159, 161, 165, 166, 169, 172–75, 177, 205, 207, 210, 212, 262, 268, 276, 282, 283, 287, 293
Le Donne, Anthony, 12, 23, 24
Legge, Dominic, 7, 33, 34, 38, 65, 96, 98, 285
Leithart, Peter, 160–62

Levenson, Jon, 105, 106, 150, 240, 291, 292
literal sense, 2, 3, 12, 13, 18, 19, 20, 60, 128, 266, 278
Litwa, M. David, 75
Logos, 36, 37, 72, 257
Lonergan, Bernard, 38, 63, 64, 285
Luz, Ulrich, 120, 162

Magi, 120, 151, 251, 255, 272
Maimonides, 130, 131
manna, 129, 146, 157, 164, 173, 207
Mansini, Guy, 47, 48
Marian interpretation, 43
marriage, 103, 215
Mattison, William, 172
McDonnell, Kilian, 181, 200–202, 210, 225
McKnight, Scot, 284, 289, 294
Meeks, Wayne, 163, 164
Meier, John, 3, 4
Melchizedek, 9, 18, 24, 25, 148
Melito of Sardis, 123, 125, 141
Messiah, 2, 12, 71, 150, 154, 155, 171, 227, 229–33, 242–46, 248–52, 254–58, 263, 270–72, 276–79, 283, 287, 291, 292
Messianic age, 198
Messianic kingdom, 262
metaphysical realism, 48–50, 56, 57
microcosmos, 66
Miura, Yuuru, 228–33, 283
monophysitism, 33
Mount of Olives, 235, 236, 276
Mount Sinai, 144, 148, 153, 158, 171, 177
Mount Zion, 193, 240, 241, 245, 255, 278, 290
mystical body, 4, 101, 281, 282
mystical sense, 278

Naaman the Syrian, 208, 213, 215
natural theology, 49, 51
Nazareth, 11, 30, 70, 168, 239, 247, 256, 270, 287, 290
Nestorianism, 46
Nichols, Aidan, 16, 47, 62
Nietzsche, Friedrich, 54, 56
Nile River, 209, 214

INDEX

obedience, 16, 49–51, 65, 67, 73, 77, 86, 94, 96, 105, 106, 111, 115, 116, 122, 124, 133, 138, 250, 269, 280, 284, 293
Oliver, Isaac, 180, 234
Origen of Alexandria, 25, 72, 123, 126–29, 142–44, 181, 184, 201–15, 220, 221, 224, 257, 285–87
original justice, 92, 93, 99
Ounsworth, Richard, ix, 180, 183–97, 219–20, 224–25

Palm Sunday, 227, 244, 245, 274, 275
Paschal lamb, 211, 292
Paschal mystery, 42, 141, 225, 293
Passion, 33, 94, 98, 104, 105, 121, 135, 137, 142, 168, 216, 218, 219, 223, 234, 235, 238, 243, 245, 247, 261, 267, 269, 277, 280, 290
Passover, 11, 23, 113–15, 118, 129, 138, 142, 158, 173, 207, 211, 289, 292
patricide, 116
Pawl, Timothy, 44
perspectivalism, 55
Pharaoh, 151, 152, 172, 177, 209
Philo, 77, 78, 115, 152–54, 163, 204, 230, 257
Pilate, 238, 239, 245
Pinckaers, Servais, 30, 169, 172
Pitre, Brant, 6, 15, 16, 23, 79, 140, 141, 170, 171, 173, 289
Pius XII, Pope, 20
Pope Benedict XVI. *See* Joseph Ratzinger
predestination, 73, 247, 280
pride, 86, 95, 211, 262
priesthood, 18, 24, 25, 171, 247, 268, 269, 276, 280
Promised Land, 11, 16, 17, 149, 153, 177, 179–89, 191–97, 199, 201–207, 209–17, 220–26, 286, 287, 293
prophet, 4, 15, 22, 122, 131, 140, 141, 143–51, 154, 155, 163, 164, 168, 169, 171, 173, 177, 183, 191, 205, 229, 230, 232, 233, 237, 240, 249, 255, 257, 267, 268, 271, 274, 277, 279, 287, 288, 294
Psalms of Solomon, 229

Pseudo-Jubilees, 115
Pseudo-Philo, 116

Qumran, 71, 115, 150, 154, 229, 230

rational soul, 64
rationalism, 32
Ratzinger, Joseph, 2, 7, 8, 68, 181, 199, 247
Rebekah, 110, 111
recapitulation, 2, 3, 13, 14, 19, 72, 144, 157, 161, 197, 216, 286
Red Sea, 148, 191, 201, 203, 206, 209, 211–14, 216, 221, 226
reign of God, 3, 281
Reno, R. R., 111, 112
Ressourcement movement. *See* Ressourcement Theology
Ressourcement Theology, 18, 19, 21, 48
Resurrection, 14, 16, 22, 42, 49, 50, 57, 75, 78–82, 85, 88, 93, 95, 98, 101, 104, 105, 108, 113, 116, 117, 120, 124, 130, 133–38, 161, 170, 175, 180, 186, 196, 199, 202, 204, 212, 230, 234, 247, 250, 251, 254, 261, 266, 271, 280, 283, 284, 287–90, 292
Riches, Aaron, 46, 47, 74
Rome, 64, 234, 270, 271
Rowe, Kavin, 70

Sabbath, 189, 192–94, 224
sacra doctrina, 18, 21, 52, 69, 108, 136, 181, 228
Sacrament, 59, 84, 141, 173, 180, 181, 200, 202, 206, 210, 211–26
sacrifice, 23, 24, 41, 105–108, 113–21, 123, 124, 128–31, 133–35, 137, 138, 183, 186, 211, 287, 291
sacrificial offering, 16, 115, 123, 129
salvation history, 10, 11, 59, 125, 180, 194, 216, 286
Sanders, E. P., 8–13, 15, 289
Satan, 70, 72, 117, 120, 153, 233, 272, 280, 282
Saul, 230, 237, 264–69, 274
Savior, 24, 31, 66, 151, 220, 225, 257, 275, 284, 287, 293

Scheeben, Matthias Joseph, 41, 67, 176
Schillebeeckx, Edward, 53–55
Schleiermacher, 49–51
Schreiner, Patrick, 141, 200
Schreiner, Thomas, 14, 182, 185, 186
Scott, Matthew, 251
Scroggs, Robin, 9
Second Council of Constantinople, 13, 47
Second Vatican Council, 29
Seitz, Christopher, 16, 17
Sermon on the Mount, 144, 145, 153–55, 157, 161, 162, 167, 169
shepherd, 15, 85, 164, 171, 198, 229, 234, 235, 237, 238, 242, 251, 252, 257, 280, 283
Siker, Jeffrey, 15
slavery, 148, 177, 184, 293
Sobrino, Jon, 29, 30
Solomon, 9, 14, 23, 24, 158, 161, 231, 232, 240–43, 259
son of Abraham, 115, 119, 120, 227, 277, 292
Son of David, 13, 15, 23, 24, 71, 119, 120, 161, 227–29, 231, 233, 244, 245, 251, 263, 273–75, 277, 283, 292
Son of God, 49, 65, 67, 70, 71, 83, 87, 91, 97, 101, 103, 113, 115, 161, 232, 233, 245, 249, 250, 253, 270, 274, 280–82
Son of Man, 63, 72, 146, 167, 227
soteriology, 28, 35, 58
Spirit Christology, 34, 58
spiritual sense, 18, 19, 126, 212, 261, 266
state of glory, 4, 173
Stump, Eleonore, 42–44
suffering, 11, 17, 23, 33, 35, 40, 42, 43, 47, 59, 72, 89, 126, 129, 132, 135, 137, 139, 170, 211, 226, 230, 232, 236, 238, 242, 243, 245, 246, 252, 260, 264–66, 280, 281, 284, 288, 292

Tabernacle, 14, 177
temperance, 86
Temple, 2, 5, 6, 8, 10, 11, 14, 23, 24, 59, 71, 76, 104, 108, 114, 117–20, 122, 123, 131, 133, 135, 136, 138, 154, 163, 182, 184, 192, 193, 212, 219, 229, 230, 231, 233, 234, 240, 243, 245, 246, 248, 249, 251, 259, 287, 289, 290, 293
Theodore of Mopsuestia, 13
Third Council of Constantinople, 47, 64
Torah, 8, 16, 94, 128, 131, 139, 140, 143–45, 147, 149, 153, 154, 156, 157, 161, 163, 164, 166, 167, 255, 288, 293
Torrell, Jean-Pierre, 7, 27, 31, 32, 33, 83
Transfiguration, 149, 158, 160, 162, 167, 170, 244, 247
Trinity, 28, 31, 36, 37, 39, 52, 57, 65, 87, 89, 101, 102, 132, 166, 177, 217, 218
typology, 1–12, 14–16, 18–25, 59, 60, 66, 70, 74, 75, 77, 80, 83, 85, 87, 88, 123, 125, 140–42, 145, 146, 149, 151–54, 157, 160–64, 176, 181, 183, 184, 186, 190, 197–200, 202–210, 213, 214, 229, 230, 232, 233, 261, 266, 269, 276, 283, 285–87, 291, 292, 294

Vatican II. *See* Second Vatican Council
Venard, Olivier-Thomas, 44, 45
Vidu, Adonis, 7, 35–38, 285
virtue, 42, 86, 99, 123, 211, 279
von Balthasar, Hans Urs, 28, 68, 215

Watson, Francis, 14, 15
Weinandy, Thomas, 30
White, Thomas Joseph, ix, 1–3, 7, 47–57, 64, 132, 177–78, 285
Whitfield, Bryan, 182, 183, 188, 193, 197
Wilken, Robert, 74, 90
Williams, A. N., 38, 39, 58
Williams, Rowan, 7, 39
Witherington, Ben, III, 91, 140, 161
Wolter, Michael, 70, 71
worship, 120, 131, 138, 148, 155, 212, 229, 249, 256, 283, 289
Wright, N. T., 5, 6, 13, 14, 76, 77, 228, 233, 234, 250, 284, 288, 290

Yom Kippur, 186, 197

For EU product safety concerns, contact us at Calle de José Abascal, 56–1°,
28003 Madrid, Spain or eugpsr@cambridge.org.

www.ingramcontent.com/pod-product-compliance
Lightning Source LLC
LaVergne TN
LVHW011758060526
838200LV00053B/3630